LEFT BEHIND

LEFT BEHIND

THE DEMOCRATS' FAILED ATTEMPT
TO SOLVE INEQUALITY

LILY GEISMER

PUBLICAFFAIRS

New York

PublicAffairs
Hachette Book Group
1290 Avenue of the Americas, New York, NY 10104
www.publicaffairsbooks.com

@Public_Affairs

Printed in the United States of America

First Edition: March 2022

Published by PublicAffairs, an imprint of Perseus Books, LLC, a subsidiary of Hachette Book Group, Inc. The PublicAffairs name and logo is a trademark of the Hachette Book Group.

The Hachette Speakers Bureau provides a wide range of authors for speaking events. To find out more, go to www.hachettespeakersbureau.com or call (866) 376-6591.

The publisher is not responsible for websites (or their content) that are not owned by the publisher.

Print book interior design by Trish Wilkinson.

Library of Congress Cataloging-in-Publication Data

Names: Geismer, Lily, author.
Title: Left behind : the Democrats' failed attempt to solve inequality / Lily
    Geismer.
Description: First edition. | New York : PublicAffairs, 2022. | Includes
    bibliographical references and index.
Identifiers: LCCN 2021031191 | ISBN 9781541757004 (hardcover) | ISBN
    9781541756984 (ebook)
Subjects: LCSH: Democratic Party (U.S.) | Poverty—Government policy—
    United States. | United States—Social policy—1980–1993. | United
    States—Social policy—1993– | United States—Social conditions—1980– |
    United States—Politics and government—1989–
Classification: LCC JK2316 .G343 2022 | DDC 324.273609/049—dc23
LC record available at https://lccn.loc.gov/2021031191

ISBNs: 9781541757004 (hardcover), 9781541756984 (ebook)

LSC-C

Printing 1, 2021

For Michael, Gabriel, and June

CONTENTS

ABBREVIATIONS

AFDC	Aid to Families with Dependent Children
AFT	American Federation of Teachers
AIP	Apparel Industry Partnership
BRAC	Bangladesh Rural Advancement Committee
CDFI	Community Development Financial Institution
CGAP	Consultative Group to Assist the Poorest
CHA	Chicago Housing Authority
CMO	Charter Management Organization
CPE	Congressional Committee on Party Effectiveness
CRA	Community Reinvestment Act
DLC	Democratic Leadership Council
EITC	Earned Income Tax Credit
EZ	Empowerment Zone
FLA	Fair Labor Association
GFF	Good Faith Fund
HHS	US Department of Health and Human Services
HOPE	Home Ownership for People Everywhere
HUD	US Department of Housing and Urban Development
IDA	Individual Development Account

INS	Immigration and Naturalization Service
NAFTA	North American Free Trade Agreement
NewSchool	NewSchools Venture Fund
NOW	National Organization for Women
NPR	National Performance Review
OEO	Office of Economic Opportunity
PPI	Progressive Policy Institute
PRWORA	Personal Responsibility and Work Opportunity Reconciliation Act
PUSH	People United to Serve Humanity
SEWA	Self-Employed Women's Association
Southern	Southern Development Bancorporation
TANF	Temporary Assistance for Needy Families
TARP	Troubled Asset Relief Program
USAID	US Agency for International Development
WSEP	Women's Self-Employment Project

INTRODUCTION

Doing Well by Doing Good

On a steamy day in July 1999, President Bill Clinton rested in a plastic lawn chair in front of a ramshackle prefabricated home in the Whispering Pines trailer park in Tyner, Kentucky. The economically depressed coal town lay deep in the Appalachian Mountains. While drinking from a can of Mountain Dew, Clinton talked with sixty-nine-year-old Ray Pennington, a self-described "old-timer" with severe emphysema who required a portable oxygen tank to breathe. Pennington had recently lost his wife of fifty-one years and had moved in with his daughter Jean. Four generations of the family lived in the rented double-wide now. Jean quit her job flipping burgers and swirling soft serve at a local Dairy Queen to care for her father. The family was now entirely reliant on the $6.30 per hour her son-in-law earned making plastic safety glasses at the Mid-South Electric Company, one of the only employers in the area.[1]

The Pennington home was Clinton's first stop on a four-day tour. He went on to Clarksdale, Mississippi, and ended in Watts, California, with stops in East Louis, Illinois, the Pine Ridge Reservation in South Dakota, and a Phoenix, Arizona, barrio. Like Tyner, these places had some of the highest rates of poverty in the nation. Like the Pennington family, residents suffered from health problems, unemployment, and a lack of adequate transportation and housing. It was the first and only time that Clinton would visit many of these communities during his presidency. His travel plans usually took him to the expansive mansions and office parks of Silicon Valley and the skyscrapers of Wall Street, the places that represented the success of his agenda to stimulate a "New Economy" based in tech, finance, and real estate. First Lady Hillary Clinton, who had stayed behind in Washington, explained, "Ray Pennington's story should remind us that, although this has been a great time for America, not every American has benefited from our country's success."[2] The administration aimed to target the people and places like Pennington and Appalachia that were being "left behind" by the forces of the New Economy.[3] This descriptor reinforced the administration's contention that these places were anomalies in the boom times of the late 1990s and evaded the fact that the poverty of their residents was in large part the result of the forces of the New Economy, which Clinton helped to unleash.

Clinton's trip drew immediate comparisons both to Lyndon Johnson's visit to Appalachia in 1964 to build support for the War

Bill Clinton visiting Tyner, KY, resident Ray Pennington outside his home, 1999, and President Lyndon B. Johnson meeting with Tom Fletcher and his family on their porch in Inez, KY, 1964

Credit: Getty Images and Clinton Library/Sharon Farmer

on Poverty and Robert Kennedy's high-profile poverty tours of Kentucky, the Mississippi Delta, Pine Ridge, and Watts in the mid-1960s.[4] Clinton's conversation with Pennington evoked the iconic image of Johnson squatting on the porch of a rundown cabin in Inez, Kentucky, to talk with Tom Fletcher, surrounded by the eight children he supported on $400 per year.[5] Clinton traversed much of the same ground as his Democratic predecessors, but his purpose was different. The Clinton tour aimed to do more than expose the problems of the "Other America." He wanted to draw attention to their profit-making potential. As Clinton explained during his 1999 State of the Union address: "Our greatest untapped markets are not overseas—they are right here at home. And we should go after them [by building] a bridge from Wall Street to Appalachia to the Mississippi Delta, to our Native American communities."[6]

Clinton and his staff compared the New Markets tour, as the four-day journey was called, to the trips they orchestrated for corporate executives throughout the 1990s to explore investment opportunities in emerging markets in Southeast Asia, Africa, and Latin America. For this so-called domestic trade mission, Clinton invited CEOs and representatives of several major corporations and financial institutions including Bank of America, Citigroup, Aetna Insurance, Walgreens, and Fannie Mae. As Clinton explained to an audience in Appalachia, not far from the Pennington home, he was showing corporate leaders that they should "take a look at investing in rural and inner-city America. It's good for business, good for America's growth, and it's the right thing to do."[7] Selling the New Markets program to Wall Street and Silicon Valley executives during the last two years of his presidency, Clinton would frequently tell them that it was a "win-win" and a way that they could "do well by doing good."[8]

The tour marked the culmination of Clinton's enduring effort to promote private sector investment, market-based tools, and opportunity—rather than redistribution, government assistance, and economic security—as the best route to address poverty, economic inequality, and racial segregation. As Clinton explained to an audience at a factory in Clarksdale, Mississippi, in the heart of the Delta, he had been cultivating this approach to poverty, economic growth, and governance since his time as governor of neighboring Arkansas. In the 1980s, he invited Muhammad Yunus, the founder of the pioneering Bangladeshi microfinance organization Grameen Bank, and Mary Houghton and Ron Grzywinski of the ShoreBank Corporation, a community development bank based in Chicago, to set up a bank and microenterprise program in the Delta aimed at helping poor Black women on welfare become entrepreneurs. Clinton carried this model with him in his successful 1992 campaign for president as part of his quest to prove that he was a "new kind of Democrat." Once in power, the Clinton administration implemented this market-based approach in its economic empowerment, international development, and welfare, housing, and school reform efforts. These efforts crested at the end of Clinton's presidency with this attempt to bring capital investment to places like the Appalachian hamlet where Ray Pennington lived.

Clinton was aided in this measure by many of the other figures who joined him on his journey to these so-called left-behind places. In addition to the corporate executives, Clinton was accompanied by cabinet secretaries like Andrew Cuomo, several members of Congress, Democratic Leadership Council (DLC) head Al From, and civil rights activist Rev. Jesse Jackson. It was fitting that From joined Clinton on tour since the DLC played a critical role in shaping Clinton's market-based vision to poverty and governance. From and a group of Democratic politicians, including Clinton and Al Gore, founded the DLC in 1985 with the explicit goal of reinventing the party through a new electoral strategy and policy agenda. Calling themselves "New Democrats," the DLC declared that Democrats should make it their fundamental mission "to expand economic opportunity not government," which would be achieved through free markets and free trade.[9] They also called for introducing choice, competition, and market incentives into the public sector and stressed that market-oriented solutions could encourage individual responsibility and empowerment among the poor.

It was more jarring to see Jesse Jackson as part of the entourage scouting out new markets in economically distressed and racially segregated communities. The civil rights activist and two-time Democratic presidential candidate had served as the most prominent face and voice for the left wing of the Democratic Party for much of the previous two decades. Jackson had also been one of most vocal critics of the New Democrats. He dismissed the DLC as "Democrats for the Leisure Class" and accused them of trying to "suburbanize" the Democratic Party. He had also routinely castigated Clinton for trading in race-baiting politics and ignoring marginalized groups, deeming his reforms to the welfare system as a "war on the poor." By 1999, however, he had done an about-face and become one of the most enthusiastic participants on the New Markets tour, affirmatively celebrating how Clinton was launching a "war for profits."[10] Jackson's ringing endorsement symbolized how dominant the faith in market-based thinking had become by the end of the 1990s and how much a progressive vision advocating equity and justice rather than opportunity, individual responsibility, and profits had diminished.

Accounts of politics in the late twentieth century have tended to focus on conservatives and the Republican Party. In this telling, a powerful coalition of right-wing businesspeople and activists used the economic and social chaos of the late 1960s and early 1970s as an opportunity to gain political power through the election of Ronald Reagan in 1980. Reagan's victory offered conservatives the chance to implement an agenda that combined free market, antigovernment, socially conservative, and racially reactionary policies.[11] These efforts became critical in destroying both the electoral coalition and social welfare commitments that had defined the Democratic Party since the New Deal. When Democrats appear in these accounts, they are largely disorganized and weakened, defensively creating policies and electoral strategies in reaction to Republicans.

Left Behind dispels this narrative of the Democratic Party and the political history of the United States since the late 1960s. It reveals how Bill Clinton and the New Democrats helped to fundamentally remake many of the priorities and policies of the Democratic Party and liberalism during this period. The New Democrats' adoption of market-oriented approaches to address inequality was not a defensive reaction to the Republicans. Rather, it was based on a genuine belief in the power of the market and private sector to achieve traditional liberal ideals of creating equality, individual choice, and help for people in need. This approach, and the ideas and policies that flowed from it, propelled the Democratic Party's increased focus on economic growth and the tools of the private sector rather than on direct government assistance and economic redistribution as the main means to address persistent poverty and structural racism. This emphasis pushed comprehensive social welfare programs further off the table and blunted the power of the labor movement and other progressive groups. Even more significantly, by placing poor people at the whims of the private sector, it put them and their communities at risk for financial instability and predation, as became all too clear in the 2008 financial crisis and its aftermath.

The philosophy and ideas of Bill Clinton and other politicians, policymakers, and economic actors who circulated around the DLC is essential to understanding both the precarity of low-income people of color today and the current tensions within the Democratic Party. It is tempting to lay the blame for the problems of inequality and the seeming paralysis of the Democratic Party on the Republicans. It also tempting to see the New Democrats as purely cynical operators with little concern for the poor. Both explanations are incomplete and miss a bigger and messier truth. While Clinton and his allies worked within the constraints of their historical and political moment—including many inherited from the Reagan administration and imposed by Republicans in Congress—they were not without agency or power and made deliberate choices about how to address inequality. The pursuit of these policies did not solve inequality, but it did ensure that a faith in market-based solutions became a pervasive and endemic feature of Democratic thought and policy that has persisted to the present day. On the way, the New Democrat agenda blocked the development of policies that created meaningful structural change and limited the influence of progressives on the direction of the party. The political, economic, and social crises of the twenty-first century have led the party and nation to grapple with the consequences of this focus on markets, opportunity, and individual responsibility and for the first time in decades to consider alternatives. Taking better stock of who and what was left behind by these past choices is essential to charting a different path forward.

In recent years, the term *neoliberalism* has reverberated across academia and Twitter, even making a cameo in a *Saturday Night Live* skit. It has increasingly become shorthand for describing and dismissing the centrist and corporatist bent of the Democratic Party, symbolized by Bill and Hillary Clinton. This popularization has also stretched it thin. Broadly, neoliberalism describes the theory of political economy that free markets and government austerity are the best way to create individual freedom and choice. The term also has become a way to define the historical period since the 1970s when these ideas of market fundamentalism, disseminated by Milton Friedman and the Chicago school of economics, came to structure seemingly all aspects of governance and spheres of human activity in the United States and much of the world.[12]

The seeming pervasiveness of these ideas has produced a tendency to treat neoliberalism as monolithic and totalizing, which obscures the spectrum of market-oriented thinking and policy. The New Democrats' distinctive view of the market and the role of government has been consistently overlooked. The roots of this Democratic version of neoliberalism were rooted less in the free-market conservatism of Ronald Reagan and Milton Friedman and more in the liberalism of the New Deal and the Great Society, with its commitment to public-private partnerships and its faith in technocratic expertise to solve social problems and capitalism to create economic stability, security, and growth.[13] In fact, a faith in markets as a vehicle for social change was not "new" to the New

Democrats but a fundamental feature of liberalism through much of the twentieth century.

More than the increasingly fraught term *neoliberalism*, the phrase *doing well by doing good* better crystallizes the approach of the New Democrats. The phrase has become so frequently invoked in the speeches of Silicon Valley executives and the mission statements of their companies that it seems like a timeless adage.[14] Yet, it came into popular usage in the 1990s largely through the help of Bill Clinton, who readily adopted it. Clinton used it to describe both his administration's approach of enlisting the private sector to address poverty domestically and using free trade and globalization to promote freedom, democracy, and human rights around the world.[15] The phrase encapsulates the aspirational belief that it is possible for the market to do good and to achieve traditional liberal goals of equality and providing for those in need.

Since the New Deal, liberals had advocated for doing well *and* doing good. However, the form of political economy enacted during the New Deal and, later, the New Frontier and Great Society understood these as distinct goals. The architects of mid-twentieth century liberalism believed that stimulating capital markets was the best path to creating economic growth and security (doing well).[16] The job of the federal government, as they saw it, was to fill in the holes left by capitalism with compensatory programs to help the poor, like cash assistance and Head Start, and to enact laws that ended racial and gender discrimination (doing good). In contrast, the New Democrats sought to merge those functions and thus do well *by* doing good. This vision contended that the forces of banking, entrepreneurialism, trade, and technology, which had created the economic growth and prosperity of the 1990s, could substitute for traditional forms of welfare and aid and better address structural problems of racial and economic segregation. In this vision, government did not recede but served as a bridge connecting the public and private sectors.

The New Democrats treated poverty and other forms of discrimination largely as a market failure. In response, its adherents looked for ways to both bring the market to poor people of color and to integrate them into the capitalist system. This thinking led to the promotion of programs like microenterprise, which aimed to transform marginalized people into entrepreneurs and savers, and inspired initiatives such as Empowerment Zones and New Markets, which sought to make distressed urban and rural places profitable. The New Democrats also applied market-based tools to areas like public housing, education, and regulation of business, where capitalism had been seen as the problem, not the solution. Clinton and his allies extended the values of what historians call racial liberalism: the argument that for marginalized groups, especially African Americans, inclusion in American society and the legal system provided the best means for creating racial equality.[17] At the same time, proponents contended that giving poor people of color the tools to start businesses, open bank accounts, get mortgages, and increase their purchasing power would generate profits and allow them to become engines of economic growth. This approach built on a long-standing liberal tradition of drawing on ideas from international development to address poverty in the United States and vice versa.[18] Policies trying to tap emerging markets and stimulate entrepreneurship show how ideas that see poor countries, places, and people as sites of profit came to ricochet globally.

The New Democrats were genuinely convinced that the market could improve the lives of poor people, alleviate the problems of racial segregation, improve the functioning of government, and maintain traditional liberal ideals of egalitarianism and individual choice and freedom.[19] In fact, the New Democrats often argued that they were simply using new means to achieve the same liberal aims. Unlike free-market fundamentalists like Milton Friedman, the New Democrats believed that both government and corporations had a fundamental obligation to do good. They aimed to enlist the private sector to not just line the pockets of large corporations but to also use the resources and techniques of the market to make government more efficient and better able to serve the people.

Clinton and his allies routinely referred to microenterprise, community development banking, Empowerment Zones, mixed-income housing, and charter schools as revolutionary ideas that had the power to create large-scale change. These programs, nevertheless, uniformly provided small or micro solutions to large structural or macro problems. The New Democrats time and again overpromised just how much good these programs could do. Suggesting market-based programs were a "win-win" obscured the fact that market capitalism generally reproduces and enhances inequality. Ultimately, the relentless selling of such market-based programs prevented Democrats from developing policies that addressed the structural forces that produced segregation and inequality and fulfilled the government's obligations to provide for its people, especially its most vulnerable.

Although Clinton started the New Markets tour visiting Ray Pennington, a white Appalachian coal miner, the New Democrats' agenda overwhelmingly focused on Black and brown women who had become the face of the poor in the 1980s and 1990s. In speeches and photo-ops, Bill and Hillary Clinton and their allies routinely celebrated people like a Black welfare recipient in rural Arkansas who started her own catering business, a poor seamstress in Chile who used a loan from a microenterprise organization to buy a sewing machine and provide for her family, and a Latinx charter school student in Los Angeles receiving a top score on a state achievement test. These images and descriptions of poor people aligned with the meritocratic ethos of the Ivy League graduates of Wall Street, Silicon Valley, and the White House. However, these celebrations falsely suggested that market forces could give the vast majority of poor people the power to move out of poverty, overcome racial segregation, and control their own lives.

Although the valorization of poor women of color as hardworking entrepreneurs and savers seemed more compassionate than the infamous Reagan-era image of the "welfare queen," it proved no less detrimental. The focus on transforming poor people of color into financial actors contributed to making what was left of the social safety net in the 1990s and beyond only available to those people willing or able to operate within the imperatives and strictures of market capitalism.[20] The celebration of a few individuals who managed to achieve success through market-based programs obscured the fundamental barriers and forms of structural discrimination and uneven development of global capitalism that made it impossible for most people of color in the US and around the world to succeed. Clinton's efforts to reward those "who played by the rules" also continued to stigmatize those poor people who allegedly did not. The "doing well by doing good" ethos, therefore, further legitimized—and operated hand in hand—with punitive policies like those contained in the 1996 welfare reform law. It also fit with the tough-on-crime politics of the DLC and the Clinton administration, including the passage of the 1994 crime bill, which led to the vastly disproportionate surveillance and incarceration of millions of African American men, whom the New Democrats deemed unable to become entrepreneurs, savers, or valuable contributors to the New Economy.[21]

The veneration of entrepreneurship to solve social problems also revealed the type of work and worker that the New Democrats valued and the types of constituencies to which they aimed to appeal. Beginning in the 1970s, this brand of Democrats consistently advocated that the future of both the economy and the Democratic Party lay in shoring up the entrepreneurial postindustrial economy and its college-educated nonunionized workforce. Starting in the New Deal, organized labor and working-class constituents played a pivotal role in shaping the base and values of the party. The New Democrats deliberately aimed to constrain the power and influence of the labor movement and stressed that white middle-class professionals were key to the party's viability going forward. Bill Clinton's capturing of the presidency and the soaring of the New Economy in the 1990s seemed to offer affirmation of this theory and strategy. However, it came with major long-term costs and repressions, not least of which are the current fractures within the Democratic Party.

The labor movement and other social justice groups pushed back on the electoral strategy and policy agenda of the New Democrats. These groups came out in full force to support Jesse Jackson's two presidential bids and the different future for the Democratic Party that his candidacy embodied. During the Clinton years, groups mounted protests to specific issues, such as welfare reform, charter schools, free trade, and sweatshop abuses. By the 1990s, however, the increased dominance of the New Democrats' approach prevented a unified coalition of social movements representing the interests of the poor and working class from coalescing to pressure the Clinton administration into either meaningfully shifting its policy agenda on the economy and poverty or changing its political strategy. Likewise, consistent claims by the Clinton administration and the New Democrats that they were doing good, coupled with concerns about the alternatives offered by the Republicans, blunted the power of these groups and progressive politicians of the Democratic Party to bring more redistributive solutions to the table.

More than trying to build common ground with social movements on the left, the New Democrats' commitment to doing well by doing good ushered in new partnerships among government, corporations, nonprofits, and philanthropic organizations like the Ford and Gates Foundations. The growing popularity of the notion that corporations could both fulfill social goals and make a profit meant that policymakers could rely on and often encourage business and philanthropy to perform functions that were once the domain of the public sector. This trend opened new funding streams for solving problems of social inequality. Marshaling companies like America Online, Nike, and Citicorp to improve public education, combat sweatshops, and revitalize distressed urban neighborhoods reinforced the idea that the private sector was better at solving these problems than government. In doing so, it legitimated these private actors to become central players in the development of public policy, especially concerning poverty and inequality. This leaning on large corporations, wealthy tech entrepreneurs, and large private foundations, therefore, removed important mechanisms of democratic accountability and transparency from the policy process. Upon leaving the White House, Clinton, through his own foundation, substantially refined and expanded this model. The Clinton Foundation made it its mission to "woo the world's most powerful interests to help the powerless" through partnerships among private companies, wealthy donors, NGOs, and underserved communities.[22]

The efforts of the New Democrats became critical to solidifying the idea that markets could "do good" in the popular consciousness. By the end of the 1990s, this consistent celebration of the power of markets would contribute to fortifying the belief among a generation of idealistic college graduates that the most effective path for enacting social change was to attend business school and work for a socially responsible company, rather than work in the public sector or become a union or community organizer. This trend is but one example of how Clinton and his allies ultimately did more to sell free-market thinking than even Friedman and his acolytes.

On the surface, *doing well by doing good* and *win-win* are phrases that call on corporations to assume more responsibility for social problems in ways that benefit all parties. But all the policies that flowed from vision created clear winners and losers. The commitment to doing well by doing good did little to address the unequal distribution of wealth in the United States and around the world. Indeed, this inequity has only intensified since the 1980s, in part due to the economic agenda and unyielding commitment to globalization by the Clinton administration.[23] At the heart of the call for doing well by doing good is the idea of erasing the barriers between the public and private sectors. The stories that follow show the power in resurrecting those barriers and the need for creating new ones that limit the reach of the private sector, restore faith in government, and truly create a more equal society.

PART I
CRISIS AND OPPORTUNITY

CHAPTER 1

GROWTH AND OPPORTUNITY

Democratic senator Gary Hart's upset victory in the 1984 New Hampshire primary left reporters and political strategists stumped. The cerebral and often aloof senator from Colorado had a personal and political style that differed from the classic baby-kissing, back-slapping candidate.[1] Hart's more gregarious Senate colleague Joe Biden once told him that if he didn't smile more, he didn't deserve to win office.[2] Yet, Hart's platform promising "New Ideas" and his focus on economic growth and opportunity captured the attention of large numbers of under-forty-five, white, college-educated professionals in cities and suburbs, which led him to rack up wins in important primaries in the Northeast and West. His success with this constituency made *yuppie* the hottest word of the 1984 election. The neologism seemed to aptly describe Hart's supporters as well as his own contradictory mix of liberal and conservative priorities.

Reporters had long struggled to come up with the best descriptor for Hart's vein of Democratic politics. When Hart and his cohort—which included Bill Bradley, Michael Dukakis, Al Gore, Paul Tsongas, and Tim Wirth—first arrived on the political scene in the early 1970s, they earned the label Watergate Babies. But by the early 1980s, the nickname seemed dated. Chris Matthews, then an aide to Speaker of the House Tip O'Neill, flippantly suggested they were "Atari Democrats." It was a reference to the popular video game company and the group's relentless focus on high-technology and entrepreneurial growth as the solution to all problems.[3] Journalist Charles Peters averred that "neoliberal" was a better descriptor.[4] Peters meant it not as a pejorative but as a positive. He believed the word captured the group's continued commitment to the values that long defined the Democratic Party rather than an embrace of Adam Smith. Neoliberals, he observed, "still believe in liberty and justice and a fair chance for all, in mercy for the afflicted and help for the down and out," but "no longer automatically favor unions and big government."[5]

Hart personally sought to distance himself from all these labels. When asked if he was the "candidate of the yuppies," Hart claimed he didn't know what a yuppie was, never mind trying to appeal to them.[6] He called the neoliberal label "dumb."[7] He fleetingly adopted Atari Democrat. But after the company announced that it was shifting much of its production assembly operations to developing countries with lower labor costs, he joined many other Democrats in openly rejecting the label.[8] Hart would tell reporters that he preferred to describe his politics as "Prairie Populist Jeffersonian democracy," but that did not exactly roll off the tongue.[9] He also contended that what set him and his cohort apart from the New Deal or Great Society was "not our principles, goals, aspirations, or ideals, but methods." And he chastised reporters for thinking of politics on a "linear, left-right spectrum." Instead, he argued the real dividing line, especially among the Democrats, was generational.[10]

Hart's main opponents in the 1984 Democratic presidential primary also offered distinct visions for the direction of the party. Rev. Jesse Jackson rose to national prominence in the 1960s as a leader in the civil rights movement. Constructing his campaign around the inclusive idea of the Rainbow Coalition, his platform and electoral strategy were perhaps the most progressive ever offered by a Democratic presidential candidate. He found support across a wide range of voters—whom he called the "desperate, the damned, the disinherited, the disrespected, and the despised"—who were disproportionately enduring the harmful effects of the Reagan Revolution. Walter Mondale embodied the traditional Democratic values and coalitional politics that both Hart and Jackson had long chafed against. Mondale eventually won the fierce primary battle. His historic landslide loss to Ronald Reagan in the general election offered an image of the Democratic Party in disarray. But the election also revealed a pivotal moment when the priorities and composition of the Democratic Party were at a crossroads.

In the aftermath of the 1984 election, several of Hart's allies would form the Democratic Leadership Council (DLC). The organization adopted many of the main principles and strategies of Hart's campaign, especially the focus on infusing the Democratic Party with "New Ideas" and appealing to affluent educated voters. To capture these aims, the DLCers embraced the label New Democrats. It proved more durable than Watergate Baby, Atari Democrat, or Neoliberal, all of which would fall into the dustbin of faddish political terms (yuppie would, of course, live on). Critics quickly dismissed the New Democrats as simply Reagan apologists or Republican-lites. The emergence of this group, however, was not a reaction or capitulation to the Reagan Revolution: its rise well predated the revolution, and Reagan's reelection offered new room for the group's ideas to gain ascendance. The group's larger goal was never to reject but, rather, to reformulate key aspects of liberalism. These figures demonstrated a consistent commitment to fusing government reform and economic growth with opportunity and equality. The evolution of the New Democrats and their ideas about the ability of the market and private sector to do social good would transform key aspects of the Democratic Party's policy agenda and political strategy while thwarting alternative paths on the way.

WATERGATE BABIES

Something was astir in Colorado. In the 1974 election, Democrats captured a Senate seat, a congressional district, and the governorship in this reliably conservative bastion of Western individualism.

Democrats Sen. Gary Hart and Rep. Tim Wirth both of Colorado celebrating their reelection victories, November 5, 1980
Credit: Denver Post/Getty Images

The election signaled a political realignment of the state, brought on by the postindustrial boom surrounding Denver and the influx of college-educated newcomers.[11] Yet, Gary Hart and Tim Wirth were not typical Democrats. They epitomized larger changes afoot in the Democratic Party, not just in Colorado but around the country.

The Kansas-born Hart had gone to Yale Divinity School in the late 1950s with plans to become a theology professor. John F. Kennedy's presidential bid inspired him to change paths and head to law school. Hart then moved to Denver where his admiration for the Kennedys and strong opposition to the Vietnam War propelled him into local Democratic politics.[12] He got to know George McGovern, who asked him to manage his 1972 campaign for the presidency. McGovern's landslide defeat by Richard Nixon convinced Hart that the Democrats "under the penalty of irrelevance and extinction" had to create a "new generation" of thinkers and leaders.[13] Hart saw himself as up to the task. Shifting from manager to candidate, he announced his bid for the US Senate in 1973. He ran on what he called "an honesty ticket." Kicking off his campaign, he declared that "the blunt truth is that people don't trust their leaders any more."[14] Hart's platform called for reducing both waste in government spending and the scope of its bureaucracy.[15] These themes tapped into a larger generational skepticism with large institutions and bureaucracy.[16]

Like Hart, Tim Wirth was in his midthirties and combined a laid-back style, movie-star good looks, and an Ivy League education with a commitment to government reform.[17] He made his bid for Congress as a Democrat in a district that spanned both the liberal academic enclave of Boulder and Denver's traditionally Republican-leaning affluent suburbs. Wirth's pragmatic and reformist claims that he was against the "old way, that doesn't work any more" and demands that "Congress must be reformed" contributed to voters choosing him over the Republican incumbent.[18]

Hart and Wirth were part of a historic wave of Democratic politicians that arrived in Washington and state houses around the country in the 1974, 1976, and 1978 elections, promising to stop the war in Vietnam, end corruption, and make government more efficient and transparent. In addition to Colorado's Richard Lamm, Michael Dukakis of Massachusetts and Jerry Brown of California won governors' races in 1974. Wirth was one of forty-one freshman Democrats to be sworn into Congress as part of a class that included James Blanchard of Michigan and Paul Tsongas of Massachusetts. Two years later, they were joined by Al Gore of Tennessee and Richard Gephardt of Missouri. In 1978, New Jersey's Bill Bradley won a Senate seat, and Bill Clinton of Arkansas and Bruce Babbitt of Arizona became governors of their respective states. These politicians were predominately white, male, and under the age of forty. They represented largely white middle-class suburban districts, and most had never before held political office. Like Hart and Wirth, many shared an Ivy League pedigree, which contributed to their commitment to meritocracy and technocratic solutions to social problems.

The group quickly earned the label of Watergate Babies, which implied that it was an anti-Nixon sentiment that bound them. In the aftermath of Watergate, the Republican Party was on the ropes, with rumors that it might be all but done.[19] The real target of the Watergate Babies wasn't Nixon or the Republicans but the Democratic establishment. The calls for reforming Congress, on which many of these candidates ran, represented a critique of Democrats who had controlled the body since the 1930s. Establishment Democrats had already faced a drubbing from the social movements of the 1960s, who charged they dragged the country into the Vietnam War, thwarted the progress of the civil rights movement, and were too cozy with big corporations. Although the Watergate Babies strongly opposed the Vietnam War and supported civil rights, they challenged the party establishment from a different angle.

"We are not a bunch of little Hubert Humphreys," Hart warned upon winning his Senate race. He was referring to the former vice president, Minnesota senator, and presidential candidate who was an icon of postwar liberalism.[20] Hart had started his campaign stump speech by calling for "the end of the New Deal" and railed against the philosophy of "throwing money at problems" and creating another federal program or agency.[21] "It is time to replace the New Deal, or at least the conventional thinking which is its grandchild," he told crowds.[22] Once in office, Hart continued to denounce the bedrock social programs of the New Deal and Great Society. He complained about inefficiencies in the welfare system and stressed that the time had come to "move beyond some of the old liberal solutions that have been tried and failed."[23] Hart contended that the New Deal approach didn't work anymore because "the proliferation of agencies often creates—not solves problems." He accused the regulatory agencies created in the New Deal of stifling competition, creating a morass of red tape, and being in bed with the industries they were supposed to regulate.[24] He was even more withering about the Great Society. He accused the "ballyhooed War on Poverty" of "only raising the expectations, but not the living conditions of the poor" and creating useless bureaucracies while driving up the deficit too.[25]

Hart's criticisms might have made for rousing stump-speech lines, but they represented a somewhat distorted view of both the New Deal and the Great Society. With its broad-based agenda of creating economic security, Franklin Roosevelt's New Deal fundamentally remade and expanded the federal government and ordinary Americans' relationship to it. It created new protections for workers, including the ability to bargain collectively, and established or expanded the capacity of federal agencies to regulate banking, finance, and other corporate sectors. The New Deal was, however, never fully universal. It connected key privileges like Social Security to work rather than to citizenship. It operated on a two-tiered system: providing unemployment and Social Security to male breadwinners while creating Aid to Families with Dependent Children (AFDC), which would come to be known as welfare, for poor, single mothers. The New Dealers envisioned AFDC as a small, hopefully temporary measure to provide monthly cash assistance to widowed and unmarried mothers so that they could take care of their children and not look for work. AFDC, like many New Deal programs, contained major loopholes that excluded the large majority of African Americans and other marginalized groups from many of its signature programs, thereby enhancing structural inequalities and racial segregation.

New Deal liberalism was also never as redistributive as detractors suggested. The New Dealers had started out at the height of the Depression to protect the nation against the destructive effects of capitalism. However, Roosevelt and his brain trust increasingly embraced the theories of John Maynard Keynes and shifted toward a new philosophy of managing capitalism and smoothing out the imperfections of the market through spending, taxation, and monetary policy rather than closely regulating or curtailing it.[26] Keynes argued that the key to ending the Depression rested in the government using its power to boost consumer demand, which would create more productivity, higher wages, and more growth. The post–World War II economic recovery and expansion validated Keynesian theory, which had become the received

wisdom among economists and politicians of both political parties but especially of liberal Democrats. In the 1950s the soaring
GDP, rebounding manufacturing sector, and substantial rise of
middle-class salaries and suburban lifestyles among both white-
collar executives and autoworkers offered proof that the Keynesian model of growth was successful. Liberals also advocated for
a mildly redistributive tax system that aimed to limit the concentration of wealth and prevent it from falling into the hands of a
few.[27] Many postwar liberals believed increasing revenues could
also fund social programs like welfare and social security. Yet, the
Kennedy administration, moving further away from a redistributive system, aimed to extend macroeconomic growth through a
massive tax cut along with programs to encourage business investment, increase labor output, and manipulate interest rates.[28]

Following Kennedy's assassination, Lyndon Johnson recognized that his ability to enact the Great Society depended in large
part on continuing the model of economic growth established by
his predecessor.[29] The Great Society extended the New Deal's ideal
that government was responsible for improving the lives of the
American people and addressing fundamental inequities. This set
of programs contained hundreds of legislative initiatives, including civil rights, educational opportunity from preschool through
college, health care for the elderly and poor, food stamps, environmental and consumer protection, and immigration reform. Most
famous was its War on Poverty, which sought to "eliminate the
paradox of poverty in the midst of plenty."

The War on Poverty emerged from Johnson's and his advisors'
belief that male unemployment was a driving factor in creating
poverty. But Johnson believed that it would be impossible to push
a massive jobs program through Congress and that the public
would not support a redistributive program. He also had a firm
belief that direct cash assistance programs like AFDC produced
dependency.[30] Instead, the administration advocated offering "a
hand up, not a handout" by providing poor men the skills they
needed to get jobs in the private labor market. The centerpiece of
the program was the Community Action Program, which offered

federal grants for the formation of community organizations focused on empowering poor people and giving them the tools to mobilize as political actors. The decentralized approach enabled grassroots activists to adapt the War on Poverty for their own purposes, which spawned the birth of scores of health clinics, tenants' rights groups, and job training programs, as well as welfare rights groups.[31] However, the War on Poverty was contested from the outset: Congress approved less than $1 billion for the program in 1964, as compared with, for example, the $5.1 billion granted to NASA for the space race that same year or the $2 billion per month that was being spent on the Vietnam War by 1966.[32] The lack of funding made Gary Hart's claim that the War on Poverty was to blame for the federal deficit especially unfair.

While AFDC also remained a small part of the federal budget, it did grow substantially in the 1960s. The growth came from a variety of factors—which had little to do with the War on Poverty. The combination of the loosening of eligibility and the unemployment crisis along with activists encouraging poor people to receive the benefits to which they were entitled led rolls to rise from 3.1 million clients in 1960 to over 8 million by 1970. Thus, despite Johnson's strong opposition to expanding welfare, the growth in the program would become ever associated with the Great Society—and not just by conservatives but by the Watergate Babies too.[33]

Tim Wirth suggested the Watergate Babies' problems with the liberal initiatives of the past was as much generational as it was ideological. He noted that he and most of the other Watergate Babies were barely alive during the New Deal and not in office when the Great Society passed so they had no "stake in those programs" and could view them with "more skepticism."[34] Wirth and his cohort took pains to distinguish themselves from the liberal old guard, symbolized by Humphrey, Senator Edward Kennedy, and especially Representative Tip O'Neill, who became the Speaker of the House in 1977. Unlike the younger Wirth and Hart, the ruddy-faced O'Neill came of age during the Great Depression and the experience of the New Deal instilled in him a belief that it was the responsibility of government to help people in need, especially his constituents. The coiner of the classic phrase "all politics is local," O'Neill had a reputation for generously supplying patronage jobs to the members of his Massachusetts district and for brokering deals with the leaders of various interest groups.[35] Hart and Wirth recoiled at the transactional politics of O'Neill and his allies. This approach ensured that, since the New Deal, groups ranging from steelworkers, autoworkers, and meatpackers in Chicago to Blacks in Harlem, Jews on the Lower East Side in Manhattan, and white farmers in Wisconsin remained loyal to the Democrats. But Wirth, Hart, and their allies believed that this model's time had passed. In their minds, it made the Democrats too beholden to what they dismissively called "special interest groups," such as African Americans, women, white farmers, and, especially, organized labor.

The labor movement had long served as a powerful check on corporate and government power. In the minds of many, however, the merger of the two largest unions in the 1950s to create the AFL-CIO made organized labor another bloated bureaucratic institution. Although private union membership plateaued in the 1960s, organized labor's influence on the Democratic Party continued to intensify.[36] The AFL-CIO's longtime head George Meany formed a close partnership with Johnson and an even tighter alliance with Johnson's vice president, Hubert Humphrey, which had proved critical to his securing the 1968 nomination.[37] The Watergate Babies believed the cigar-chomping Meany was calculating, corrupt, and outdated.[38] Increasingly, Hart and the Watergate Babies came to see unions and the sectors they represented as a drag not just on the party but on the economy as well.

ATARI DEMOCRATS

The roots of the economic problems of the 1970s predated the Watergate Babies' arrival in Washington. There had been many warning signs, but the 1973 oil crisis sent shock waves through the American economy.[39] The gas shortage created a particular hardship for the auto industry as consumers stopped buying cars, especially the gas guzzlers that Detroit churned out. The Big Three automakers cut back on production, closed plants, and furloughed or laid off workers. By early January 1975, when Hart and Wirth took their oaths of office, the unemployment rate in the auto industry reached 20 percent, and half of all Chrysler workers were out of work.[40]

Chuck Robichaux was one of the casualties. The white twenty-eight-year-old high school graduate had been working on the assembly line for over five years at a General Motors factory outside Boston, earning enough to support his wife and three sons when he got laid off in January 1974. Unemployment kept him going for a while, but his bills started mounting, and his job hunt turned up nothing. So in February 1975, he decided to pack his family and belongings into his old Chrysler Imperial and drive south to Winter Haven, Florida, in search of a job, a lower cost of living, and warmer weather. However, things weren't much better there. The only job he could find was at a phosphate mine hauling rock out of a mosquito-infested marshland. The work paid him less than he received from his unemployment benefits. Even though his wife was able to pick up the occasional shift at a local nursing home, with the rise in inflation, the family struggled to have enough to buy food and pay the mortgage, and they fell deeper into debt. Missing their friends and old life, the Robichauxs decided after only six months to return to Boston to wait for GM to hopefully recall him back to the line. "I'd always been proud that I could take care of my family," he wistfully observed. "But now I've got to admit to myself that I've failed. And I feel ashamed."[41] Robichaux was not alone in feeling this way.

Layoffs quickly spread to all sectors of the economy, hitting everything from steel to construction to food. The decisions of many corporations to shift operations overseas exacerbated the situation. The unemployment numbers skyrocketed with thousands of people like Robichaux added daily.[42] Welfare agencies and unemployment offices found their resources strained as they were unable to keep up with the demand for food stamps, unemployment compensation, and other forms of assistance.[43] And it was not just white men who got pink slips. For traditionally marginalized groups, the situation was even more acute. Stephen Douglas, an African American veteran in Detroit, found the job prospects in the city bleak. "I'm barely surviving," he admitted. "I've put applications in everywhere, been everywhere twice, but I can't get a job." Maranda Boyd, an African American woman who had lost her job as a clerk at a city department store, complained that the few jobs available in the Detroit area were in the suburbs, and she had no means of transportation to get there.[44] As the unemployment rate reached 13.4 percent and continued to climb for people of color and women of all races, it raised concerns that the recession would thwart many of the gains of the civil rights movement and second-wave feminism.[45]

With people crisscrossing the country in search of jobs and standing for hours waiting for state relief, the situation brought back painful memories of the Great Depression. For those Americans who kept their jobs, the inflation rate's surge from 4 percent to 12.1 percent between 1973 and 1975 consumed paychecks.[46] The costs of staples from milk and meat to mortgages and car loans doubled, and income and property taxes swelled as well. Some families simply skipped luxuries like steak and weekly bowling outings, while others took to the streets or ballot boxes to protest the cost of basic goods and expanding tax bills.[47] Even though the worst of the recession abated slightly, it was clear the underlying economic problems were far from resolved. A widespread sense of hopelessness sunk in.[48] For an American society still recovering from the chaos and unrest of the late 1960s, the Vietnam War, and Watergate, stagflation was particularly unsettling. For the first time in a generation, opinion polls showed a substantial decline in optimism about the future among Americans of all income levels, races, and geographic areas.[49] Throughout the political turmoil of the 1960s, at least the country's economic prosperity and growth remained uninterrupted. Sally Martinez, a nursery schoolteacher trying to support her four children and husband who lost his job at a Chevrolet plant, captured the mood of many when she declared, "You get the feeling that everything's rotten." Rosie Washington, a twenty-seven-year-old African American single mother in Buffalo who had to turned to welfare after losing a string of administrative assistant jobs, was even more pessimistic. "This country thinks it's so damn great. It's not."[50]

For many Democrats—the Watergate Babies included—the recession proved not just an economic crisis but an intellectual and political crisis as well, which led to questioning the basic shibboleths of Keynesian theory.[51] Hart and Wirth initially advocated anti-inflationary measures and deficit reduction but realized those were only stopgap measures and they needed a bolder and more comprehensive solution. On the right, the free-market ideas of libertarian economists like Milton Friedman and Frederich von Hayek were gaining new traction and credibility. On the left, civil rights and welfare rights activists and their progressive allies in Congress were calling for an expansion of the social welfare state, including national health insurance, a substantial increase in the minimum wage, and a massive public service employment program to achieve the interrelated goals of racial and economic justice.[52] Hart, Wirth, and the other Watergate Babies were, nevertheless, dubious of both approaches. For them, the oil crisis coupled with the nation's trade deficit had laid bare the interdependency of the global economy and showed the need to look outward by accelerating the global flow of goods.[53] Similarly, the free fall of the manufacturing sector confirmed that heavy industry was not a sure way to provide jobs or economic growth. Instead, the Watergate Babies began to believe that the future for the economy and the Democrats lay in a new model of growth that focused on bolstering trade and the postindustrial sector, especially high-tech entrepreneurship.

Paul Tsongas became one of the fiercest advocates for high-tech growth. Although he was born and bred in Lowell, Massachusetts, Tsongas had little nostalgia for getting the city's famed textile mills and shoe factories humming again. As a college student, he'd been inspired by John F. Kennedy's calls for national service. After graduating from Dartmouth, he enlisted in one of the first classes of the Peace Corps and spent two years in rural

Ethiopia. He described his time in the village of Wolisso as the "most formative experience of my life" and said it instilled in him a commitment to public service and helping the poor in the United States and around the world. Yet, he approached problems of economic inequality as more of a technocrat than a social worker. After graduating from Yale Law School, he returned to the Peace Corps, but he dreamed of running for public office. He went home and successfully earned a position on the Lowell City Council and quickly advanced to Congress in 1974 and the Senate in 1978.[54]

As a city councilor, Tsongas helped devise an ambitious redevelopment plan for the city, which drew on building partnerships with local businesses and banks. The plan contributed to the turnaround of the city, especially after the minicomputer company Wang Laboratories relocated its operations to Lowell.[55] The success of the program inspired Tsongas's dogged insistence—to which he held firm in his Washington years—that Democrats should be focusing on public-private partnerships and economic growth rather than redistribution and expanding social welfare programs. "Government money has but one purpose: to foster an environment that will attract private money, giving disadvantaged sectors of society a chance to reap the rewards provided by economic growth," he maintained.[56] Tsongas contended that the political battles of the past thirty years had concentrated "on the distribution of the golden eggs" when they should have been focusing on "the health of the goose." The economic turnaround of Lowell and the state of the Massachusetts as a whole bolstered his belief that tech and trade might be the best way to keep the goose healthy.[57]

MIT economist Lester Thurow strongly influenced Tsongas's and his cohort's growing commitment to tech and other postindustrial industries. Thurow's 1980 book *The Zero-Sum Society* could be found on the shelves of many a Capitol Hill office and became something of a guidebook for Tsongas and other Watergate Babies. Thurow argued that the solution to the multifaceted problems of the 1970s lay in accelerating productivity. He believed this speedup could happen by investing public and private resources in "sunrise industries" like computing and biotechnology rather than "sunset industries" like automobiles, steel, and electronics, which had been hardest hit by the recession.[58]

It was the work of Thurow's colleague a few miles down the Charles River—Harvard professor Robert Reich—that was perhaps most significant in shaping the economic policy of this group of politicians. Reich entered Dartmouth College just a few years after Tsongas and was a standout student, balancing academics, student government, and theater. This impressive résumé led *Time* magazine to select Reich and seven others for a cover story in June 1968 called "The Graduate." *Time* called him the tiniest "Big Man on Campus" in reference to his four-foot, nine-inch frame, but Reich told the magazine he was in complete opposition to "status quo-ism."[59] Soon after the story appeared on newsstands, he was on his way to Oxford on a Rhodes Scholarship, where he overlapped and became close friends with Bill Clinton. The relationship continued when both enrolled at Yale Law School. As Clinton headed to Arkansas to launch his political career, Reich did a stint in the Carter administration before arriving at Harvard's Kennedy School of Government. Reich's wry sense of humor and candor made him a popular professor and a favorite interview subject among Washington reporters. However, it was his ideas, more than his jokes, that piqued the interest of politicians and policymakers.

Reich believed that in seeking the root causes of and solutions for the economic crisis of the 1970s, policymakers failed to pay enough attention to the issue of international competition and the structural changes in the economy. He argued that the nation's industrial base was in the midst of a transformation from less profitable and more labor-intensive sectors like automobiles, steel, and textiles to more lucrative, highly skilled, entrepreneurial, and technically intensive areas.[60] Reich contended this shift needed support from the government to speed it up. He observed that the US's biggest competitors in Western Europe and Japan had adopted industrial policies by which their governments made targeted investments in specific industries.[61] The US needed its own industrial policy. Reich and other proponents of this idea carried on the tradition of public-private partnership and using government incentives to fuel private sector growth that had been a hallmark of liberal political economy since the New Deal. In fact, Reich suggested that industrial policy was nothing more than connecting the dots among myriad existing federal programs and translating them into a more coherent plan.[62] Reich's industrial policy did, however, mark a key departure from the Keynesian model and its focus on stimulating demand. Instead, Reich emphasized increasing investment in the private sector to create productivity. Unlike conservatives like Milton Friedman, who emphasized expanding capital and letting the invisible hand of the market rule without government oversight, Reich argued that the government should direct the investment and direct it toward high-tech industries.[63]

Reich contended that the US should not try to stop industries like textiles, steel, and automobiles from shifting their production overseas. Moving production of labor-intensive work to Asia and Latin America would help those regions modernize while enabling the United States to shift its resources into sunrise industries. He recognized that this transition would leave manufacturing workers like Chuck Robichaux out of jobs. In his book *The Next American Frontier* he made a strong case for government policies that would help ease the adjustment to a high-tech, knowledge-based economy. He called for worker retraining programs, which would give people like Robichaux the skills appropriate for this new economy. He also proposed making the public education system more focused on preparing students for technologically intensive careers.[64]

The idea of an industrial policy, especially Reich's formulation of it, drew criticism from all sides. For conservatives, the idea violated the basic tenets of the free market and gave too powerful a role to the federal government. Republican staffer Bruce Bartlett derided Reich's ideas as "just new rhetoric to disguise economic planning," fearing it was a step on the road to socialism.[65] Reich's theory invoked even stronger outrage from the labor movement who worried it would make unions and their members obsolete.

A United Steel Workers representative angrily chided Reich at a Washington meeting: "You cannot glibly write off whole segments of industries."[66] Reich countered that he was by no means heartless and that he firmly believed that "social justice is not incompatible with economic growth, but essential to it."[67] He defined social justice less to mean equity for historically marginalized groups and more to include equitable distribution of income, a quality education, a clean environment, safe workplaces, and other protections and benefits for workers.[68] Reich thus believed that balancing social justice and economic growth through strategic government intervention and investment provided the best means for a successful economy and more equitable society.

Reich's ideas had immediate appeal for the Watergate Babies and was a large part of what led to their rechristening as Atari Democrats. The Watergate Babies became especially drawn to the aspects that focused on entrepreneurial-based growth. Hart deemed small businesses "the most active, innovative, and diverse sector of the economy" and suggested "we should put our money where we can use it—within the reach of American entrepreneurs." This call embodied a shift away from the macroeconomic worldview of Keynesian economics and its postwar liberal promoters like John Kenneth Galbraith, who had focused on an economy primarily comprised of large corporations and institutions.[69] In fact, encouraging entrepreneurship represented a distinctly microeconomic approach to economic growth. Yet, the ideals of entrepreneurship aligned with other aspects of this breed of Democrats' ideology, especially their belief in meritocracy and opposition to large bureaucracies. Entrepreneurship also connected to the "small is beautiful" ethos and focus on individual creativity and the self that was rampant in the 1970s. Building on Reich and Thurow's ideas, the so-called Atari Democrats began advocating for tax incentives and funding for research and development and training that would foster entrepreneurial growth in high-tech areas like computers and information technology.[70]

The focus on bolstering the growth of the high-tech economy gelled with Hart's, Wirth's, and other Atari Democrats' critique that the Democratic establishment was relying on an electoral strategy suited for the industrial past rather than the postindustrial present and future. Wirth did little to hide the fact that this kind of growth would benefit his own constituents, the type of people who he saw as critical to the future of the party. "Democratic constituencies used to be labor, blue-collar and minority-oriented," Wirth declared. "Now, as in my case, they are suburban, with two working parents—a college educated, information-age constituency."[71] Wirth, Hart, and Tsongas recognized that these white college-educated voters had also grown increasingly skeptical of New Deal and Great Society programs, which they feared they were paying for with high taxes and growing deficits but were reaping few personal benefits from. The tax revolts that were spreading around the country in the late 1970s offered one indication of this attitude. So, too, would Ronald Reagan's presidential victory.

Reagan's win over Jimmy Carter in the 1980 election confirmed the Atari Democrats' criticisms of their fellow Democrats. Tsongas accused Carter and the Democrats more broadly of "living off" the "New Deal tradition of pump priming" and their record of Social Security and Medicare, which failed to meet "realities of the 1970s and 1980s." Tsongas and his cohort sought to develop a clear alternative both to the liberalism of their fellow Democrats and antigovernment and free-market ideas of Reagan and the right. As they did so, "the solutions of the thirties will not solve the problems of the eighties" would become one of their central rallying cries.[72]

THE ROAD TO OPPORTUNITY

Two days after the 1980 election, Al From, a longtime Hill staffer, received an invitation from Louisiana representative Gillis Long to discuss the Democrats' future.[73] Things were clearly not looking good. In addition to Reagan besting Carter, the Republicans had won control of the Senate with many liberal stalwarts like George McGovern finding themselves out of a job. Reporters were already dashing off election postmortems, discussing how the Democratic

Party was bereft of ideas or a standard-bearer. Over a lengthy dinner in the House Members Dining Room, Long and From discussed their shared concerns about the party and its future and "hit it off incredibly" despite having quite different backgrounds.[74]

Long, a member of the famed Louisiana political dynasty, came to Congress in the early 1960s. He represented a largely rural district, though he was not a typical southern Democrat or typical member of the Long family. He had broken with the rest of the southern delegation by supporting civil rights legislation, earned a reputation for being deeply principled, and become a mentor to many of the newer generation of representatives like Wirth, Gephardt, and Gore.

In contrast, From had grown up in South Bend, Indiana, in a Jewish family of loyal Democrats. He went to Northwestern University where he was editor of the *Daily Northwestern*. In 1966, he gave up a job as a reporter with the *Chicago Daily News* and joined the War on Poverty instead. Office of Economic Opportunity (OEO) head Sargent Shriver hired him to investigate how the programs were being implemented on the ground in the Deep South. From 1966 to 1969, he spent time in places like Sunflower County, Mississippi, which was the home of Fannie Lou Hamer and where she led an effort to gain control of a Head Start program from the county's white power structure. The experience of watching Hamer and other southern Black grassroots activists gain control over antipoverty programs and earn a voice in politics led him to believe that personal empowerment—not direct cash assistance—was the best way to help marginalized groups. While he thought that government had an important role to play by giving people opportunities, poor people had to accept the responsibility of helping themselves.[75] It was a selective interpretation of the War on Poverty programs because many poor people used their empowerment to demand the government assistance to which they were entitled.[76] His time with the War on Poverty, nevertheless, would have a lifelong impact on From. In addition to meeting his wife, Ginger, while in Wilcox County, Alabama, and picking up a bit of a southern drawl, working for the OEO made the ideas of "opportunity and responsibility" core to his own political philosophy and later to that of the New Democrats.[77]

From went on to spend almost a decade working for Senator Edmund Muskie, a Democrat from Maine, who had a reputation for fierce independence and was a leading voice on fiscal discipline and government reform. From's work on budgetary and economic issues at the height of the 1970s convinced him that inflation was the primary source of middle-class voters' growing dissatisfaction with the Democratic Party.[78] At the tail end of the Carter administration, he went to the White House where he served as an advisor on inflation. However, he found the experience frustrating, and it solidified his belief that the Democrats needed a new approach.[79] Around the time he met with Long, he had heard Paul Tsongas talk about the need to worry about the health of the goose rather than the distribution of the eggs. The metaphor had stuck with him. "It isn't enough any more simply to pluck the feathers from the bird and redistribute them," he began to think. "The emphasis has to be on growth and investment."[80]

During their dinner, Gillis Long shared with From his view that the 1980 election represented a clear rejection of the Democrats' platform and principles. Long believed that the party needed to develop a more coherent message to be successful going forward.[81] He had decided to become chair of the House Democratic Caucus and offered From the position as its staff director. From accepted, and they immediately got to work. Long and From hoped to turn the caucus into what From described as an "incubator of ideas" to rejuvenate the Democrats.[82] To fulfill that goal, they created the congressional Committee on Party Effectiveness (CPE), which could develop a platform to give the party new meaning and purpose. Long deliberately made the thirty-member group encompass the philosophical and geographical spectrum of the party—from Boll Weevils like Charlie Stenholm of Texas to liberals like Barney Frank of Massachusetts, as well as a healthy dose of Watergate Babies, including Wirth, Gore, and Gephardt.[83]

While members of the CPE were meeting weekly over lunch in a cramped, windowless office space on the seventh floor of the

House's Longworth Office Building, less than a mile away staffers at the White House were transforming Reagan's campaign promises into a set of policies that would come to be known as Reaganomics. The agenda rested in large part on the supply-side economic theory of economist Arthur Laffer. He argued that cutting taxes especially on the highest earners would unleash investment and creativity that would "trickle down" to the rest of society and cure both inflation and unemployment. Since his first entry into politics, Reagan had made attacking poor Black welfare mothers a steadfast part of his agenda and political brand. He regaled audiences with stories of Cadillac-driving welfare queens who were defrauding the system. These claims became amplified by a growing chorus of conservative commentators who argued that AFDC encouraged dependency on the state, discouraged family stability, and contributed to an intergenerational cycle of poverty, which was simultaneously driving up crime and creating the drug crisis.[84] The Reagan administration did not fully abolish welfare but did push through sharp cuts to a large swath of means-tested domestic programs, including AFDC, unemployment benefits, Medicaid, food stamps, school lunches, and other public services intended for the poor.[85] The groups disproportionately affected by the combination of supply-side policies, social spending cuts, and the Federal Reserve's manipulation of the interest rate responded in protest. The opposition reached its apex in September 1981 when a racially and economically diverse crowd of over 250,000 people participated in a demonstration at the Capitol organized by the AFL-CIO and two hundred other organizations called Solidarity Day.[86]

As the country headed ever deeper into recession in 1982 and the protests continued, Gillis Long's committee decided to develop a policy statement that offered a clear view of the Democratic Party's vision and goals and how they were distinctly different from Reagan and the Republicans.[87] The resulting document, *Rebuilding the Road to Opportunity: A Democratic Direction for the 1980s*, was intentionally noncomprehensive and focused primarily on creating a long-term economic policy focused on growth.[88]

Along with Wirth, Al From played a major role in authoring key components of the document. While drafting it, Wirth and From consulted Robert Reich and Lester Thurow, and the influence would become clear. The section headings had names like "Investments in Our Economy" and "Investing in Our People." This redundant emphasis on "investment" was not due to the authors' limited vocabulary but their conscious effort to make the word a central theme for the Democrats in the 1980s.[89] While the authors acknowledged that investment was at the center of the economic policies of the Reagan administration, Wirth and From dismissed Reagan's faith in tax cuts as "merely a bonanza for the rich," which brought the country deeper into recession. Instead, *Rebuilding* offered an alternative investment policy that focused on building public-private partnerships that would foster postindustrial entrepreneurialism and would create "new, challenging jobs in prospering, competitive industries" like computer technology. It was up to the Democrats, the authors contended, to "rekindle the entrepreneurial spirit in America, to encourage the investment and risk taking—in the private industry and in the public sector [in order] to maintain leadership in the world economy."[90] If *investment* was the word most present in the report, the phrase *industrial policy* was the term perhaps most notably absent. However, the recommendations together essentially amounted to Reich's vision of industrial policy with a few add-ons.

At the press conference to release *Rebuilding*, Wirth deemed the document a significant shift for the Democrats. He explained that it represented a move away from the party's focus on "redistribution" and toward "growth and opportunity."[91] Wirth overstated the Democrats' tradition of redistribution and understated its history of growth policies. His use of the word *opportunity* was important. One of the goals of Wirth, From, and the other main architects of *Rebuilding* was to propel the party away from a language of *fairness*, which they felt intimated redistribution, and toward a focus on *opportunity*, which signaled the meritocratic ideal that everyone would have an equal chance to advance.[92] The term was in large part inspired by the lessons From gleaned working for the War on Poverty in the Deep South. However, it marked a deliberate effort to evade the long-standing demands of the civil rights and welfare rights movements for racial and economic justice, including a racially conscious reallocation of resources. Instead, many Democratic politicians would join in and offer a deliberately colorblind and nonredistributive path.[93]

This choice of words did not escape the notice of the *Washington Post* editorial staff who wrote an editorial accusing the Committee on Party Effectiveness of "Skirting the Fairness Issue."[94] The *Post* expressed surprise at the near absence of core Democratic issues like welfare or civil rights in *Rebuilding*. The document had no separate sections on civil rights or social welfare, which was especially notable given Reagan's sharp cuts to the social safety net and the outrage and large demonstrations those cuts had engendered. The only part of *Rebuilding* to even mention these issues was a chapter buried deep in the document called "Expanding the Role of Women in Our Economy." Drafted by a committee that included Geraldine Ferraro and Shirley Chisholm, the chapter discussed how Reagan's budget cuts caused "the safety net [to] unravel for thousands of poor women and their families with minority women the hardest hit."[95]

The lack of attention in *Rebuilding* to organized labor or to the concerns that union leaders voiced about industrial policy was also striking. From described how someone asked him how he got union leaders to sign off on something so "forward looking." He responded: "It's pretty easy. I didn't ask."[96] However, From privately advised Wirth and politicians involved to tell reporters that they believed "rank and file labor union members will embrace this program [because] it could bring about economic growth and that means more and better jobs."[97] In effect, From was trying to do an end run around labor's brass.

Rebuilding, nevertheless, gave new ammunition for unions and other liberal and left critics. Arthur M. Schlesinger Jr., an icon of postwar liberalism and close advisor to John F. Kennedy, publicly accused Wirth and allies like Gary Hart of simply "rejiggering" the ideas of Reagan, while journalist Robert M. Kaus in an article for

the *New Republic*, titled "Reaganism with a Human Face," suggested there was little difference between Ronald Reagan "and the
Democrats as Tsongas would remake them."[98] Wirth and others
bristled at the comparisons to Reagan, perhaps because they
failed to recognize that he and his allies did not think that all government intervention was wrong. "It's not a question of getting the
government off our backs," Wirth explained, but considering its
"appropriate" role and the specific areas where "the federal government does have an aggressive role to play."[99] Tsongas similarly
advocated a leaner but *more* activist government that spent less
on big social programs and instead intervened to direct private
investment toward addressing problems like capital flight, poverty, and racial segregation in urban areas.[100] While the members
of the Reagan administration saw the market as a means to shrink
the size and reach of government, Atari Democrats like Tsongas
thought market mechanisms could be adopted to make government more effective. Wirth, Tsongas, and others, in fact, spoke
forcefully against allowing government to abdicate its responsibility of protecting individuals from hardships of the market system,
which they believed the Reagan administration was doing.[101]

The debate about whether these ideas would offer salvation
for the Democrats only intensified when Gary Hart announced
his bid for the presidency in the 1984 election. Hart adopted the
slogan "New Ideas" as the organizing theme of his presidential
run. Many of his ideas, however, were those that he and the other
Watergate Babies had been promoting for the past decade.[102] Hart
spoke of the need "to adapt to enormous change at home and
abroad by devising new solutions to sustain old principles."[103] He
maintained a commitment of "compassion and caring" for those
in need, and he called Reagan's supply-side approach cruel. But
he criticized programs like cash assistance and Social Security.
He contended that establishment Democrats were too focused
on creating new agencies that "sent people checks." Instead, Hart
argued for "market mechanisms, nonbureaucratic, nonprogram-
matic methods" that could achieve the same ends.[104] "There are
other ways to help senior citizens, to help poor people, to help

unemployed people, than creating an agency and throwing dollars at that problem," Hart declared.[105] His platform also called for
stimulating investment by exempting savings from taxes, encouraging more math and science curricula in public schools, retraining workers displaced by technological changes, and promoting
arms control and energy independence.[106] In his stump speech,
the forty-seven-year-old Hart framed the election in generational
terms. "It is not a choice between Democrats and Republicans or
liberals and conservatives, but a choice between the past and the
future," he declared. "It is time for the old order to pass, for the old
establishment politicians to give way. It is time for our voices to
be heard at last."[107] Hart's message and ideas would find currency
among white, college-educated professionals who appreciated
his seemingly nonideological, pragmatic approach to problems
and commitment to economic growth.[108] Hart's campaign also
excited people like Al From who saw Hart as embodying the generational and ideological changing of the guard that he had been
long clamoring for. "Even more than his specific ideas," From explained, "it was that he challenged the old orthodoxies, the old
political arrangements"—including his explicit unwillingness to
practice "interest group politics."[109] While Hart's approach might
have earned the approval of From and the yuppies, it found little love from the labor movement and African Americans.[110] Exit
polls showed Hart capturing around 3 percent of the Black vote
in many primaries.

Hart's priorities and voter outreach strategy marked a notable
contrast to his primary opponent Jesse Jackson. Throughout his
career the forty-two-year-old civil rights activist had been controversial even among his allies, who questioned his tactics and
feared he was often too motivated by personal opportunism.[111]
Born in Jim Crow South Carolina, Jackson had become a leader
of the sit-in movement as a college student. After graduating from
seminary, he became the head of the Southern Christian Leadership Council's economic program Operation Breadbasket. In the
early 1970s, he created PUSH (People United to Serve Humanity), which emerged as a leading force in the Black struggle for

economic empowerment and justice. Announcing his candidacy, he declared: "A black candidate does not mean an exclusive black agenda, but an inclusive agenda that grows out of the black experience in America." Jackson built his campaign message and strategy around a recognition that the recession, cuts to social spending, and the social conservatism of Reagan's policies had hurt large swaths of Americans of all races. He had a firm belief that the Democratic Party could be a way to channel the aspirations and demands of historically oppressed and marginalized groups. His 1984 campaign sought to bring those groups together in a unified Rainbow Coalition of Blacks in the urban North and rural South, white farmers in the upper Midwest, labor unionists, peace activists, feminists, gay and lesbian groups, Asian Americans, Mexican Americans, and Native Americans.[112] Jackson's agenda of restoring and expanding the nation's commitment to social welfare and reducing its spending on defense galvanized the political left. With the help of a committed cadre of grassroots organizers, the Jackson campaign also inspired hundreds of thousands of people from marginalized groups, especially African Americans, to register to vote. This outpouring helped Jackson to win the DC, Louisiana, South Carolina, Mississippi, and Virginia primaries and garner 80 percent of all African American voters. As he vied for second place with Hart, Jackson's bid put the fire under the feet of Walter Mondale during the spring primary season.

Mondale embodied the traditional Democratic values and strategy that Hart and the Watergate Babies long chafed against. Despite being less than a decade older than his opponents, he seemed of a different generation. The protégé of fellow Minnesotan Hubert Humphrey, Mondale followed the footsteps of his mentor to Washington as a senator and later became Jimmy Carter's vice president.[113] Mondale had close ties to the AFL-CIO, and in 1984, the union saw him as their chance to redouble its political power and actively mobilized on his behalf.[114] Mondale also earned early and enthusiastic endorsements from Democratic lions like Tip O'Neill. This support only increased Hart's charges that Mondale was the candidate of special interest liberalism.

Mondale famously retorted by asking about Hart's New Ideas platform: "Where's the beef?" AFL-CIO head Lane Kirkland accused Hart of abandoning the labor movement for the "fabricated futurism of microchip minds."[115] The former vice president eventually narrowly won the fiercely fought race for the nomination in large part due to his support from the labor movement along with the superdelegates, who were mostly made up of party stalwarts.

Heading into the Democratic convention in San Francisco, Mondale selected Geraldine Ferraro as his running mate, and his team gave Jesse Jackson a prime speaking slot at the event in an effort to project an image of inclusivity. In his nearly hourlong address, Jackson spoke of the necessity of spreading the message that "all of us count and all of us fit somewhere." He insisted that reallocating defense spending to building bridges, schools, and hospitals and providing jobs and better social services for all was the best way forward for the Democrats and the nation.[116] Mondale's campaign largely jettisoned these ideas as well as those of Hart for tech-based economic growth. In the general election, Mondale instead called for another $29 billion cut in social expenditures and a tax hike on all families earning more than $25,000.[117] These proposals failed to inspire the larger electorate, and Mondale suffered one of the greatest defeats in presidential election history. In the end, the 1984 election did not heal the party's ideological fissures. It only sharpened them.

THE NEW DEMOCRATS

Even before the delegates officially nominated Mondale, Gillis Long and Al From invited a group of politicians in San Francisco for the Democratic National Convention to Long's hotel suite for a private meeting. On the first day of the convention, From had started a minor firestorm when he told the *Wall Street Journal* that the convention marked "the last hurrah for Mondale's part of the party."[118] The purpose of the meeting was to develop an alternative. The attendees included several members of the Committee on Party Effectiveness, senators Lawton Chiles of Florida and

Sam Nunn of Georgia, and governors Bruce Babbitt of Arizona and Charles Robb of Virginia, who shared From's frustration.[119] Long and From started the meeting by repeating their belief that the Democrats needed to restructure and focus on ideas rather than special interests. Robb and Nunn made a parallel argument that, to have any future in the Sunbelt, the party needed to make a deliberate shift to the ideological center and cater more directly to white middle-class voters. As they huddled in the cramped hotel suite, the group contemplated a range of strategies, including trying to make a bid for chair of the Democratic National Committee, forming a think tank, and establishing an independent organization.[120] The group made no decisions at this initial meeting. But Mondale's rout in the November election served as further confirmation to the participants that they needed to take charge.

In the weeks after election day, Robb hosted a series of meetings in Washington and Virginia for "fellow travelers" to develop a strategy for going forward.[121] The son-in-law of Lyndon Johnson, Robb was a retired marine captain who had a reputation for seriousness and action. The participants in these discussions included many of the same people in attendance at the hotel room powwow. The group eventually decided that the best way to push for change would be outside the formal structure of the party and they should create their own institution. Al From agreed to come up with the initial plan. He issued a memo suggesting the creation of an independent body called the Democratic Leadership Council whose purpose would be to "develop an agenda strengthening the Democratic Party and making it competitive again in national elections."[122] Robb supported the idea of staying independent as a way of avoiding what he called "the Noah's Ark approach," where "every interest group caucus has [to] be represented."[123] The independence from the party would also enable them to avoid certain campaign finance regulations. From stressed that the independence and unorthodoxy would allow the group to be more "entrepreneurial" both in their securing of funding and in their approach to policy and political strategy. From later would anoint the group as "entrepreneurs of the political ideas industry."[124] Since there was no existing organization on which to model themselves, they were stepping into what one early staffer described as "an institutional vacuum."[125]

During the DLC planning process, Gillis Long was watching the Super Bowl in his apartment at the Watergate complex when he suffered a fatal heart attack. His death left the House Democratic Caucus without a leader and From out of a job. Robb cajoled him to take the post as executive director of the nascent organization. From initially demurred because he worried about being able to pay for his children's college education without a federal paycheck. He agreed only after Robb personally guaranteed his salary for the first year.[126] From then hired Will Marshall as policy director; Marshall had served as a staffer at the Committee on Party Effectiveness where he demonstrated a knack for policy analysis. The DLC staff remained quite small during this initial stage and operated on a shoestring budget. For the first several months, Marshall received his salary through unemployment checks.[127]

The architects recruited as founding members a lineup of fourteen senators, including Nunn, Chiles, and Gore (who had just moved chambers); seventeen representatives, like Wirth, Gephardt, Leon Panetta of California, and Les Aspin of Wisconsin; and ten governors, such as Robb, Babbitt, James Blanchard of Michigan, Richard Lamm of Colorado, and Bill Clinton of Arkansas. The founding members reflected the architects' goal of "twist[ing] together" three strands of Democratic elected officials—House, Senate, and governors—who often remained in separate spheres.[128] The demographic composition reflected many of the DLC's other aims. Of the total forty-one inaugural members, there were no women, two were men of color, and only four came from outside the Sunbelt.[129] Although Robb was the most central early player, the founders decided Gephardt should be the first chair in part because he was from Missouri, and it would deflect criticisms that the group was only led by southerners and westerners. While some saw the group as an incubator for "the next Gary Hart," Hart himself opted not to join.[130]

In a clear homage to Hart, at their first press conference, Robb explained that the DLC was committed to creating "fresh ideas" for the Democratic Party.[131] He declared they hoped to create a movement of Democrats who would "change the party rather than changing parties."[132] With that idea in mind, Robb and other members adopted the term New Democrats to describe themselves. When talking to the press and public, From and Marshall counseled DLC members to define New Democrats as different from both "Old Guard Democrats and from the Republicans" and explain they would serve as a "counterweight" to the special interest groups.[133] This definition was revealing of the larger aims of the DLC and would provoke strong outrage from other factions of the Democratic Party.

In its early days, the DLC had more detractors than supporters. Arthur Schlesinger labeled the organization "a quasi-Reaganite formation" and accused it of "worshipping at the shrine of the free market." Victor Fingerhut, a longtime union pollster and strategist, called them "crypto-Republicans," and Texas populist Jim Hightower observed, "If the meek shall inherit the Earth, these timid voices will be land barons."[134] Others pointed to the DLC's race, gender, class, and geographic composition as evidence that it was a second coming of the Dixiecrats. Douglas Wilder, a Black Virginia politician, accused the council of being a divisive force whose members were making a "demeaning appeal to Southern white males."[135] Others started calling them the "conservative white caucus" or the "southern white boys caucus."[136] When the DLC served quiche and croissants at an early event and only had white male politicians speak, it intensified claims of the organization's elitism and homogeneity.[137]

Menu selections aside, it was hard not to interpret the calls of the DLC (like the Watergate Babies before them) to shift away from special interest groups as an effort to minimize the influence and voices of organized labor and African American, Latinx, feminist, and gay and lesbian groups in the party. Charlotte Taft, a committed Democrat who ran an abortion clinic in Dallas, said the DLC's opposition to interest group politics struck "a little panic in my heart," as she feared it meant the Democrats increasingly would marginalize people like herself and the issue of reproductive rights.[138] It did not help the DLC's assurances that Taft's fears were unjustified when members like Florida governor Robert Graham explained that the group sought "to give hope to people who felt they had been permanently cast aside." He was referring not to the people to whom Jesse Jackson appealed but primarily white middle-class men in Sunbelt states like his own.[139]

It was Jackson himself who offered the sharpest and most prominent condemnations of the DLC. He accused the group of "trying to push the Democratic Party to the right" and said it was "sending a clear signal" by "traveling around the country as a group of all whites." Jackson started saying that DLC actually stood for "Democrats for the Leisure Class" and its members "didn't march in the '60s and won't stand up in the '80s."[140] He urged members of the council to reject the idea that special interest groups were to blame for the party's problems. He said that environmentalists, women, Native groups, peace advocates, and farmers were not "special interests, but members of our family."[141]

In response to the criticism from Jackson and others, the DLC made a concerted effort to diversify its membership base. The leaders successfully recruited to their ranks mayors Tom Bradley of Los Angeles and Henry Cisneros of San Antonio, Texas representative Barbara Jordan, and Mississippi representative Mike Espy. The DLC convinced Rep. William Gray III, then one of the most prominent African Americans in Congress, to serve as vice chair.[142] These inclusions did not assuage skeptics. Jesse Jackson and many of his allies would continue to critique and protest the DLC in the years to come.

The DLCers decided better defining their policy agenda would offer another way to build support and defuse criticism. Over the next few years, the leaders enhanced their commitment to economic growth through free trade and high-tech entrepreneurship. Although the DLC did not directly call it industrial policy, they spoke of creating labor-management-government partnerships to improve international competitiveness in key sectors, which they presented in contrast to the Republican commitment to free markets.[143] Deflecting charges that they had entirely abandoned the core concerns or constituencies of the Democratic Party, the New Democrats decided to make poverty another central focus. Charles Robb, who became the chair of the DLC in the spring of 1986, became especially committed to the issue of urban Black poverty. His perspective and discourse often veered quite close to Daniel Patrick Moynihan's famed discussion of the problems of the Black family and the culture of poverty. Robb charged that the Democratic Party had to end their "conspiracy of silence and start a frank discussion about the obstacles to black progress," which meant grappling with the "self-defeating patterns of behavior," including teenage pregnancy, family disintegration, dropout rates, drugs, crime, and incarceration.[144] He declared the time had come for a substantial reform of the welfare system and the development of the new targeted social initiatives designed to foster self-help, self-sufficiency, and a stronger sense of reciprocal responsibility between beneficiaries and government.[145] Placing these ideas into more abstract terms, the DLC began calling for "a new opportunity offensive against poverty and dependence," contending "the best social policy of all is economic growth."[146] This idea would become one of its central exhortations in the years to come. In the mid-1980s, however, the DLC was still using broad strokes to describe its agenda of combining economic growth with opportunity to combat poverty. Its leaders decided that they had to find and develop more specific policies and programs that upheld these goals. This search would lead them to Chicago, Bangladesh, and Arkansas.

CHAPTER 2

THE POWER OF CREDIT

"We thought they were out of their minds," said ShoreBank's Mary Houghton, remembering her and her colleague Ron Grzywinski's reaction to a phone call from the Ford Foundation asking them to go to Bangladesh in 1983.[1] A decade earlier, Houghton and Grzywinski, along with two other colleagues, cofounded the ShoreBank Corporation, which established a unique model of leveraging capital from deposits at a commercial bank to create economic redevelopment in Chicago's South Shore neighborhood. ShoreBank's mission was to show that private capital could be invested to achieve social objectives and that the banking system could be used to help people of color in underinvested communities join the economic mainstream. The model proved successful in reinvigorating South Shore and had earned the bankers substantial notice and support from funders, including the Ford Foundation. Now Ford was enlisting them to consult on another innovative program started several years earlier by Muhammad Yunus. Grameen Bank, which would become one of the world's most iconic microenterprise organizations by the 1990s, used a peer-based system to offer small loans to poor women in Bangladesh to help them finance their own business endeavors.

Houghton and Grzywinski were not wrong to be skeptical about what they could offer to a program in a poor, rural, and largely Muslim country, about the size of Wisconsin but with a population of over one hundred million people. Neither had been to Asia much less Bangladesh, but it "seemed kind of exciting." Plus, Ford was an investor in ShoreBank, and they didn't want to disappoint the foundation, so they agreed to go.[2] Like many people who visited Grameen's operations, Houghton and Grzywinski were inspired watching poor women, dressed in colorful saris, huddle together on thatched mats in village centers, calculating loan payments and distributing money. They were also stirred by their conversations with Yunus about the transformative power of private capital, especially credit, to change the lives of poor people. It was rare to meet someone with such a "big idea."[3] Houghton and Grzywinski offered Yunus their banking expertise and returned to Bangladesh several more times to help him formalize his operations. The trips also led the ShoreBank founders to consider whether Yunus's model of microenterprise might work in the United States.

If the Atari Democrats and the Democratic Leadership Council offered one response to the economic crisis and contraction of the welfare state in the 1970s and 1980s, ShoreBank and Grameen Bank provided another. These organizations crafted their own versions of entrepreneur-driven economic growth that focused on applying private sector tools and funds to help poor and low-income people.

ShoreBank and Grameen's fusion of antipoverty and economic development goals was almost a political unicorn: their methods combined liberal priorities like eliminating poverty and conservative ones like leveraging capital while rejecting aspects of both big government liberalism and the Reagan Revolution's adulation of the free market. It was this orientation that would attract Bill Clinton and key members of the DLC, who recognized that Shore-Bank and Grameen might just be the political and policy solution they needed.

AN UNTESTED EXPERIMENT

It all began with happy hour. Starting in the late 1960s, a group of four thirty-something coworkers at the Hyde Park Bank in

The founders of ShoreBank clockwise from
top right: Ron Grzywinski, James Fletcher,
Mary Houghton, and Milton Davis, 1984
*Credit: Special Collections, University of
Illinois Chicago/Fred Leavitt*

Chicago met each Friday at the Eagle Bar. None of the four looked
like traditional bankers or had the usual path into working in finance. Ron Grzywinski, who was the bank's president, was in his
midthirties and had a soft-spoken and thoughtful demeanor. He
grew up in a Polish American industrial neighborhood on Chicago's South Side surrounded by steel mills even though his father
drove milk and bread delivery trucks. After working as a butcher
to pay his tuition at Loyola University, Grzywinski got a job at IBM
selling large-frame computers to banks. He eventually switched
over to banking, becoming president of a suburban bank before
transferring to Hyde Park Bank.[4] The new job brought him back
to the South Side at the height of the 1960s. Grzywinski had a
long-standing interest in civil rights and racial justice: in 1967, he

started a minority small business loan program, which was the
first of its kind in Illinois and only second in the country.[5] He recruited Milton Davis, the former chair of the Chicago chapter of
the Congress of Racial Equality, to run the division. Davis brought
along his friend James Fletcher who was the assistant director
of the Great Lakes Region Office of Economic Opportunity. Mary
Houghton also came aboard. The Milwaukee native had recently
received a master's degree in international policy from Johns
Hopkins University; she was in search of a job and thought what
Grzywinski and Davis were trying to do sounded exciting.[6] The
division was successful—even creating a few millionaires when
it financed several Black McDonald's franchise owners—and it
still gave all four the time to remain involved in local community
organizations.

On Friday afternoons, the foursome cut out early and headed
to the Eagle, which billed itself as "Hyde Park's Only Quiet Bar."
At their favorite corner table, while drinking beer and eating
pretzels dipped in mustard, conversation would often turn to the
problems of urban neighborhoods.[7] All around them, the neighborhoods of Chicago's South and West Sides were undergoing
rapid racial and economic turnover. People, capital, businesses,
and social services were leaving; poverty and unemployment
were increasing; and more and more residents felt disillusioned
and disempowered.[8] Federal programs had not stemmed the tide;
in fact, the bankers feared they might be making things worse.
Urban renewal had wreaked havoc. The Great Society and War
on Poverty had created a wide array of new programs for poor
communities, from Head Start to Legal Aid organizations, but the
programs had created a situation where local actors, especially in
Chicago, fought for political control over them, which left many
poor urban residents empty-handed.[9] The foursome were dubious
of Richard Nixon's Black capitalism agenda, which seemed a cynical way to convince African Americans to abandon the quest for
meaningful racial justice in exchange for business opportunities.
Regardless, they worried such programs—including their own—
were not meeting the demand and were missing the most serious

issues because they focused on individuals rather than on entire neighborhoods.[10] "We should do something bigger," Houghton later remembered of their thinking.[11]

The happy hour discussions also turned to the community-based organizations in which they were involved. The foursome believed that such organizations knew best about the specific needs of communities, but because, according to Grzywinski, "they didn't have an endowment like a university or hospital and weren't privately capitalized like a business, they never assembled the resources commensurate with the problem."[12] Community development corporations (CDCs) were another popular approach in the late 1960s and early 1970s. The organizations, which often grew out of religious congregations or grassroots groups, offered economic development and social services in low-income urban areas.[13] CDCs, nevertheless, spent an enormous amount of their time and resources trying to get government, philanthropic, and corporate grants, which often made them less effective in fulfilling their larger goals.[14]

The group began to discuss an alternative that neither government officials and foundation officers nor activists had thought to consider: a commercial bank.[15] The bankers knew from experience that bank managers and loan officers had important knowledge about local areas and neighborhood economies, and they had to focus on the bottom line in a way that other nonprofits often did not.[16] Plus commercial banks were self-sustaining, which meant they did not have to rely on government funds for capital. And unlike a community development corporation, a bank could issue credit, which the foursome recognized as a critical factor in fueling redevelopment. Yet, a bank that focused on community development could also counter the trends of the commercial banking industry, which had been avoiding urban neighborhoods since the 1950s. Those banks that remained in urban areas tended to make investments outside the neighborhoods in which they were located.[17]

The foursome turned their happy hour daydream into an actual plan for a community development bank that would use the capital from ordinary deposits toward redevelopment projects in the surrounding neighborhood. It could be self-sustaining and would bring both basic banking services and investment back to urban areas and community participation into the decision-making process.[18] The model they developed was rooted in their knowledge of the intricacies of banking law. It especially rested on an understanding that if they organized as a holding company rather than just a commercial bank, they could serve as both lender and initiator of projects and would be able to operate a nonprofit arm that could receive and administer social services.[19] They first named the holding company the Illinois Neighborhood Development Corporation and later changed the name to Shore-Bank. The hope was that this model would prove to banks and businesses that investing in low-income urban neighborhoods could be profitable. It could also force banks to acknowledge that redevelopment was not just the responsibility of the government but of the private sector as well.[20] Grzywinski was a firm believer in the idea that because banks had public licenses and charters, they had a responsibility to help to make society more equitable.[21] In some ways, the idea connected with the urban reinvestment movement taking root in Chicago at the same time, with which Grzywinski later became affiliated. The efforts eventually led to the passage of the Home Mortgage Disclosure Act of 1975 and the Community Reinvestment Act of 1977. These pieces of legislation enabled public scrutiny of lending records and recognized the obligation of banks to lend in communities where they do business.[22] In a deviation from the reinvestment movement, Grzywinski and his team planned to do the lending themselves.

It turned out that the ideal laboratory for the experiment was in South Shore, which was only an eight- to ten-minute drive from their offices at Hyde Park Bank.[23] Resting on the shore of Lake Michigan, South Shore contained 250 square blocks of wide boulevards and tree-lined side streets with a mix of modest brick bungalows, three-story limestone courtyard apartment buildings, and Tudor-style mansions. It had been a coveted spot for prosperous white middle-class families during the first half of the twentieth century, and 71st Street was one of Chicago's premiere shopping destinations.[24] However, the roughly 80,000-person neighborhood experienced rapid demographic change in the late 1960s. It looked very different from the early 1950s, when Grzywinski worked as a produce clerk and butcher at a South Shore Kroger supermarket to pay his way through college.[25] Between 1960 and 1972, the population shifted from 98 percent white to 75 percent Black (it would be 98 percent Black by 1980), attracting a mix of teachers, bus drivers, postal workers, and maintenance workers. Michelle Obama's family was one of the many who moved to South Shore during this period; she lived on the second floor of her aunt's bungalow on Euclid Avenue until leaving for college.[26]

The racial turnover created a chain reaction, leading the neighborhood to spiral into economic crisis. Banks stopped offering mortgages or home improvement loans, and landlords increased rents while performing less maintenance, which caused many of the apartment buildings to deteriorate. By the early 1970s, several houses and apartment buildings lay abandoned. Local businesses faltered or moved, and over a hundred storefronts sat vacant.[27] These dynamics proved attractive to Grzywinski and his team to test their theory. "We were going to a neighborhood where we were not going to have to try to overcome decades of segregated disinvestment," Houghton explained. Since they were getting there "just when the change had occurred," they thought they might have "a better chance of having a success."[28] The neighborhood also had a commercial bank for sale.

The South Shore National Bank had been in operation since the late 1930s and sat at the heart of the neighborhood's commercial center, but in the late 1960s, its assets and deposits dwindled and so, too, did its services. Milton Davis, who had moved to South Shore around that time, had tried to set up an account there and gave up after waiting in line for more than two hours.[29] Other residents experienced similar frustrations trying to get a mortgage. By the early 1970s, South Shore National was issuing only a handful of mortgages every year. In 1972, the owners petitioned the comptroller of the currency to move to a downtown Chicago location on the grounds that South Shore residents could no longer support the bank.[30] A group of residents protested that claim and even started a Stop the Bank Move Committee. The comptroller rejected the owner's application, leaving the owners eager to sell the bank.[31]

Grzywinski quickly got to work to raise the funds to purchase South Shore National. It was difficult to find people willing to invest in what they admitted was an "untested idea" to see if a bank could do what governments had failed to do and successfully rehabilitate an urban neighborhood.[32] They managed to secure $800,000 of equity capital from a group of foundations, individual private investors, nonprofits, and religious institutions. With this money and a $2.25 million loan personally guaranteed by Grzywinski and his wife, the sale went through. On August 23, 1973, Grzywinski, Davis, and Houghton became the bank's new managers. Grzywinski later said that when they arrived in South Shore, he and the team felt like they were confronting a "tornado-like, self-feeding spiral of deterioration."[33] It didn't help that they took over just months before the start of the oil crisis and recession.

After getting the keys and balance sheets of South Shore National, the new managers realized that the first way to confront this tornado would be to concentrate on getting local residents to bring their money to the bank.[34] As South Shore National's services declined, most residents had shifted their accounts to larger downtown banks in the Loop near where they worked.[35] In response, the new managers started by distributing flyers and ads throughout the neighborhood declaring "Don't Go to Strangers" and "Plant your Money Close to Home."[36] Despite the fact that Davis lived in South Shore, many residents viewed the new managers as strangers and were suspicious of their motives.[37] Davis and Grzywinski decided to take a page from Chicago's famed local aldermen and pound the pavement. In the fall of 1973 and winter of 1974, they held over eighty community meetings to recruit potential patrons.[38] Sitting in church basements, living rooms, and schools, they underscored their commitment to their neighborhood.

The new managers also made changes to the bank itself. They remodeled the lobby, which Houghton described as "grubby and depressing," and spruced up the exterior.[39] The renovations were a conscious effort to send a message to the community that they were there to stay, which was important as everything from grocery stores to government services were leaving.[40] They also hired more tellers, created a drive-through window, lengthened operating hours, lowered the minimum deposit amount, created new types of accounts that better suited the needs of the community, and substantially increased the approval of home mortgage applications.[41] These efforts worked to draw in deposits from local residents, which helped turn the bank's fortunes around.[42]

Once they were able to get the bank back on track, the management set about creating nonprofit and for-profit subsidiaries that aligned with their larger mission. The team launched a nonprofit focused on job training and counseling and other social services, a for-profit real estate development corporation that initiated projects the private market might avoid, and a minority enterprise small business investment corporation that provided venture capital for new projects.[43] The executives staffed these ventures with people who, like them, did not have traditional banking experience but were pragmatic, hardworking, dedicated, and focused on the mission.[44] Grzywinski was especially committed to recruiting people he thought were "really bright" and had "their heart in the right place" based on his conviction that the model would only work with the "right talent" running it.[45] Early hires included George Surgeon. A PhD student in sociology at the University of Chicago, he got an internship at ShoreBank in the mid-1970s with the hope of writing an ethnography of banking. He became instantly attracted to ShoreBank's mission, especially its efforts to address racial inequities in mortgage and small business lending and enjoyed working for "really cool" and inspiring people like Grzywinski and Houghton.[46] He also found that his social science quantitative skills, like making spreadsheets and using computers, translated to banking, and he enjoyed the work. He never returned to the University of Chicago and remained at ShoreBank for the next thirty-five years, starting as a loan officer and eventually becoming chief financial officer, among other roles.

ShoreBank's management quickly recognized that it could not rely solely on deposits from local residents to maintain these various components and their staffs and achieve the bank's economic development goals. The viability of the bank depended on bringing in larger, more profitable deposits from outside sources. The bankers decided their best bet was to tap into the growing interest in socially responsible investing. The movement first took shape with religious institutions who wanted to avoid investing their endowments in companies that made weapons used in the Vietnam War or did business in South Africa. Socially responsible investing quickly spread beyond religious orders as many individuals in the 1970s were looking for ways to reconcile their moral values with their financial imperatives.[47]

The South Shore team developed a program called Development Deposits to attract outsiders to open accounts at the banks. Susan Davis, who ran a feminist newsletter, came aboard as the first head of the program. She orchestrated a campaign to target people and institutions with records of giving to liberal causes through direct mail and taking ads out in publications like the *New Yorker* and the *Atlantic*.[48] The campaign promised potential depositors that South Shore could provide the same services, interest rates, and depositor insurance as a traditional bank. But, by having an account at South Shore, the depositor could also "do good" by helping inner-city residents.[49] Unlike most banks, which were redlining areas by restricting the flow of mortgages and other forms of credit and investment, Davis promised investors that they could help ShoreBank "greenline" urban neighborhoods like South Shore.[50]

It turned out there were many people and organizations interested in such an opportunity. The fund grew from $863,000 in 1974 to $7,300,000 by the end of 1976.[51] By 1978, the list of institutions with significant deposits at South Shore ranged from corporations, like Amoco Oil, Avon, General Mills, Philip Morris, United Airlines, and Xerox, to seventy-five religious groups and nonprofits like the Center for Community Change and the Legal Assistance Foundation of Chicago.[52] Individuals from all over the country (and eventually the world) set up accounts, enticed by the prospect of having their bank deposits assist in addressing the problems of an urban area that was hundreds or thousands of miles away and that they never visited. By 1981, Development Deposits represented a quarter of the bank's deposits, and that percentage increased over the 1980s.[53]

Despite this influx of outside funds, ShoreBank initially struggled to get its redevelopment efforts off the ground. In its early years, the bankers focused primarily on reviving commercial activity in South Shore by providing loans to the owners of food and liquor stores, cleaners, and repair shops. The loans tended to be time intensive for the bank's staff, and experienced high rates of delinquency and default, which was impinging on other aspects of ShoreBank's operation as well as its ability to provide even a modest return to its investors. Most of the businesses did not survive, save for a few fast-food franchises, which at best provided minimum wage jobs.[54] By 1980, South Shore's main shopping strip, which sat on the same stretch of 71st Street as the bank, looked in worse shape than a decade earlier. The bankers realized, however, that they had overlooked another type of potential entrepreneur in their midst, one that could provide another revenue stream for the bank.

The discovery happened somewhat accidentally. While 70 percent of the land area of South Shore was covered by single family homes, 70 percent of the residential stock consisted of three-story walkup apartment buildings.[55] Most of the buildings had been built in the 1920s and needed major renovations. The owners were usually absentee, and many of the buildings were hovering near foreclosure.[56] Local electricians, plumbers, and city employees who either lived in or near the buildings began applying to the bank to purchase and renovate them and then rent out the units. Management realized that this was a golden opportunity to not only encourage local entrepreneurship but also revitalize the neighborhood's real estate stock.[57]

ShoreBank set up an entire program focused on giving out loans to the these "ma-and-pa rehabbers," as the bankers began to call them. Most of the rehabbers would not have qualified for a loan at another bank because the amount they needed was too low or they could not offer enough collateral or because of the color of their skin. ShoreBank staff instead decided to rely on "old-fashioned character lending," seeking out borrowers who were reliable and had home renovation skills and a sense of business acumen, especially the "street smarts" to select reliable tenants.[58] The loans offered to the rehabbers were not contingency-free. The loan officers required that the borrower make specific improvements, such as sandblasting a façade, installing new lighting or windows, and putting up wrought-iron fencing to improve security to increase the value of the property.[59] The ma-and-pa rehabbers often performed these tasks themselves after work and on the weekends.

Keith Banks was one of the first borrowers. A turbine operator at Commonwealth Edison for more than twenty years, he took his life savings of $14,000, got a $40,000 mortgage and a $15,000 rehab loan from South Shore Bank, and invested it all into a rundown multiunit building, which he spent the weekends renovating.[60] By 1984, Banks had quit his day job, expanded his real estate portfolio to four buildings, and later doubled his holdings again. "Every place I buy a building," he observed, "I also see neighbors starting to fix up their buildings and it makes me feel good."[61] As Banks described, the program created a chain reaction that would have a dramatic effect in transforming the real estate stock of the neighborhood while also providing a means of employment and wealth generation for local residents.

ShoreBank management saw the ma-and-pa rehabbers as an important way to challenge most financial institutions' and investors' attitudes about urban residents. The bankers proved that low- and moderate-income people of color were "actually credit

ShoreBank borrower Jim Taylor performing maintenance on a unit in the South Shore apartment building he owned and managed with his wife Rita, 1984

Credit: Special Collections, University of Illinois Chicago/Fred Leavitt

worthy, they want to improve their own life conditions."[62] In fact, management reported that Banks and his fellow rehabbers revealed that private credit was "the single most important element" in creating capital-generating opportunities for local residents, restoring market forces in disinvested neighborhoods, and assuring the financial stability of cities.[63] ShoreBank thereby developed its own version of coupling growth and opportunity in a moment when the traditional forms of both were in short supply from the state and local governments.

ShoreBank's lending practices paralleled the meritocratic ethos of the New Democrats. The bank consciously sought out local residents, who it recognized had the "capacity to succeed" and were "winners."[64] ShoreBank officials told prospective borrowers: "If you've got the talent, we've got the money. If you don't have the talent, all the money in the world won't help."[65] This approach undoubtedly created winners and losers among residents and still assumed that there were local residents who were unworthy of credit and who would not reap the full benefits from the bank's model. It pointed to the fundamental constraints of Shore-Bank's market orientation and focus on bottom-line discipline to address the structural problems of racial segregation and capital disinvestment.

While ShoreBank may have been a socially conscious firm, it did not have the radical commitment of Saul Alinsky, Black Power groups, or even the Community Action Programs of the War on Poverty. Several figures in Chicago's vibrant network of community organizations, in fact, raised concerns that ShoreBank prioritized banking and the bottom line over the priorities and political empowerment of local residents.[66] "We don't see organizing the community as our job," Grzywinski later quipped in response to such criticism. "We try to be a professional bank organization—bank writ large—that behaves professionally and delivers money and talent to the neighborhood and helps the neighborhood compete."[67] That comment sharply delineated the ways in which ShoreBank's model deviated from many community-based and civil rights organizations of the 1960s. To others, including the New Democrats, it was that very fact that would make the model so attractive.

Even among detractors, it was hard to deny ShoreBank's contribution to the transformation of South Shore. After a decade in operation, not only did the neighborhood's residential streets look better, but property values and median family income had also increased.[68] ShoreBank's real estate corporation developed a $25 million apartment complex project called Parkways, which consisted of twenty buildings spread over twelve square blocks in the community's northwest corner.[69] Other financial institutions, which had shunned the area, were now eager to offer mortgages and do their own real estate development in South Shore.[70] Eventually, other banks would open up branches in the neighborhood. Grzywinski took the competition as a sign of success, fulfilling their goal "to make markets work again" in the area.[71] South Shore had also managed to avoid many of the traditional patterns of gentrification and experienced minimal displacement of local residents or an influx of white residents coming back into the community. The bank struggled and came "close to the edge" in the late

1970s, as it had to contend with the economic recession and the spike in interest rates, which affected the entire banking industry.[72] Yet, by the early 1980s, it was consistently turning a profit.

Management maintained that these successes proved that "the best way to achieve a community development agenda is with the hard discipline of business."[73] This contention gained national recognition. ShoreBank became the subject of stories in several major news outlets, and the bank received inquiries, invitations, and funding from policy experts, bank regulators, politicians, and philanthropic foundations.[74] It was an appreciation of South Shore's vision and business and banking expertise that led an officer at the Ford Foundation to suggest that Mary Houghton and Ron Grzywinski could help a project that Ford was supporting in Bangladesh.

DISCIPLINE, UNITY, COURAGE, AND HARD WORK

Muhammad Yunus's path into banking was as unexpected as that of ShoreBank's management team. Born into an affluent Bengali Muslim family in 1940, Yunus grew up in the port city of Chittagong. He received a Fulbright scholarship in 1965 to go to the United States to pursue a doctorate in development economics at Vanderbilt University. He then accepted a teaching position at Middle Tennessee State University. But, inspired by the Bangladesh War for Independence in late 1971, he returned home, hoping he could apply his economic expertise to help build the new country.[75] He first took a job with the government planning division but quickly found the new government equal parts bureaucratic, ineffectual, and corrupt. He soon left to become chair of the economics department at the University of Chittagong. Witnessing firsthand the devastating famine that killed several hundred thousand Bangladeshis between 1973 and 1974, he found his research and teaching on econometrics frustrating and useless. He decided that he should focus instead on the problems of hunger and poverty and that he and his students should learn economics not from textbooks but from actual people.[76] He thus started taking groups

of graduate students into villages in the Bangladeshi countryside
to study the habits and practices of the poor.

In a story that would eventually become part of Yunus's personal legend, one day on a visit to the village of Jobra in 1976, he
stopped in front of a thatch-roof hut. He saw a woman squatting on
the dirt floor intently weaving a bamboo stool. Her name was Sufiya Begum. Though her stools were sturdy and expertly crafted,
Begum only made a profit of two cents per stool because she had
to purchase her supplies from a middleman or borrow from the
village money lender who charged interest of 10 percent a week.
She also could not get a loan from a formal financial institution. In
1970s Bangladesh, banks did not give loans to women much less
to a poor villager like Begum, who was illiterate and could not put
up any collateral.[77]

Yunus approached the problem as a neoclassical economist
and identified that a lack of access to capital was the main con-
straint keeping Begum and her fellow villagers in poverty.[78] Thus
he reasoned access to small amounts of credit would provide poor
rural villagers the means to propel themselves out of poverty. To
apply this theory, he came up with an experiment that vaguely
resembled a word problem from an introductory college economics course. He would provide very small loans that allowed villagers in Jobra to translate skills like making stools, taking care of
cows and other livestock, and husking or puffing rice into income-
generating activities. He cobbled together funds from a commercial bank in Bangladesh and the Ford Foundation and relied on
the labor of his graduate students to launch the experiment. He
named it Grameen, the Bengali word for "village."

Yunus took a leave of absence from the university, and over
the next few years, he hired more permanent staff members and
set up branches throughout Bangladesh.[79] In the process, he and
his staff refined aspects of the project. Yunus studied existing
credit cooperative programs in Bangladesh and India and realized
many failed because they gave loans that were too large and had
a long repayment schedule.[80] Instead, Grameen distributed small
amounts of money and required borrowers to make repayments

weekly. He also adapted a peer-group model where borrowers created groups of four or five. The group members offered one another both support and peer pressure. If one of them failed to make a repayment, it meant they all did, and the group could not take out a larger loan. The approach shifted the responsibility of supervision and monitoring onto the other members of the group, which not only reduced the work of Grameen employees but also encouraged the discipline and self-reliance of the borrowers.[81] Grameen charged an interest rate of about 20 percent, which was significantly higher than most commercial rates in the United States but lower than the average loan shark in rural Bangladesh. The high rate offered a way to make the project potentially self-sustaining and to remind borrowers that it was not a charity.[82]

Grameen saw results immediately. Yunus liked to tell the story of an extremely poor woman who took a loan that equaled one dollar to sell bangles and hair ribbons door to door.[83] Most borrowers took out the equivalent of sixty dollars to buy a goat or a cow or a machine or fabric for making saris. After they paid back their first loan, a borrower's next one might be larger, which they would use to buy a cart or a loom.

Bhagyarani, an early borrower, followed that pattern. The mother of four lived in the village of Kuttalypara in a small hut entirely made of hay with no furniture. Since the war for liberation, she had hovered near starvation, which worsened when her husband contracted tuberculosis. She tried to support the family by doing odd jobs for her neighbors, but it was not nearly enough to feed her children or buy her husband his medicine. She routinely went three days without food. Grameen became a lifeline. Bhagyarani took out her first loan to start a rice-husking business and paid it off in six months. She then took out another larger loan and bought a pregnant cow whose milk she used to sell and feed her family. Through her small enterprises, she was able to feed and dress her children and send them to school and to give her husband the medical care he needed. She also became a leader of her borrowing group, making sure none of the other members missed a meeting or payment. Bhagyarani celebrated how

Grameen brought her not just material wealth but also a sense of self-worth. "Before joining the bank I did not think of myself as a human being," she declared, "but now things have changed."[84]

Thanks to the commitment and discipline of borrowers like Bhagyarani, Grameen experienced, almost from the start, a 98 percent on-time repayment, and less than 1 percent of borrowers defaulted. These results were especially impressive given the bank's high interest rate. Many of the borrowers' family incomes increased over just a couple of years, and their asset bases grew as they acquired new animals and machines and made improvements to their homes. Yunus was convinced the results dispelled the myth that people were poor because they did not work hard or lacked skills. Women like Bhagyarani and Sufiya Begnum, in his estimation, worked "very hard—harder than anybody else, but did not receive the full worth of this work."[85] The women also disproved the common assumptions that the poor could not save money and that the banking system required collateral. In fact, Grameen's experimental approach showed that peer pressure could be its own form of collateral. Grameen's results suggested that access to even a small amount of capital could serve as an effective pathway out of poverty, especially for women.[86]

While the Grameen experiment initially included both male and female borrowers, the project increasingly concentrated just on women. This focus emerged in part to challenge many of the traditional customs of the largely Muslim country.[87] Most women in Bangladesh lived in rural villages, were illiterate, and got married and had children before the age of eighteen. They also abided by Muslim practices that left them relatively secluded and unable to earn an income.[88] Women who lost their husbands to war, famine, or abandonment faced further marginalization and desperation. Yunus believed that self-employment opportunities would help women confront this undervaluing, repression, and lack of independence because rather than learning a new skill, a borrower could "do whatever she does best, and earn money for it."[89]

Yunus had another reason for favoring women. A few years of running the project led him to believe that women were by nature more responsible borrowers than men. He found that women did not just make payments more regularly, but also used the funds in more responsible ways. "Credit given to a woman brings about change faster than when given to a man," Yunus frequently explained. "When a poor father starts making extra income, he starts dreaming about himself, [but] a woman sees much further into the future than a man does. She wants to have a better life for her children."[90] Thus, lending to women, he believed, could have a greater multiplier effect and would offer a better means to address poverty and create upward mobility among poor rural families. This reasoning connected to a movement gaining ground in the 1970s in the fields of economics and international development called women-in-economics, which emphasized the role of women in economic development. Advocates, like Danish economist Ester Boserup, argued for gender equity in development and for programs that integrated women into the economy.[91] Yunus's model combined this economic theory with a stronger dose of gender essentialism. It treated a poor woman as a rational economic actor who operated in the best interest of herself, her family, and society. Yunus and Grameen thereby both challenged and reproduced key ideas about poor women's place in Bangladesh society.

Yunus's vision of entrepreneurship was equal parts progressive and neoliberal. His understanding of entrepreneurship drew upon his graduate school reading of economic theorist Joseph Schumpeter, who argued that entrepreneurs acted as important agents of change and could reshape entire industries and economies.[92] Schumpeter articulated that the traits of entrepreneurship were held by only a select few and exclusively by white males. Yunus adopted a definition that was far more expansive and included, if not focused on, poor brown women. Although Yunus's idea was on the surface a radical idea, his thinking suggested the core neoliberal principle that entrepreneurship and the market offered the best path toward individual freedom. Sounding an awful lot like a Chicago School economist, Yunus would frequently declare, "If we imagine a world where every human being is a potential entrepreneur, we'll build a system to give everybody a chance to materialize

A Grameen Bank borrower in Bangladesh receives her loan, 1983
Credit: Rockefeller Archive Center

his or her potential."[93] Like ShoreBank, Grameen's model celebrated the meritocratic dimensions of entrepreneurship.[94] On the
one hand, the focus on meritocracy challenged Bangladesh's caste
system. Yet, on the other hand, it stigmatized and did little to help
the poor people who might not possess the qualities of hard work
and resilience or a natural urge to provide for their families.

When explaining Grameen, Yunus often told the stories of individual borrowers like Bhagyarani and how joining the program
changed their lives.[95] The tactic in part aimed to make the project's
purpose accessible and reinforce the importance of entrepreneurship in motivating poor rural women to achieve their potential.
Despite relating the experiences of dozens of different women in
various villages throughout Bangladesh, the narratives followed
a linear trajectory of desperation to self-sufficiency and personal
empowerment, which made the individual women relatively alike.
The simple, almost fable-like style of the narratives failed to meaningfully analyze other aspects of the women's experiences or provide the full range of their attitudes about the program.[96] The tool,
nevertheless, became a key aspect of Grameen's presentation and
increasingly other microcredit programs as well.

As Grameen evolved, Yunus began to think about how the program offered an entry point to addressing a range of other social problems. The project adopted a pledge called the Sixteen Decisions, which all participants had to memorize and say in unison at the start of every meeting. The decisions revealed how the credit and social dimensions of Grameen became increasingly inseparable. The list focused specifically on behavioral norms. It made borrowers promise to practice "discipline, unity, courage, and hard work in all parts of our lives," "not to give or take dowries," to "keep our families small," to "not live in a dilapidated house," "to grow and eat vegetables," to "build and use pit-latrines," and to engage in physical exercise.[97] Grameen imposed discipline by making attendance and promptness mandatory at every meeting, and borrowers had to demonstrate that they understood the rules and regulations of the organization by taking an oral exam. It also demanded borrowers use a salute as greeting for one another to further encourage a sense of self-esteem and empowerment. Some development experts raised eyebrows that these requirements and practices were veering close to indoctrination.[98] Yet for many of the borrowers, it evidently solidified both their loyalty to one another and the program. "The Grameen Bank saved us all," Bhagyarani declared. "As long I live, I shall not let anybody break its rules." A borrower named Samina went even further and told a staffer: "I am prepared to die for the bank. If necessary I'd work night and day to keep the group . . . going."[99] The commitment of Bhagyarani, Samina, and countless other women made it difficult for Yunus to consider returning to the academy. By 1982, Grameen had a presence in over 480 villages and extended loans to 25,000 borrowers.[100] Yunus decided to resign from the university so that he could expand the project significantly and convert it from an NGO into a formal independent bank. To fund these new plans, he reached out to several institutions, including the Ford Foundation.

Ford had been Grameen's earliest and most critical donor. The foundation's Bangladesh office recognized how aspects of the project fit in with the mandate sent by Ford's leadership in the 1970s and 1980s to support innovative programs that could empower a large number of poor people and shift toward funding NGOs instead of government programs.[101] Following the pulse of the time further, Ford had begun to have an interest both domestically and internationally in funding organizations that had a more businesslike orientation and adopted techniques from the private sector.[102] This focus clearly made Grameen additionally attractive. Ford had also begun deliberately prioritizing women's issues starting in 1979, doubling its allocation for grants aimed at female advancement and dispatching staffers with a specialty in women's issues to its international offices.[103] Adrienne Germain, who became head of Ford's Bangladesh field office in the early 1980s, was interested in expanding the foundation's focus on women in Bangladesh beyond population control and family planning. Germain was immediately taken with Grameen's commitment to enhancing the economic independence and social power of poor women.[104] She and the officials back in New York were supportive of Grameen's plans to expand, but both they—and Yunus himself— thought he needed help to scale up and become a formal bank. As he was preparing to get a bank charter, he asked Germain to recommend a list of Indian and American bankers he could talk to.[105] From that list, Yunus selected Ron Grzywinski and Mary Houghton of ShoreBank.

The ShoreBank executives arrived in Bangladesh in April 1983 for a two-week trip. They stayed at the Ford Foundation's guesthouse in Dhaka, which was in a rare quiet neighborhood in the crowded and chaotic city. Each morning, Yunus picked them up in a car, and they would travel out to various villages to observe borrowers' weekly meetings and meet with bank employees at Grameen's branches.[106] In the car and at night when they came back to Dhaka, Grzywinski, Houghton, and Yunus would talk.[107] The conversations led the ShoreBank executives to better recognize why Yunus had selected them to assist him. "We were thunderstruck by how much we had in common," Houghton recounted.[108]

Though they operated in very different environments, the three shared a belief in harnessing private sector methods to address problems of inequality. Grzywinski and Houghton, like Yunus, had seen firsthand how the very basic tools of the banking system could create a self-generating revenue stream and a sense of discipline that would make both their programs and their borrowers self-sufficient. All three also recognized the power of credit to address inequality and empower low-income people, be it a rehabber like Keith Banks in South Shore or a paddy husker like Bhagyrani in rural Bangladesh.[109] At the time of the ShoreBank founders' visit, Yunus was developing an argument that credit should be considered a fundamental human right along with food, clothing, and medical care. In fact, he maintained that it was the *most basic* right since it led to all other rights.[110] Turning another principle of poverty experts on its head, Yunus was convinced that self-employment was preferable to wage employment for poor women. Self-employment had flexibility so women could do it in their homes and around the demands of their other household duties. Yunus believed it had more chance for upward mobility than working in the fields or a factory.[111] (This same argument would later be used to celebrate the gig economy in the 2000s and 2010s).

Ford officers had only expected that Yunus, Grzywinski, and Houghton would chat and learn from one another. But the Shore-Bank executives decided they should use the last part of their time in Bangladesh to write a report with some recommendations for Yunus and the Ford Foundation to follow.[112] A Ford field officer stationed in Bangladesh reported back to the New York office that their work "was a stunning success" and "their experience and skills was exactly what Yunus is looking for and we believe helped him considerably."[113]

While Grzywinski had been drafting the recommendations, Houghton described that she got "totally bored" sitting around the Ford Foundation's Dhaka guesthouse. Starting with a little handheld calculator, she began trying to figure out the financial projections for the Grameen Bank.[114] She tabulated what its balance sheet would look like and what its internal expense statements would be if it continued on the same path of growth. Houghton's area of expertise was in small business lending, so she was a bit far afield. She taught herself as she went drawing on things she had picked up from a decade at ShoreBank. She decided to keep working on it when she got back to Chicago. ShoreBank had just gotten its first personal computer, and she used the early spreadsheet software VisiCalc to convert what she had tabulated on her handheld calculator into a set of financial projections to help Yunus plan for the growth of the bank.[115] The numbers and modeling became crucial to Yunus's ability to negotiate with Ford and other funders for additional money. Grzywinski and Houghton's involvement with Grameen continued after that. The two returned to Bangladesh several times over the next few years and were able to assist Yunus with financial modeling using their newfound appreciation for computers. At the time of their visits, Grameen employees were keeping track of transactions by hand, which had become ever more challenging as the bank added more customers, especially because Grameen required weekly repayments. Grzywinski and Houghton developed a computerized system that enabled Grameen management to monitor the bank's lending disbursements and performance and create financial projections.[116] Yunus immediately embraced the system. It appealed to his previous incarnation as a social science researcher, and he became a strong advocate of the use of microcomputer capacity at Grameen.[117] Houghton maintained the system was critical to Grameen's ability to manage "a high-volume, far-flung operation" and "delive[r] capital and support to the poor."[118]

EVERY PERSON AN ENTREPRENEUR

As Grameen grew, Yunus became increasingly convinced that its microenterprise model had the potential not just to reconceptualize banking for the poor but also international development more broadly. He staunchly criticized what he called the "big bang" theories of international development, like modernization and the Green Revolution. These approaches focused on large projects, such as building bridges, dams, and large factories and spawning large agribusinesses, rather than distributing it directly to the people who needed it most.[119] He offered a scorched earth perspective of traditional forms of development aid, which he suggested merely expanded and enriched government bureaucracies and armies of private development consultants. He contended that the billions of dollars in aid allocated to Bangladesh rarely reached or helped the poor and only intensified poverty and inequality.[120] Yunus advocated offering credit to poor women, saying it was a preferable way of addressing the problems of hunger and deprivation than building an impressive bridge or providing credit to a large government program.

Although Yunus arrived at these ideas from a very different perspective, they had a lot in common with those of the New Democrats launching the Democratic Leadership Council around the same time. Yunus offered similar critiques of bureaucracy and promoted the notion of empowering the poor and making them more independent and responsible by relying on market-based techniques. Yunus, like the DLC founders, was also interested in finding alternative means of generating macroeconomic growth. He started to argue that self-employment programs were an overlooked means of economic development. Sounding an awful lot like Al From and Charles Robb, Yunus started arguing that microenterprise programs could transform "men and women who were a burden to the society at large" into "productive and earning members contributing to the economic well-being of the nation."[121]

Yunus's ideas about the potential of poor entrepreneurs to fuel economic development also paralleled those of Peruvian economist Hernando de Soto, who was simultaneously taking the development world by storm.[122] De Soto's influential book *The Other Path: The Invisible Revolution in the Third World* argued that capitalizing on the entrepreneurial practices of the poor could address the problems of underdevelopment in Peru and other parts of the Global South. Yunus shared de Soto's criticism of the ways that countries like Bangladesh and Peru were assuming major amounts of debt from foreign banks and institutions and feared it was creating a system of dependency. Yunus, nevertheless, maintained that when distributed in more micro ways, to organizations like Grameen and to poor women, credit could be liberating and empowering.[123]

Yunus was not alone in recognizing the potential of small businesses, self-employment, and credit to help the poor in the Global South in the 1970s and 1980s. The growing shift toward export-oriented production, industrialization, and large agribusinesses led to a decline in family-level subsistence farming.[124] People in places like Peru, Bolivia, and the Dominican Republic were turning to self-employment, such as street vending and sewing, for survival. Other countries like Egypt had a long and vibrant tradition of small informal workshops operated by craftsmen.[125] By the mid-1970s, it was estimated that the informal sector comprised 30 to 70 percent of the labor force in developing countries and 80 to 90 percent of the economic activity in many poor villages and barrios.[126] NGOs like Accion in Latin America, the Self-Employed Women's Association (SEWA) in India, and the Bangladesh Rural Advancement Committee (BRAC) in Bangladesh launched credit programs to help the members of the informal sector. These organizations were also experimenting with a solidarity group model directed toward women around the same time that Yunus was getting Grameen off the ground.

The imposition of structural adjustment policies further contributed to the surge in microenterprise programs.[127] From Bangladesh to Argentina, countries borrowed large sums from international creditors to fund their industrialization efforts in the 1960s and 1970s.[128] However, the combination of the oil crisis and the prolonged recession led most of these countries to go into significant debt by the early 1980s. Recognizing that the situation threatened the stability of the international financial system, the International Monetary Fund and World Bank offered bailouts. But in exchange, they administered a harsh medicine of austerity and privatization, free trade, and sharp cuts to social services.[129] Many countries and international aid organizations actively encouraged the poor to rely on NGOs like microenterprise programs for services once offered by the state.[130]

The idea of microenterprise was especially appealing to the US Agency for International Development (USAID), the central development aid organization in the United States. Founded during the Kennedy administration, the agency initially focused on modernization and industrial development.[131] At the height of the Vietnam era, this focus endured extensive pushback, especially for the ways it did not reach or involve the poor. In response, Congress passed the Foreign Assistance Act in 1973, which mandated USAID's focus on the very poor's "basic human needs" like food and nutrition, health, population planning, and education. Bangladesh had been at the receiving end of some of this shift in priorities.[132] In addition, women-in-development advocates and feminist groups pressured Congress to add the Percy Amendment to the Foreign Assistance Act, which required USAID to make women's issues a priority in funding decisions and program design.[133] It led the agency to establish a Women in Development Office to fulfill this requirement. When Reagan took office, his administration sought to impose its own priorities onto USAID. The White House pressured the agency to make private sector growth central to all its projects and channel more of its activities through private voluntary organizations that were businesslike in their operations.[134] Microenterprise offered USAID a way to square the circle between the requirements of Congress to focus on poor women and the Reagan administration to focus on the private sector.[135] USAID began to sponsor studies and pilot programs in countries ranging from Egypt and Kenya to the Dominican Republic and Costa Rica.[136] The agency confronted a shrinking budget under Reagan, and USAID staffers acknowledged these programs had the additional advantage of being cheaper than traditional aid programs because they operated on loans and had the potential to become self-sustaining. Finally, USAID recognized how microenterprise aligned with the growing excitement about entrepreneurship, which in the 1980s was spanning business, society, and both sides of the political aisle, from Ronald Reagan to the New Democrats of the DLC. This converging set of factors led interest in microenterprise to spread from USAID to the chambers of Congress and the national press by the mid-1980s.

Muhammad Yunus's gift as a salesperson and spokesperson for Grameen and microenterprise directly contributed to the increased attention. His charisma and commitment mesmerized journalists and politicians, much as they had captivated Ron Gryzwinski and Mary Houghton and Ford Foundation officials. Journalists and development experts began to make the pilgrimage to rural Bangladesh to witness Grameen borrowers in action and speak with the man who had purportedly cracked the code of poverty in the Global South with a simple and inexpensive solution. In early 1986, Yunus accepted an invitation to travel from Bangladesh to Washington to testify before a congressional subcommittee hearing about microenterprise. He captivated representatives on both sides of the aisle with stirring testimony that intertwined his personal narrative and that of several of his borrowers with the bank's practices and his own philosophy on poverty alleviation.[137]

Yunus deftly embraced the language and ideas of the 1980s zeitgeist to present microenterprise to US audiences. This strategy further elicited the praise of politicians and positive media coverage. In addition to liberally adopting the term *entrepreneur* to describe the borrowers, he underlined that Grameen was not a charity "doing any favors. We are in business." Positive stories about Grameen and Yunus started running in many major news outlets, including the *New York Times* and *Washington Post*, putting him on the fast track to international celebrity status. Reporters praised how Grameen was a revolutionary approach to solving the problem of global poverty and compared him to Gandhi, as they breathlessly adulated that "no other banker in the world is like Muhammad Yunus."[138] The reports about the success of Grameen in Bangladesh sparked many people to wonder whether microenterprise might work to help the poor in the United States. Ron Grzywinski and Mary Houghton were ahead of the game and got the chance to experiment with microenterprise domestically after they received another unusual request. This time it came from Arkansas.

CHAPTER 3

BE YOUR OWN BOSS

D orothy Quarles achieved an impossible dream when she opened a small takeout restaurant and catering business called DQs in the late 1980s.[1] Quarles, an African American divorced mother of five, lived in Pine Bluff, Arkansas, one of the poorest cities in the second poorest state in the United States. She had worked for over forty years as a cook in private homes and long dreamed of starting her own business where she could her sell her casseroles and custard pies. But she had no savings or form of credit to receive a conventional loan from a commercial bank.

Quarles found a solution when the Good Faith Fund (GFF), a microenterprise organization directly modeled on Grameen Bank opened in Pine Bluff in 1988. Quarles secured an initial loan of $1,500 from GFF to purchase a commercial oven and steam table. She later received another $1,800, which she used to buy a station wagon to expand her catering business.[2] The organization's head praised her as "one of our hardest workers." Despite the long hours, Quarles declared, "I prefer this to working anywhere."[3] She proudly wore a T-shirt made by another member of the organization with the words: "Make Your Own Job."[4] "I wanted to be my own boss," she said. "The Good Faith Fund was really a lifesaver."[5] GFF had enabled her to do just that, not only by providing loans and the support network of the peer group but also by teaching her bookkeeping and cash management.

The Good Faith Fund was one part of the Southern Development Bancorporation. The Arkansas-based community development bank was founded in 1986 through a seemingly unlikely collaboration between the Winthrop Rockefeller Foundation, the executives of ShoreBank, and the administration of Governor Bill Clinton. It built directly on the models of economic development forged by ShoreBank and Grameen Bank. Like ShoreBank, Southern (as people referred to it) used a commercial bank to catalyze economic development and job opportunities in a distressed area. It focused especially on helping low-income residents in the Arkansas Delta launch small, homegrown businesses like Quarles's DQs.

The physical landscape and history of rural Arkansas was quite different from that of the South Side of Chicago or Bangladesh. It was surprising, perhaps, that it would become the testing ground for implementing ShoreBank's approach outside Chicago and for Muhammad Yunus to bring the Grameen model of microenterprise to the United States. However, the ShoreBank staff, Yunus, the Clintons, and philanthropic underwriters saw it as an important opportunity to show how market-oriented antipoverty programs could be adapted to rural parts of the US. Supporters also believed it could serve as an important prototype for proving how the structures of the private sector, especially the banking system, could be used to address problems like unemployment, economic development, and poverty, which had long been the domain of the public sector.

The program's double bottom-line goals and focus on encouraging individual responsibility and independence among low-income people and communities would generate a considerable amount of national attention. The idea eventually became especially popular with the members of the Democratic Leadership Council, as the type of approach to economic development, poverty, and welfare reform they believed the country should adopt. The project established an important version of partnership between government, nonprofits, philanthropic foundations, and businesses. This particular interrelationship would become influential as the Clintons later made the shift from Little Rock to Washington. Yet, the actual practice of making community development banking and microenterprise into a solution to rural poverty and welfare dependency proved easier said than done. And rural Arkansas would prove itself to be a challenging testing ground.

BUILDING ARKANSAS FROM THE INSIDE OUT

Bill Clinton just missed the chance to join the Watergate Babies in Washington in 1974. After narrowly losing his bid for Congress, the ambitious twenty-eight-year-old Rhodes scholar pressed on. He decided that state politics was really where he could make a difference. Combining a political style that one reporter called as "smooth as Arkansas corn silk" with a wonkish interest in the finer details of policy, he became, in 1978, the youngest governor in state history.[6] In his first term, he displayed a bit too much ambition and commitment to change for many Arkansans. In what proved to be an unexpected last straw, he pushed through a major highway repair program paid for in part by doubling the tax on license plates.[7] Voters were outraged, and Clinton lost his first reelection bid. By the time he reclaimed the job in 1982, he was slightly chastened and narrowed his focus to addressing the state's economic problems.

Arkansas's landscape had always made it a challenge for those trying to strike it rich or even just survive. Most of the state was too rocky to farm. The Delta area in the southeastern part of the state was filled with swamps, but was fertile ground for growing rice and soybeans. Yet, by midcentury, with the rise of agricultural mechanization, the region had fallen into a state of chronic poverty.[8] In the 1950s, the state government responded to Arkansas's economic difficulties by implementing a model of economic development called "smokestack chasing," which used public subsidies and the promises of a low-wage and nonunionized workforce to recruit manufacturers. This approach lured many national companies to open branch plants in Arkansas. Six hundred new industrial plants opened there in less than a decade. It also created a surge in "one-company towns," with companies like Levi Strauss and Reynolds Metals Company (manufacturer of Reynolds Wrap) arriving in towns and small cities throughout the state.[9] Beginning in the late 1970s, however, these same companies found even cheaper labor outside the United States, mostly in the Pacific Rim. The shift in production overseas benefited Arkansas-based Walmart. It also boosted Tyson Foods, the state's largest private employer, since, as Clinton would say, "so far the Japanese have not figured out how to import chickens" to the US.[10] In fact, the northwest part of the state, which housed the headquarters of Walmart and Tyson, flourished by the time Clinton took office. But globalization devastated many of the state's smaller rural towns, especially in the Delta region, where even industrial poultry plants were few and far between. Arkansas experienced a sharp increase in its rate of unemployment and the length of its welfare rolls, especially among African Americans. The sharp cuts that Reagan administered to federal social spending in the early 1980s further compounded the hardship.

Even if he had not joined Tim Wirth, Al Gore, and the other Watergate Babies in Washington, Clinton shared their conviction that the solution to the dual problems of economic crisis and persistent poverty lay in the postindustrial sector. "Smokestack chasing is dead," he confidently announced.[11] Yet, Clinton proved to only partially believe that bold statement: he was committed to bringing business to Arkansas, just not of the type that had actual smokestacks. His efforts to lure high-tech companies convinced him that the poor quality of the state's education was creating a major obstacle to economic development. Since his days in Oxford, he had remained close friends with Robert Reich, which made him well versed in the Harvard professor's arguments about the importance of postindustrial innovation and the need for the public education system to prepare students for a high-tech, knowledge-based economy.[12] Clinton also recognized that focusing on education enabled him to maintain a traditional Democratic commitment to the poor and equal opportunity. But he could combine it with a new model of economic growth.[13]

Clinton's interest in education coincided with and was bolstered by the release of the National Commission on Excellence
in Education's report *A Nation at Risk* in 1983. The Reagan-
appointed commission offered an ominous diagnosis of the state
of American public schools. The authors demonstrated that academic test scores of American students paled in comparison to
economic rivals in Japan and Western Europe, especially in math
and science.[14] Coming on the heels of a decade of economic recession and fears of national decline, the commission's conclusion
that poor education was contributing to the nation's global economic woes caused panic and made education reform seem all
the more urgent. The problem was particularly acute in Arkansas.

"Thank God for Mississippi" was a long-running joke in Arkansas because its neighboring state scored last place on most measures, saving Arkansas from that fate.[15] But by the early 1980s,
even Mississippi was besting Arkansas on education. A report
bluntly declared that students would be better off in any other
state.[16] Studies showed that Arkansas schools were the worst in
the nation: the state devoted the smallest percentage of funding
to schools, the lowest rate of students went on to college or vocational school, and many schools did not offer physics, chemistry,
or foreign languages. In addition, more than half of adult Arkansas residents did not have a college degree, and 35 percent of the
state workforce was estimated to be functionally illiterate.[17] Upon
returning to the governor's mansion in 1983, Clinton announced
that education would be the first priority of his economic development agenda. He created the Arkansas Education Standards
Committee, chaired by Hillary Clinton, who took a leave of absence from her job as a law partner.[18] The findings of the committee motivated Bill Clinton to push through an ambitious education
reform package. The proposal was condemned by state and national teachers' unions, who were especially outraged at a requirement that every teacher take a basic skills test as a condition of
keeping his or her job. Because a high percentage of the state's
teachers were African American, Clinton faced charges of racial

discrimination.[19] Clinton stood his ground and maintained that
Arkansas could not improve its poverty rate unless its students
had a better education.[20] He secured the first sales tax increase in
decades to provide teachers with better pay by persuading voters
that education, upward mobility, and economic growth were all
inextricably linked.[21] "Do you really believe that God meant for us
to drag up the rear of the nation's economy forever?" he asked in
speeches.[22] It was hard to argue with that.

Clinton and his staff began experimenting with other ways
to stimulate postindustrial growth, such as deepening public-
private partnerships and stimulating entrepreneurship. In addition to implementing a series of large tax incentives for expanding
industries, Clinton created several new agencies, including the
Arkansas Development Finance Authority, the Arkansas Capital
Corporation, and the Arkansas Science and Technology Authority, which all used state power to direct private capital toward
new ventures, rural development, and job creation.[23] He publicly
announced his goal of transforming Arkansas into "an environment for entrepreneurs second to none," by making government
more of a partner with the private sector, and pledged to place
a particular emphasis on small business.[24] Clinton and his staff
were very much on the lookout for new ideas for how to stimulate homegrown entrepreneurship and jobs, especially in the
Delta, where poverty and unemployment remained unbending.[25]
It was these priorities that made the ShoreBank model especially
attractive.

Clinton first heard about ShoreBank during a conversation
with an old friend. The path to that discussion was somewhat cir-
cuitous and involved multiple continents and cities. When Shore-
Bank's Mary Houghton and Ron Grzywinski were planning to go to
Bangladesh for the first time to advise Muhammad Yunus, Houghton decided to contact a woman she knew named Jan Piercy who
was working in Dhaka for a family planning organization.[26] The
three instantly hit it off. When they learned that Piercy was thinking of moving back to the US, Houghton and Grzywinski decided
to try and recruit her to work at ShoreBank. Piercy happened to

be Hillary Clinton's close friend from college and was planning to spend Thanksgiving with the Clintons in Little Rock.

On her way to Arkansas, she had a layover in Chicago, and Houghton and Grzywinski met her at O'Hare Airport. In addition to talking in more detail about the potential job, Grzywinski handed her a draft report he had just received, prepared for Arkansas by an economic development expert named Belden Daniels, that mentioned ShoreBank.[27] Sitting at breakfast in the Arkansas governor's mansion, Piercy started flipping through the report. When Bill Clinton came to breakfast, he asked, "What are you reading?" When she told him it was a report for him, they started talking about it. He then called his economic development chief Bob Nash and told him to come over. The conversation quickly expanded to include Hillary as well. Both Clintons were captivated, and Bill thought it might be just what he and his advisors had been looking for. The Clintons also convinced Piercy to accept the job at Shore-Bank and help bring the model to Arkansas.[28]

Bill Clinton's model of public-private partnership extended to nonprofits and philanthropic foundations.[29] He especially encouraged staffers to develop close ties with the Winthrop Rockefeller Foundation, which was the biggest philanthropic organization in the state and one with a somewhat unique mandate. In the 1950s, Winthrop Rockefeller, in an act of modest family rebellion, moved to Arkansas and quickly became a key force. He chaired the Arkansas Industrial Development Commission and then served as governor (the first Republican to do so since 1872). He also set up an eponymous foundation, which he charged to focus on economic development, education, and poverty in his adopted state. By the early 1980s, the foundation and its president, Tom McRae, were firmly committed to revamping the state's economic development policy to focus on new ways of stimulating growth and jobs opportunities in rural areas.[30] McRae and his staff had been working with Clinton's economic development team on the effort.

Soon after Piercy's Thanksgiving visit, Bob Nash related his boss's interest in the ShoreBank model. McRae was already familiar with the Chicago organization, which several people in the philanthropic world had recommended to him.[31] McRae and Nash decided to arrange a phone call with Grzywinski and Houghton. Talking to them, McRae felt for the first time that he had found "people who understood the comprehensive approach we felt necessary to make a difference in development" and "had the know-how to make it work."[32] McRae asked if ShoreBank was willing to create a version of their bank in Arkansas.

Grzywinski and Houghton were intrigued by the request. While other senior staff members at ShoreBank were more incredulous and thought the organization should stay focused on South Shore, Grzywinski and Houghton were always on the hunt for new chances to experiment and innovate. As Grzywinski later explained, he almost pathologically "never saw an opportunity that I didn't like [and] Mary was a coconspirator all along the way."[33] The Arkansas invitation was especially appealing, according to Grzywinski, because we "really believed that we had a model, a bank holding company with nonbank subsidiaries that could really do a lot of good stuff," but they hadn't been able to implement it beyond the South Side of Chicago.[34] Arkansas seemed an enticing challenge since the project would encompass the entire state and not just a single neighborhood. It was also an exciting chance to test out their model in a rural place, but one that, like South Shore, had a large African American population. The ShoreBank founders immediately recognized that their focus of offering loans to individuals to rehabilitate apartment buildings would not work in rural Arkansas.[35] But this situation actually made the endeavor more alluring. As George Surgeon explained, ShoreBank had not yet "solved the riddle" of how to create a lot of jobs and small businesses outside real estate.[36] Grzywinski and Houghton were hoping they could experiment with new techniques for small business growth in Arkansas and apply what they learned back to Chicago and other parts of the country. It was additionally attractive that they would have the political and financial support of the governor and the state's biggest private foundation.[37]

Grzywinski, Houghton, and several other ShoreBank staffers spent the summer of 1985 traveling through Arkansas to gain more insight into the social and economic dynamics of local communities and the state as a whole. For Houghton and Grzywinski, both lifelong midwesterners, the experience was a "huge eye opener." The Chicago bankers observed firsthand the extreme economic and racial inequality of the state—both visiting a town in the Delta suffering from deep poverty and meeting Sam Walton at the Walmart headquarters in Bentonville and venture capitalist Witt Stephens in his cavernous Little Rock office.[38] The Shore-Bank founders discovered many cultural differences between Illinois and Arkansas, including the cuisine, climate, race and gender dynamics, and colloquialisms. But one of the biggest was that, unlike their home state, they had close access to the governor and First Lady.[39] Like many who encountered Bill Clinton, Houghton found him a "very charming, relaxed, policy wonk genial person."[40] Clinton responded enthusiastically to the preliminary ideas the ShoreBank officials presented to him. The project was particularly attractive to him because it served many public sector goals but was privately operated and would require little, if any money, from the state government. In their first meeting, Clinton provided the Chicago bankers with detailed profiles of the economic conditions in various communities in Arkansas and an extensive explanation of the state's employment and industry trends.[41]

Clinton also became genuinely interested in the ShoreBank founders' vision of community development banking. On a few Saturday afternoons, Clinton invited Grzywinski and Houghton to the governor's mansion to discuss economic development and learn more about ShoreBank itself.[42] While sprawled out on the couch with a Diet Coke in hand, Clinton showed, according to Grzywinski, that "he really cared about economic development and opportunities for poor people." It was also clear that the Shore-Bank model "appealed to his more general idea of government doing less for people, but enabling them to do more for themselves."[43] The Clintons eagerly accepted Grzywinski and Houghton's invitation to come to Chicago and tour the South Shore community and the bank. A bank staffer recounted that during the visit Bill

Clinton "wanted to know everything" from how they managed risk to how they made a profit.[44]

Hillary Clinton was also deeply involved in ShoreBank's Arkansas project. As Jan Piercy put it, her old friend was "tremendous" and "totally behind it."[45] She volunteered for the Rose Law Firm, where she was a partner, to serve as the project's lawyers and personally provided her expertise of corporate law to address many of the project's legal issues.[46] She also agreed to serve as one of the project's founding board members and drew on her extensive contacts to recruit other members. She and the other planners recognized that getting Arkansas business leaders to sign on was an important way of gaining the project legitimacy. Early recruits included Walter V. Smiley, head of Systematics, Inc., one of the state's first tech-based companies, and Thomas "Mack" McLarty III, the CEO of a Fortune 500 natural gas company who was a childhood friend of Bill Clinton (he would later serve as his first chief of staff at the White House).[47] Hillary had recently joined the board of Walmart and invited Rob Walton, Sam Walton's oldest son and heir apparent, to join the ShoreBank project. Grzywinski described the early board meetings feeling "like family gathering" since the Arkansas members "all knew each other." The ShoreBank contingent often felt like "outsiders" looking in, even though they were doing much of the heavy lifting in getting the project off the ground.[48]

During the planning stages, the project changed names several times—from the Arkansas Development Bank to ArkRock, Arkansas Development Bank Holding Company, and Southbank—before settling on the Southern Development Bancorporation. The different names in part reflected the project's changing relationship to ShoreBank. The Winthrop Rockefeller Foundation and governor's office had assumed that Chicago bankers would run the project and assume permanent equity ownership.[49] However, interstate banking laws and Federal Reserve policies prevented ShoreBank from assuming an ownership position, though its management and staff could serve as the main advisors and handle most of the other technical issues involved in starting and operating a community development bank. The pivotal involvement of the ShoreBank team in the planning process directly shaped the structure of Southern. Like ShoreBank, Southern would serve as a bank holding company. At the center of the effort would be a local commercial bank, which would help to sustain a combination of for-profit and nonprofit subsidiaries. The only substantial departure from ShoreBank's model was the microloan fund from which Dorothy Quarles received her loan. The design was based on the ShoreBank officials' recognition that in order to stimulate entrepreneurship and small business growth in distressed areas, they needed a variety of different ways to deliver capital.[50]

In the documents circulated to investors, Arkansas officials, and bank regulators, the planners emphasized the benefits of locating an economic development project in the private sector rather than the public sector. The founding proposals stressed that "profit-motivated, privately capitalized businesses and non-profit organizations" were "more flexible and resourceful than comparable government agencies."[51] These institutions could be self-sustaining and permanent, which most government antipoverty programs had been unable to achieve. George Surgeon and other ShoreBank officials more candidly explained to local businesspeople in Arkansas: "We're not do gooders. We want to make money. The difference is we're not greedy."[52] Surgeon meant the characterization in part to caution locals that they were not a government program, charity, or philanthropic foundation that would simply distribute grants to poor people.[53] The statement, nevertheless, encapsulated the larger ethos of ShoreBank. Surgeon captured how the approach focused on using the private sector and market as a means to an end but was not looking to make a substantial profit beyond what would allow it to be self-sustaining. In fact, ShoreBank staffers like Surgeon believed that a community development bank had to make money to satisfy bank regulators, but if the bank made a large sum of money, its management was not abiding by the larger mission of helping low-income people.[54] It was this approach and outlook that would make community development banking so appealing to figures like Clinton and the New Democrats.

The Southern organizers set out to find investors who would not necessarily want to lose money but whose primary motivation would not be trying to maximize a return on their investment.[55] Piercy, who was basically working full-time in Arkansas on raising capital, acknowledged that selling the bank holding company, which was a "kind of Rube Goldberg invention," was a tough sell.[56] Several foundations did prove amenable. The Ford Foundation provided a $2 million loan to assist in the capitalization process and provided subsequent loans and grants as well.[57] Ford was one of the main underwriters of both ShoreBank and Grameen Bank and wanted to see if the programs had applications beyond Chicago and Bangladesh.[58] Southern also received commitments from the MacArthur Foundation, the Mott Foundation, the Levi Strauss Foundation, and the Sam and Helen Walton Foundation.[59]

It was the Winthrop Rockefeller Foundation that provided the majority of the initial funding for the $12 million project. The foundation's $5 million investment, which was a significant portion of their $35 million endowment, signaled their commitment to the endeavor. Bill Clinton directed one of the state's economic development agencies, which had been actively involved in the planning, to provide $300,000 in funding and act as a coinvestor on projects.[60] More significantly, Clinton helped raise both attention to the project and money from the Arkansas business community. "Bill twisted a lot of arms of local investors," Surgeon recounted.[61] He and Hillary made the calls to get the ShoreBank team in the door with major corporations.[62] Clinton, Tom McRae, and Walter Smiley made personal appeals to members of the "Good Suit Club," which was how the leaders of Arkansas's major companies referred to themselves. According to Surgeon, Clinton told them: "This is important. We think this will be really good for Arkansas. If it's good for Arkansas, it'll benefit you."[63] While Sam Walton, and a lot of the other "Good Suits," might not have necessarily fully understood the project, it was hard to say no to the governor, and they agreed to find $150,000 or more on their balance sheets to invest in it.[64] Clinton also publicly promoted Southern in speeches as a symbol of what he was doing for economic development in rural Arkansas. These references attracted increased attention, but they also raised expectations of what the project would do.[65]

The Southern team found that harder than raising the money was finding a bank to anchor the project. The planners initially planned to position their project in the Delta region, which had the state's highest rate of poverty and largest African American population. However, they were unable to find an appropriate or profitable commercial bank at a reasonable price. Many of the bank presidents that ShoreBank management met with viewed the "Yankees" from Chicago with suspicion.[66] Eventually, a bank consultant to the Walton family stepped in and helped them secure a deal to buy Elk Horn Bank, whose owner, James Harrington, was drawn to Southern's mission.[67] Elk Horn was located in Arkadelphia, the seat of Clark County, about sixty miles southwest of Little Rock. Arkadelphia and its surrounding counties still had the potential to fulfill many of its objectives. The area stretched into Hope, the small town where Bill Clinton was born, and Hot Springs, the larger community where he grew up. The region's clay soil had sustained generations of soybean and cotton farmers, and Arkadelphia had once been a manufacturing hub. But it had recently experienced significant economic turmoil. Reynolds Metals, Munsingwear, Levi Strauss, and Fafnir factories in the area had shut down in rapid succession. At the time of the bank's purchase in August 1987, the county's unemployment rate had reached 12 percent, which was double the national average.[68] The downtown storefronts in Arkadelphia sat vacant, as retail activity had shifted to a Walmart and a few chain supermarkets on the community's periphery.[69] There was "grass growing in the cracks in the sidewalk," ShoreBank staffers recalled when they first visited the bank's midcentury headquarters.[70] Management believed that Arkadelphia would provide a sound base of operations for their project. And since it was only three miles from a major interstate, it was easily accessible for the ShoreBank management, who were commuting almost weekly from Chicago to supervise activities.

With the bank in place, the organizers set out to get the project off and running. In addition to hiring receptionists, accountants, and administrative assistants from Arkadelphia, they deliberately recruited a racially diverse management team, many of whom had roots in Arkansas, in an effort to prove they were not a bunch of "carpetbaggers."[71] ShoreBank's George Surgeon eventually stopped taking the Monday morning 7:15 a.m. Delta flight from Chicago and relocated full-time to Arkadelphia to became Southern's CEO. He and other Southern management also joined local organizations like the 4H, Chamber of Commerce, and Kiwanis and Rotary clubs and became members of the local country club (even though none of them played golf) to earn the trust of Arkadelphia's leaders.[72] The team then set out to address the requests that had been rapidly rolling in. Even before Southern opened its doors, it had a backlog of over a thousand applications. Many of them came from people who had learned about the project in the newspaper or from a speech by Clinton and heard that the bank wanted to focus on providing credit to people who had previously been blocked from getting it.[73] In addition to business plans, some of the requests came from individuals who had fallen on hard times and wanted $500 to help with their car payments or rent.[74] The applications demonstrated that Southern had its work cut out for it. As the Southern team set out to fulfill its early slogan of "Building Arkansas from the Inside Out," it was the microloan fund that quickly proved the most novel and most challenging aspect of achieving that goal.

GOOD FAITH

During the planning and start-up of Southern, the indefatigable Houghton and Grzywinski were not just commuting from Chicago; they were also continuing to travel to Bangladesh to advise Muhammad Yunus and Grameen Bank. After learning more about the economic landscape in rural Arkansas, Grzywinski and Houghton began to consider if the Southern project offered an opportunity to bring the Grameen model of microenterprise to the United States. Despite all the attention ShoreBank had garnered, it had not been able to meet the capital needs of the smallest of business owners, nor reach the very poor. Houghton and other members of the management were interested in experimenting with other ways to use finance to assist the small businesses of low-income people. Grameen looked like "a very big idea about how you could reach" this population.[75] Houghton, in particular, was concerned about the increasing feminization of poverty, evidence of which she saw firsthand not just throughout the South Side of Chicago but also in the small towns throughout Arkansas she visited while doing due diligence for Southern.[76] She had been deeply impressed with Grameen's success rate with poor women.[77] ShoreBank staffers began to discuss how starting a microenterprise fund might be a stepping-stone to a larger company that would employ not just themselves but dozens of others and address the chronic unemployment problem in inner-city Chicago and rural Arkansas.[78]

Houghton and Grzywinski invited Yunus to come to Arkansas and travel around with them and Jan Piercy on a "listening tour" to consider whether the Grameen model could be adapted to address the needs of the state's poor rural communities and welfare recipients.[79] Piercy recalled that though Yunus acknowledged the myriad ways that poverty in Arkansas differed from Bangladesh, he talked, during their drives on rural back roads, about how he recognized a similar "poverty of the spirit" and sense of social exclusion among the poor people in both places.[80] The tour took them to a community center in the struggling Delta town of Pine Bluff. During a meeting there, Yunus explained the premise of Grameen and asked the local residents assembled what they would do with a small loan. One woman, who had lost her job at a textile factory after it moved to Taiwan, told him she would borrow a few hundred dollars to buy a sewing machine to "make clothes and sell them to my neighbors." Another woman said she wanted a loan to buy a pushcart to sell her homemade tamales, which "were famous."[81]

Yunus later stated the responses of the Arkansas residents proved to him that "the aspirations of the really poor Americans that I had met had a lot in common with the poor in Bangladesh, Malaysia and Togo."[82] Mary Houghton reported to other planners that the "meetings reinforced our conviction that very small enterprise creation can be promoted in the small towns and rural areas of Arkansas with loans of not more than $5,000 per person." She described how they "witnessed an outpouring of ideas" and "found a willingness and sometimes enthusiasm to participate in a peer group process that would work to assure a high rate of loan repayment and provide psychological support for entrepreneurs."[83] The ShoreBank staff also commissioned a study by Jeffrey Ashe, one of the leading experts on microenterprise, who persuaded the project's architects with his prediction that "micro-entrepreneurs of rural Arkansas will respond to innovative credit programs in a way similar to that of Asia, Africa, and Latin America."[84]

Grzywinski, Houghton, and Piercy then orchestrated a meeting in Washington, DC, in February 1986 between Yunus and Bill and Hillary Clinton.[85] Yunus's story, philosophy of poverty alleviation, and model of microenterprise immediately captivated both Clintons. Bill Clinton had become increasingly interested in finding ways to reform the welfare system in Arkansas and nationally. He was especially interested in work-oriented approaches to welfare, which he believed would reduce dependency and empower recipients.[86] During his first stint as governor, Arkansas participated in a Carter administration workfare experiment that made work a condition for food stamps. Clinton later supported a program that required all welfare recipients with children over three to sign a contract committing themselves to a course of independence through literacy, education, and job training.[87] By the time of his meeting with Yunus, Clinton had been working with his fellow governors to make work requirements and job training part of the federal welfare law. These efforts were earning him a reputation as a national leader on welfare.

Clinton recognized how Yunus's ideas fit in with his efforts to promote work and independence among welfare recipients. "It was obvious what the parallels were," Bill Clinton later said. "He made enterprise work. He promoted independence, not dependence."[88] With typical Clintonian enthusiasm, he declared, "I mean, I just loved it. I loved it." Yunus recalled that at their first meeting Hillary was even more "gung ho."[89] She asked him a series of detailed questions and then declared: "We want it. Can we have it in Arkansas?"[90] The answer was yes, and pretty quickly.

The microenterprise organization, which came to be called the Good Faith Fund, relied heavily on the design and philosophy of Grameen and the advice of Yunus. Julia Vindasius, who served as Mary Houghton's assistant at ShoreBank, became the first director of the organization. The twenty-eight-year-old California native, who had recently received a master's degree in urban planning from MIT, impressed Yunus with her passion and interest in microenterprise during one of his US visits and he recommended she lead the program.[91] Vindasius, nevertheless, had very little experience in the South and had not stepped foot in Arkansas until after she accepted the position. Before setting up shop, she did, however, travel to Bangladesh to observe the practices of Grameen, and she brought to Arkansas what she learned.[92]

The organizers initially planned to call the program the Grameen Fund, but this name confused many people in Arkansas, and they changed it based on the notion that the program distributed loans on "good faith."[93] "We look past bankruptcies and bad credit," Angela Dooley, GFF's first loan representative explained. "[We] see collateral in a person's character."[94] Mirroring Grameen Bank's famed model, GFF adopted a peer-lending system, where four to six people created a group and were collectively responsible for paying back the loan.[95] GFF required that loan be paid back on a weekly installment system at an 11 percent interest rate. Although lower than the 20 percent interest rate Grameen charged, it was still significantly higher than most conventional loans in the US. In fact, it was the maximum allowed under Arkansas's usury laws.[96] The high rate drew on Yunus's theory that a relatively high interest rate was essential to absorb credit losses, cover operating costs, and send the message to borrowers that they were not receiving free or easy money.

The planners decided to position the headquarters of the GFF in Pine Bluff, which was more than 1.5 hours from Arkadelphia on country roads. The "Gateway to the Delta," Pine Bluff was located on the Arkansas River and Cotton Belt Railway Line and had once been a bustling transportation and commercial hub. By the mid-1980s, its fifteen-block downtown was filled with boarded-up storefronts. The acid smell of emissions from a factory that produced materials for plastic-coated milk and juice containers, which was one of Pine Bluff's remaining employers (and which only stayed due to the strong-arming of Bill Clinton), would often fill the entire city.[97] From Pine Bluff, the staff was able to spread out into the five surrounding counties, which were among the poorest in the nation. Per capita income ranged from $7,064 to $10,544 and unemployment rates from 6.1 to 11.0 percent. There was a high percentage of welfare recipients, with payments from Aid to Families with Dependent Children (AFDC) or disability representing roughly 32 percent of total personal income.[98]

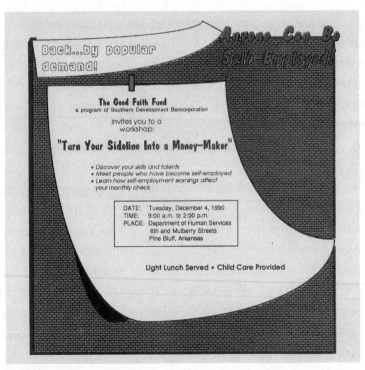

A flier for the Good Faith Fund distributed in the Pine Bluff, Arkansas, area, 1990

Credit: Special Collections, University of Illinois Chicago

The GFF staff spent their early days trying to attract borrow-ers in the small Delta towns that surrounded Pine Bluff. In these places, the central business district often consisted of a gas sta-tion and a couple of shops. The long history of social and racial divisions remained both physically and ideologically etched into the landscape.[99] The staff held seminars on how to "Turn Your Sideline into a Money-Maker" and distributed flyers and leaflets in parking lots, advertising a chance to "Make Your Own Job."[100] During the first year of operation in 1988, GFF established nine borrowing groups with forty-six members and dispersed thirty-two loans.[101] The inaugural borrowers were 85 percent African American and 55 percent women. The percentage of female par-ticipants increased in the ensuing years as the staff aimed to ful-fill aspects of Yunus's directives. The bulk of the initial borrowers were not "the poorest of the poor," which Grameen targeted, but they operated at a state of relative poverty. They fell below the national median income but above the national poverty line.[102] In addition to Dorothy Quarles, the early borrowers included people like Diane Grayson who started a BBQ business out of a trailer in the small town of Hamburg and Lucille Spiller, a sixty-year-old for-mer factory seamstress with plans of turning her small house into a home day-care center.[103] Several of the borrowers already had ventures and wanted to expand them. Fanny Slater ran a small dress shop in Dumas, Arkansas, but had been unable to secure a loan to expand her inventory until she joined a borrowing group. The $2,500 loan she received helped her buy a new line of clothes and advertise for the first time.

The dynamics of the fund were ideally tailored to the human-interest stories popular in the press. Journalists and TV producers tended to focus on the individual experiences of the various bor-rowers. Dorothy Quarles became a frequent interview subject and the unofficial poster child of the fund. She was featured in articles in a variety of national news publications and on NPR's *All Things Considered*. The stories of Quarles and her fellow borrowers were crucial in helping to expand the image of entrepreneurship—which usually evoked white men like Arkansas's own Sam Walton—to

Fanny Slater, a Good Faith Fund client, in her dress shop in Dumas, Arkansas, August 1989
Credit: Rockefeller Archive Center/Theodora Lurie

include poor women of color. Like Yunus, the GFF presented their potential borrowers as rational economic actors with the skills that would make them successful businesses operators. Vindasius stressed its would-be entrepreneurs were "not just guys whose faces are on the cover of *Fortune*—it's women, people who live in low-income communities, displaced workers, minorities."[104] Such descriptions countered the long-standing discourse about the undeserving poor as well as stereotypes about African American single mothers often used in the underclass and welfare debates of the 1970s and 1980s.[105] In its promotion of Quarles and other borrowers, the GFF directly sought to offset images of poor Black women, especially those on welfare, as passive, lazy, or trying to cheat the system.

The inspiring stories of women like Quarles and the creativity and dedication of the GFF staff pulled attention away from the fact that the organization struggled substantially in its first years of operation. Even the work of employees like Sheila Middleton, who put 21,000 miles on her car in a year driving on dusty and ditch-filled country roads visiting borrowing groups and conducting seminars for potential clients, wasn't enough.[106] The fund experienced difficulty attracting participants and faced higher than anticipated default and delinquency rates. Ten borrowers defaulted on loans totaling $17,000 in 1989 alone.[107] In its first two years, the fund experienced severe default rates.[108]

The problems revealed that the fund's staff and advisors like Yunus had not fully appreciated the differences between Bangladesh and rural Arkansas. Although both rural, Bangladesh boasted one of the largest, if not the largest, population densities in the world, with 814 people per kilometer. The Arkansas counties surrounding Pine Bluff averaged about 9 people per kilometer.[109] The lack of density made it a challenge to create borrowing groups, much less a cohesive borrower network, and for the microentrepreneurs to create client bases for their enterprises. In addition, barriers of entry were much greater in the US than Bangladesh. Unlike most Grameen borrowers, GFF members had to get permits and licenses to start their businesses, had to go through routine inspections, and faced much higher costs of supplies.[110] Even in rural parts of Arkansas, microentrepreneurs had to compete with national chain stores and deal with customers who were more used to buying products from the grocery store rather than their neighbor. And as credit card companies were increasingly penetrating areas like Pine Bluff by the late 1980s, it offered residents a form of credit that was unavailable in Bangladesh and didn't require having to create a peer lending group and make weekly loan payments.[111]

The GFF found the peer-lending aspects of the Grameen model especially hard to emulate. "Peer pressure isn't as significant as it might be in a place like Bangladesh," Vindasius admitted."[112] Several foundation officials and researchers and USAID officials had, in fact, begun to question whether it was some of the unique social and cultural dynamics of Bangladesh that made Grameen successful there. Others started to doubt the efficacy of the program even in Bangladesh. The businesses of Grameen microentrepreneurs were rarely innovative or had the potential for significant growth and scale. These factors meant that the enterprises had little potential to meaningfully contribute to Bangladesh's economic development and offered borrowers little opportunity for true upward mobility and freedom from debt relationships.[113] Such doubts and criticism about Grameen and microenterprise more broadly would intensify in the ensuing years.

In the Arkansas context, Yunus and the other GFF architects overestimated the interest in entrepreneurialism and small business ownership in the Pine Bluff area. Staffers quickly discovered the majority of residents still preferred wage work and their old factory jobs to self-employment.[114] Loan officers saw borrowing groups fall apart when a local lumber mill or paper factory added a second shift. George Surgeon recounted that "the pull of being your own boss was strong if you didn't have options" but not if the person could get "a job at International Paper or Weyerhaeuser or Georgia-Pacific" with a steady paycheck and benefits.[115] The problems demonstrated that despite celebrations of Arkansas's entrepreneurial spirit, the state, like the country, had much stronger roots in formal sector employment. Even among the people who came to their seminars and wanted to join the program, it was rare for them to have reliable means of transportation, childcare, and enough formal education to participate.[116] Yunus and several other practitioners believed that a greater impediment was actual welfare laws. Chicago's Women's Self-Employment Project (WSEP) became one of the fiercest critics of how welfare rules inhibited microentrepreneurs, developing an argument that would eventually make its way to Washington.

PRISONERS OF POVERTY

WSEP had its origins in ShoreBank and Grameen's collaboration. At the same time Mary Houghton was helping to set up Southern, she, along with several other women entrepreneurs and foundation officials, decided to start a Chicago nonprofit to offer low-income women in the city access to the tools they needed to take care of their families and achieve economic self-sufficiency.[117] It was in part inspired by Grameen and Muhammad Yunus's theories of the power of self-employment. WSEP also drew inspiration from the interest in entrepreneurship among white middle-class women in the 1980s. Press coverage abounded, with headlines such as "Torn Between Family and Career?: Give Birth to a Business."[118] Advocates celebrated how entrepreneurship, especially home-based businesses, provided women with more control over their lives, a way to balance the demands of work and family, a path toward increased self- esteem, and a means to feel more fulfilled and passionate about their work. WSEP wanted to see if self-employment could offer many of the same benefits of empowerment, autonomy, and balance to women of color who were either unemployed or earning minimum wage, toiling in pink-collar jobs.[119] Houghton served as the president of the board and played an integral role in launching the effort. Yunus acted as a consultant and offered his guidance and expertise. He and Houghton served as important mentors to WSEP executive director Connie Evans.[120]

For Evans, the goals of WSEP made immediate sense both personally and professionally. She herself was the product of a self-employed mother. Her father had died two weeks before she was born, and by running a catering business from their home in Franklin, Tennessee, her mother had been able to purchase a house and put Evans and her three siblings through private school and college.[121] Her mother's story impressed upon Evans the value of self-employment for women of color. Her previous professional experiences helping run Chicago's first public housing tenant management program had also demonstrated the power of business ownership and collective action for low-income Black women.[122] Soon after setting up the WSEP headquarters in downtown Chicago, Evans placed at the front a statue engraved with the motto "She who learns, teaches," which she saw as representative of the organization's goals.[123]

WSEP had plans to start a peer-lending program in the style of Grameen, but it got its sea legs in 1986 by offering a training program for women interested in self-employment.[124] The twelve-week program included topics like bookkeeping, cash flow, taxes, net-working, and creating a business plan. Once a woman completed the program, she was eligible to receive loans of $500 to $5,000 to finance specific aspects of her business. The early participants had a range of business ideas from childcare and jewelry making to a motorized hotdog stand and a lingerie store called Hidden Secrets.[125]

With its training program off the ground, WSEP decided to launch its microenterprise program. WSEP's microcredit program, named the Full Circle Fund, adhered even more closely to the Grameen model than the Good Faith Fund. The Full Circle Fund began in 1988 by offering loans of $300 to $1,500 to low-income women who started peer groups or "circles." In an effort to fulfill Yunus's mission of helping the "poorest of the poor," the program concentrated on the Englewood neighborhood. One of the most economically distressed and racially segregated parts of the South Side, Englewood had a reputation for entrepreneurs of the illicit kind.[126] Evans was steadfast that the program had to include women receiving state aid since "you can't get too much more low income than being on welfare."[127] Like Arkansas, Illinois had begun establishing work requirements as a condition for aid. Evans worried that these programs shuttled women into dead-end jobs in hotel cleaning and data processing, in which most women lacked interest or which gave little chance for advancement.[128] She thought a better alternative would be to give women the opportunity to start their own businesses doing something they were interested in. Evans believed that the experience of creating something of their own—even if it involved data entry or cleaning—would help to change welfare recipients' outlook and give them a mental and material shot at upward mobility.[129] At the time, however, the federal government and many states limited the assets a recipient could have to $1,000 and did not distinguish between personal and business assets. This rule meant most of the equipment people needed to start and run a small business would exceed the ceiling.[130]

WSEP launched a campaign to challenge this rule. WSEP made its case by emphasizing the entrepreneurial drive and desire for independence and self-reliance of its borrowers. The organization did not disclaim the culture of poverty argument but instead used it to its advantage. In promotional material, WSEP laid out the many advantages of self-employment: "Children of these entrepreneurs become exposed to ownership and business. Exposure to role models then becomes a factor in breaking cycles of dependency."[131] An ally of WSEP discussed how welfare recipients' existing skills would make them successful businesses operators: "Show me a welfare mother alone with two kids who manages a family on $600 a month and I'll show you a financial wizard," she declared.[132] Yunus himself joined the effort. During his visits to Chicago, he promoted the benefits of credit and its ability to help poor women achieve self-sufficiency and encouraged state officials to give welfare recipients who joined WSEP programs a waiver from the asset limit and the ability to keep their cash assistance for three years as they launched their businesses.

Such tactics proved effective as the state granted the request not just for WSEP but adjusted the asset ceiling to $5,000 for all welfare recipients wanting to start businesses, making Illinois the first state to do so. Evans described the change as "huge" and "very beneficial" in enabling women on welfare to start and run businesses.[133] Illinois also commissioned WSEP to create a demonstration program "to show entrepreneurship as a viable means of transition from welfare."[134] The program enabled the Full Circle Fund to recruit women like Dorothy Wallace. The Englewood mother of two teenagers had not held a steady job in years and was on welfare. Like many of the women who signed up for the program, Wallace had a dicey credit history and had exhausted opportunities to get a conventional loan or receive a credit card. Her experience revealed both the hardships imposed by the increasingly predatory aspects of financial institutions in the 1980s and why the Full Circle Fund's offer of an alternative pathway to receiving a loan was enticing.[135] Wallace found other aspects of the program equally attractive and important. She joined a borrowing circle and borrowed $800 to start a business peddling perfume and lotions in downtown office buildings and on Chicago's "L" trains.[136] The loan and the moral support of other women in her group gave her hope that she could leave welfare.

For Yunus the experience of working with WSEP was also transformative. He later stated that through his involvement he "saw in practice how welfare law in the United States created disincentives for the welfare recipients to pull themselves out of welfare. If you are on welfare . . . you are a virtual prisoner not only of poverty but those who would help you."[137] He told a local reporter during one of his visits to Chicago: "I'm against handouts—they kill initiative. They take away dignity." Instead, he proposed "giving each welfare recipient the option of credit."[138] In subsequent years, he intensified this argument and began opposing any form of direct government support, including unemployment benefits and state-provided health care and education, and instead argued people should have the opportunity to support themselves. His ideas and microenterprise continued to gain steam in Washington, especially because both parties were scrambling to offer ways to reform the welfare system.

In March 1991, Dale Bumpers happened to be driving in his car one weekend afternoon when he heard the NPR interview with GFF borrower Dorothy Quarles.[139] The chance listening proved significant because Bumpers was not just a senator from Arkansas and the state's former governor, he was also head of the Senate Committee on Small Business. The story about his home state inspired him to consider the ways in which microenterprise programs might help people to get off welfare. In the summer of 1991, he pushed Congress to approve a $15 million five-year demonstration program.[140] "The idea is to help others, get people off welfare, give people who have an idea, the opportunity to make it," Bumpers explained.[141] Although GFF and WSEP were the only ones directly to replicate Grameen, several other microenterprise organizations had begun appearing across the US during the 1980s in places ranging from Los Angeles to Iowa, a Sioux reservation in South Dakota, and along the border in Arizona. In addition to providing GFF, WSEP, and more than two dozen other programs with modest funding, Bumpers's legislation offered an important endorsement of microenterprise as a form of domestic poverty alleviation and potential means of welfare reform.

As they learned more about microenterprise, several members of Congress grew outraged to learn that AFDC's $1,000 asset limit prevented most welfare recipients from joining a program. "We subsidize microenterprise programs overseas, but we actually block them here in America," Rep. Tony Hall (D-OH) lamented.[142] In response, he and Rep. Mike Espy (D-MS) introduced a bill that would have raised the asset ceiling for a welfare recipient if she was starting a business. Espy was a rising star in the Democratic Party and a member of the Democratic Leadership Council who demonstrated a particular concern for the problems of poverty, in large part because his Mississippi district included some of the poorest census tracts in the country. He recognized that microenterprise had particular political appeal for the Democratic Party. In 1991, Espy publicly suggested to fellow Democratic members of Congress that microenterprise should become a central part of "the Democratic national platform, because it has got all the elements that we want to push, as a national party." He stressed that the party needed "to push this really hard as we move into a presidential race. There are a lot of advantages for Democrats."[143] Bill Clinton, who was beginning to prepare his bid for the White House, was already heeding Espy's advice.

The growing enthusiasm by politicians did not always match the success of the microenterprise and community development banking programs. The Arkansas experiment was a case in point. Elk Horn Bank, a branch of Southern, was itself profitable, earning a record $730,000 or 1.05 percent return on assets in 1991. Other parts of Southern struggled.[144] Many Arkansas residents welcomed the new money Southern provided as it was the only venture capital institution in the state willing to invest in small businesses. Yet, it became clear that the project had been vastly undercapitalized.[145] While it was able to help some individuals and their businesses, Southern had made little transformation in the economy of rural Arkansas by the early 1990s.

The Good Faith Fund especially continued to falter. "We've gone through some tough times," Julia Vindasius conceded in 1992. She noted that the fund had spent its early years "focused as much on building entrepreneurial energy and interest as in actually making loans." But she was cautiously optimistic that even if the fund was not exactly following its lending mission, it was helping people in the Pine Bluff area gain business and leadership skills.[146] The WSEP's Full Circle Fund in Chicago was more successful but faced its own hurdles. It boasted a 98 percent repayment rate and experienced not a single default in its first years. However, it struggled to get women to join. Of 350 Englewood women who initially signed up, only 50 stayed through the end of the orientation period and 35 joined borrowing groups.[147]

The rocky start of Southern and the Good Faith and Full Circle Funds exposed the challenges in transferring ideas tailored for one place to a different region or country. It also became apparent to many on the ground that capital alone was not enough to solve the more structural problems of poverty in the rural South. Towns like those surrounding Pine Bluff and their residents needed far more substantial intervention from the state and federal government to address their interlocking problems.[148] The experiences of these programs might have served as more of a cautionary tale.

The lessons the programs offered became largely ignored, however, especially as Bill Clinton agreed to serve as head of the DLC and began to position himself to run for president. As he did so, Clinton continued to place community development banks and microenterprise at the forefront of his agenda, selling what were small-scale and not entirely effective programs as novel ways to address the structural problems of capital disinvestment, economic inequality, and racial segregation. Thus, the fates of ShoreBank, Grameen, and Clinton became ever more entwined as community development banking and microenterprise became key examples of the new approach to poverty and inequality that Clinton and the DLC promised they could offer.

CHAPTER 4

REINVENTING LIBERALISM

In May 1991, the Democratic Leadership Council staged its annual convention in Cleveland. After a processional led by a local fife and drum band, DLC chairman Bill Clinton strode to the lectern to give what would prove to be a dry run of his presidential announcement. "Our burden is to give people a new choice rooted in old values" and one that "offers opportunity, demands responsibility, gives citizens a say, provides them with responsive government," he declared to the nearly eight hundred DLC members in attendance. He asserted the DLC's agenda rejected "old categories and false alternatives" and was "not liberal or conservative" but instead "is both and is different."[1] Concluding the speech, he announced, "We are not here to save the Democratic Party. We are here to save the United States of America."[2]

Despite the speech's references to unity, the DLC had pointedly excluded two-time presidential candidate Rev. Jesse Jackson from the event. DLC chair Al From explained that Jackson represented the "old" politics of the Democratic Party that the DLC was trying to be a departure from. The snub led Jackson to redouble his charge that the DLC stood for "Democrats for the Leisure Class." He decided to come to Cleveland anyway and spent the week staging counterevents. Under the surface of the name-calling and the public relations stunts festered a deeper split about the different political strategies and policies that the

DLC and Jackson's Rainbow Coalition believed the Democratic Party should pursue.

Since its founding in 1985, DLC leadership had been working to develop a more aggressive strategy and a coherent set of principles and policies to help achieve their goals of modernizing both government and the Democratic Party. By 1990, the DLC had issued a statement called the New Orleans Declaration that deemed the "fundamental mission of the Democratic Party is to expand opportunity, not government," "economic growth is the prerequisite to expanding opportunity for everyone," and the "free market, regulated in the public interest, is the best engine of general prosperity."[3] These ideas would become essentially the DLC mantra in the 1990s, and it worked to develop specific policies that supported these larger market-oriented principles. Many of the proposals drew on innovative programs operating at the state and local level—including microenterprise and community development banking—that the DLC hoped to scale at the national level. The DLC simultaneously cultivated an electoral strategy with a laser focus on winning the presidency by appealing to white moderate and working-class swing voters who had defected to the Republicans in the previous election cycles.

The DLC leaders recognized that Bill Clinton offered the ideal fusion of their policy ideas and political strategy. Clinton's appointment as DLC chair in 1990 marked an important turning point for the organization. Clinton, nevertheless, did not merely want to become a mouthpiece for the DLC or adopt its agenda whole cloth but also to play an active role in shaping both its message and policy proposals. He drew on the strategy, philosophy, and specific programs he cultivated as governor of Arkansas, pushing the council to take a more forceful stance on issues like education and welfare reform. The coalescing of Clinton and the DLC's agenda became critical to Clinton's bid for the presidency in 1992. Clinton's run with fellow New Democrat Al Gore was a clear victory for the DLC. The presidential campaign gave the relatively small organization an outsize means to influence both the Democratic

Party and its policy agenda in the future. But the path was never completely smooth with Jackson continuing to put up the biggest fight. The New Democrats' quest for control of the party and the presidency, nevertheless, ensured that Jackson and the left's vision of the future would get pushed to the wayside.

THE POLITICS OF EVASION

Al From began the 1988 presidential election season optimistic. He was especially enthused in November 1987 when Gary Hart, the presumed frontrunner in the Democratic race, became ensnared in a salacious scandal of marital infidelity and dropped out. Since four of the other candidates in the race—Sens. Joe Biden of Delaware and Al Gore of Tennessee, Rep. Richard Gephardt of Missouri, and Governor Bruce Babbitt of Arizona—were all founding members of the DLC, the odds were good one of its own would be the nominee.

The hard part was picking which candidate to back. Gephardt had served as the organization's inaugural chair. But as he set his sights on the presidency, Gephardt distanced himself from the DLC for fear it might alienate labor leaders and the rank and file whom he saw as critical to winning the nomination.[4] Biden's tough-on-crime politics and often hawkish position on foreign policy aligned with that of many members of the DLC. He also shared the New Democrat critiques that the party had been captured by special interests. But Biden was not fully as committed to the organization's larger ideological agenda, and the leadership saw him as too much of a maverick to fully serve as their mouthpiece in the primary. In fact, many observers saw Biden's lack of clear political identity and ideology as one of his major liabilities.[5] Babbitt looked like a long shot from the start.

Gore emerged as the candidate most committed to the DLC's philosophy. Gore first arrived in Congress at the age of twenty-eight in 1976 as part of the second wave of Watergate Babies. He had already cultivated an impressive résumé as the son of a prominent senator, Harvard graduate, and Vietnam veteran, who had even served briefly as an investigative reporter.[6] His promotion of science and technology as a means toward both knowledge and economic growth quickly earned him the reputation as the most quintessential Atari Democrat.[7] Gore was also one of the behind-the-scenes architects of the DLC and drafted its first official press release. Since then, he remained an active player in DLC events, especially those on the environment and foreign policy. Gore's platform combined traditional New Democrat issues, like competitiveness in trade and reducing the federal deficit, but added a focus on arms control, military preparedness, and a hard line on the Soviet Union.[8] By the late fall of 1987, reporters anointed him as the "virtual standard-bearer for the DLC."[9] Despite a strong start, his campaign sputtered by the spring of 1988, and he decided to drop out of the race. Part of Gore's problem was that Jesse Jackson had decided to make another go for the Democratic nomination.

Not one to pull punches, Jackson called his campaign a "struggle for the direction of the party."[10] Building on the infrastructure and message from his 1984 run, Jackson returned to the fray in 1988 with a stronger organizational base and a bolder and more specific set of economically populist policies. He denounced the "economic violence" enacted on vulnerable groups during the Reagan years, including the loss of manufacturing jobs, closure of farms, rise of homeless people on the streets, and spike in children going hungry. In what he labeled "the opposite of Reaganomics," he called for both eradicating the supply-side tax cuts for a fairer system that made wealthy Americans and corporations pay more and dramatically reducing military spending.[11] Jackson contended doing so could expand the social safety net and provide more funding for Aid to Families with Dependent Children, Medicaid, Social Security, childcare, drug treatment, education, public housing, and emergency shelter for the homeless.[12] He also proposed a creative plan to use federal guarantees to shift a portion of public pension funds to invest in housing, small business development, and infrastructure like roads, mass transit, and water systems, particularly in cities.[13] The Jackson campaign contended such a program would be a major source of jobs and could create both economic growth and economic justice. Jackson's proposal suggested that that economic growth and redistribution were not as contradictory as the DLC long claimed.

Jackson coupled these ambitious economic ideas with proposals such as a moratorium on family farm foreclosures, civil rights legislation to protect the LGBTQ community, the ratification of the Equal Rights Amendment, a workers' bill of rights, and ending the war on drugs. He also endorsed a universal, single-payer health-care system administered by the federal government and funded by raising taxes on corporations. These promises once again brought him a broad-based, economically, racially, geographically, and ideologically diverse set of supporters. He secured over seven million votes and won fourteen primaries, finishing behind Massachusetts governor Michael Dukakis, who From and the DLCers saw as a far safer bet.

Dukakis never served as an official member of the DLC, but he had long been identified as one of the main Atari Democrats. He largely staked his presidential bid on how he had used postindustrial growth to fuel the economic turnaround of Massachusetts.[14] From applauded Dukakis's technocratic and "growth-oriented" approach and commitment to "using government to enhance opportunity," but still felt he fell a bit short.[15] When asked to comment about Dukakis, From quipped to the *Wall Street Journal* that "we've erased the graffiti from the wall" but still needed to "paint the mural."[16] It was From's way of suggesting that Dukakis was an improvement over Walter Mondale, but he still lacked a clear vision or message of what he and the party stood for.[17] When Dukakis lost to George H. W. Bush in the general election, it reinforced to the DLC's leaders that they had not fundamentally changed the Democratic Party. Realizing they had to become more focused and powerful, the DLC leadership decided to shift strategies and cultivate a presidential candidate of their own.[18]

Just after Bush's inauguration, From met for breakfast at his favorite Capitol Hill restaurant with William Galston, a political scientist with experience working on several presidential

campaigns.[19] During the breakfast, Galston outlined a theory he
had been developing. He postulated that the Democratic Party
blamed its defeats in presidential races on bad candidates or the
media and failed to see that its real problem was that it was not appealing to key swing voters. From strongly agreed with Galston's
hypothesis, which upheld his own theory of the party's problems.
Throughout the 1988 race, From had been telling the press that
the Democrats shouldn't try to get "the dispossessed to vote. To
win, we have to go where the people are." And by "people" he
meant the "aspiring middle" who lived in suburbia.[20] From commissioned Galston, along with political scientist Elaine Kamarck,
to write a formal report for the DLC, which they entitled "The Politics of Evasion." Relying on a variety of polling data and other demographic information, Galston and Kamarck contended that the
Democrats needed to focus on trying to lure back northern white
ethnics and southern white protestant males—whom they deemed
"the heart" of the electorate—rather than trying to increase turnout among marginalized groups.[21] The Democrats could not just
rely on the fact that they controlled Congress and many state and
local offices, Galston and Kamarck maintained, but needed to also
capture the presidency to ensure political power and viability as
a party.

Galston presented the findings of "The Politics of Evasion" at
a panel at the DLC's 1989 annual conference in Philadelphia. The
organizers were clearly trying to stir the pot for the panel by also
inviting DLC founder Charles Robb and Jesse Jackson to participate. The discussion exacerbated the sharp split between Robb
and the DLC and Jackson, which had been simmering for years.
Robb strongly supported Galston. "It is the swing voters—the
disaffected Democrats—we have to bring back to the party," he
maintained.[22] Jackson vigorously disagreed. He reiterated the argument he had been making for years that the Democrats' future
lay in "pursuing the vast number of people who feel they've been
left out—blacks, Hispanics, women."[23] The argument between
Robb and Jackson continued after the panel formally concluded
and got increasingly heated. Jackson and Robb moved closer to

Rev. Jesse L. Jackson discussing the "Politics of Evasion" at the Democratic Leadership Council's annual conference, 1989. Jackson is seated between Sen. Charles Robb (L) and Gov. James J. Blanchard (R).
Credit: The LIFE Images Collection via Getty Images/William Foley

each other and even stuck their fingers in each other's chests. As the media swarmed and created a circle around them, it looked ever more like a boxing match and not a staid panel in a hotel convention center.[24] While never again getting physical, the fight over the best direction for the party would intensify as "The Politics of Evasion" became the DLC's political playbook going forward.

CREATING "PROGRESSIVE" POLICY

The DLC recognized that it had to match its political strategy with a sharper policy agenda. The organization also wanted to hold true to its claim that it represented the "idea development wing" of the party.[25] From and his sidekick Will Marshall decided the best way to do so would be to establish their own think tank. From and Marshall recognized the critical role think tanks like the Heritage Foundation, American Enterprise Institute, and Cato Institute had played in the conservative revolution of the 1970s and 1980s and in shaping the policies and principles of the Reagan administration.[26] Like the Heritage Foundation, Marshall and From envisioned their think tank would allow the DLC to "have its ideology and governing agenda form the intellectual and programmatic underpinnings for the Administration of a future president."[27] Hedge fund manager Michael Steinhardt agreed to provide a large part of the financial backing for the outfit and became chair of the board.[28] From served as vice chair, and Marshall left his post as policy director of the DLC to become the director of the think tank.

From and Marshall decided to call the new organization the Progressive Policy Institute (PPI). Reporters and critics frequently labeled the DLC as conservative. Marshall and From felt that descriptor missed the fact that their goal was not (at least intentionally) to push the Democrats to the right but rather to modernize the party and liberalism more broadly. Thus, they selected the name in part to reflect its roots in the progressive and pragmatic tradition.[29] Extending this theme, Marshall described the institute's goal as "fill[ing] a void in today's national policy debate by advancing progressive alternatives in public policy that challenge the orthodoxies of both the left and the right."[30] PPI would not be neutral, but rather, as Marshall explained, it would be an "analytic guerrilla group" devoted to "proselytizing" policies that aligned with the aims of the larger New Democrat movement.[31] In order to do so, the DLC also launched a magazine called *Mainstream Democrat*, which largely featured the policy proposals of PPI. It served as an important way to spread their ideas and principles to their elected official members.[32] The magazine was edited by Bruce Reed, who also served as the DLC's new policy director. The not yet thirty-year-old Idaho native and Rhodes scholar had worked as a speechwriter for Al Gore and on the Dukakis campaign before accepting the post.[33] He was convinced the Democratic Party "had just run out of steam, run out of ideas" and was excited to take a position where he could help develop and promote new policies and approaches.[34]

The DLC's and PPI's small staffs devoted their energy to identifying and supporting ideas that represented their efforts to

modernize liberalism with a particular focus on those that combined growth and opportunity. PPI publicly launched in June 1989
with a policy paper that embodied its efforts to break with traditional liberal shibboleths on poverty. Many Democrats had long
clamored to raise the minimum wage—it was a key plank of Jackson organized labor—and were engaged in a fierce debate with the
Bush administration about doing so. The PPI report, written by
fellow Robert Shapiro, called the minimum wage "anachronistic"
and "regressive" and would help the middle class rather than the
working poor who would be saddled with higher costs of goods.
Rather, Shapiro suggested the best way to help low-income people would be through the Earned Income Tax Credit (EITC). The
EITC was established in 1975 and expanded in 1986 and essentially
served as a subsidy or grant to working people with incomes up
to $19,000 per year.[35] Increasing the EITC, Shapiro argued, would
eliminate poverty among all families of full-time workers and also
promote and reward a work ethic. And by inducing more people
into the paid workforce, it could contribute to overall economic
growth.[36] The proposal aligned with the New Democrats's core
faith in growth over redistribution and financial incentives over
cash assistance. It also connected to the DLC's idea that social
policy should be structured around a sense of reciprocal responsibility and not handouts.[37] Journalist E. J. Dionne dubbed Shapiro's
argument as "heretical" for Democrats, and Ted Kennedy even
tried to prevent the paper from being released.[38] Many observers
saw the proposal as a veiled attack on organized labor. Marshall
publicly countered criticisms by contending the EITC offered a
way for the Democrats to show it could "still be the party that
cares about the problems of poor people," just through growth-
oriented and incentive-based means.[39] The stance indicated more
of what was to come from the think tank.

The PPI also became one of the earliest promoters of asset-based
welfare policy, which was another market-based approach. The
policy was the brainchild of social worker and professor Michael
Sherraden, who recognized that the poor lacked the same tools for
savings and asset accumulation as the middle class.[40] He proposed

Individual Development Accounts (IDAs), where the government could match the deposits in tax-exempt accounts made by low-income families, which could later be used to purchase a home, start a business, or pay for college.[41] Sherraden believed his approach could give more low-income citizens a stake in the market economy. It could also bolster the entire economy since it would create new bank customers, mortgage holders, small business owners, and educated employees. The PPI embraced Sherraden's work, recognizing how it had the potential to fuse antipoverty policy with economic growth and could burnish the DLC's reputation for providing a new approach to traditional liberal governance.[42]

REINVENTING GOVERNMENT

David Osborne, an early fellow at PPI, was especially important in shaping the mission and philosophy of the DLC and linking it with market-based programs like ShoreBank and the Southern Development Bancorporation. Osborne followed a different path than many others involved in the organization, as a journalist rather than a party operative. He had been a campus activist at Stanford, which instilled in him suspicions about large and centralized bureaucracy. He did not have particularly deep roots or alliances to the Democratic Party. In fact, the self-described "left-winger" had chosen third-party alternatives over Democratic candidates throughout the 1970s.[43] By the 1980s, he was convinced that the party had "intellectually" run out of steam and was selling an outdated 1960s and 1970s version of liberalism that failed to confront the realities of the present and future. He aligned with the future-oriented bent of the Atari Democrats and believed that technological advances and the rise of the global economy were making centralized government ineffective and increasingly obsolete. By that time, he had decided to write about public policy as a "way to change the world."[44]

In his reporting, Osborne sought out programs and politicians at the state and local level he believed were the ones delivering true innovation. His list of subjects included Bill Clinton, to whom he devoted a chapter of his 1988 book *Laboratories of Democracy*, and he was an ardent champion of ShoreBank, writing pieces about it for several national media outlets. He believed that ShoreBank was a powerful example of the power of combining the investment methods of the private sector with the social goals of the public sector. He would dub it the "perfect model for the '90s, inexpensive, market oriented, and entrepreneurial."[45] He later went further amd declared that ShoreBank "taught me more about development in low-income communities than any other institution in America" contending its "combination of social purpose and market methods has enormous power."[46] He was equally effusive about the Southern Development Bancorporation. In an article for *Inc.* magazine, as the bank was just beginning, he praised it as nothing less than "the reinvention of rural economic development." Osborne was particularly taken with the Good Faith Fund, which he celebrated as the "most radical experiment in rural economic development since the Tennessee Valley Authority."[47] He would bring his commitment to these organizations with him to PPI, which contributed to making community development banking and microenterprise priorities for the think tank.

At the time he joined PPI, Osborne had been developing both a critique of government and an alternative approach that substantially influenced the philosophy and messaging of the DLC. Osborne abided by a variation of the DLC's mantra that solutions of the 1930s did not work for the problems of the 1980s. "Governments that developed during the industrial era, with their sluggish, centralized bureaucracies, their preoccupation with rules and regulations, and their hierarchical chains of command," he argued, did not meet the needs of a "postindustrial, knowledge-based, global economy." Although his critique might have sounded libertarian, Osborne's solution was not. He did not believe that government should be eliminated but, rather, "reinvented" to become more entrepreneurial.[48]

Osborne's "entrepreneurial government" model envisioned a government that was innovative, results oriented, less costly, and more decentralized; injected competition and other market principles into the public sector; and redefined citizens as customers. Osborne also contended that governments should "steer" and let others do the "rowing."[49] In other words, government should create policies but look to the private sector to distribute services. He proposed calling on private actors, including companies, voluntary organizations, and nonprofits, to provide many services, especially to the poor. Osborne rarely acknowledged that there was a long tradition of such arrangements dating back to the New Deal if not earlier, but he advocated for this approach to be used more expansively than before.

Osborne deflected criticism that his model and support for organizations like ShoreBank and Southern was a pitch for privatization. Instead, he would repeatedly argue that government should serve as the "catalyst" that would spark private action for public purposes. He urged governments to "use their immense *leverage* to structure the market so that millions of businesses and individuals have incentives" to meet needs like childcare, job training, and environmental protection. In his mind, this was the opposite of leaving matters to the free market and was, instead, "a form of intervention in the market."[50] Overall, Osborne's view of entrepreneurial government itself aimed to meld the public and private and to use resources in new ways to maximize productivity and effectiveness. Osborne developed these ideas into a book, cowritten with Ted Gaebler, called *Reinventing Government: How the Entrepreneurial Spirit Is Transforming the Public Sector*, which was released in 1992.

The idea of entrepreneurial government had immediate currency for the New Democrats of the DLC who, since the 1970s, saw entrepreneurship not just as an economic growth strategy but a worldview. It was one of the reasons that Clinton and others had become so drawn to the microenterprise model. The DLC directly applied Osborne's ideas of reinventing government and of market-oriented, entrepreneurial techniques to its mission and policy proposals. The organization began releasing papers and articles suggesting replacing environmental regulations with market incentives and mechanisms like tradeable permits and reforming the health-care system through market mechanisms.[51] Under Osborne's guidance, the DLC became one of the first political organizations to explore charter schools as a means of improving public education. Charters, along with the other programs, became a critical part of the new approach that DLC promised it would provide as the nation was starting a new decade.

TURNING POINT

The DLC hosted its 1990 conference at the Fairmont Hotel in New Orleans attracting over seven hundred people. Although the grand hotel was most notable for serving as the headquarters for legendary Louisiana politician Huey Long in the 1920s, the DLC sought to focus on the Democratic Party and the nation's future. The moment was ripe to make a case that times were changing. The event occurred at the dawn of a new decade and just a few months after the fall of the Berlin Wall. Communism was ending throughout Eastern Europe, which increased the stakes for the DLC to set forth a new agenda and argument for why it was best suited to lead the Democratic Party in the post–Cold War era. In the lead-up to the convention, the DLC leadership decided to develop a statement that would "give a clearer definition of our policy and principles" and what it meant to be a New Democrat and a member of the DLC, which it could release at the conference.[52] From explained in a private memo to key elected officials that the New Orleans Declaration was part of their effort to stage "a bloodless revolution in our party" akin to what conservatives had accomplished in the Republican Party.[53]

Updating the long-standing New Democrat refrain for the new decade, the declaration opened by announcing: "The political ideas and passions of the 1930s and 1960s cannot guide us in the 1990s." Instead, it declared the DLC believed first and foremost that the "fundamental mission of the Democratic Party is to expand opportunity, not government," "economic growth is the prerequisite to expanding opportunity for everyone" and the "free market, regulated in the public interest, is the best engine of general prosperity."[54] The statement stressed how the values of growth, opportunity, and freedom applied to foreign policy aims, especially as the Cold War was ending. The DLC wanted to make clear that with the fall of the Berlin Wall, US foreign policy needed to make its main focus encouraging the spread of democracy in the world.[55] It called for expanding international trade, opening markets to US goods, and moving beyond traditional forms of economic and military aid by providing new forms of democratic assistance. The DLC, therefore, found a new justification for its long-standing promotion of international, open markets and enhanced technological innovation and investment. Now it would also serve not just domestic aims of increasing economic growth and opportunity but also the foreign policy goals of spreading peace and democracy. This vision was actually closer to the priorities of the Reagan and Bush administrations than the DLC might have cared to admit.

Bruce Reed, one of the declaration's primary drafters, explained that "unlike most party platforms, which tend to blur ideological differences," the statement "set forth a distinct new ideology." He confidently called it "a declaration of independence from old ways of thinking . . . and on the forces of inertia and complacency in both parties."[56] Although bold, the declaration reiterated many of the core ideas that this wing of Democrats had been advocating since the 1970s about combining opportunity and growth, reforming government, opening markets, and enhancing trade. The New Democrats' dogged efforts to distinguish the DLC from the Great Society, like the Watergate Babies before them, failed to address that this focus on growth was more a continuation of than break from the liberal priorities of the past.

The declaration included other points to demonstrate how the DLC represented a departure from the liberal agenda. The statement endorsed "equal opportunity, not equal outcomes," which was a not-so-subtle rejection of Affirmative Action.[57] It called for implementing social welfare programs that "bring the poor into the nation's economic mainstream, not maintain them in dependence," which implied that means-tested programs disincentivized work and saving. It also supported "preventing crime and punishing criminals, not explaining away their behavior," which was a rebuke of the call by many liberals that it was important to understand the social conditions and context that produced crime. In these cases, the DLC was trying to show a hard-nosed and pragmatic approach to issues of race and poverty, but in ways that clearly had the potential to further harm vulnerable groups. The declaration was also notable for the issues it did not address, including reproductive and LGBTQ rights (save for an oblique commitment to a right to privacy). It discussed "workers," but made no mention of organized labor. These oversights looked deliberate, and they were. Even more than trying to distinguish themselves from Republicans, the drafters were making a conscious effort to "draw sharp lines" between the DLC and the rest of the party.[58]

The New Orleans event "left a lot of blood on the floor," Marshall recalled, which had been its very goal.[59] The declaration especially rankled Jesse Jackson who was in New Orleans for the conference. He publicly denounced the statement's commitment to "equal opportunity, not equal outcomes" as "a perversion of the Democratic tradition" and a clear effort to undermine Affirmative Action.[60] Speaking before the crowd, Jackson offered a contrasting vision of the future of Democratic policy, which included deep cuts in military spending and higher taxes on the rich, as well as major new domestic spending programs on welfare, jobs, and infrastructure. Bill Clinton shot back that Jackson's calls for higher taxes resembled class warfare.[61] It was looking increasingly like Jackson and Clinton and the DLC were losing the ability to find any middle ground.

Clinton's bold attack on Jackson was also an effort to assert himself as the new chair of the DLC. Clinton had been one of the original members of the DLC and in the late 1980s had become increasingly involved in the organization. Clinton demonstrated both a genuine interest in policy and ideas and shared the DLC's belief that the Democratic Party and government had to modernize. From and his staff believed appointing the charismatic and committed Clinton as chair could help avert charges that the DLC was just a group of Washington insiders and could raise its profile beyond the beltway. As governor of Arkansas, Clinton demonstrated a keen ability to communicate and appeal to moderate and conservative voters, but he also had connections and credibility with liberal Democrats dating back to his days working on the McGovern campaign. From and Marshall realized that Clinton's rare ability to reach multiple constituencies could potentially make him a viable presidential candidate as well.[62] When From offered Clinton the post, he readily accepted. Clinton appreciated that, like him, the DLC was "genuinely interested in ideas and issues and reforms that were percolating at the state and local level" and were trying to convert them into national policy.[63] He also recognized that chairing the organization would provide him with an important platform as he considered a bid for higher office.

In his first speech as chair, delivered at the 1990 conference, Clinton built on the themes of the New Orleans Declaration. He defined being a Democrat as believing "there's a role for government in solving common problems" and "that whenever government does something with or for individuals who are disenfranchised, it must empower them, and that whenever the government does something with individuals who are irresponsible, it must require responsibility from them."[64] He admonished the audience that "any political resurgence for the Democrats depends on the intellectual resurgence of our party." Clinton also aimed to prove that he was not an Arkansas hayseed who favored a protectionist approach to foreign and economic policy. Clinton had been in fact working hard to bolster Arkansas's international stature, taking multiple trips to Asia in the 1980s to lure international companies to open up factories or invest in the state.[65] In his speech, he noted that the end of communism was bringing new market economies and political democracies, which were "creating a whole new raft of economic opportunities." Clinton sought to connect these new dynamics of US foreign policy to two of his own pet issues. He deemed "education and economic growth the national security issues of the 1990s" and the best way to take advantage of the new opportunities. Thus, like the DLC as a whole, he aimed to show how domestic growth and opportunity had new global stakes.

After the speech, Clinton explained to reporters that "one reason I took this job is to define and communicate what we are. People don't know what a Democrat is. Until they know what we stand for we are not going to win elections."[66] In order to abet this process, Clinton and From barnstormed the country during 1990 and 1991 to build support for the DLC and its ideas. With crammed itineraries, which often left them racing to get on planes before the doors closed, the trips proved important for Clinton in honing his own message.[67] At events with local politicians and civic groups, Clinton delivered speeches about the need to rebuild the Democratic Party around themes that did not fit onto a liberal-conservative continuum.[68] Osborne's idea of "reinventing government" served as an organizing theme as Clinton disseminated the key principles of the DLC. "We believe the job of government is to expand opportunity, not bureaucracy," he told audiences. "We believe in responsibility. . . . We have to recognize that entrepreneurial, antibureaucratic revolution spreading across the world . . . has to come to government here."[69] During the stops, Clinton and From would often take time out to visit innovative programs like a community policing initiative in South Carolina or efforts to reform public housing in Chicago.[70] Clinton would then incorporate these specific examples into his speeches.

Clinton did not merely want to become the puppet of the DLC; he wanted to play an active role in shaping both the message and the policy proposals of the organization. He drew on the strategy, philosophy, and specific programs he had developed as governor of Arkansas and fused them with that of the DLC. By the time he took the helm of the DLC, Clinton was a firm believer in school reform as the best way to simultaneously improve the nation's education system and the nation's productivity. Both Marshall and Reed described Clinton's ideas as "far and away more compelling" than what they developed, and they quickly made them part of the DLC agenda.[71]

Clinton directly shaped the DLC's position on poverty and welfare as well. Like Osborne, Clinton encouraged DLC and PPI staffers to look more seriously at issues like microenterprise and community development banking, which he had supported in Arkansas. In 1991, Marshall commissioned a study entitled *Microenterprise: Human Reconstruction in America's Inner Cities*, written by Lewis Solomon, a law professor and PPI fellow. Solomon praised microenterprise as "truly an empowering strategy" and contended that "this inexpensive, market-oriented, entrepreneurial solution can help alleviate poverty and promote economic development."[72] The PPI staff also explored community development banks like ShoreBank and Southern. The DLCers began to recognize how the idea fit with their efforts to make the private sector a more central partner of the Democratic Party to improve overall economic growth and help people improve their situation. These banks also aligned with the New Democrat belief that private sector assistance and involvement was not just what was needed to help low-income people move up the economic ladder, it was also what they wanted too.[73]

Clinton forcefully urged the DLC to make welfare reform a more prominent part of its agenda. By the early 1990s, AFDC's initial rationale to keep women out of the workforce had continued to be one of the major strikes against it. Ronald Reagan's systematic attacks on Black welfare queens further heightened the sense that the welfare system zapped recipients of self-sufficiency. Fueled by Charles Murray's 1984 book *Losing Ground*, Reagan and other conservatives contended that welfare should be abolished because it produced dependency and laziness among recipients and prevented them from getting jobs or getting married. Welfare recipients themselves had also long argued for reforming the system. Beginning in the late 1960s, recipients and their advocates contended the welfare system was stigmatizing and dehumanizing and the payments were too meager.[74] By the early 1990s, the packages had become even stingier: with the combination of cash, food stamps, and health insurance a recipient received an average of $7,600 a year, which was nearly $4,000 below the poverty line.[75]

Clinton believed in reforming the welfare system to focus more on work and responsibility. In Arkansas, Clinton had pushed for several laws that required women to enter the workforce or skills training courses. Clinton did not originate this idea. Many states—including California under Ronald Reagan—had instituted workfare type programs beginning in the 1960s. Clinton advocated for a less punitive model that offered skills and education along with supplementary supports such as childcare, transportation, and Medicare benefits.[76] He became a national leader in the conversation on work-based welfare as the chair of the National Governor's Association. In 1988, he helped draft the first major federal welfare reform law, which required every state to enroll some of its recipients into a jobs or training program.[77] Clinton recognized that work requirements aligned with the DLC's larger ideals since it constituted an effort to promote responsibility, opportunity, and economic growth. Clinton believed it could also both turn former recipients into productive contributors to the economy and reduce the welfare bureaucracy. Moreover, Bruce Reed and the other members of the DLC-PPI staff understood that to many Americans the welfare system was a symbol of the failures of the Democratic Party. Adopting Clinton's ideas for reforming the system could, therefore, help the DLC to show they were a new kind of Democrat.

Clinton played an equally critical role in shaping the organization's message as its policy priorities. He encouraged the DLC to shift away from its rhetorical emphasis on being "mainstream" and "centrist."[78] Instead, he advocated the DLC accentuate the label of New Democrat, which was more optimistic and future oriented and had the potential to galvanize more people.[79] Similarly, Clinton helped DLC staffers realize, according to Reed, that they would not win the battle for the "soul of the party if we tried to define it as a conservative vs. liberal or moderate vs. liberal fight. We had to make it a fight between new and old."[80] The DLC sought to put this new strategy on display at its 1991 convention in Cleveland, making "New Choices" the theme. The convention organizers decided one clear way to illustrate that theme would be to exclude Jesse Jackson from the lineup.

NEW CHOICES

Al From had to know he was inviting controversy when he said Jackson would not be invited to the DLC's convention. From slyly maintained it was not personal, but because Jackson was "representative of old-style politics" from which the DLC was consciously trying to move the party away.[81] Jackson, of course, took the bait and welcomed the chance to denounce the DLC once again in a series of speeches and interviews. He charged that the DLC "was trying to suburbanize the party" and did not care about the issues of marginalized people, and he called African American members like Mike Espy and William H. Gray "fig leaves."[82] He suggested the conference "New Choices" theme was a "code word for exclusion" and marked a covert effort "to shift the political center away from the moral center of racial justice, gender equality and peace."[83] Demonstrating his public relations prowess, Jackson came to Cleveland anyway and staged a series of rival appearances. The events included a speech at a nearby Union Hall in front of a banner with the slogan "Jobs for Justice."[84]

Jackson was not alone in openly protesting the DLC and its 1991 convention. Liberal senator Howard Metzenbaum (D-OH) had been trying to organize a rival faction called Coalition for Democratic Values, which aimed to reaffirm the party's New Deal and Great Society legacy and supported issues like tax fairness, campaign finance reform, and defending women's rights. Metzenbaum's group held a convention of their own in Iowa the same weekend as the DLC's conference in an explicit effort to highlight the differences between the groups.[85] Organized labor also saw the Cleveland convention as an opportunity to oppose the DLC's support for free trade and its increasingly cozy ties to big business. Representatives of the United Auto Workers positioned themselves outside the entrance to the Cleveland convention hall where they handed out leaflets opposing DLC's position on both.[86]

The people filtering into the hall further validated the union members' suspicions. Lobbyists from the National Rifle Association, the Tobacco Institute, AT&T, Boeing, RJR Nabisco, and

Bill Clinton delivering the keynote address
at the Democratic Leadership Council convention in Cleveland, May 6, 1991
Credit: AP Photo/Mark Duncan

Philip Morris saw the convention as the ideal opportunity to rub
elbows with the many public officials in attendance.[87] Several of
the companies ponied up thousands to underwrite the three-day
event. The presence of corporate sponsors also heightened the
predominately white and male tilt of the attendees.

The controversy surrounding the convention put even more
pressure on Clinton to prove the mettle of himself and the DLC.
On the convention's eve, he pulled an all-nighter to rewrite his
opening speech. Despite his lack of sleep, he was remarkably
relaxed as he addressed the crowd, rarely looking at his single
page of handwritten notes. He used the "New Choices" idea as

a point of departure and refined the points he had been making while stumping for the DLC. He focused on the themes of opportunity, responsibility, growth, and streamlining government and connected them to the changing global economy. He defined opportunity to mean "first and foremost a commitment to economic growth," which would be achieved by "expanding world trade" and investment in "emerging technologies" and "world-class skills" for workers. Yet, he maintained that opportunity had to be paired with responsibility through initiatives like reforming the welfare system through education and workfare. "We should invest more money in people on welfare to give them the skills they need to succeed," Clinton declared, "but we should demand that everybody who can go to work do it, for work is the best social program this country has ever devised."[88] A version of this claim would become one of Clinton's pat lines and embodied both a continuation and break of the New Deal vision of social welfare. Clinton addressed Jackson's criticisms head on and contended "choice is not a code word for elitism and racism."[89] He then listed off the DLC proposals to address the problems of poverty with programs like childcare vouchers, public school choice, job training programs, and community policing. Drawing directly on Osborne's work, Clinton also stressed that such programs would "reinvent government" by eliminating bureaucracy, empowering people, and increasing accountability.

Clinton would later call it one of the best speeches he ever gave. As the room erupted in a standing ovation, it was clear to the DLC operatives that they had found their presidential candidate. The speech laid out clearly and concisely the messages and themes the DLC had been trying to promote for years. In fact, the DLC decided that "opportunity, responsibility, community" so pithily distilled its key themes and goals that they made it their official slogan.

"The New American Choice Resolution" put to the delegates for approval filled in Clinton's message with specifics.[90] The DLCers hoped that these proposals would not just help to define their organization but could also serve as the template for a presidential platform in the upcoming election. The platform thereby included policy ideas perceived to appeal more directly to moderate white middle-class voters that "The Politics of Evasion" had argued were so central to the Democrats winning back the White House. Playing to the racialized fears of many white moderates, the DLC adopted an even more punitive position on crime, calling for heightened mandatory minimums for gun-related crimes and military-style boot camps for young first-time offenders convicted of nonviolent crimes. The platform also asserted the importance of promoting strong family values, strengthening the heteronormative two-parent family, and intensifying child support laws and access to day care. Welfare reform became another major focus. The DLC proposed as an alternative to the existing welfare system market-based programs like the Earned Income Tax Credit and Individual Development Accounts and providing government support and capital for microenterprise programs in urban and rural communities. These programs, the DLC maintained, would help to "liberate the poor from poverty and dependence," and by turning them into productive workers, it would help the US "succeed in a global economy."[91]

The New Choices Resolution went more brass tacks on Clinton's argument that increasing global trade and opening markets would help economic growth and individual opportunity domestically. The collapse of the Soviet Union—which looked all but inevitable by the spring of 1991—meant that the US was going to have to redefine its place in the world. The DLC contended the nation should lead the global march toward democracy and free enterprise, which could help achieve domestic goals.[92] In particular, the DLC urged Congress to give the Bush administration fast-track negotiating authority for the creation of a free trade zone with Mexico, which would come to be known as the North American Free Trade Agreement (NAFTA). This stance was controversial since the Democratic establishment had taken a much less conciliatory stance and the labor movement strongly objected to the agreement. The DLC contended, however, that the agreement would lead to higher income and more employment for workers in Mexico and the United States. The resolution called on Congress to provide training, education, and other services to people displaced by liberalizing trade so that they could "compete in the future."[93] Such arguments would fail to convince union leaders, who continued to voice outrage at the DLC's position on free trade.[94]

Despite the protest from Jackson, labor unions, and other liberal Democrats, the three days in Cleveland made clear that the DLC had found its stride and that its chair had a shot at the presidency. Soon after the convention, Clinton announced that he was resigning his post so that he could form a presidential exploratory committee. On October 3, 1991, he stood on the steps of the Arkansas State House and formally declared his candidacy.

THE NEW COVENANT

Watching Clinton during the 1992 Democratic primary, *New York Times* reporter Gwen Ifill observed that his "most reliable campaign applause lines seem borrowed from the council [DLC]'s speech writers," especially the relentless invocation of buzzwords like opportunity, responsibility, and community.[95] Members of DLC staff in truth probably had helped write the speeches. Several of the DLC-PPI staff and fellows joined the campaign, including Bruce Reed who became policy issues director. Al From did not have an official role, but he remained a close advisor and continued to exert considerable influence over Clinton and his message and strategy. From would step in especially when he believed that Clinton was straying from his New Democrat roots.[96]

Clinton immediately followed up on the announcement of his presidential bid with a series of speeches at his alma mater Georgetown University. The speeches portended how the goals and philosophy of the DLC would come to shape Clinton's run and message.[97] The first speech aimed to establish the central themes of the campaign. He called it the New Covenant, which was an intentional variation of Democrat slogans of yore like the New Deal and the New Frontier. In the speech, he defined the New Covenant as "a solemn agreement between the people and their government, to provide opportunity for everybody, inspire responsibility throughout our society, and restore a sense of community to this great nation."[98] He then followed it up with more specific policy proposals. Reed, who served as main drafter of the speech, recognized that Clinton needed to distinguish himself and thought welfare reform was an important way he could do so. He believed the issue represented "the best opportunity to outline the new social bargain" that Clinton and the New Democrats had been working on and how they offered a new way to address poverty.[99]

Clinton had already called for work requirements for welfare recipients, and he and his DLC advisors wanted something even bolder for his Georgetown speech. A few days before the speech, Will Marshall handed Bruce Reed a policy paper that had been lying on his desk by a Harvard professor named David Ellwood about welfare time limits.[100] Ellwood developed an idea of limiting the duration of cash support in exchange for an expansion of health care and other social services, as well as the supply of more government-created jobs.[101] Reed and Clinton quickly adapted the most controversial (and conservative) part of Ellwood's concept. At Georgetown, Clinton pledged to "end welfare as we know it" by establishing a two-year limit before recipients had to get a job either in the private sector or performing community service.

The pledge would become the defining part of Clinton's Georgetown speech and one of the key and most controversial features of Clinton's campaign more broadly. Amid all the attention the phrase received, many missed that Clinton was not calling for the eradication of the welfare system but a revamping of it to make it more efficient and decentralized and, above all, to give recipients more choice and responsibility. The pledge extended Clinton's belief in the psychological power of work and his firm conviction that no one who worked should be poor. No matter how Clinton diced it, however, it was still a call for limiting the social services and benefits for low-income women. And as would quickly become clear, it was difficult for welfare recipients to exert much choice or responsibility with no safety net, when well-paying jobs were in short supply and the minimum wage was not enough to lift anyone out of poverty.

In a sign that Clinton and the New Democrats recognized they were overlooking these deeper structural realities, the campaign offered small-scale market-based tools like community development banking and microenterprise as an alternative to welfare and a solution to poverty. "We need special efforts to empower the poor to work their way out of poverty," he told the audience at Georgetown, "by supporting private and public partnerships to give low-income entrepreneurs the tools to start new businesses, through innovative institutions like ShoreBank in Chicago and its rural counterpart, the Southern Development Bancorporation in Arkansas."[102] Throughout his presidential run, Clinton spoke of plans to replicate the ShoreBank model around the country and hailed how microenterprise programs revealed that "the power of the government can be used to create market forces that work."[103] He suggested that the programs integrated a commitment to using the private sector in important ways and would both eliminate bureaucracy and empower the poor. The plan thereby upheld Clinton's continued calls to reinvent government, which was another main campaign theme.[104] In fact, when David Osborne and Ted Gaebler released *Reinventing Government* in early 1992, Clinton emerged as the most influential advocate praising it as a "blueprint" to "revitalize government." His support contributed to making the book a *New York Times* best seller and practically required reading among public officials around the country.

Throughout the campaign, Clinton also extended the New Democrat commitment to economic growth. Clinton's advisors included PPI's Robert Shapiro who played a key role, especially in the first part of the race, in encouraging Clinton to focus his policies on the idea that financial markets should be harnessed to deliver more opportunity and equality to an increasing share of the American people.[105] The rest of Clinton's economic advisors offered a range of priorities but all shared a commitment to growth. "We're Democrats, which means we have concerns about social

justice," advisor and Clinton's Rhodes scholar classmate Ira Magaziner revealingly observed. "But when you have an economy that's
growing at seven-tenths of one percent per year per person, it's
hard to solve the other problems."[106]

Robert Reich, another Rhodes scholar friend of Clinton who
had been critical of many of the early ideas of the Atari Democrats,
became especially influential in shaping the campaign's economic
agenda. Just before the launch of the Clinton campaign, Reich released a book called *The Work of Nations*, which reinforced his
long-standing argument that to succeed in the global economy, the
United States had to invest in the education and skills of its citizens. Reich injected these ideas directly into Clinton's economic
platform, which often looked like the same vision of industrial
policy the Atari Democrats had been calling for since the early
1980s. However, Clinton overlaid it with a folksy gloss by talking
about small business growth and using catchy slogans like "What
you earn depends upon what you learn," which made it more appealing to voters.[107] Reich also persuaded Clinton not to obsess
over deficit reduction as advocated by Goldman Sachs executive
Robert Rubin and a few of Clinton's other advisors.[108] Instead,
Reich urged significantly greater spending by the government on
roads, bridges, and other major infrastructure projects. This idea
would sit at the heart of Clinton's campaign book *Putting People
First*, which was largely written by Reich in a hospital bed while
he was recovering from hip surgery. The book contended that
investing in communication, transportation, and environmental
systems—including a national information network—would not
just provide jobs, but also contribute to making the country more
globally competitive.[109]

At the same time that the Clinton campaign was promoting
the international benefits of domestic construction projects, it
also continued to tout the domestic benefits of free trade. During
the 1992 election, NAFTA emerged as a central campaign issue.
The agreement became a symbol for unions about job loss and
declining wages. These fears became amplified after third party
candidate Ross Perot made the negative effects of NAFTA one

of the organizing issues of his own campaign. Environmental groups joined the labor movement in opposing NAFTA, concerned that Mexico did not have the same environmental standards as the US. In contrast, the DLC and PPI issued articles and policy reports promoting trade liberalization and NAFTA. PPI fellows stressed that free trade was a "win-win," which would encourage the spread of democracy and the market economy in Mexico and increase the incomes and employment opportunities for US workers.[110] Clinton largely adopted this position too. He promised that, if elected, he would negotiate a better deal than Bush, which would have tougher environmental and worker safety standards.[111] Yet, he continued to argue that NAFTA would benefit the US economy and American workers.[112]

The issue of free trade showed the difficult position of the labor movement after Clinton became the presumed Democratic presidential nominee. Labor officials and the rank and file both had strong objections with Clinton's position on free trade and were well aware of the New Democrats' long-standing hostility toward unions.[113] Labor leadership was not surprisingly rankled when Clinton announced plans to reduce the size of government by eliminating 100,000 jobs from the federal payroll. In an appearance at a United Auto Workers meeting, Clinton suggested labor should accept more flexible hours and cooperate more with the private sector.[114] Even though union members had gained more than a quarter of the delegate seats at the 1992 Democratic Convention, labor leaders made a conscious decision not to demand that Clinton openly advocate for unions in the platform or to temper his support for free trade. This calculation rested on their sense that Bush was a bigger threat to unions, and the movement should focus their energy on defeating him.[115]

Clinton's relationship to Jesse Jackson and the Rainbow Coalition was even more fraught and revealed deliberate calculations as well. After deciding not to join the 1992 race himself, Jackson continued to push the Democratic Party to embrace many of the key issues from his two presidential runs. With the Cold War over, he redoubled his calls for a national investment and jobs program that would direct military spending along with public pensions to remake the country's basic infrastructure.[116] Once Clinton was safely the frontrunner, Jackson invited him, in early June, to address the Rainbow Coalition convention, the theme of which was Rebuilding America. Clinton picked up on the Rebuilding America theme, focusing on the need to take new steps to bring private sector money to inner city communities. He suggested that what the urban African American poor wanted was not "more government" but "more jobs and small businesses." He advocated nurturing free enterprise through community development banks like ShoreBank in places like Baltimore, Washington, and Detroit, in the same way the US was advocating for free enterprise in Eastern Europe, the former Soviet Union, and China.[117] Clinton also offered his own version of a national infrastructure project focused on things like high-speed rail, airline transportation, water, and sewer systems. While not quite as ambitious as Jackson's, Clinton contended his project would provide more jobs and economic growth.

The more substantive aspects of Clinton's speech quickly got buried, however, beneath something he said later. At the end of his remarks, Clinton shifted gears and denounced another speaker in the convention lineup. He accused the Black rap artist Sister Souljah of sowing racial division with her lyrics, which were "filled with hatred." Clinton suggested she advocated that Black people have a week where they kill white people.[118] He compared her comments to the views of Klan leader David Duke and to Clinton's own mistaken decision to golf at a Little Rock country club that had no African American members. The digs at Sister Souljah created a firestorm, especially after Clinton refused to apologize for them. Jackson took the remarks less as an attack on the rap artist and more on him. He called the comments part of a "consistent attempt to provoke me" and suggested that Clinton used the platform of the convention to establish distance from the Rainbow Coalition and "embarrass us."[119]

Many others saw the speech in less personal terms and suggested that Clinton had used the forum to appeal to white moderates and was trading in culturally conservative tropes about rap music to prove he was not beholden to "special interests."[120] It looked like a tactic culled directly from "The Politics of Evasion" playbook. The speech, and the strategy behind it, also suggested that the decision of Clinton and his DLC advisors to make ShoreBank and microenterprise programs a part of his campaign agenda was less about trying to secure the votes of the poor people of color served by the initiatives. Instead, these market-oriented entrepreneurial programs were types of approaches to poverty that they believed would be most appealing to politically moderate upper-middle-class whites.

Jackson and many other members of the Black community struggled with how best to deal with Clinton's presidential bid, which was rife with downright racist moments. In addition to the Sister Souljah fracas and the calls for welfare reform, Clinton left the campaign trail and returned to Arkansas to oversee the execution of a Black mentally impaired prisoner named Ricky Rector. The stunt was a bald effort to show he was not "soft on crime," with clear racial overtones.[121] Yet, many African American politicians and civil rights leaders advocated for giving Clinton a chance. As Rep. John Lewis (D-GA) explained, he and his predominately Black Atlanta constituents first and foremost wanted a Democrat in the White House and believed the only way to do so was by reaching out to white swing voters.[122] Eventually, even Jackson grudgingly came around to this position and tepidly endorsed Clinton, though he did not drop his complaint that the New Democrats were misguided for focusing so intensively on white middle-class voters.[123] For his part, Clinton increasingly embraced Jackson's economic populist rhetoric and ideas for tax fairness, suggesting that under Reagan and Bush "government has served the rich and special interests." However, Clinton concentrated more on how the system had become "rigged" against the "forgotten middle-class," rather than concentrating on the people who comprised Jackson's Rainbow Coalition.[124]

While Clinton's campaign strategy showed the influence of the DLC, the Democratic platform revealed how the New Democrats had come to assert dominance on the Democratic Party as a whole. Unlike years past when the platform at least tried to reflect the goals and issues of the various factions of the party, the Clinton campaign successfully lobbied for the platform to reflect the nominee's agenda. The resulting document—the very DLC-named "New Choices"—contained the themes and issues the organization had been developing for more than a decade. It included calls for growth over redistribution, streamlining government, and using the private sector and the market to address social needs. The platform continued to provide a false caricature of the New Deal and the Great Society and explicitly rejected "the outdated faith in programs as the solution to every problem."[125] Instead, it declared that "expanding the entrepreneurial economy of high-skill, high-wage jobs is the most important family policy, urban policy, labor policy, minority policy and foreign policy America can have."[126] In keeping with the DLC's long-standing efforts to shift the party away from "special interests," it made no explicit mention of unions or bolstering organized labor as a pathway to ensure fairness or full employment or of achieving racial and economic justice. Instead, the platform followed the lead of Clinton's campaign and put a strong emphasis on the colorblind and class-evasive category of "forgotten hard-working middle-class Americans."[127]

A further symbol of the DLC's influence came in Clinton's choice of a vice presidential running mate. He elected not to balance the ticket and instead chose fellow southern New Democrat and active DLC member Al Gore. Clinton defended his decision by explaining that "we share a common philosophy that it's time to move beyond old ideas."[128] The DLC founders took the decision as confirmation they had achieved their "bloodless revolution." Robert Shapiro proudly declared that with Clinton's nomination and the platform, the DLC group had conducted "an intellectual leveraged buyout" of the Democratic Party.[129] It was an especially impressive feat given the fact that by 1992, the DLC still only had about 3,000 members, roughly 750 of whom were elected officials. As Al From strolled the floor of Madison Square Garden, the site of the 1992 Democratic National Convention, with an FOB (friend of Bill) button on his lapel, accepting handshakes and even

Al From and Hillary Clinton share a laugh at a Democratic Leadership Council dinner in Washington a month after the 1992 election, December 8, 1992
Credit: AFP via Getty Images/Chris Walkins

hugs and kisses from attendees, it was a sign of just how far the DLC had come in a few short years.[130] Looking out at the flood of Clinton-Gore signs around the convention floor, From almost got choked up.[131]

Clinton and Gore's victory in the November election was even more cause for celebration. Third party candidate Ross Perot had thrown a curveball into the race. The billionaire's antistatist populism, antipathy toward free trade, and siren calls about the deficit directed the race ever more to economic issues and shaved off support from both Clinton and George H. W. Bush. But in the end, Clinton captured 43 percent of the popular vote and 370 electoral college votes. He secured 83 percent of the African American vote and 61 percent of Latinx voters (though turnout among both groups was low) and won back many of the so-called Reagan Democrats as well and moderate Republicans in places like Philadelphia's Main Line and Southern California.[132] The politics of evasion were over.

The DLC hoped to find a way to continue their influence on Clinton now that he was headed to the White House. From and Marshall wanted to play an analogous role to the Clinton administration that the Heritage Foundation had served for the Reagan administration. After Reagan's 1980 victory, the Heritage Foundation produced a guide to public policy called *Mandate for Leadership*, which Reagan distributed to every member of his cabinet at their first meeting. PPI decided to create a similar book, which they called *Mandate for Change*, which could provide Clinton a way to translate the ideas that the DLC had been developing for the past few years into a governing agenda. As many of his colleagues were out on the campaign trail, Marshall spent 1992 in the PPI's office working on the book, which was released in early December.[133] *Mandate for Change* emphasized the five themes of opportunity, responsibility, community, democracy, and entrepreneurial government. Marshall and From wrote the preface, laying out a version of what they would later brand as the "Third Way." Once again overstating how redistributive the Democratic Party's agenda had previously been, Marshall and From stated the New Democrats explicitly rejected "the recent liberal emphasis on redistribution" and the "right's notion that wealthy investors drive the economy."[134] *Mandate for Change*, like the New Democrats, instead focused on progrowth policies and "innovative, non-bureaucratic approaches to governing." It called for "introducing choice, competition and market incentives into the public sector," "reciprocal obligation between citizens and government," and "protecting our national interests by promoting democracy and free markets."[135] In many ways, the book served as culmination and synthesis of the work that PPI had been producing over the previous three years.[136]

Mandate for Change served as the more public-facing policies and advice that the DLC offered more privately to Clinton as he made the move to the White House. Clinton asked Al From to oversee his transition's domestic policy plans, with Bruce Reed serving as his deputy. The responsibility solidified the DLC's reputation as an idea generator and gave them an important opportunity to shape the president's domestic agenda. For a month, From and Reed and their team feverishly worked out of a cramped office space in downtown Little Rock. Just before Christmas, they sent Clinton a large book called *The Clinton Revolution: A Domestic Agenda for the First 100 Days*. The title alluded to both Franklin Roosevelt and Ronald Reagan, though they encouraged Clinton to transcend "the tired and predictable left-right debate."[137] In a memo attached to the front of the volume, From and Reed urged Clinton to hold true to his promise "to be a different kind of Democrat." The larger book included a set of specific policies and clear agenda for action, much of which were culled from DLC and PPI policy reports.[138]

Clinton's presidential campaign had given the DLC their long-awaited opportunity to redefine the basic contours of the Democratic Party's message and electoral strategy. But with Clinton headed to the Oval Office, they had an even bigger opportunity. The New Democrats now had the chance to reinvent government from the inside and insert their philosophy of growth and opportunity and market-based solutions to social problems directly into public policy and popular common sense. Their arrival at the White House, nevertheless, would leave both the more redistributive approaches to addressing inequality offered by figures like Jackson along with poor people of color who had made up the Rainbow Coalition further in the cold in the 1990s.

PART II
WIN-WINS

CHAPTER 5

BETTER THAN WELFARE

During the spring of 1992, the acquittal of the white police officers accused of beating African American motorist Rodney King in Los Angeles ignited the largest and most destructive urban uprising of the twentieth century. For five days, the nation's second most populous city turned into a cauldron of frustration, anger, and fear. The protests began in South Central, the city's poorest and most heavily African American and Latinx area, which had been hit hard by decades of declining economic opportunities and rising poverty.[1] But it quickly spread to Koreatown, Hollywood, swaths of the San Fernando Valley, and other immigrant communities throughout the city where the recession of the early 1990s tripled unemployment. Mayor Tom Bradley issued a dusk-to-dawn curfew, and George H. W. Bush ordered six thousand national guard to stand by. By the time the violence abated, there were more than fifty deaths, over two thousand injuries, 4,500 fires, 16,000 arrests, and over a billion dollars of property damage.[2] "It was definitely inevitable," observed Howard Barnes, a twenty-seven-year-old Black tow truck driver from Inglewood. He warned that an even worse conflict would occur unless there was a solution to the economic problems of South LA.[3]

In contrast to the boarded-up storefronts, rundown houses, and gang violence that marked South LA, Chicago's South Shore area in the early 1990s had a low crime rate and was bustling with entrepreneurial activity. Freshly painted apartment buildings lined the streets, and a shopping center opened in the heart of the neighborhood, anchored by a large supermarket. Nearby, an artist incubator and community center had also recently opened. These developments largely could be credited to the intervention of ShoreBank.

Juxtaposing South LA with South Shore served as a key part of Bill Clinton's antipoverty, civil rights, and urban redevelopment agenda during the 1992 presidential race. On the stump, Clinton stressed the importance of increasing private sector activity by creating enterprise zones and providing more credit in urban areas. In an extended interview with *Rolling Stone*, Clinton declared the solution to poverty and urban unrest was "to create a small-business entrepreneurial economy in every underclass urban area and rural area in the country through the use of banks like the South Shore Bank."[4] He explained how as governor he helped start "the first rural version of the South Shore Bank" in Arkansas and declared that as president he wanted "to create one of those banks in every urban area of any size and every rural area."[5] Clinton refined this lofty vision to a succinct pledge that if elected he would create a hundred new community development banks around the country based directly on the ShoreBank model.[6]

In office, the Clinton administration responded to the moment of racial reckoning and concerns about concentrated poverty provoked by the uprising in LA with an economic empowerment agenda. The plan included Empowerment Zones, which used tax incentives to lure business into distressed areas, and a community development banking program. The administration also championed strengthening the regulations of the Community Reinvestment Act to provide new credit and economic opportunity to areas like South LA. The programs collectively treated poverty and racial discrimination as a market failure. Their main architects saw a lack of access to capital and credit—not the evisceration of the social safety net, rising incarceration, and historical patterns of segregation—as the primary problem poor communities of color faced. These initiatives rested on the premise that access to the

private sector, especially the banking system, could replace traditional forms of aid and that credit was an elixir that would magically erase years of exploitation and racial segregation.

The economic empowerment agenda helped insert into policy
and popular consciousness that markets and private investment
could serve as a tool to address poverty and racial discrimination.
It smacked of the New Democrats' philosophy and influence. In
fashioning their plan, Clinton's advisors drew on ideas long circu-
lating in urban policy circles and advocated by both the left and
the right. The administration then linked them with New Democrat principles such as public-private partnerships, reinventing
government by reducing bureaucracy, individual empowerment,
and personal responsibility. The programs all abided by the belief
that government should serve as a catalyst for private economic
growth to help achieve public sector goals. The agenda also continued Clinton's and the New Democrats' long-standing efforts to
prove that their model of governance was a departure from the
liberalism of the past. Clinton even touted his approach as "much
better than welfare" (the ultimate liberal bogeyman) because it
utilized private sector investment and purportedly fostered self-
sufficiency rather than give cash to individuals or expand government bureaucracy.[7] This market-based solution to poverty proved
far less controversial than welfare and generated far more support
from Republicans.

The Clinton administration often promoted its economic empowerment agenda as a win-win that offered the private sector incentives to invest in areas and people that "had been left behind."[8]
It routinely stressed how these programs had multiple benefits
with few downsides since they required relatively little funding
from the federal government, provided capital to underserved
areas, empowered the poor, and integrated them into the mainstream economy. The administration also contended that the initiatives offered private companies and banks with an opportunity
to make money and do good at the same time. It would eventually
become apparent that these programs were not such a "win-win"
and were creating clear winners and losers. It was also quickly

clear that the Clinton administration was overselling relatively small-scale programs like ShoreBank as the solution to large-scale structural problems. In the short term, however, ShoreBank itself proved one of the primary winners from Clinton's efforts to peddle this approach, as it garnered further renown and interest from investment banks.

GETTING BEYOND THE WAR ON POVERTY

The turmoil in Los Angeles made the already tense presidential race in the spring of 1992 even more contentious. While the Bush administration scrambled to come up with an appropriate response, Clinton quickly sought to get in front of the issue. As residents and storeowners took to the streets armed with brooms and shovels to sweep charred rubble, Clinton arrived in the city where he toured the damage and met with local community activists, religious leaders, and residents. He told them that the violence reinforced the need to heal the nation's racial divisions and stimulate the "economic and political empowerment of the people who are most disadvantaged."[9]

Soon after this visit, Clinton and Bush's discussions of the LA riots moved from platitudes about national healing into a partisan referendum on past approaches to urban poverty and racial segregation.[10] "We believe that many of the root problems that have resulted in inner-city difficulties were started in the '60s and '70s," Bush's press secretary announced.[11] He maintained the violence and destruction in LA proved once and for all that the Great Society had failed.[12] Clinton instead blamed the situation on years of neglect by the Reagan and Bush administrations. Yet, he also relied on a canard of liberalism to make his point. "Throwing money at a system that is profoundly broken," he said, was not the answer. "We literally have to empower and connect these people to the life we want them to live or they will be lost forever," Clinton urgently warned.[13] Through the remainder of the campaign, Clinton sought to show how he was not just another big government liberal who wanted to pour money in the inner city. Instead, he outlined plans to revitalize urban America by doing what ShoreBank had pulled off in South Shore. At a range of forums—including his infamous speech to the Rainbow Coalition—Clinton advocated stimulating private sector activity by creating enterprise zones and community development banks to rebuild neighborhood economies, empower residents, and heal the nation's racial tensions.[14]

After the November 1992 election, Clinton's advisors recognized that the credibility of his domestic and economic agenda rested, in part, on proving he could address the problems represented by places like South LA. An energy filled staffers who felt after twelve years of Republican control of the White House the moment was ripe to make meaningful change. The DLCers were particularly excited to have the opportunity to prove the Democratic Party had moved away from Great Society liberalism and could provide solutions suited for the 1990s. Clinton appointed DLC members Lloyd Bentsen, Mike Espy, and Richard Riley to cabinet posts. DLC staffers and fellows from its think tank the Progressive Policy Institute, like William Galston, Elaine Kamarck, Robert Shapiro, and Paul Weinstein, got plum positions in the arenas of domestic and economic policy.[15] Bruce Reed's role as campaign issues director and deputy of the domestic policy transition team earned him a post as the assistant domestic policy advisor. He and the other DLC-PPI alumni all brought their copies of *Mandate for Change* with them to the Executive Building and continued to talk back and forth with Will Marshall and Al From, who stayed behind at the DLC and PPI.[16] Weinstein, who joined Reed at the Domestic Policy Council, explained that the DLC and PPI continued to "set the tone" on a number of policy issues and served as a useful countervailing force to the "groupthink" that would often take hold over the administration.[17] Weinstein and other alums of the DLC and PPI believed that one of their main responsibilities was to ensure that Clinton remained true to the ideas of growth, opportunity, and responsibility that he had been touting since his time as the organization's head.[18]

Clinton and his senior advisors recognized that addressing the growth part of that trifecta had to be their first priority. Yet, even before Clinton left Little Rock, his advisors clashed over the best pathway to achieve economic growth.[19] During the campaign, Clinton had promised a substantial investment in infrastructure, worker training, and jobs, advancing ideas long promoted by Robert Reich and the Atari Democrats. However, Goldman Sachs executive Robert Rubin, whom Clinton appointed as director of his newly created National Economic Council (NEC), believed that the key to economic growth and stability lay in rebuilding the trust of Wall Street. Rubin argued Clinton had to lower interest rates by reducing the federal deficit.[20] Clinton was dubious of arranging his economic agenda around the desires of bond traders.[21] But Rubin, along with deficit hawks Bentsen and Panetta, finally persuaded the new president that creating a proinvestment climate would not just help Wall Street, but also make borrowing easier for the larger swath of middle-class Americans whom Clinton had centered his presidential bid upon. Reich, who had been appointed labor secretary, found his economic stimulus and infrastructure plan left on the wayside. Clinton did embrace the long-standing Atari Democrat position that global trade was a critical ingredient to creating a high-wage, high-growth economy. During his first year in office, Clinton completed the North American Free Trade Act deal and successfully pushed it through Congress.[22]

From the beginning, the president's advisors recognized he had to pair the issues of community development and economic empowerment with his approach to economic growth. Just after Clinton's inauguration, Rubin and Domestic Policy Council chair Carol Rasco set up an interagency working group with the goal of breaking the traditional walls between the domestic and economic policy arenas. The group resembled what one *Wall Street Journal* reporter dubbed a "think tank of talent," drawing the best and the brightest from the executive branch offices and various agencies.[23] Bruce Reed oversaw the task force along with Gene Sperling, the deputy director of the National Economic Policy Council. Like Reed, Sperling was in his midthirties, had a firm belief that the Democrats needed to combine social spending with strong private sector economic growth, and had the trust and respect of Clinton.[24] Sperling also had a reputation for his attention to policy detail and his workaholic tendencies. Both he and his workspace often looked like they were fresh off an all-nighter.[25] He brought this work ethic and energy to the interagency group.[26]

The working group also included Andrew Cuomo, an assistant secretary of HUD, who would quickly take on a leading role. The thirty-four-year-old was one of the youngest assistant secretaries, but his Democratic royal pedigree as the son of Mario Cuomo and husband of Robert Kennedy's daughter made him perhaps the most prominent.[27] He had firsthand experience working on issues of urban redevelopment as head of a low-income housing organization in New York. He combined this expertise with strong political instincts, which would prove useful for the group's work.[28] Cuomo joined Reed, Sperling, and other players in the working group in recognizing that their efforts offered a real chance to shape Clinton's antipoverty agenda.

It was both a daunting and exciting endeavor. Paul Dimond, a staffer charged with overseeing the day-to-day workings of the group, observed at the outset that "urban economic and community development has been a graveyard for liberal democrats for decades" and had "consumed much public treasure and many political careers for little return."[29] The interagency working group set out to prove that Clinton could succeed where three decades of previous presidents—both Democrats and Republicans—had failed.[30] The group made "economic empowerment" the top priority since on that issue "more than any other, the old answers don't work anymore and we need to launch a new *era* of bold, persistent, experimentation."[31] The group aimed to develop, as Sperling and Reed explained to Clinton, a set of ideas that "move beyond the old left right debate" and that focused on getting the private sector to invest in distressed communities.[32] Yet, in its effort to show how it was a departure from the past, the signature component of the plan actually drew on the urban policies of Clinton's predecessor.

FROM ENTERPRISE TO EMPOWERMENT

The idea of enterprise zones had been kicking around since the 1970s. It first emerged in England developed by Peter Hall, a leftist urban planner who suggested turning abandoned industrial areas into free trade zones. Margaret Thatcher's government implemented the plan, renaming them "enterprise zones."[33] The concept soon captured the attention of supply-side economics crusaders like the conservative Heritage Foundation and Ronald Reagan.[34] Rep. Jack Kemp (R-NY) became enterprise zones' most avowed champion based on his belief that cutting taxes and regulation could spur economic growth throughout the nation's impoverished urban core. He introduced annual versions of enterprise zone legislation throughout the 1980s, but they consistently stalled out. Many states took up the idea, but the programs varied widely in scope, size, and effectiveness since state governments could offer limited tax incentives.[35]

When George H. W. Bush appointed him secretary of HUD in 1989, Kemp intensified his crusade for federal enterprise zones. Observers compared his zeal for the idea to a teenager who had just read *The Fountainhead*.[36] Kemp's enthusiasm for enterprise zones as well as his calls for launching a "conservative war on poverty" alienated many Republicans, and he quickly found himself ostracized in the Bush administration.[37] Yet, the 1992 Los Angeles riots gave the former pro-football player a chance to make one final drive. This time enterprise zones legislation passed in Congress, but Bush vetoed the bill in October 1992, largely out of fear that it might hurt his reelection bid.

Throughout the 1992 presidential race, Clinton signaled support for Kemp's enterprise zone idea but always cautioned that tax incentives could not do the trick alone and had to be paired with social programs.[38] Channeling his Arkansas roots, Clinton proposed enterprise zones for rural areas as well. This expansion both broadened the appeal politically and made it appear more race neutral by mitigating the stigmas associated with a program targeting poor urban communities. The modification also built

on Clinton's understanding of the urgent need for economic redevelopment in places like Pine Bluff and the Arkansas Delta. The
interagency working group assumed the task of turning these
pledges into a workable policy. The group considered the possibility of simply reintroducing the bill Bush vetoed but instead opted
to create a new bill that would be "broader than the Kemp concep-
tion."[39] The members believed developing a bolder and bigger plan
would provide Clinton a means to take an ambitious stance and
show how his approach differed from his predecessors. The group
worked in something of what staffer Sheryll Cashin described as
"a vortex," leaving the Executive Building at 11 p.m. and returning at 7 a.m. to craft a plan in just a couple of months.[40] The frenetic schedule gave the staffers no "luxury of reflection" and left
them "exhausted," but they managed to put a proposal together by
early April.[41]

The modifications that the working group made to the enterprise zone idea purposefully reflected a New Democrat approach.
Kemp advocated making tax incentives available to any business
willing to move into a designated depressed area and envisioned
very little government involvement or provision of social services.
The model the Clinton administration developed had far more
of a role for government. The working group was skeptical that
tax breaks alone could provide residents in places like South LA,
the South Bronx, or the South Side of Chicago the services they
needed. "It's misleading to say, once I.B.M. moves to the South
Bronx everything's going to be rosy," Cuomo explained.[42] Instead, Cuomo and other working group members believed the tax
breaks had to be paired with increased social services like job
training, education, nutrition, day care, and affordable housing.
These services would be delivered in a block grant approach that
echoed the urban policies of the administrations of Gerald Ford
and Jimmy Carter. In another important deviation from the Republican version, the working group's proposal offered payroll tax
relief, rather than the capital gains tax cuts Kemp championed, to
businesses that employed Enterprise Zone residents. The working
group believed that payroll credits would serve as a better way to

encourage job creation. The idea thus extended Clinton and the New Democrats' strong focus on work as the best solution to economic growth, welfare dependency, and poverty.

While Kemp saw enterprise zones as an opportunity to reduce government, the Clinton administration saw the program as a chance to "reinvent" it.[43] This delineation was one of the major distinctions between the traditional neoliberalism of conservatives like Kemp and the more Democratic version offered by Clinton and the DLC. Reed and other staffers recognized how popular the promise of "reinventing how government does business" had been during the 1992 campaign and how committed to it Clinton was. The enterprise zone project served as one of the administration's first opportunities to implement David Osborne and Ted Gaebler's theory of governance, and the working group determined early that it would be one of the central themes of their proposal.[44] The group sought to adhere to Osborne and Gaebler's vision of making federal and local government more efficient, entrepreneurial, and results oriented by borrowing tactics from the private sector. Rather than simply bestowing an enterprise zone onto a city, the group decided to turn the designation into a competitive grant.[45] The application required creating what they called "public-private-community partnerships" and urged applicants to secure commitments for investment from the private sector and matching grants from state and local governments.[46] The working group believed these requirements would both encourage innovation and stimulate closer cooperation between the public and private sectors. The task force also hoped the approach would transfer much of the responsibility for designing, administering, and funding the program to local actors.[47]

Running counter to pledges that it was streamlining government processes, the working group developed a complex two-tiered program that would make communities compete for ten awards but formally acknowledge roughly a hundred more. The staffers believed that the competitive aspect would be a way to leverage private investment and encourage public-private cooperation in a wide range of municipalities. In an effort to win over skeptics, task force members started comparing the design to "Dumbo's magic feather"; just as Dumbo did not need the feather to fly, these stakeholders already had the ability to come together but just needed the enticement of federal tax incentives and grants.[48] In addition, the process was a way to bring attention and resources to disinvested communities that had been all too often ignored.[49]

To further distinguish the proposal from the earlier enterprise zone models and "put the Clinton stamp" on it, the working group decided they needed to rebrand it.[50] After running through a series of potential terms, the staffers eventually decided the word *empowerment* best signaled that the proposal aimed not just to restore private enterprise but empower poor people. *Empowerment* was a somewhat odd choice given that it was preferred by Kemp. The word also harkened back to one of the main goals of the War on Poverty, the legacy of which Clinton was working so assiduously to distance himself from. Yet, staffers saw that the term's most immediate connection was to Clinton's 1992 campaign, where it was closely linked to personal responsibility, freedom, and choice.[51]

The administration's efforts to present the program as a bold departure failed to persuade everyone. Several liberal Democrats worried that it was just old wine in a new bottle and opposed the heavy focus on tax incentives.[52] Jack Kemp voiced few substantive criticisms but made a political decision to distance himself from the proposal. He denounced it as "a throwback to the top-down, paternalistic policies, which have dominated liberals' thinking on poverty since the Great Society."[53] Even others in the administration voiced skepticism. The staff of the Office of Management and Budget were especially concerned about the ways the program tried to use the tax code to create social impact. The tax experts warned, according to Cashin, the tax code was a "very blunt instrument" and a "very weak substitute to just spending money for some real anti-poverty programs."[54] Even Robert Rubin had concerns about the design of what his staff cooked up with its two tiers of grants. He struggled to fully understand the program, which Cashin referred to as a "big, complicated beast."[55] Despite these reservations, Clinton approved the proposal, and the Empowerment Zone (EZ) program became part of his first budget, which he sent to Congress in the summer of 1993. Rep. Charles Rangel, whose Harlem district stood to benefit substantially from the program, became its most dogged proponent on Capitol Hill.

The EZ program turned out to be one of the least controversial parts of the $500 billion package. The budget also included the administration's initial stab at lowering the deficit by cutting spending on defense and entitlement programs. It marked Clinton's effort to hold to the economic populism of his campaign with a small tax increase on corporations and the top 1 percent, and it included a significant expansion of the Earned Income Tax Credit to help the working poor. To get the budget through, however, Clinton abandoned his campaign promise to enact a middle-class tax cut and agreed to trim down requested allocations for social programs, including food stamps and Head Start.[56] Despite these concessions, the plan cleared Congress without a single Republican vote. It only passed in the Senate through the magic of the budget reconciliation rules and after Vice President Al Gore broke a 50-50 tie.[57] Despite this very narrow victory—and charges that he was just another "tax-and-spend liberal"—the plan would become one of Clinton's greatest achievements.[58] The reduction in spending and tax increases enabled government revenues to grow steadily and eventually start running a surplus. The inclusion of Empowerment Zones in the landmark package marked an important step toward fulfilling the belief of advisors like Sterling and Reed that economic empowerment initiatives could be directly linked to the overall growth of the economy.

Many members of the Black community and the left were less convinced by this equation. Just after Clinton's inauguration, the Citizens' Commission on Civil Rights sent Clinton a memo emphasizing that focusing on economic recovery without specifically targeting the needs of African Americans would do little to address racial segregation or the urban crisis. Other groups renewed calls for a "Marshall Plan" for cities.[59] Many leaders were particularly disappointed that the Clinton administration had elected to forgo the stimulus and infrastructure program he had promised during the campaign. This idea had long been a key plank of Jesse Jackson who believed it could bring critical jobs to residents in South LA and its counterparts.

Jackson and other members of the civil rights community were outraged at the trade-offs in the budget, which scaled back funds for a variety of programs that had a direct impact on inner city communities, including transportation, Medicare, food stamps, and Head Start. Jackson deemed EZs a "half measure" that would do little to address the serious problems of racial segregation and concentrated poverty that the uprising in LA had brought into sharp focus. In general, the bill looked to Jackson and others like a sign of Clinton's apathy on urban issues and sent a message that he and the Democratic Party only had use for marginalized groups on Election Day.[60]

Just weeks after the budget cleared the Senate, a hundred thousand people descended on the Capitol Mall to commemorate the thirtieth anniversary of the March on Washington. Standing in front of the Lincoln Memorial, several of the speakers directed their remarks to the White House, as well as to the crowd, even though they knew Clinton was vacationing on Martha's Vineyard at the time. Civil rights and labor representatives reminded Clinton that he owed his victory to their constituencies, and they were expecting him to provide urban aid and job creation.[61] Jackson offered the rhetorical high point of the event. He stressed that in the thirty years since the original March on Washington "there are more poor people" and "the ghettos and barrios of our cities are more abandoned, more endangered." He sharply denounced Clinton's decision to reduce the budget rather than pursue a jobs and infrastructure program and offered a list of steps to "rebuild urban America."[62] The bold but clear list did not mention EZs but did include full employment, universal health care, an end to police brutality, and criminal justice reform.

The members of the Clinton administration were more effusive about the potential of Empowerment Zones. To mark the passage of the program, Cuomo hosted a lavish cocktail party at Hickory Hill, Robert Kennedy's famed Northern Virginia estate, where he lived with his mother-in-law during his first year in Washington. Members of the task force and other guests like Al Gore, George Stephanopoulos, Janet Reno, Robert Reich, and Robert Rubin ate petit fours with the abbreviation EZ spelled in chocolate while listening to Cuomo toast how Empowerment Zones would carry on Robert Kennedy's commitment to addressing poverty with the help of the private sector.[63]

Gore oversaw the review process, which was far less glamorous. The administration received over five hundred applicants, ranging in size from large cities like New York and Chicago to sparsely populated rural counties like Mingo County, West Virginia, and Harmon County, Oklahoma.[64] In municipalities across the country, the competition created unlikely coalitions of city officials, community activists, business executives, foundation officers, and university administrators.[65] What the task force claimed was a "new way of doing business for the federal government" resulted in a rigorous and lengthy selection process undertaken by staffers at HUD and the Department of Agriculture.[66] In December 1994, the administration announced that it was bestowing the vaunted Empowerment Zone status on New York City, Chicago, Baltimore, Philadelphia, Atlanta, Detroit, Kansas City, the Mississippi Delta, and the Kentucky Highlands.[67] Los Angeles was notably absent from the list.

In the minds of LA officials, Clinton and other members of his cabinet had all but guaranteed that South LA would be the focus of its urban redevelopment efforts.[68] However, the belief that LA was a shoo-in made LA officials overly complacent, and their application lacked rigor.[69] HUD officials had sent a warning that the initial application would not pass muster and was too short on details about how the city would spend the funds and how non-profit and private sector groups would participate.[70] The city did revise its application, peppering it with references to reinventing government and other favorite Clinton buzzwords.[71] Politicians ranging from LA mayor Richard Riordan to Rep. Maxine Waters

(D-CA) also launched an aggressive eleventh-hour lobbying campaign.[72] Even Commerce Secretary Ron Brown warned Al Gore it was political suicide not to give something to LA. But Gore was insistent that political pressure from LA politicians or anyone else would not taint the process and repeatedly told staffers "this is going to be done by the books."[73] In the end, HUD decided that the revised LA plan was still too vague, especially compared to proposals offered by cities like New York, Chicago, and Detroit, which all showed much more concretely how the public and private sectors, state and local government, and community groups would work together. Aware of the necessity of including Los Angeles in the plan, HUD created a consolation prize, a new category called "a supplemental empowerment zone" for the city. The designation came with $200 million in grants, which enabled Riordan and HUD officials to save some face.[74]

The situation in LA would portend the difficulties of the EZ program around the country in the coming years. Atlanta, Philadelphia, and Mississippi all confronted questions of management, which delayed and constrained the implementation of the program,[75] and local community groups in Chicago and New York complained about being left out of the planning process.[76] Persistent problems of chronic unemployment and poverty in South LA and its counterparts served as a clear sign of the need for a more comprehensive solution and one that offered jobs with a living wage and adequate social services.[77] Community groups continued to decry the EZ program as one of the many signs that Clinton was doing little to advance the fortunes of the Black community.[78] The Clinton administration's focus on credit, which formed the other main component of its economic empowerment agenda, did only a little to mitigate that sentiment.

MARKETS MAKE COMMUNITIES WORK

While the grants attached to Empowerment Zones might have garnered the interest of urban mayors, the issues of credit and community development banking were what captured the heart of Bill Clinton. "Clinton straight up had religion on South Shore," Sheryll Cashin recalled.[79] It was clear the Saturday afternoon conversations at the Arkansas governor's mansion years earlier with Ron Grzywinski and Mary Houghton had made more of an impact on Clinton than they realized. The ShoreBank founders were surprised at Clinton's frequent allusions to their bank during the presidential race, especially since they had in no way suggested to Clinton to make their model so central to his campaign message. They suddenly found themselves in the spotlight with a reputation as "Clinton's favorite bank" and fielding a stream of calls and visits from reporters and officials from other cities hoping to understand the bank's recipe for success. Stories about the bank appeared on the front pages of newspapers across the country throughout 1992. Headlines like "Bank with a Conscience Still Makes Money" and "Bank Shows It Can Profit and Follow a Social Agenda" captured the bank's commitment to both profit and social purpose. Reporters celebrated how ShoreBank combined "old-fashioned community spirit, fiscal conservatism and a 1960s-style social consciousness."[80]

The ShoreBank founders began to worry that Clinton was overpromising what a community development bank could do. Ron Grzywinski was careful to point out that their model was "not a cure-all for all the most depressed areas in America." It could not magically transform places like the South Bronx or South LA.[81] Grzywinski underscored that a bank could not by itself address problems like better schools and employment training desperately needed in disinvested communities.[82] He and other Shore-Bank officials emphasized that a community development bank was not a "quick fix" and that it had taken them almost two decades to achieve the success they had in the single neighborhood of South Shore.[83] Despite their collaboration with Clinton in Arkansas, ShoreBank's founders also maintained their skepticism about government programs.[84] Government grants and regulations, Grzywinski and other senior staffers maintained, did not compare to the discipline imposed by running a profitable bank.[85] "Development works better," Grzywinski explained to a reporter, "when government is not cushioning mistakes, when everyone—banks included—has something to lose."[86] Yet, Clinton made it clear throughout the 1992 election cycle that, if elected, he would make community development banking a part of his solution for addressing the structural problems of urban disinvestment and racial segregation.

The members of Clinton's community empowerment working group sought to build on the momentum from the campaign and make banking and credit key components of their economic empowerment agenda. Clinton's staffers quickly discovered what ShoreBank officials had been saying for years: the banking landscape in low-income communities was bleak. "Across the country," staffers noted, rural and urban communities were "starved for affordable credit, capital and basic banking services." Millions of Americans were living in areas that had no bank or ATM, did not have savings or checking accounts, and lacked access to reliable forms of credit.[87] Commercial lenders avoided low-income areas because they believed they had higher transactions costs. Lenders were also deliberately denying mortgage loans to borrowers from underrepresented groups despite the stipulations of the Fair Housing Act. It was even worse for people of color seeking commercial loans.[88] The Treasury Department estimated that unmet credit needs in low-income areas totaled a whopping $15 billion.[89] Staffers suggested the problem would in part be addressed by Clinton's decision to focus his economic agenda on reducing the ballooning federal deficit, but he needed to take additional steps to address "credit deprivation" in low-income areas.[90] Community development banks looked like the perfect way to do so.

Even before Clinton came to Washington, his staffers had realized the idea of creating "a hundred ShoreBanks" was a nice stump speech line but a logistical headache. Not only would it be challenging to capitalize that many new banks, but many of the conditions that made ShoreBank successful would be difficult to replicate. Clinton's campaign promise to create a hundred new banks also stirred outrage within the larger economic development community. While ShoreBank and Southern were two of the few strictly community development commercial banks, hundreds of community development credit unions, community development corporations, and revolving loan funds operated in both urban and rural places. These institutions did not want to miss an important opportunity and decided to create a unified front organizing around the name Community Development Financial Institutions (CDFI). They then launched a campaign to convince the administration that rather than trying to start a hundred new organizations, it would be better to support existing ones.[91] Ron Grzywinski and George Surgeon were concerned that including such a broad range of organizations in the program might dilute the model ShoreBank had worked hard to perfect. The ShoreBank officials did not, however, campaign hard to convince the Clinton administration to maintain a stricter definition or abandon the project. And Grzywinski, Surgeon, and other management officials at ShoreBank continued to consult with the administration staffers as they developed their plan.[92] The working group's proposal created the CDFI Fund, which would award money on a competitive basis, provide technical assistance, and serve as a clearinghouse for information.[93]

Although deviating from Clinton's original idea of a hundred ShoreBanks, the recommendations for the CDFI Fund remained true to the DLC's principles and ideas of governance. The proposal stressed the government should be a source of equity investments, favorable interest rates, and deposits but would not directly run community development banks.[94] Similar to the Empowerment Zone program, applicants would have to present a strategic plan and also prove that they had secured matching private investment money for any dollars loaned by the fund.[95] Bruce Reed and Gene Sperling explicitly celebrated the plan, proclaiming that it upheld "the New Democrat approach to helping distressed communities create jobs and spur economic growth" by leveraging federal money to get the private sector involved.[96] In a memo to Clinton, Reed and Sperling contended the program would prove "government cannot do the whole job—but we can be a catalyst for the private sector and bottom-up innovation in local communities."[97] Placing this idea in concrete terms, the administration predicted that the fund could create $5 billion in new investments to distressed communities and could provide upward of forty thousand loans to entrepreneurs, small business owners, and potential home buyers.[98] It would prove a very ambitious calculation.

The task force's decision to place the fund under the control of the Treasury Department marked another effort to prove the administration was putting a market-oriented spin on its antipoverty agenda. Members of the task force believed that Treasury officials—many of whom were part of the revolving door between Wall Street and Washington—had the best technical knowledge and expertise to oversee the program. Staffers also recognized that placing it at the Treasury could legitimate the CDFIs as "real" financial institutions. It would give the idea credibility with finance-oriented administration officials, like their boss NEC chair Robert Rubin, as well as the Republicans, whose support was needed to get the program passed.[99] The choice bucked precedent and ruffled some feathers.[100] The Treasury Department had, in fact, never before played a significant role in a federal antipoverty or urban redevelopment initiative. Traditionally, HUD or Health and Human Services (HHS) oversaw antipoverty and economic development programs, and both those agencies had campaigned to gain control of the CDFI Fund.

The legislative process delayed the passage of the law authorizing the CDFI Fund until August 1994 when both chambers voted for the Riegle Community Development and Regulatory Improvement Act.[101] The legislation remained largely unchanged from the administration's original proposal save for the inclusion of a program called the Bank Enterprise Awards, which provided incentives for traditional financial institutions to increase their equity investments in CDFIs. It cleared both the House and the Senate with wide bipartisan margins and received enthusiastic endorsements from many Republicans who favored its market-oriented approach.

The September 23, 1994, signing ceremony for the CDFI legislation occurred in a windowless auditorium of the Agriculture

Department. The somewhat drab setting did not temper the energetic mood of the event.[102] Clinton's excitement was palpable as he claimed that "the possibility to sign this act into law and, more importantly, to unleash the energies of millions of Americans too long denied access to the mainstream economics of our country, was one of the things that drove me into the campaign of 1992." He joked that he had come to mention ShoreBank in almost every speech he'd given as a candidate and president. "I've long admired the way they steered private investments into previously underprivileged neighborhoods, to previously undercapitalized and underutilized Americans," Clinton explained, "proving that a bank can be a remarkable source of hope and still make money."[103] He celebrated the CDFI Fund as an "example of what I hope and believe must be the goal of Government in the future." He explained the fund demonstrated his belief that government cannot be "society's savior" nor "sit on the sideline" but would have "to be a more effective partner." Clinton took extra pains to prove that the fund was not a throwback to antipoverty programs of the past. It's "not about bureaucracies, and it's certainly not about distributing handouts," Clinton extolled, but "making the private sector work in places where it had not gone before."[104] His comment reflected how the approach embodied his belief that markets and the private sector could help those places in need and the people who lived there.

Robert Rubin proved a similarly passionate champion. Just as the CDFI Fund set up shop in early 1995, Rubin transitioned from head of the National Economic Council to become treasury secretary. The former cochair of Goldman Sachs was not familiar with ShoreBank before joining the Clinton campaign, but he had long been concerned about the problem of urban poverty.[105] During his investment banking days, he served on the board of a Harlem community organization. As he left Wall Street for Washington, he said that the inner city was the political issue he cared most passionately about.[106] "I don't think we can have a truly successful economy if we have a large, alienated inner-city poor," he declared.[107] Rubin would later say that it was his concern about urban poverty and racial inequality, and a sense that markets could not alone address the problem, that made him a Democrat.[108] He believed in trying to make financial markets work for more people and to give more people the opportunity to engage in the financial system to gain access to credit. He was clearly no big government liberal and maintained a finance-oriented perspective and commitment to fiscal responsibility.[109] The community development banking model was especially appealing to him since it required a relatively small expenditure, which would not offset his larger commitment to deficit reduction.

Rubin's enthusiastic support and promotion of the fund gave it important credibility.[110] While Congress never appropriated the full amount promised by the enabling legislation, in 1996 and 1997, the fund had awarded $77.6 million to eighty-one CDFIs around the country and leveraged $273 million in investment from banks and other financial institutions.[111] In addition to several projects affiliated with ShoreBank, the awardees ranged from Community Capital Bank in Brooklyn to the First American Credit Union in Window Rock, Arizona, which served tribes and reservations throughout the Southwest.[112] Under Rubin's direction, the Treasury Department put its own slant on the project and ensured that it fell even more squarely within a market-based framework. The majority of the fund's staff had private sector backgrounds, and few had worked at ShoreBank or other CDFIs. They, in fact, prided themselves on how they used the traditional tools of finance to evaluate applicants rather than the rules federal agencies usually adopted to administer grants.[113] Rubin and his staff liked to tout how the CDFI Fund reached "market niches" that have not been adequately served by financial institutions.[114] Rubin explained the purpose of CDFIs was to help address the "market inefficiencies which exist in distressed communities."[115] But treating poverty and disinvestment as "a market inefficiency" and poor people and their communities as "market niches" meant that the officials did not view CDFIs as a means of restructuring or regulating the banking system to more meaningfully address the problems of racial inequity in the market economy. Instead, in their minds, CDFIs merely established a tool to fill the void created by the competitive forces of an increasingly deregulated financial sector. And, perhaps more detrimentally, the CDFI Fund validated the idea held by Rubin and others that the banking system could fill the void left by the scale-back in government spending.[116]

DOING WELL

The Clinton administration recognized that to get buy-in from the major commercial banks for its market-based initiatives it had to prove there was something in it for them as well. That is where the efforts to reform the Community Reinvestment Act (CRA) came in. Like community development banking, the CRA had roots in Chicago-based community activism of the 1970s. As ShoreBank was setting up shop on the South Side, a multiracial group on Chicago's West Side was forging a grassroots movement to stop the practices of redlining and mortgage discrimination in their communities.[117] The grassroots activists' efforts resulted in the passage of the CRA in 1977, which required that financial institutions "serve the convenience and the needs of the communities in which they are chartered to do business"—including low-income areas. The law also gave activists the ability to deny or delay an institution's request to merge with another lender, open a branch, or expand any of its other services if it was not in compliance with the law.[118] Ron Gryzwinski had served as the only banker to testify in favor of it, and ShoreBank had remained a strong advocate ever since.[119] But the CRA had garnered strong opposition throughout much of the banking industry.

Clinton's staff recognized that the CRA was "probably the most effective tool the federal government possesses for increasing private lending" in distressed areas "and the best way to leverage the private sector"; however, its "full potential" was unrealized.[120] Not surprisingly, the enforcement of the CRA had been spotty under Reagan and Bush, and bankers complained the documentation it required was unnecessarily arduous. Since the mid-1980s, Democratic policymakers recognized the law was ripe for reform, and

Clinton had included his intention to do so in all major campaign documents.[121] The working group took up this case and called for "breath[ing] new life and new purpose into the law." It urged sharpening the CRA's teeth by focusing on "performance not paperwork," meaning focusing less on documentation and more on accountability and results.[122] In July 1993, Clinton tasked federal banking regulators to develop a set of reforms that would make it easier for banks to implement the CRA, create new standards to ensure lending and investments in low- and moderate-income areas, and institute stronger sanctions for noncompliance.[123] The administration framed these reforms as a win-win that would channel more money into disinvested communities, reduce the burden on banks, and potentially offer an opportunity for profit.

Since the CRA's passage, bankers had complained the CRA would force them to make unprofitable and risky loans. The administration worked vigorously to counter that assumption. Comptroller of the Currency Eugene Ludwig, who had taken the lead on the reforms, stressed that greater lending to low- and -moderate income borrowers, among other measures the CRA required of banks, was "not only the right thing to do, it was fundamentally good business for the bankers."[124] Clinton similarly celebrated the reforms as a way to enable financial institutions to "discover new, profitable lines of business" by lending in low-income areas. Clinton noted as an added benefit: "it doesn't cost taxpayers a dime."[125] Ludwig and Clinton's emphasis on the profit-making potential of low-income communities overlooked the fact that the urban core had long been a site of economic investment and extraction for the real estate and banking industries.[126] The focus also revealed how the administration's process of "breathing new life" sought to transform the CRA from a mechanism of redistribution intended to rectify a historical injustice into a win-win that required little sacrifice by the banks or the taxpayers, many of whom were the direct beneficiaries of redlining and other practices. Along with Empowerment Zones and community development banks, the CRA reforms became, nevertheless, a critical part of the Clinton administration's exhortation that market-based solutions offered private companies a way to simultaneously fulfill their social obligations and improve their bottom lines.

The Clinton administration pursued this approach on a larger scale as it sought to show that loosening constraints on markets was the best way to help Americans and increasingly people around the world. In addition to the steadfast pursuit of lower interest rates through deficit reduction, the administration enthusiastically endorsed the Riegle-Neal Interstate Banking and Branching Efficiency Act in 1994, which legalized interstate banking and eased merger and acquisition requirements. Clinton explained the law as a way of reinventing government to make it more efficient and contended it would help the banking industry better meet the needs of the American people.[127] The law paved the way for increased consolidation of the banking system and became an important step in the process of financial deregulation, which would culminate in the modernization laws passed at the end of the 1990s. Clinton consistently contended that such banking deregulation was not a sign that government was relinquishing its basic duties. Instead, he made the somewhat dubious case that deregulation offered tools to advance traditional liberal social causes.[128]

The Clinton administration took a similar stance toward NAFTA and other free trade policies. The administration maintained that the relaxation of trade barriers would help fuel overall economic growth, provide more options to consumers, and lift the fortunes of people in developing countries. These ideas started to come full circle. "If we simply can apply our international economic policy to south central Los Angeles, Harlem, Milwaukee, Detroit, you name it, the Mississippi Delta, south Texas," he optimistically suggested soon after the passage of NAFTA, "we're going to do just fine in this country."[129] Financial deregulation and trade liberalization, nevertheless, would have a series of negative long-term consequences for distressed communities and the organizations like ShoreBank established to serve them. But, in the immediate future, Clinton's agenda brought ShoreBank a flurry of new attention and capital.

"WE ARE IN THE '90S"

"I think we're 14 1/2 minutes into our 15 minutes of fame," Shore-Bank executive Charles Rial half joked in early 1993.[130] The organization sought to make the most of its remaining thirty seconds and capitalize on several aspects of Clinton's economic empowerment program. While ShoreBank itself received little money from the CDFI Fund, the attention it received brought it both new interest and investment capital.[131] At the end of 1993, Shore-Bank reported assets of $271 million and a $1.7 million profit, up more than 85 percent from the previous year.[132] The bank's Development Deposit program grew substantially in just a couple of years. By 1994, the program constituted 60 percent of the bank's $261 million in deposits, and it continued to offer customers a solid return on their investment.[133] ShoreBank also experienced a flood of applications from recent business school graduates who wanted the opportunity to work at the now fabled institution. "I think people are yearning for a way to combine their business skills and personal values," executive Joan Shapiro mused. "We are in the '90s."[134] Robert Weissbourd, another top official, explained ShoreBank was attractive because it had transcended "the old-fashioned dichotomy of charity and business."[135] Another official put that juxtaposition in slightly different terms: "Here at the bank we say we've got Democrats doing the talking, but Republicans making the loans."[136]

ShoreBank's blend of business acumen and social values would also make it increasingly attractive to large investment banks. While the creation of the CDFI Fund offered ShoreBank attention, the CRA reforms brought an influx of new funds. Many of the nation's major financial institutions saw investing in ShoreBank as an effective way to fulfill their CRA compliance. The banks were able to exploit loopholes in the law to get more credit for investing in ShoreBank than in a smaller institution. In the mid-1990s, Goldman Sachs, J.P. Morgan, and Continental Bank (which would soon merge with NationsBank and soon after Bank of America) all made large investments in ShoreBank, which enabled the institution to scale up significantly.[137] ShoreBank decided to use the money to expand its reach in Chicago by purchasing Inde-corp, which was the nation's biggest Black-owned bank. Some members of the city's African American community raised strong objections to the purchase since they believed Indecorp should remain a fully Black-owned institution and were wary of the white presence in ShoreBank's management and board of directors. Several Black community and religious leaders tried to block the sale.[138] The resistance campaign ultimately failed, and the 1995 purchase enabled ShoreBank to double its assets, substantially increase its presence throughout the city, and achieve a size and scale that would also expand its ambitions.

The combination of its new investment and easing of interstate banking restrictions also meant that ShoreBank could expand its reach nationally. A contingent of the management and staff objected and thought the institution should stay focused on Chicago.[139] But Ron Grzywinski and Mary Houghton firmly believed their unique model had the chance to do a lot of good in other parts of the coun-try and could provide them new chances to innovate.[140] ShoreBank first brought its model to Cleveland in 1994 at the urging of busi-ness executives, philanthropic organizations, and the mayor. Then ShoreBank expanded to Detroit, setting up its operation in the heart of the city's Empowerment Zone in 1996. It gradually phased out its role in the Southern Development Bancorporation, which would flourish as it expanded deeper into the Arkansas Delta in the late 1990s. ShoreBank instead launched another rural proj-ect in Michigan's Upper Peninsula and established a partnership with Ecotrust, an environmental organization in Oregon, to use its community development banking model to promote environmen-tally focused businesses.[141] ShoreBank stretched its focus interna-tionally as well, forming a for-profit consulting company in 1988 called ShoreBank Advisory Services to consult banking and de-velopment projects in the US and around the world. This arm rode the wave of economic globalization in the 1990s and spread Shore-Bank's model of community development internationally.[142] The consultants cultivated a particular expertise on postcommunist countries. ShoreBank Advisory received contracts from USAID, the World Bank, and the Ford Foundation to teach "western style banking" to local bankers in Poland, Russia, and the Caucasus and help facilitate entrepreneurship and small business growth.[143]

In 1998, *Crain's Chicago Business* reflected the attitude of many when it observed that "if there ever was an example of doing well by doing good, it is Chicago-based Shorebank Corporation." The trade newspaper celebrated how the bank had proven that it was possible "to use capitalist tools as the force of good."[144] Shore-Bank had clearly secured its reputation and spread its message. The bank's expansion also demonstrated the increased opportunities that the Clinton administration's economic development programs made available to private organizations that abided by market-oriented principles, even if the Clinton administration had essentially appropriated the ShoreBank idea to suit their own needs.

Despite the effusive language that Clinton used to describe institutions like ShoreBank and initiatives like the CRA and Empowerment Zones, these programs all remained very small in comparison to the very large problems of concentrated poverty and racial segregation that they were intended to address. In this way, the programs actually had more in common with the War on Poverty than Clinton would have cared to admit: they were a relatively small response to a very large pressing problem. By not pairing the credit and investment initiatives with more comprehensive social welfare services, the programs were poised to make little difference in the lives of the vast majority of people living in economically distressed areas. The smallness of these market-oriented approaches would become ever more apparent as Clinton sought to fulfill his campaign promise of drastic reform to the welfare system.

CHAPTER 6

CHANGE THEIR HEADS

In February 1997, more than 2,900 people from 137 countries gathered at the International Microcredit Summit in Washington, DC, to launch a campaign to extend microcredit to 100 million poor people, especially poor women, around the world.[1] The attendees included the leaders of Bangladesh, Mali, Uganda, Mozambique, and Peru; the presidents of Monsanto, Citibank, and the World Bank; Muhammad Yunus; and borrowers from Kenya, Bolivia, and India. Together they listened as Hillary Rodham Clinton delivered the inaugural address.[2] "Although it is called 'microcredit,' this is a macro idea," Clinton asserted. She dubbed it "an invaluable tool in alleviating poverty, promoting self-sufficiency and stimulating economic activity . . . [with] potential to transform the lives of individuals, their families, their communities and their nations."[3]

Hillary Clinton took pains to emphasize the potential of microcredit not just internationally but in the United States as well. The speech came just as states were implementing the requirements in the 1996 welfare reform act, which fulfilled Bill Clinton's campaign pledge to "end welfare as we know it." The law terminated the assistance for women and children in place since the Roosevelt administration and served as a potent symbol of the Clinton administration's attempt to put a nail in the coffin of New Deal liberalism.

Since she first helped bring Muhammad Yunus and ShoreBank to Arkansas to start the Good Faith Fund, Clinton had a belief that microcredit could be a critical tool in the effort to help women get off welfare. In her speech, she renewed that hope, celebrating microcredit's potential for "lifting people out of poverty and moving mothers from welfare to work" and giving them "a path to the economic mainstream."

Just a couple of weeks after the summit, Hillary Clinton visited the Chicago headquarters of the Women's Self-Employment Project (WSEP), the microenterprise organization started by Shore-Bank's Mary Houghton based on the principles of Yunus and Grameen Bank. The WSEP had recently received an award from the White House for its innovative work in helping welfare recipients become entrepreneurs. During her visit, Clinton met several of WSEP's clients, including Arinez Gilyard. A single mother of three young children, Gilyard used the training and a small loan from the organization to start a day care called Child Care Crew in her South Side apartment. She had not only repaid the loan she had received but had also expanded her business into the apartment across the hall and hired a couple of employees.[4] She also joined a matched savings program that WSEP ran, which added two dollars for every one dollar Gilyard saved. She hoped to buy a single-family home to house her family and her business. Clinton remarked how women like Gilyard defied stereotypes of poor women of color as lazy. She reaffirmed that organizations like WSEP would be critical "if we are going to fulfill the promise of welfare reform and not just pass a bill and walk away from people."[5]

At the dawn of his second term, Bill Clinton confronted the Gingrich Revolution's quest to roll back any vestiges of the New Deal and Great Society and outrage from progressive groups over his pursuit of terminating the assistance for women and children in place since the Roosevelt administration. Microenterprise offered his administration a way to combine its pursuit of market-oriented solutions for streamlining government with its commitment to helping the poor, especially women of color. The issue also helped

to fuse domestic and foreign policy objectives, especially surrounding poverty. In practical terms, microenterprise would remain a relatively small aspect of both the welfare reform agenda
and efforts to address issues of global poverty and international
human rights. However, it played an outsized ideological role in
solidifying the New Democrats' ethos. Microenterprise helped
Clinton and the New Democrats justify the retrenchment of welfare and other social services. It also bolstered their argument
that the private sector, especially entrepreneurship, could solve
the problems of poverty and create economic growth in the United
States and around the world.

The New Democrat promoters of microenterprise made the
case that the market's power to "do good" lay not just in its economic benefits but also in its ability to change the behavior and attitudes of the poor and low-income people of color and make them
feel more independent and empowered.[6] Like Muhammad Yunus's
discussion of the Grameen borrowers in his talks and books, Hillary and Bill Clinton relentlessly celebrated the stories of women
like Gilyard as "agents of change" who had power over their own
lives to move out of poverty and off welfare. By commending a
few exemplary individual borrowers and former welfare recipients, the administration sought to prove the effectiveness of these
techniques while signaling their concern for issues of economic,
racial, and gender inequality. These stories served as a deliberate
counterpoint to typical stereotypes of poor African American single mothers as lazy and irresponsible, which Hillary Clinton refer-
enced in her visit to the WSEP. Yet, the image of the hardworking
entrepreneur and saver that Clinton and her allies evoked did not
avoid depicting poor women in gender-laden and racialized terms.
It also did not erase the line between the undeserving and deserving poor and acceptable and unacceptable forms of assistance in
the postwelfare reform era.[7] Instead, it just reinforced the line.

The focus on transforming poor women of color into financial
actors and integrating them into the mainstream financial system
contributed to making social welfare benefits only available to
those able to operate within the imperatives of market capitalism.[8]

In doing so, it caused the same harm as the demonization of welfare mothers by Ronald Reagan and other conservatives. This elevation of hardworking poor women of color implicitly stigmatized people who could not or would not participate in the market economy. As these celebrations coincided with the passage of major crime legislation in 1994, it provided justification for cutting off benefits to and incarcerating those who did not "play by the rules." It also circumscribed efforts to develop antipoverty policies that countered market-based principles, strengthen the social safety net, and address structural racial and gender inequities.[9]

The New Democrats, moreover, significantly overestimated the ability of microenterprise to address the problems of inequality, especially as hundreds of thousands of families confronted the loss of their welfare benefits. The challenges faced by WSEP and its Arkansas counterpart the Good Faith Fund brought into further relief the limitations of market-based tools like microenterprise to create meaningful relief and revealed the inability of small nonprofit organizations to do the work of the government.

ENDING WELFARE

One of the first things Bruce Reed did when setting up his new office at the White House Domestic Policy Council was to tape the words "end welfare as we know it" to the wall. In his mind, those words and phrases such as "two years and you're off" and "make work pay" should not have just been campaign slogans but also the guiding principles of the reform effort.[10] The former DLC staffer believed that it had been these promises above all that had helped Clinton get elected, and he urged Clinton to make welfare reform his top domestic priority. Clinton ignored the advice and decided to make health care and crime his first major domestic issues instead.

Universal health care had been on the liberal agenda since the Truman years, and in the ensuing years the problem had only intensified. When Clinton took office, more than fifty million Americans had incomplete or no coverage at all, while the costs of private health care were prohibitive for many. He tasked Hillary Clinton and his longtime friend management consultant Ira Magaziner to lead the effort to create a plan to achieve universal coverage. Hillary and Magaziner's task force quickly jettisoned the push for a single-payer government-run plan, which Jesse Jackson and others on the left advocated. Instead, the team developed a complex equation to achieve universal health care by requiring businesses to pay for most of their employee's benefits while the government would provide insurance for the unemployed. The plan envisioned setting up regional insurance purchasing alliances, which would create "managed competition" among private insurers and thereby use market forces to lower premiums. Despite its focus on market-based tools, the complex, technocratic plan made even many DLCers scratch their heads. The private sector was even more affronted. Business owners grew fearful that having to provide health care for employees would hurt their bottom line, while the health-care and insurance companies resisted reform. A trade group of insurance companies sponsored television ads featuring the fictional white middle-class couple "Harry and Louise" who described how the plan would create a large government bureaucracy and deprive them of their right to choose their own doctors. The ads contributed to swaying public opinion and gave the Republicans the ammunition to decry the plan as "socialized medicine." The opposition grew so strong that the proposal never even came up for a vote in Congress, and the Clinton administration eventually abandoned it.[11]

Clinton had more luck—at least on Capitol Hill—with his anticrime agenda. In 1994, Congress passed the Violent Crime Control and Law Enforcement Act. It was largely the handiwork of Joe Biden, who had been advocating for major crime legislation since the 1970s.[12] The law's provisions included expanded use of the death penalty; life sentences for nonviolent offenders (the infamous three-strikes rule); elimination of federal funding for inmate education; truth-in-sentencing provisions, which facilitated longer prison stays; funds to place one hundred thousand more police on the streets; and $10 billion for new prison construction.

The bill passed by a large bipartisan margin—including the support of several members of the Black Congressional Caucus. But it engendered strong outrage among civil rights and criminal justice activists who argued that the policies targeted Black communities where unemployment and a reduction in social services, coupled with the introduction of crack cocaine, had spurred a rise in crime and gang violence in the early 1980s through the early 1990s.[13] Clinton himself had said as much by repeatedly bemoaning how Black people were "murdering each other with reckless abandonment."[14] While Jesse Jackson had done his fair share of moralizing on the issue of crime and drugs in the Black community over the years, he joined those decrying the legislation as "race-bait politics" and rightly predicted that it would disproportionately impact young Black men.[15] Jackson also voiced outrage at the $33 billion price tag, especially the significant line item for prison construction. This expenditure was particularly galling given the cuts to social services like food stamps and Head Start that the Clinton administration and Congress had enacted.[16]

It was within the heated political climate of the health-care and crime initiatives that the administration finally released its welfare plan in the summer of 1994. An interagency task force, cochaired by Bruce Reed and HHS undersecretaries Mary Jo Bane and David Ellwood, had worked for over a year to turn Clinton's campaign pledges into a workable policy that would also align with the administration's larger deficit-reducing priorities. The proposal, which took the form of a 431-page bill, coupled a two-year time limit on direct cash assistance with billions of dollars in spending that would help people make the transition into the workforce. It included a promise that government would serve as an employer of last resort for those who couldn't find private sector employment. Reed advocated for making microenterprise part of the plan.[17] He believed that in many communities microenterprise could be a solution where the lack of job opportunities made it difficult to transition off government assistance.[18] The proposal acknowledged one way to leave welfare was "to turn a hobby such as providing child care, making jewelry or styling hair into a business," proposed expanding the existing federal microloan programs, and called on states to start their own.[19] These ideas quickly got lost in the larger opposition to the bill.

Many Democrats on Capitol Hill were deeply suspicious of the time limits, while public sector unions voiced fears about creating a new army of community service workers who would threaten their members' jobs.[20] Others stressed that a better path lay in pursuing full employment and creating a program on par with the New Deal's Works Progress Administration. "There will never be real welfare reform without jobs, jobs, jobs," Rep. Maxine Waters (D-CA) consistently argued.[21] On the other side, Republicans denounced the price tag and accused the plan of encouraging out-of-wedlock birth with the hope of denying Clinton a major legislative win during an election year. The bill quickly stalled out, and Clinton lost the chance to pass a major reform before the November midterms.

Clinton knew that the 1994 election would be significant, but he and his team didn't quite anticipate how decisive it would be. On Capitol Hill, conservative firebrand Rep. Newt Gingrich (R-GA) set his sights on controlling Congress.[22] Plotting a coordinated attack, he brought Republican congressional candidates together around a ten-point program called the Contract with America, which included a balanced budget amendment, even more crime control, a stiff reduction in the capital gains tax, and a stringent welfare-to-work plan. The strategy worked. Republicans won big, picking up eight seats in the Senate and over fifty in the House. It gave the GOP control of Congress for the first time in forty years, and Gingrich was elected Speaker of the House. Even though Gingrich had deliberately avoided including divisive social issues like abortion in the contract, the 1994 election would come to symbolize the larger political and cultural polarization afoot. Clinton interpreted the results as a referendum on his presidency. The DLC did too.

While most Democrats mourned Gingrich's victory, the heads of the DLC saw it as an opportunity. "The 1994 elections have wiped the slate clean and liberated Democrats from special-interest liberalism," Al From and Will Marshall announced to fellow DLCers in early 1995.[23] The DLC's leaders believed that Clinton strayed from his New Democrat roots during his first two years in office in an effort to appeal to traditional Democratic constituencies.[24] The DLCers were particularly concerned about some of his appointments. Clinton followed through on his pledge to have the most diverse administration in history by giving prominent cabinet posts and other high-level positions to people of color, including many who had notably liberal credentials. Marshall wrote in a May 1993 memo to From that he feared Clinton's "placement of 'PC' activists in key policy positions" would "drive white moderates out of the party, not to mention alienating swing voters."[25] The DLCers also took issue with the health-care reform plan and believed that the administration's tax measures abandoned the "forgotten middle class" who were so critical to his 1992 win.[26] The DLC leadership stressed that focusing on welfare reform, especially promoting a work-based approach, offered one of the best ways to bring Clinton back to the New Democrat fold.[27] In the aftermath of the midterm election, the DLCers laid out a case to the White House that passing a major reform bill would not just create a better welfare system, but would also earn back the trust of middle-class voters, especially independent voters whom the DLC believed were critical to Clinton's reelection bid.[28]

Dick Morris agreed with the DLC's assessment. Following the election (and much to the chagrin of many others at the White House), Clinton brought his longtime political strategist back on board. Morris, who had a reputation for ruthlessness and opportunism, convinced Clinton that to counter Gingrich and ensure he was not a one-term president, he should adopt a strategy of triangulation.[29] In Morris's formulation, triangulation largely meant co-opting features of the conservative agenda, such as reducing the deficit and welfare reform. Many of these were things that Clinton more or less wanted to do anyway. Yet, he confronted a challenging road ahead. In addition to forcing two shutdowns of the federal government, Gingrich did not want to give an inch on welfare.

It enraged Gingrich that Clinton's promise of "ending welfare" during the 1992 election had undermined one of conservatives' best issues. Gingrich wanted to reclaim it, and he had the majority in Congress to do it.[30] The Contract with America promised to introduce legislation that would cut spending for welfare programs, enact a two-year lifetime ban on cash assistance, implement work requirements to promote individual responsibility, deny welfare support to teenage mothers, and refuse any additional money for women if they had more children. After winning control of the House, Gingrich shifted course and began to advocate for a block grant approach that both restricted federal funding for welfare and devolved power to the states.[31] Over the next year, Republicans offered various versions of welfare reform in the House and Senate. The bills all kept Clinton's proposal of strict time limits, but scrapped the training, health care, day-care programs, and public-sector jobs intended to help ease women into the labor market. Democrats on Capitol Hill offered swift condemnation of the plans, focusing especially on the impact that such reforms would have on the children of welfare recipients. Daniel Patrick Moynihan famously predicted if Gingrich had his way, it would lead to "children sleeping on grates," evoking something out of a Charles Dickens novel.[32] The Republican plans were a step too far for Clinton, and he twice vetoed welfare bills sent up to him from Congress.

After months of back-and-forth, Congress narrowly passed another version of welfare reform, which landed on Clinton's desk in the summer of 1996 at the height of his reelection race. The bill was far from ideal even to Bruce Reed and the other DLC alums in the West Wing pushing for welfare reform. It had stricter time and term limits than Clinton advocated and also included a $24 billion cut in food stamps. In a particularly harsh measure, it barred most immigrants—even those with authorized status—from receiving even basic welfare assistance. Carol Mosely Braun (D-IL), the only Black member of the Senate, voiced the attitude of many when she called it a "draconian attempt to separate Americans one from another, again, and leave the poor to their own devices."[33] Civil rights, antipoverty, religious, feminist, and labor groups—who included many of the Democratic Party's core constituencies—all

Eleanor Smeal of the Feminist Majority, Rev. Jesse Jackson, and National Organization for Women president Patricia Ireland at a demonstration in front of the White House urging Clinton to veto the welfare reform bill, August 1, 1996

Credit: AFP via Getty Images/Joyce Naltchay

publicly urged Clinton to veto the bill and tried to inundate the White House with telephone calls and letters.[34] The National Organization for Women (NOW) began holding daily demonstrations and nightly candlelight vigils, and Patricia Ireland, the president of NOW, launched a hunger strike, vowing not to stop until Clinton vetoed the bill.[35]

Clinton agonized about what to do. Most of his cabinet—including Robert Reich, Robert Rubin, and Donna Shalala—all advised he veto it. His main political advisor took a different stance. Even though Clinton had a double-digit lead over Republican opponent Bob Dole, Dick Morris advocated that the bill offered "insurance" for his reelection. Bruce Reed made the case from another angle and suggested that it was the best chance for Clinton to fulfill the mantra taped to Reed's office wall to end welfare.[36]

On July 31, 1996, Clinton held a press conference announcing that he would sign the legislation.[37] Entitled the Personal Responsibility and Work Opportunity Reconciliation Act (PRWORA), it formally terminated the New Deal's AFDC with a time-limited block grant program called Temporary Aid to Needy Families (TANF), which required recipients to find a job two years after they enrolled and put a five-year lifetime limit on receiving benefits including health care. PRWORA gave states wide leeway in developing programs, but new federal funding formulas and rules offered financial incentives if states cut their rolls. The law also encouraged states to create contracts directly with for-profit and nonprofit intermediaries and included a series of other provisions, including allocating funds for marriage promotion and "chastity training." Microenterprise was not as prominent in PRWORA as many had hoped, but it enabled states to include microenterprise as one of the work options available and allowed welfare recipients the opportunity to retain their benefits for a set period while starting their own businesses.[38]

The DLC applauded the president's decision, suggesting it would transform the welfare system "from one that creates dependence to one that creates opportunity and promotes responsibility."[39] This praise underlined the fact that the act's name itself contained two of the main planks of the New Democrat philosophy: responsibility and opportunity. PRWORA's focus on transferring power away from Washington to the state and local level and the private sector and imposing performance-based principles also upheld the vision of government that the DLC had long advocated.

Others were outraged. Three high-ranking officials at HHS resigned in protest, while another anonymously accused the president of sending the poor "into the abyss."[40] The *Nation* issued a scathing editorial charging Clinton with "seeking reelection by further afflicting this nation's most defenseless citizens." The *Nation*'s editorial board asked the question on the minds of many: Where exactly would all these people terminated from welfare work? In many communities with high numbers of AFDC recipients, the unemployment rate was around 30 to 50 percent, which was one of the reasons why many women had applied for assistance in the first place.[41] Encouraging some microenterprise programs clearly could not fill this void.

Few liberal politicians missed the symbolism of Clinton terminating a bedrock New Deal program and accused him of issuing a deadly blow to Roosevelt's legacy.[42] John Sweeney, head of the AFL-CIO, called the reforms "anti-poor, anti-immigrants, anti-women and anti-children" and bemoaned how a Democratic president was dismantling the New Deal social safety net.[43] Jesse Jackson had long criticized welfare-to-work programs as wrongly assuming "a deficiency in Black and poor people" and called the welfare reform bill "a war on the poor."[44] Yet, the scale of the protest in no way matched the demonstrations that occurred in opposition to Reagan's budget cuts in the early 1980s when a coalition of progressive groups brought over two hundred thousand people to the Capitol. The lack of visible protest was less a reflection about the law's severity and more about the relationship of the party's progressive wing to Clinton in the mid-1990s.

The 1996 Democratic National Convention held in Chicago just a couple of days after Clinton formally signed the welfare reforms brought into focus just how scared many liberal politicians and progressive groups were after the 1994 midterm elections and how much they feared being left behind. All the members of Congress who had criticized Clinton days earlier showed up at the convention and offered their full support. The AFL-CIO, which had over eight hundred delegates at the convention, decided to give Clinton its full endorsement, despite his position on welfare and NAFTA, both of which the union strongly opposed. John Sweeney, then president of the AFL-CIO, believed Clinton was labor's only line of defense against Gingrich and his allies' desire to eradicate union protections and rights, and he wanted to stay in the president's good graces.[45] Jesse Jackson made a similar calculation. In the lead-up to the event, Jackson drew parallels to the last time the Democrats held their convention in Chicago in 1968, which famously became engulfed in protest. Jackson contended the chaos had contributed to Richard Nixon winning the presidency. He urged left-wing groups that they needed to avoid a repeat.[46] Jackson did not just attend the convention; he spoke at it. In his speech, Jackson did pointedly criticize Clinton for abandoning "Franklin Roosevelt's six-decade guarantee of support for women and children." Yet, the self-appointed standard-bearer of the left declared that "in 1996, Bill Clinton is our best option."[47] NOW and other feminist groups followed suit. Patricia Ireland of NOW abandoned her hunger strike, and with a note of resignation declared, "I will hold my nose and vote for Bill Clinton."[48] Jackson, Ireland, and other progressive leaders even decided not to push for planks in the party platform calling for tying welfare reform to job creation or to demand a living wage. Instead, like four years earlier, the platform looked like it had been crafted by DLCers (which largely it had been).[49]

Clinton did go on to win the November election by a wide margin. It is unclear how much the lack of pushback from the left helped with his reelection but probably not all that much. Clinton continued to face fierce opposition from progressive groups, labor unions, and politicians on particular issues and policies. Yet, for much of his second term, Clinton did not experience coordinated or sustained resistance from the left. The combination of the left's fear of the growing power of the right coupled with Clinton's consistent promise that his market-oriented approach would work prevented a unified progressive coalition to fully coalesce and progressive alternatives to take shape. This lack of a cohesive movement on the left undoubtedly had implications for the administration's agenda on welfare and poverty—among other things—in the coming years.

GIVING AN ANSWER

Clinton subsequently demonstrated some regret about the severity of the welfare law. He and his sympathizers retrospectively argued that his hands were largely tied because of the strong opposition he faced from Gingrich and the Republicans.[50] It was true that the right was becoming more powerful in the mid-1990s and had ever-deepening pockets, thanks to strong and wealthy libertarian donors who railed against welfare and other government programs. Yet, many aspects of the reform and the ways in which Clinton framed it fell directly in line with the New Democrat principles that he had been promoting for more than a decade. While Clinton may have thought some of the requirements in the reform bill were too stringent, his long-standing commitment to work requirements and microenterprise underscored his firm belief in the power of market-based solutions to help poor welfare recipients become more independent, self-sufficient, and empowered.

To showcase these aspects of Clinton's support for welfare reform, the White House decided to invite some former recipients to the signing ceremony held in late August just a few days before the Democratic Convention. Staffers solicited suggestions from organizations like Chicago's Women's Self-Employment Project and culled Clinton's old speeches for anecdotes.[51] Eventually, aides came upon a story that Clinton often told about a recipient he encountered a decade earlier when he was governor of Arkansas. The woman was enrolled in the state's work program and had gotten a job as a cook at a Best Western. When asked what she liked best about her job, the African American mother of three answered: "When my boy goes to school and they say 'What does your mama do for a living?' He can give an answer."[52] Clinton used her story to illustrate that no one disliked welfare more than the recipients themselves.

Administration staffers tracked down the woman, whom they learned was named Lillie Harden. She was living in North Little Rock and now worked in the deli department at a supermarket. Her children were all employed or excelling in school, and she remained supportive of Clinton and his welfare reform efforts.[53] The White House asked her to come to Washington and introduce the president at the signing ceremony. A few weeks later in the Rose Garden, Harden stood at the podium and gave her version of the story that the president had used many times before. She concluded by calling Clinton "the man who started my success and the beginning of my children's future."[54] After enveloping her in

President Bill Clinton signing the Personal Responsibility and Work Opportunity Reconciliation Act into law. Lillie Harden stands to his right, August 22, 1996.
Credit: Reuters/Stephen Jaffe

a bear hug, Clinton spoke of how Harden had been even more influential to him, recalling how she had inspired his attitude about welfare.

Standing by Clinton's side as he put his pen to the legislation, Harden served as an effective symbol of what the administration sought to suggest the law would do. Her hard work, desire to provide for her children, and sense of success exemplified Clinton's long-standing commitment to challenging the view of poor women of color as lazy and irresponsible. Clinton later remarked he sincerely thought the new law would "diminish at least a lot of the overt racial stereotypes." Jason DeParle has suggested that Clinton sincerely believed he was giving welfare recipients an opportunity to show that they did not want to be dependent on government support.[55] Yet, his invocation of women like Harden also reinforced his strong support of poor Black and brown women who abided by middle-class meritocratic norms and ideals—those "who worked hard and played by the rules," as he would often say.

These celebrations inherently stigmatized those people who did not uphold these norms and justified the termination of their support from the state. Women like Harden served as a direct counterpoint not just to the image of the welfare recipient unwilling to work, but also to the Clinton administration's racialized demonization of drug dealers and other criminal offenders, which it used to justify the harsh penalties in the 1994 crime bill.

Clinton's repeated embrace of Harden's story about her son also reflected his view that the benefits of having a job, starting one's own business, and saving money were as much psychological as material.[56] Since his time in Arkansas, he had spoken of the ways in which a job offered a sense of purpose and discipline. A paycheck rather than a welfare check, he stated repeatedly, would offer poor women of color an important sense of self-worth and help integrate them into the market economy. Muhammad Yunus and other advocates of microenterprise had made a similar case, which was in large part why Clinton had been a champion of those tools and the women enrolled in programs like the Good Faith Fund and WSEP. Microenterprise would not evoke the same controversy as other aspects of the welfare reform law in large part because it was a small piece of the larger legislation. The debate surrounding the 1996 reforms, nevertheless, further solidified welfare's connection to microenterprise and the idea these tools offered a route toward both personal empowerment and economic growth. These links would become important as microenterprise became ever more integral to the administration's efforts to promote economic development and women's rights across the world.

CAGED BIRD

Bill Clinton initially did not make microenterprise central to his foreign policy agenda. USAID, nevertheless, recognized that microenterprise was crucial to its ability to stay relevant in the post–Cold War era, especially as the Clinton administration increasingly placed spreading free markets and democracies at the center of its foreign policy priorities.[57] Representatives from the agency routinely deemed microenterprise "the building block of capitalism" and suggested that it "builds a safety net for many of the world's poor," including those who risked being "left behind" by the rise of globalization.[58] In June 1994, USAID launched the Microenterprise Initiative, which established an "enduring commitment to microenterprise by the agency," especially helping poor women "increase their incomes, assets, skills and productivity," which, in turn, could "facilitate the creation of economic democracies."[59] This commitment aligned with the work of a set of development economists—including future treasury secretary Lawrence Summers—who argued that investing in women offered the most efficient way to end poverty and promote economic development in the Global South.[60] Like the rationale undergirding Clinton's and the New Democrats' support for microenterprise domestically, USAID adopted a focus on growth and investment over redistribution and treated the market as a salve for the pressing problem of global poverty.

USAID became the world's largest funder of international microenterprise programs in the mid-1990s. While the Clinton administration significantly cut funds for foreign aid, it increased the budget for microcredit. By early 1997, USAID was spending $130 million a year on microenterprise, funding about 150 institutions in forty countries and estimated it was reaching about twenty million people, most of whom received loans of under $300.[61] "We are out ahead of the revolution that's occurring around the world," USAID administrator Brian Atwood proudly declared.[62]

Soon enough the World Bank was right at its side. Clinton appointed his old friend and former ShoreBank official Jan Piercy, who had been instrumental in the creation of Southern Development Bancorporation and the Good Faith Fund, to serve as the leading US official at the bank. When Piercy told Clinton she was humbled by the appointment, he chuckled and said, "Jan, I thought it was time that the World Bank looked more like ShoreBank . . . I know the World Bank is doing these big, huge structural adjustment loans, but any national economy is only as strong as the robustness of its local economies and that is what you understand because of ShoreBank."[63] Her arrival at the World Bank in 1995 directly coincided with its taking up the issue of microfinance. Many World Bank officials had resisted supporting microcredit because they believed it violated the bank's mission of doing macro-economic development and distributing large rather than small loans.[64] Drawing on her experiences with the Good Faith Fund and at ShoreBank, as well as the years she spent living in Bangladesh, Piercy persuaded the World Bank to establish the Consultative Group to Assist the Poorest (CGAP). The division provided micro-enterprise organizations not just more funding, but also validated microcredit as a major feature of international development.[65] The support abetted the growth and visibility of the microcredit field, leading to the expansions of long-standing organizations like Accion, FINCA (Foundation for International Community Assistance), SEWA, Women's World Bank, and Grameen Bank and further burnishing the international stature of Muhammad Yunus.

The efforts to spread the microenterprise revolution earned further legitimacy and attention as Hillary Clinton made it increasingly central to her policy agenda as First Lady. After the 1992 election, she formally resigned from the Southern Development Bancorporation's board, though she pledged to continue to show "interest and concern" in issues of economic development and microenterprise.[66] During the first years of the administration, however, she remained almost fully consumed by health-care reform. After the health-care plan failed to pass, Clinton cautiously shifted her attention to microcredit. The topic enabled her to address issues of women's rights and foreign policy, and by focusing on poor women in the Global South, Clinton could circumvent the contentious culture wars and potentially avoid attacks from the right.[67]

In the spring of 1995, Hillary and Chelsea Clinton embarked on a twelve-day trip to Southeast Asia intended to highlight efforts to empower women in the region.[68] In addition to visits in Pakistan and India, the trip included a stop in Bangladesh, where Muhammad Yunus gave the Clintons a tour of a Grameen branch. Despite her involvement with the Good Faith Fund and an almost

Hillary Clinton and Chelsea Clinton meeting with Grameen Bank borrowers in the village of Moshihati in Bangladesh, April 3, 1995
Credit: Getty Images

decade-long relationship with Yunus, it was Hillary's first visit to an international microenterprise organization and the first time she closely interacted with poor women in the Global South.[69] By the time Clinton made her trip, Grameen had expanded to more than a thousand branches and had over two million clients.[70]

Clinton found the experience of going to the Grameen branch in the small village of Jessore worth the ride on the very bumpy dirt roads to get there.[71] She and Chelsea watched the solidarity groups in action and attended a meeting of over three hundred women. She also met with a smaller group of borrowers who asked Clinton questions about her status as a woman and her independence from her husband.[72] She was particularly inspired by a conversation she had with one borrower who told her how with her first loan she bought a cow, with her second loan she bought another cow, and with her third loan she bought a rickshaw for her husband "to do something to help the family."[73] For Clinton, the story encapsulated the version of feminism she was committed to advancing, which focused on empowering oppressed women around the globe by providing individual rights and economic opportunities.

Following on the heels of the visit to Bangladesh, Clinton started using her bully pulpit to bring attention to microenterprise. Her appearance at the 1995 United Nations Conference on the Status of Women in Beijing is most memorable for her iconic statement that "human rights are women's rights and women's rights are human rights." Yet, during her time in Beijing, she made several references to microenterprise as an important means of women's empowerment and poverty alleviation and pledged to increase its spread in the United States.[74] In the next few years, she increased her travel schedule and sought out opportunities to visit microenterprise organizations throughout the world, going from Denver to Bolivia, where a borrowing group she met with decided to rename itself "Hillary" to honor her.[75] These trips provided her with more anecdotes to include in the many speeches she gave on the topic. In the coming years, it was in fact rare to find a speech by Hillary that didn't mention microenterprise. Bill Clinton publicly praised her "for beginning this obsession, almost, that we have with microenterprise" and convincing him to "go national with this micro idea in a very macro way."[76]

It was a sign of Hillary Clinton's commitment that the organizers of the 1997 Microcredit Summit selected her to deliver the keynote address at the event. To express her devotion visually, she included a PowerPoint with pictures of her talking with and observing borrowers at various microenterprise organizations around the world.[77] As she flipped through the slides, Clinton recounted some of her favorite anecdotes from her visits over the previous two years. The women in the stories would become Hillary's own Lillie Hardens. She told of a borrower she spoke to at a Denver organization called Mi Casa who helped Latina welfare recipients translate their skills into income. The woman, who wanted to start a bakery, told Clinton of the challenges of gaining start-up funds and loans without collateral and wistfully stated "too many great ideas die in the parking lots of local banks." She included another favorite story of a seamstress she met in

Santiago whose new sewing machine, purchased through a loan from a local microenterprise organization, made her feel "like a caged bird set free."[78]

The anecdotes of the Denver baker and Chilean seamstress helped humanize the topic of microenterprise and also brought international attention to the experiences of these women. At the same time, Hillary's descriptions reduced the complex life histories of these women into simple and uplifting parables. Like Bill Clinton's routine mention of Harden, the stories served as a counterpoint to stereotypes of low-income women of color and shifted their image away from that of lazy, dependent, or helpless victims and into hardworking entrepreneurs. Yet, by valorizing the borrowers' hard work and success despite adversity, this approach suggested that poverty was an individual problem that could be solved through personal initiative and a line of credit.[79] The particular stories and images Hillary used in her speech at the summit clearly intended to show the universal applicability of microcredit. Yet, her travelogue flattened the individual circumstances and context of each place she visited. It erased the fact that there were clear differences in the conditions of poverty in Chile and Denver, just as there were in Bangladesh, Chicago, and Arkansas, which all required their own local solutions. In fact, even as Hillary Clinton aimed to stress its universal applicability, US policy on microcredit was increasingly diverging on international and domestic lines.

In the international sphere, US aid agencies increased spending on microcredit in the late 1990s but focused on lessening the dependence of microenterprise groups on international donors and encouraging self-reliance through privatization and financialization. USAID adopted the position that the only way for microcredit to have an impact in addressing global poverty was to "go beyond the limited bounds of public funding, to full integration within the private financial system."[80] Several leading microcredit organizations were already moving in that direction. Accion, which focused on Latin America, started to believe that the only way to assist microentrepreneurs out of poverty was by connecting them with international capital markets. Under the direction of former private equity executive Michael Chu, Accion began concentrating on helping the NGOs it worked with become established regulated financial institutions.[81] In partnership with USAID, Accion facilitated the opening of BancoSol in Bolivia in 1992. It was the world's first commercial bank solely dedicated to the microenterprise sector, and by 1997 it had become the largest and most profitable bank in Bolivia.[82] Accion leaders marveled that international financial markets now had in circulation loans to female street vendors in La Paz and suggested these connections symbolized the market system of the future.[83] USAID similarly celebrated the success of BancoSol and Accion's larger financial services approach. In the late 1990s, USAID contracted Accion to provide technical assistance to help other microenterprise organizations move toward financialization and also teach conventional banks how to run microfinance programs.[84] This approach would have a major impact on the shape of microfinance internationally in the new millennium.

The Clinton administration's domestic microenterprise policy focused primarily on ensuring the self-reliance of individual low-income people, especially those transitioning off welfare.[85] By the late 1990s, several different federal agencies—from the Small Business Association and the CDFI Fund to HHS—were running microenterprise programs. Many of the initiatives directly targeted TANF recipients. To further advance this effort, the Clinton administration established the Presidential Awards for Excellence in Microenterprise Development. The lengthy named award was an outgrowth of Hillary Clinton's promise at the UN conference to spread microenterprise in the US. The Treasury Department oversaw the award, which honored "outstanding and innovative" organizations.[86] While the awards brought new visibility to the movement and to organizations like the Women's Self-Employment Project (which was one of the inaugural awardees), it reified the Clinton administration's relentless depiction of microenterprise as an effective and successful solution to the hardships of low-income women. In doing so, the awards obscured the many

challenges microenterprise organizations like WSEP and the
Good Faith Fund endured in the post–welfare reform era. In fact,
it was notable that the Clintons rarely provided specific details
about their involvement in setting up the program in Arkansas or
told uplifting stories about its borrowers.

AFTER WELFARE

"Any job is a good job." That was the motto of the Pine Bluff social
services agency as it struggled to abide by the mandates of the new
federal and state welfare-to-work requirements.[87] Clinton's home
state felt the pressure to fulfill, if not exceed, the directives of his
welfare reform law. Not long after Lillie Harden's trip to the Rose
Garden, the Arkansas legislature passed its own version of the
welfare-to-work program, which was one of the most stringent in
the country. The law established a two-year lifetime limit on cash
assistance (five for childcare, medical care, and transportation).
It granted exemptions in only the most severe cases. Arkansas received a great deal of national attention after it saw a 45 percent
reduction in its caseloads in the first year of the program. The
drop was in large part due to its unyielding requirements.[88] The
law, however, created havoc in the Pine Bluff area where roughly
sixteen thousand people on welfare confronted losing their aid.
In a region that had suffered from capital flight, high unemployment, rising incarceration rates, and chronic poverty, fulfilling
the mantra to find any job proved difficult. The Pine Bluff–based
Good Faith Fund started by ShoreBank and the Clintons in the
late 1980s sought to help.

The Good Faith Fund and the Southern Development Bancorporation had undergone a series of internal changes by the time the
Arkansas law took effect. ShoreBank executives Mary Houghton
and Ron Grzywinski had relinquished much of their involvement
with Southern. At the same time the bank had shifted its attention
to expanding its work in the Delta region. The GFF had a new executive director named Penny Penrose who was an Arkansas native with a background in social services. Penrose was distressed

about the severity of the state's new welfare law. She recognized
that the GFF's existing experience working with AFDC recipients
could give them leverage with state officials to potentially change
and modify the law. Traveling frequently from Pine Bluff to Little
Rock, she earned a reputation as a thorn in the side of state legislators. She and the GFF played a critical role in cajoling Arkansas
to provide more services to people leaving the welfare system and
would later fight for fair credit and against predatory lending.[89]

The GFF matched its policy work with a series of new programs
intended to address more directly the needs of women transitioning off welfare. These programs focused less on self-employment
and more on wage employment. The GFF recognized that health
care was one sector of the economy that was growing in the Arkansas Delta and one that offered entry-level workers the possibility for advancement.[90] In 1997, the GFF established Careers in
Health Care, which trained individuals leaving the welfare rolls as
certified nursing assistants and home health care aides and then
helped participants find jobs in hospitals, home health agencies,
nursing homes, and rehabilitation facilities.[91] The participants included women like Donna, an African American thirty-five-year-
old single mother of three. After graduating from the program, she
got a job providing physical therapy to nursing home residents.
She earned $7.50 an hour—$2.00 above the minimum wage—and
also received benefits. The program quickly received a positive
reputation in the Pine Bluff area as a source of reliable health-care
workers. It was also popular with participants like Donna, who
stressed how it brought not just financial security but also helped
her grow personally.[92]

At the same time, the GFF significantly revamped its microenterprise program, eliminating the Grameen-influenced peer-
lending component. The program had struggled throughout the
first part of the 1990s. The GFF experienced defaults on many of
its loans, and peer lending never succeeded in capturing the imagination of the local residents it was meant to assist. Low-income
residents in the Delta were uncomfortable being responsible for
making lending decisions for their peers and sharing sensitive

personal financial information with nonrelatives.[93] Initially, the GFF staff believed the problem might be that they had made adaptations to the Grameen model, and they shifted course to follow it even more strictly.[94] By 1996, GFF leaders acknowledged, however, that "there was no easy way to fit the Grameen model and its cultural 'props' to Arkansas."[95] Soon after, the fund ended the peer-lending program and decided to instead focus on assisting individual borrowers with a "more decisive degree of business-readiness" than the poor Black welfare recipients who it initially focused on.[96] GFF also changed its definition of a microloan, raising its loan limit to anything less than $25,000.[97] The typical borrower shifted from being a Black single mother starting a catering or childcare business to the owner of a successful Pine Bluff restaurant and bakery looking to expand his business.[98] In justifying such alterations, the GFF acknowledged that most microlending organizations had begun to focus on "safer investments."[99]

WSEP corroborated the claim that the challenges of peer lending were not unique to rural Arkansas and also existed in Chicago. The organization received a great deal of attention for its Grameen-based Full Circle Fund, but by the middle of the 1990s, the program had not fulfilled these high expectations. Executive Director Connie Evans and the rest of WSEP's staff came to terms with the fact that among their borrowers peer pressure was not serving as an effective substitute for collateral.[100] While they did not have the same high rate of defaults as the GFF, the women in the WSEP program did not borrow with the frequency needed to make the fund sustainable. As Evans explained, "the social component of the program worked really well and gave many women the social capital and encouragement to change their lives."[101] But WSEP was unable to make it work successfully as a lending program, and those positives proved not enough to keep the program in operation.[102] WSEP decided to phase out the Full Circle Fund, though it continued to offer loans to individual women starting small businesses, including those making the transition off welfare.

When welfare reform went into effect, the city of Chicago had more people on welfare than the combined client populations of the nation's thirteen least populous states.[103] While local antipoverty and services organizations decried the law's time limits and work challenges, Evans and WSEP saw it as an opportunity. Unlike her colleagues at other organizations, Evans described herself as "incredibly single-focused" on helping women of color achieve "economic self-sufficiency" and ensuring that "even women receiving welfare could start businesses if they wanted to" by taking away the "shackles . . . within the public aid system that prevented them from doing that."[104]

WSEP began to explore matched savings accounts as another way to help women transitioning off welfare achieve self-sufficiency and empowerment. Based on the asset-building theories of Michael Sherraden, matched savings had become a favored idea of many in Washington, especially the members of the DLC in the early 1990s. Sherraden argued for shifting welfare policy away from its narrow focus on direct cash assistance and toward asset accumulation.[105] He proposed creating Individual Development Accounts (IDAs), modeled on Individual Retirement Accounts (IRAs), where government would match the deposits made by low-income people in tax-exempt accounts to be used for purchasing a home, starting a small business, or paying tuition. Sherraden contended a matched savings account would provide financial education for the poor and also channel their savings into the financial system. Similar to Muhammad Yunus's and the Clintons' arguments about microenterprise, Sherraden primarily stressed the psychological benefits of asset accumulation. "While incomes feed people's stomachs," he contended, "assets change their heads."[106]

When Sherraden met with Evans and suggested she consider experimenting with his idea of IDAs for welfare recipients, she immediately said yes.[107] Since its formation, WSEP had emphasized the benefits of savings. The organization required all of its loan recipients to establish savings accounts for their businesses to create equity in their microenterprises.[108] According to Evans, WSEP saw the accounts as way to instill "a culture of savings" among borrowers and make them more responsible and future-oriented.[109] WSEP launched the effort even before Clinton signed the welfare-to-work requirements into law in partnership with the Chicago-based Harris Bank, which matched the women's savings on a 2:1 basis. The early participants in WSEP's IDA program included many of the women whom the organization helped to launch their own cleaning, day-care, and hairstyling businesses, including Arinez Gilyard.[110]

TUNED INTO SAVINGS

With the dawn of welfare reform, IDA programs became more widely available to many other women who, like Gilyard, were transitioning off public assistance. The idea had strong champions in Congress from both parties. The 1996 welfare reform law included IDAs as one option states could adopt. In 1998, Congress passed the Assets for Independence Act, which provided $125 million to states and community groups to test the validity of IDAs to help low-income people, especially those receiving TANF, achieve financial independence. The laws provided funds, but even more important, they legitimated asset building as a tool for addressing economic inequality.[111]

Asset building and matched savings also became a pet interest of several major private philanthropic organizations, most notably the Ford Foundation.[112] During the 1990s, Ford played a critical role in stressing that one of the best ways to address the problems of global and domestic poverty was to help poor people become more integrated into the market system.[113] In 1996, the same year as the passage of welfare reform, Ford decided to place all of its domestic and international antipoverty initiatives under the rubric of Asset Building and Community Development. Ford officials believed that making assets an organizing principle would direct the foundation to think about poverty less as a problem and a negative and instead focus on the future and solutions to "empower" poor people to succeed.[114] As part of its new focus on assets, the foundation made IDAs a major priority. In 1997, it spearheaded a group of philanthropies to commission Michael Sherraden to test the effectiveness of IDAs both financially and for changing the behavior of poor people. The experiment, called the American Dream Demonstration, involved IDA programs at thirteen organizations around the country, including WSEP and ShoreBank. The 2,350 participants were primarily women of color with children who received some sort of public assistance. In addition to making monthly deposits, the program required them to attend monthly economic literacy courses. The courses focused on skills like balancing a checkbook, making a budget, and how making small changes in habits, such as taking a sack lunch to work, could add up to big differences.[115]

Through the courses and monthly deposits, the experiment aimed to provide, in the words of WSEP's IDA program coordinator, "not just wealth creation, but a change in long-term behavior."[116] The financial system, therefore, could achieve the forms of social control and discipline that had been a feature of programs for the poor since the nineteenth century. Program participants themselves described how the accounts altered their outlook. Gilyard explained how the program "turned on that area of my brain that was not in tune to savings" and made her more "disciplined and focused on savings." She also spoke of the sense of pride she felt when she received her monthly bank statements.[117] After a year in the program, Gilyard amassed more than $2,000 and withdrew some to pay for a summer tutoring program for her teenage daughter.[118] Sonia Soto, a welfare recipient, had worked in salons since coming to Chicago from Puerto Rico two decades earlier. She had long wanted to open up her own salon, but it proved only a pipe dream until her welfare case manager told her about WSEP's IDA program. Saving money proved a challenge since she was supporting her two children and her husband on a salary of six dollars per hour and had no health insurance. Yet, she quite remarkably managed to put aside fifty dollars monthly in her savings account and dutifully attended all the economic literacy and entrepreneurial training courses. Revealing how she inculcated the messages of the courses, she described how the program "disciplined her" and "helped her change her life," especially by teaching her "not to throw away money" and "save for your dream."[119] Eventually, Soto put away enough to convert an old barbershop into her own salon. After a year in business, she had built a steady client base and her weekly income had more than doubled. "This place was a gold mine," she proudly reported of her salon.[120]

For many of the participants in the WSEP program and the larger Ford-funded experiment, however, it became extremely difficult to put away small amounts of money even with the promise of matched savings. WSEP found the greatest challenge was preventing women from making early withdrawals from their accounts to address emergency situations.[121] The decision of a participant to give up two dollars in the future for an immediate dollar was not from a lack of discipline or financial knowledge but because she needed the money for urgent necessities like rent, food, or medicine. Most of the participants lacked stable health insurance (in part the consequence of the failure of Clinton's health-care reform), and many found medical bills to be the biggest impediment to savings. Several people accumulated thousands of dollars in medical debt over the course of the experiment.[122] In sum, 48 percent of the participants in the larger experiment saved less than a hundred dollars.[123]

While proponents of asset building frequently touted the psychological benefits of saving money, this emphasis often motivated participants to measure their self-worth in financial terms and blame themselves if they did not meet their goals. One participant in the national experiment explained: "I've been really disappointed, you know, in myself—not with the program because the program I think is wonderful . . . just disappointment with myself and—just still being in that same rut, that rut that I've been in pretty much all my life."[124] The titles of the economic literacy courses—"Master Your Money," "Making Your Money Work," "All My Money"—reflected how the programs encouraged participants to think primarily in microeconomic and individualistic terms.

Even the title of the tool—IDA—was meant to evoke IRAs, focused on individual development rather than trying to make collective change.[125] By continuously trotting out the few success stories of people like Gilyard and Soto and using them to speak for the whole, the WSEP and other program operators did not fully acknowledge that while saving fifty dollars per month was impressive, in most cases it still made purchasing a house, starting a business, or paying tuition all but impossible.[126]

Michael Sherraden and other asset-building proponents would frequently bemoan how the US spent billions annually to subsidize the asset acquisition of the nonpoor in the form of home mortgage deduction, preferential capital gains, and pension funds exclusions.[127] This critique joined the growing discussions of the hidden welfare state and how the state contributed in fundamental ways to producing structural inequality.[128] Yet, for Sherraden, the solution lay not in abolishing those benefits for white middle-class people and redistributing the surplus funds to low-income families; rather, he and other asset-building proponents argued poor people should have the same access to savings and subsidies as white middle-class families. In many ways, therefore, the entire theory rested on the idea that a main source of economic inequality—asset accumulation—could be used to combat it.

The results of the IDA experiments tempered some of the enthusiasm matched savings programs initially received. Policymakers and practitioners adopted a cost-benefit critique and argued that the limited amount poor people were able to save in the programs did not meet the outsize amount of attention asset building received from policymakers, foundations, and think tanks.[129] Microenterprise programs, especially those operating domestically, increasingly received similar criticism.

The number of microenterprise training and development programs in the US grew from 108 in 1992 to 427 by 2002.[130] Many of the leading international organizations like Accion and FINCA established programs in the US. Microenterprise's advocates continued to promote it as a less expensive alternative to welfare and other social programs, especially because it operated through private and independently run organizations.[131] Yet, few of the programs were self-sufficient; most continued to rely heavily on funding from foundations and government grants. Many began to question whether the programs were worth the cost, especially when they helped such a limited number of welfare recipients and other low-income people.[132] The explosion of microenterprise internationally, which only increased after the 1997 Microcredit Summit, compounded the skepticism about domestic microlending organizations. GFF, WSEP, and others found themselves routinely compared to organizations like Grameen, which had always operated at a much larger scale.[133] In addition, critics raised concerns that the domestic programs put too strong an emphasis on building the self-esteem of participants and gave them the false hope that if someone wanted something badly enough she could make her dreams come true.[134] But it was these very messages, coupled with the promise to empower poor Black and brown women, that made microenterprise and asset-building programs so attractive to Bill and Hillary Clinton.

Bill Clinton routinely stressed the real value of microenterprise and asset-building programs lay in their ability to promote self-esteem and independence. In 1999, he declared:

> What does it mean to a single mom's life when she goes to the mailbox in the morning and sees a bank statement instead of a welfare check? What does it mean to a child when he or she can go to school and say, when they ask, 'What does your mother do for a living?' She owns a beauty shop.[135]

This hypothetical scenario updated Lillie Harden's story to fit the conventions of microenterprise and asset building. It implied that poor women could find their sense of self-worth and validation of their parenting ability through entrepreneurship and a savings account. Fusing the material with the psychological, Clinton contended that "a shortage of confidence . . . is just as debilitating as a shortage of cash."[136] This framing directed blame for poverty away from the forces of capitalist restructuring and the policies of his administration and instead treated it as a psychological and individual problem. This celebration also created a distorted view of the effectiveness of the microenterprise programs. The hypothetical story Clinton offered, like the many of the real ones he would use, ignored or underplayed the realities of the microentrepreneurs who struggled to stay out of the red or people who could not successfully save for a house. It thus provided another means to stigmatize the thousands of people who had tried and failed to create a sustainable business or never had the resources to do so at all.

From his first declarations to end welfare as we know it and on through the late 1990s, Clinton repeated the meritocratic mantra that "people who work shouldn't be poor." Though it was undoubtedly a noble ideal, the programs that the Clinton administration offered to achieve it all too often shunted people into low-wage and unstable work that made basic economic security, much less upward mobility, unattainable. Many children in poverty may have been proud of their mothers for working, as Clinton contended; however, for many it meant that they lost a reliable source of care and supervision. Studies would come to reveal that the best way to address the problem of childhood poverty was not through welfare-to-work programs but rather through means-tested cash assistance and the other social safety net mechanisms that became substantially curtailed by the 1996 welfare act.[137]

These dynamics became all too clear in Clinton's home state. The Clinton administration joined Arkansas officials in celebrating the sharp drop in the state's welfare rolls as a sign of the success of the welfare-to-work initiatives.[138] However, more than a surface-level glance at the statistics revealed that the Arkansas program helped the most employable get off the rolls, and whites transitioned at a much higher rate than Black and Latinx women. It became increasingly difficult to find opportunities for those who were not work ready or who were more susceptible to employment discrimination. Even many of the women in Arkansas who did find work continued to struggle. A 1999 study conducted by the Good Faith Fund found that 84 percent of people enrolled in Arkansas's welfare-to-work program worked part-time in low-wage jobs, earned well below the federal poverty line, and lacked childcare, health care, and other supportive services.[139] Even Lillie Harden, Clinton's poster child for the success of welfare-to-work programs, experienced substantial hardship following her trip to the Rose Garden. After suffering a stroke, she lost her job at a Little Rock supermarket, found herself unable to receive Medicaid, and could not pay for her prescription drugs.[140]

Harden's story reflected that of thousands of others, including many of the women WSEP's programs targeted. Like Arkansas, Illinois saw a sharp drop in its welfare rolls beginning in 1997, but many women did not find stable or well-paying employment.[141] Chicago case workers celebrated women like Englewood resident Daneen Clark. The thirty-three-year-old former welfare recipient found work as a cook at a local fast-food restaurant. She earned $5.15 per hour to stand over a 350-degree deep fryer. The exhausting job still left her under the poverty line and stuck living in a cramped, hot, roach-filled apartment with her three teenagers without enough money to pay for gas in her own stove. "I'm struggling," she admitted in 1999. "You have to make more than minimum wage to make it."[142] Further evoking concern, the implementation of welfare-to-work programs had occurred during a moment of economic boom, and many experts worried what would happen during the next downturn.

Microenterprise ultimately became less of a substantial option for women like Harden or Clark than proponents had hoped at the outset of the 1990s. Yet, it played a critical ideological function in spreading the notion that entry into the mainstream financial system as an entrepreneur or saver could replace traditional forms of aid and could change the behavior of poor women of color. The persistent celebrations of microenterprise and asset building bolstered the thinking that the private sector and financial system offered the best route for addressing poverty and racial and gender discrimination. These celebrations elided examination of the structural origins of those problems, which further foreclosed the pursuit of structural solutions.

This market-based vision of antipoverty policy continued to globalize. By the early twenty-first century, USAID, the United Nations, the World Bank, the International Monetary Fund, and several leading philanthropies all made microfinance and financial inclusion for the poor a central priority. The United Nations declared 2005 the International Year of Microcredit, and the following year Muhammad Yunus won the Nobel Peace Prize for his work combating poverty and empowering women. By that time, Grameen had expanded beyond just microcredit to offer a wide array of financial services, including housing loans, pensions, and insurance. It had forged partnerships with companies like Danone Yogurt and created its own cell phone company.[143] The trend toward privatization and financialization in microfinance also increased. For-profit microcredit companies spread rapidly through Africa, Asia, and Latin America, extending loans to poor villagers with exorbitant interest rates. In India, SKS Microfinance raised more than $350 million in its initial public offering, with the founder personally making millions. However, in the state of Andhra Pradesh, where SKS concentrated most of its business, scores of women became buried in a mountain of debt, and a large number began committing suicide.[144] The news of the deaths ignited questions about whether microfinance was just another predatory way to scam the poor.

Yunus for his part was sharply critical of the shift toward the financialization of microcredit.[145] He believed it represented a betrayal of the original purpose of microcredit, which, he contended, was meant to focus on sustainability, not profit maximization. "Microcredit should be seen as an opportunity to help people get out of poverty in a business way," Yunus chided a group of financial officials at the UN, "but not as an opportunity to make money out of poor people."[146] The controversy and criticism undoubtedly removed some of microfinance's luster, but USAID continued to invest significantly in microenterprise and other forms of financial inclusion.[147] So, too, did many leading philanthropic organizations—from the billions donated by the Bill and Melinda Gates Foundation to the thousands of people who donated twenty dollars to Kiva to support poor women around the globe.

These international efforts further codified the idea that providing entry into the financial system could replace a comprehensive social safety net. It ushered in a new vision and language to address inequality and poverty based on the idea that the market could do good and could help discipline the behavior of poor Black and brown women. Yet, as they confronted other market-based reforms, especially the remaking of public housing, poor and low-income people in places like Pine Bluff and the South Side of Chicago (as well as Bangladesh, Bolivia, and Chile) stood in an even more precarious position.

CHAPTER 7

FROM A RIGHT TO A REWARD

Juanita Williams refused to leave. The seventy-four-year-old lived in the Hole, the most troubled part of Chicago's Robert Taylor Homes, the largest and, according to many, worst public housing project in the nation. Despite the gangs, violence, broken elevators, graffiti, garbage, and vermin infestations, and the fact she had recently entered her apartment to find four strangers making packets of heroin at her kitchen table, the Hole had still been her home for twenty-five years.[1] She ignored the eviction notice she received in 1998 and endured having her water and gas shut off. Eventually, Chicago police officers had to remove her and her furniture from the unit. Her fellow resident Katie Sistrunk was more accepting of her eviction. The mother of thirteen and grandmother of twenty-eight had seen so many people get killed at Robert Taylor and did not want it to happen to any of her children.[2]

Similar scenes and conflicted emotions occurred across the city of Chicago and the nation in the late 1990s. Williams and Sistrunk were just two of the tens of thousands of mostly Black and brown residents forced to leave public housing buildings as part of the Clinton administration's Housing Opportunities for People Everywhere (HOPE VI) program. HOPE VI razed large, distressed high-rises like the Robert Taylor Homes and replaced them with new mixed-income, low-density developments created in partnership with private developers. Former residents like Williams and

Sistrunk had the option of applying to return to the newly renovated buildings, move to another public housing development, or
receive a Section 8 voucher to use in the private housing market.

By the time Clinton took office, housing projects like Robert
Taylor had become to some monuments to the failures of the
public sector and New Deal liberalism while to others they were
symbols of decades of neglect of the poor by federal and local government. The HOPE VI program became a key piece of the New
Democrats' efforts to change the Democratic Party's image and
secure the support of the white moderate voters while simultaneously altering the image and function of public housing. Just as
the 1996 welfare reform legislation pledged to "end welfare as we
know it," HOPE VI promised to "end public housing as we know
it." It is in many ways the clearest example of the Clinton administration's restructuring of a core aspect of the social safety net
and privatization and marketization of a previously public service.

Chicago was the city that enthusiastically embraced the
HOPE IV program the most. The city boasted some of the na-
tion's most iconic and notorious projects, which, in addition to
the twenty-eight high-rises and four thousand apartments of the
Robert Taylor Homes, included such household names as Cabrini-
Green, Henry Horner, and Ida B. Wells. In partnership with the
Department of Housing and Urban Development, the Chicago
Housing Authority orchestrated a plan to demolish the vast majority of these high-rise developments. The HOPE VI program and
Chicago's adoption of it symbolized the convergence of the types
of market-based solutions advocated by the New Democrats. The
program sought to simultaneously make poor people into market
actors, make distressed urban neighborhoods profitable, and use
the tools of the market to make the public sector more efficient in
helping low-income people. Unlike other components of the New
Democrats' antipoverty agenda, such as community development
banking or microenterprise, the program provided the clearest opportunity for private developers and businesses to make a profit;
in fact, that was one of its main objectives. HOPE VI also offered a
chance to follow through on the DLC's and the Clinton campaign's

promises that it would "reinvent government" to make it more efficient, entrepreneurial, and reliant on the private sector. With the Republicans threatening to eliminate HUD after the 1994 midterm elections, the department embraced a radical plan for reinvention, which placed HOPE VI at the center.

By the late 1990s, HOPE VI fused with other key aspects of Clinton's domestic agenda, especially welfare reform, anticrime legislation, and efforts to boost commercial and residential real estate markets. This linking contributed to transforming public housing from a right into a reward for good behavior. Although it received less attention than welfare, the public housing reforms were equally revealing about the Clinton administration and its allies' commitment to incorporating market mechanisms and racialized behavioral norms into programs to address social problems. In the process, it left Sistrunk, Williams, and hundreds of thousands of other low-income people of color in an ever more vulnerable position. And it exacerbated racial segregation, economic inequality, and gentrification of Chicago and other major urban centers, while further circumscribing the availability of subsidized housing in smaller struggling cities like Pine Bluff, Arkansas.

CHICAGO'S WALL

No one driving into the center of Chicago could miss the four-mile stretch of high-rise public housing developments—including the Robert Taylor Homes—known as the State Street Corridor. By the 1980s, the imposing structures had become symbols of crime, segregation, and concentrated poverty. The *Chicago Tribune* began calling the corridor Chicago's Wall since it served as "a physical and psychological barrier that divides the city in an abundance of ways."[3] It wasn't supposed to be this way.

Federal public housing began as a New Deal program intended to help the recovery of both the white working poor and the construction industry. Following World War II, the federal government allocated funds for a substantial increase in the units to help urban redevelopment and address the national housing shortage. Chicago was one of the cities that most actively clamored for the federal funds, and it received money to construct thirty-three new projects and thousands of units. After confronting fierce resistance from local white residents and their aldermen, the Chicago Housing Authority (CHA) decided to place all except one of the new projects in predominantly Black areas on the city's south and west sides.[4] In the mid-1960s, CHA, like other public housing authorities, began changing their policies to allow occupancy by single-parent households and welfare recipients.[5] Further altering the development's demographics, Congress passed a law in the late 1960s capping public housing rents at 30 percent of a household's income. The change increased the rent for working families and effectively drove them out of public housing. It contributed to making developments like the Robert Taylor Homes the housing of last resort for the poorest of the poor.[6]

In the 1970s and 1980s, the problems of public housing in Chicago and the nation intensified with further changes in federal policy. In 1974, Congress approved the creation of the Section 8 program, which included a voucher program for families to use in the private housing market. Though the vouchers were supposed to be fair market value, they tended to be too meager to help residents move out of poor neighborhoods, especially for recipients who had large families.[7] The law also did not have a provision requiring landlords to accept Section 8 vouchers. Thus, while many liberals had supported vouchers as a backdoor way to create residential integration, the main effect of Section 8 was to reinforce racial segregation. The program also contributed to remaking HUD from a builder of public housing units into an issuer of subsidies to private landlords.[8] While the Reagan administration saw HUD as a symbol of the failures of the Great Society's commitment to "big government" and slashed its budget by 75 percent, it did increase the use of Section 8 vouchers, making the program the federal government's main form of housing assistance for the poor in the 1980s.[9]

These changes had a boomerang effect on Chicago and other cities. Almost from the outset, Chicago's large public housing high-rises endured severe maintenance problems, but the issues reached new and dangerous heights in the 1980s. Garbage, lead paint, vermin, broken elevators, and other hazards threatened the health and safety of inhabitants. With little funding devoted to the upkeep of its apartments, CHA started losing hundreds of units to vandalism and disrepair each year. Compounding the problems, CHA itself was in turmoil. It was the subject of several lawsuits, faced substantial debt, and between 1981 and 1988 churned through eight executive directors.[10]

Many of the vacant units in the high-rises became sites of gang and drug activity.[11] In the 1980s, the average public housing resident in Chicago had a 50 percent greater chance to be the victim of a violent crime than the average city resident, and inhabitants also endured routine burglary and other forms of harassment.[12] It was the gang and drugs that drew substantial media attention and made the Robert Taylor Homes and Cabrini-Green shorthand for the larger problems of the inner city, both locally and nationally. The notoriety created further harms for residents as delivery people, social workers, and even emergency service technicians and police refused to go there. Residents reported a sense of isolation, though most lived less than a mile away from Chicago's downtown Loop and famed Gold Coast.[13] Chicago in the 1980s had three of the nation's wealthiest census tracts and fifteen of its poorest—all of which had large public housing developments.

By the late 1980s, the federal government began raising more alarm bells about the problems of public housing nationally. When he took over as secretary of HUD in 1989, Jack Kemp put revamping public housing at the top of his agenda by encouraging residents to assume ownership of their units.[14] Kemp persuaded President Bush to support and Congress to pass a series of programs called HOPE (Homeownership for People Everywhere), which would allow for the ownership of either public housing units or homes on which the FHA had foreclosed.[15] While the idea earned praise from experts affiliated with the DLC, low-income housing advocates charged that it would not help the vast majority of public housing residents, who were too poor to participate, and would do little to address the larger problems of concentrated poverty.[16] Responding to the growing sense of a crisis, in the last days of the Bush administration, Congress passed the Housing and Community Development Act of 1992, which created a $300 million federal grant program to revitalize severely distressed public housing, especially high-rise buildings like the Robert Taylor Homes.[17] The program was officially called the Urban Revitalization Demonstration, but the architects referred to it as HOPE VI in an homage to Kemp's pet project. By the time the program was up and running, however, Kemp and Bush had left office.

Henry Cisneros, Kemp's successor, was a member of the DLC and had earned a reputation as a rising star in the Democratic Party. He had a background in city planning and as mayor of San Antonio in the 1980s oversaw an ambitious redevelopment agenda. In addition to his professional experience, Cisneros grew up in a San Antonio neighborhood that contained several public housing projects and watched as they fell into disrepair.[18] However, he would say that it was not until he became the head of HUD and toured public housing developments in Chicago that he came to understand the scope of the problem. After spending the night in a Robert Taylor Homes apartment in 1994, he pledged to turn it and places like it "from vortices of despair to fountains of hope."[19] Cisneros's efforts to do so became part of his larger vision to reinvent HUD as it faced threats from both inside and outside the administration.

REINVENTING HUD

HUD had long earned scorn from Republicans as a symbol of the bureaucratic excesses of the Great Society, but when Clinton took office, his administration also pledged to change the way the agency did business. The quest became a key component of the effort to hold true to his DLC-influenced campaign promise that if elected he would "reinvent government" to make it more efficient and entrepreneurial. Less than two months after taking office, he announced the administration would launch a comprehensive six-month review of the entire federal government led by Al Gore called the National Performance Review (NPR). Staffers internally started calling the project REGO, which was shorthand for reinventing government. The nickname was not just a way to differentiate it from National Public Radio; it was also a nod to *Reinventing Government*, the 1992 book cowritten by David Osborne, a fellow at the Progressive Policy Institute, the DLC's think tank. The book, which outlined ways to transform industrial-era public bureaucracies into leaner, more flexible, more results-oriented institutions suited to the new realities of the Information Age, had become a bible for the New Democrats in the early 1990s, and the project was a direct effort to apply these ideas. The NPR not surprisingly received strong support and involvement from the DLC and Progressive Policy Institute.[20] Gore assigned his domestic policy advisor, the former PPI fellow Elaine Kamarck, to oversee it. Osborne also came on board as a senior advisor.

Gore himself took a leading role in the project, believing strongly in the purpose of the initiative.[21] He staged visits to most federal departments as well as to private companies that had reputations for being "high-performance" and "high-profit," such as Southwest Airlines and Saturn.[22] Gore's first stop, however, was HUD. This visit was intended to acknowledge the agency's shortcomings and to signal Henry Cisneros's strong commitment to revamp it. Even before the formal unveiling of the NPR, Cisneros had announced plans to "reinvent HUD" to "change the way people think about this department."[23] Cisneros enthusiastically appeared alongside Gore in the HUD cafeteria as the vice president solicited examples from employees of excessive regulations, bureaucracy, and waste at the agency.[24]

In early September 1993, Gore presented the NPR's first report to Clinton at a formal ceremony held on the White House South Lawn. The event featured forklifts filled high with piles of papers meant to represent regulations the commission deemed

unnecessary. Standing in front of the piles, Gore pledged the report would help streamline "old-fashioned, outdated government,"
save $108 billion, and cut 252,000 federal jobs by 1998.[25] The report,
called *From Red Tape to Results*, directly aligned with the principles Osborne and the New Democrats had been advocating for
several years. Osborne, in fact, served as the report's chief author.
The report promised to make government more customer driven
and entrepreneurial and to subject it to the discipline and competition of the market.[26] In addition to these broad goals, the report
also included agency-specific recommendations, ten of which targeted HUD and its public housing program, which it called a "classic story of good intentions gone awry."[27]

Cisneros welcomed the recommendations. He agreed to cut
1,500 employees, reduce the agency's budget, and make HUD
more "decentralized, entrepreneurial, responsive" and a "partner
and facilitator and expediter."[28] However, HUD's commitment to
reform proved insufficient to placate the Republican criticism of
the agency as a bloated bureaucratic failure. In the aftermath of
the 1994 midterm elections, Newt Gingrich and his allies had the
power to act on their threats of eliminating the agency, which
made the White House nervous. On a late November plane ride,
Gore warned Cisneros that "profound changes were in order." Cisneros promised that HUD would start further "rethinking the way
it did business."[29]

In the span of just a few weeks, Cisneros and his staff developed a plan for the restructuring of the agency and its public
housing program, which took the reinventing government idea to
its extreme. The plan, called *Blueprint for Reinvention*, sought
to make public housing "subject to market forces." It would demolish the most distressed housing and shift entirely to "a market environment" through a voucher-based program modeled on
Section 8.[30] The idea of fully voucherizing public housing was
clearly an effort to assuage conservatives, who had long touted
that approach. The idea also built directly on core themes of the
DLC's and Clinton administration's approach to poverty and social welfare. HUD officials suggested the voucher approach would

give low- and moderate-income families greater power to make decisions about their lives and "provide real choice and opportunity to escape from concentrations of poverty."[31] In addition, they argued, it would force public housing authorities to compete with private developers and thereby improve their services to attract inhabitants.[32] Similar to other New Democrat–backed anti-poverty programs, like microenterprise, HUD's voucher proposal treated public housing residents as rational actors operating in an unfettered housing market and operated on the assumption that voucher recipients would both want and be able to make housing choices. It assumed that they would have no reason or desire to stay in the areas where they lived, would not face discrimination in more affluent housing markets, and would be able to move into safe and thriving middle-class communities. These assumptions would pose key challenges for voucher-based housing programs in the ensuing years.

A *Washington Post* reporter deemed *Blueprint for Reinvention* as "radical a proposal as Washington can produce" and the equivalent of a "moon shot."[33] Yet, it was not entirely out of left field and had clear roots and debts to the core ideas of *Reinventing Government*, the National Performance Review, and the Section 8 program. *Blueprint* earned high praise from the Clinton White House and even grudging respect from many Republicans in Congress.[34] While neither the full-scale reorganization of HUD nor complete voucherization came to pass, the plan marked a key change in the priorities and approach of the agency. HOPE VI emerged as a centerpiece and main vehicle for this new set of priorities.

NEW HOPE

"Hope VI is the end of public housing as we know it," HUD official Christopher Hornig boldly announced in 1996.[35] His radical statement captured how HUD was transforming HOPE VI at the same time it was considering its own transformation. In the first years of the Clinton administration, Cisneros and HUD largely operated

HOPE VI as a competitive grant program that would help local authorities to rehabilitate distressed developments.[36] Yet, even before the 1994 midterms, HUD staff already had been considering ways to revise HOPE VI to make it a tool for deconcentrating poverty and revitalizing urban neighborhoods.

The changes drew in large part on the ideas of St. Louis–based developer Richard Baron who was a leading voice in affordable housing circles. Baron sent a memo to HUD officials in December of 1993 suggesting that the focus of HOPE VI should be more on making developments mixed income and integrated into their surrounding neighborhoods. He argued this approach would not just benefit residents but could also stimulate private investment and contribute to redeveloping the surrounding community.[37] Baron argued that making HOPE VI a vehicle for public-private partnership could open up new forms of investment as well. HUD took to heart Baron's suggestions, recognizing they provided a way "to bring private sector investment into the public housing sphere."[38] HUD officials were painfully aware that the Gingrich Revolution augured for even fewer federal funds for public housing and that being able to leverage private sector funds and include more market-rate rents would serve as a critical means for underwriting new developments.[39] Keeping in line with both Baron's ideas and *Blueprint for Reinvention*, HUD began encouraging applicants to HOPE VI "to think big" both in how projects could leverage private capital, include mixed-income residency, improve neighborhoods, and create more upward mobility.[40] These suggestions revealed how HUD was gradually reimagining urban public housing authorities to serve not as social service providers but rather as real estate developers and deal brokers.[41] HUD was also envisioning how to use HOPE VI to both facilitate the privatization of public housing and stimulate private real estate markets with public funds.

HUD increasingly emphasized to HOPE VI applicants the importance of physical design and encouraged, if not required, them to adopt the principles of New Urbanism. New Urbanism, a movement within architecture and urban planning, focused on neotraditional design, nostalgia for small-town life, and creating

community, which drew on the work of writer Jane Jacobs.[42] It began in the 1980s, led by architects Andres Duany, Elizabeth Plater-
Zyburg, and Peter Calthrope to combat suburban sprawl. But in
the mid-1990s, the leaders started thinking about how they could
apply their principles to revitalizing cities as well.[43] Strongly rejecting modernist buildings, New Urbanists instead called for the
introduction of mixed-use, lower-density developments of townhouses and single-family homes. The New Urbanists argued these
changes would not just make urban areas more aesthetically attractive and promote a strong sense of community cohesion but
would also provide a way to draw more private investment to economically depressed areas.

The leaders of New Urbanism cultivated a close relationship
with HUD. Henry Cisneros spoke at its annual meeting in 1996
and the same year served as one of the founding signatories of the
Charter of New Urbanism.[44] Specifically addressing the issues of
public and affordable housing, the charter called for dispersing
developments throughout a metropolitan area and making public
housing not immediately identifiable. In addition, the New Urbanists advocated taking steps to foster safety and community, such
as clearly lighted paths and spaces for congregation.[45] The New
Urbanists put a strong emphasis on front porches as a means to
have residents themselves monitor for suspicious behavior.[46] HUD
worked with the Congress of New Urbanism to apply these ideas
to the criteria of the HOPE VI application selection process.[47]

New Urbanist neotraditional townhouses with front porches
and communal spaces would, however, create substantially lower-
density developments than those filled with modernist high-rises.
HUD thereby persuaded Congress in 1995 to suspend the federal
one-to-one replacement requirement, which allowed demolition
of a public housing unit only if it was replaced with another one.
Instead, HUD convinced Congress to allow for Section 8 vouchers
to stand in for replacing hard units. Residents of projects slated
for demolition would, therefore, receive a housing voucher to use
in the private housing market during the renovation of their developments and would then ostensibly have the choice to apply to

return to the new development or not. Thus, even if HUD failed to implement a full-scale voucherization of public housing, this change would substantially increase their usage.[48]

The suspension of the one-to-one policy and approval of more vouchers enabled the demolition of the nation's most distressed and dilapidated high-rises. Throughout 1995 and 1996, Cisneros went from Philadelphia and St. Louis to Denver to observe wrecking balls tear through high-rise developments. He called the buildings slated for demolition as "virtual reservations of poverty" and promised residents that "the urban landscape will literally change before their eyes."[49] As Cisneros ceremoniously broke ground on the new projects, it increasingly became clear HOPE VI itself was also transforming from its original mission of rehabilitating severely distressed housing to remaking public housing developments and surrounding urban neighborhoods into mixed-income oases.[50] This shift in priorities also meant that the majority of HOPE VI funding went to large cities like Chicago and New Orleans. HUD paid ever less attention to its housing in smaller cities like Pine Bluff, where residents already often lived in low-rise developments and which showed less potential for significant revitalization. The problems of disinvestment and shortage of adequate subsidized housing were no less severe in these places.[51] Several local officials accused HUD of having a big city bias and griped, in the words of one housing administrator, that HOPE VI was "really just targeting the most obsolete and desolate programs with the stereotypical horrible high rises."[52]

Cisneros would later defend the program's urban demolition and mixed-income focus by declaring that "HOPE VI posited drastic change as a way to save public housing" everywhere.[53] He and other HUD officials contended that the only way to shift negative attitudes about public housing among the larger public would be to demolish the most visible and infamous projects and build them (and the areas around them) anew. HUD thus saw the program much in the same way as the Vietnam sergeant who declared that his unit "had to destroy the village in order to save it." This model would be put to the test in Chicago.

ON TRIAL IN CHICAGO

On October 13, 1992, seven-year-old Dantrell Davis was holding his mother's hand while walking outside his building in Cabrini-Green on the way to school. Suddenly, a shot from a sniper in an abandoned apartment several stories above struck and killed him. The murder created significant national outrage and solidified Cabrini-Green's status as one of the country's most notorious housing projects and a shorthand for the system's failures. This image was corroborated by Chicago Housing Authority chair Vincent Lane, who had been brought in to reshape the agency.[54] Responding to the murder, Lane deemed Chicago's public housing to be "the worst in the world" and declared that "Cabrini symbolizes all that is wrong with public housing."[55] Immediately following the Davis murder, he released a plan of action, which included the demolition of the city's worst developments, with Cabrini-Green first in line. CHA submitted a HOPE VI proposal focusing specifically on the building where Davis lived. HUD approved the proposal in November 1993, but the plans had stalled as the problems of CHA intensified.

Lane struggled to overcome CHA's long history of mismanagement, fraud, and corruption, and HUD officials thought it needed more oversight. At a tense meeting with federal officials in spring of 1995, an exasperated Lane threw his large set of keys across the conference table at the HUD team and told them the federal government could have Chicago's public housing if it wanted it.[56] HUD took him up on his offer and Lane resigned.[57] HUD made the bold decision to not wait for a court-appointed receiver and instead immediately assumed control over CHA itself. At the press conference announcing the takeover, Cisneros declared: "The national system of public housing is on trial in Chicago."[58]

It was not just public housing but also the Democratic Party that was on trial as Chicago was the site for the 1996 Democratic National Convention. The Clinton administration and Mayor Richard Daley wanted to avoid the embarrassment of putting on display a city blemished with decrepit high-rises. It was especially urgent since the Henry Horner Homes sat just across from the United Arena, which was the site of the event.[59] In addition, HUD faced its own pressure from congressional Republicans and the administration. The seizure provided HUD an opportunity to show its value, test out *Blueprint for Reinvention*, and put on notice housing authorities in other major cities.

Cisneros tasked his undersecretary for public housing Joseph Shuldiner to take the helm of CHA. Shuldiner had previously served as director of the New York and Los Angeles housing authorities and played a key role in drafting *Blueprint for Reinvention* and the changes to HOPE VI. Like his boss, he saw the Windy City as the ideal test case for this kind of approach, declaring: "If we can make Chicago work, we can make any place work."[60] Shuldiner recognized that HOPE VI and Cabrini-Green were central to this mission. Soon after arriving in Chicago, he issued a call for new HOPE VI proposals for Cabrini-Green that would incorporate more market-rate units and mixed-income residents. Several local and national private developers readily embraced the challenge.

Cabrini-Green's proximity to the Loop and Gold Coast long served as a symbol of the segregation and isolation of its residents. Yet, from a real estate perspective, it made the seventy acres on which the high-rises sat very valuable. Starting in the early 1970s, the city had deliberately sought to attract college-educated postindustrial workers to the area to stop the flight of the white middle class to the suburbs.[61] The area began sprouting galleries, boutiques, restaurants, and renovated buildings, and realtors rebranded it "River North" and a place for the city's "creative community." In the 1980s, the neighborhood gained four thousand new white residents and a flurry of new construction and renovations, and the median home price skyrocketed. This wave of gentrification had been moving ever more rapidly toward Cabrini-Green, and private developers had long pressured CHA to sell Cabrini's plot to them.[62] Now they had a chance.

After receiving plans from several different developers, CHA released the Near North Redevelopment Initiative in June 1996. The plan proposed to knock down 1,324 units in Cabrini-Green and replace them with 2,300 new units, with half sold or rented at market rate, 20 percent for moderate-income households, and 30 percent for public housing families. Roughly half the new units would appear on the site of the Cabrini development, while the others would be spread throughout the neighborhood. The proposal also included plans to build a new park, school, police station, and commercial center on or near Cabrini. The design drew on New Urbanist principles and would replace modernist superblocks with a traditional street grid and the high-rises with neotraditional townhouses and eight-plexes. The proposal aligned with HUD's call that HOPE VI applicants creatively leverage private capital. CHA included several funding schemes that would rely on and bolster more high-end real estate investment in the area.[63]

The proposal sparked immediate indignation from residents and tenant organizers who felt a sense of double exclusion.[64] First, residents protested that they had had little role or input in the development of the proposal. Second, the plan proposed making the vast majority of the units unaffordable to current residents and would cause substantial displacement. Though the media and officials typically described public housing as lacking in community, the response proved just the opposite. In fact, Cabrini-Green boasted an active tenant rights movement and a large contingent of residents who had a strong sense of pride in the community. These resident activists quickly leapt into action. Working with the Coalition to Protect Public Housing, they staged large protests outside city hall, and in October 1996, filed a federal lawsuit against CHA and the city of Chicago.[65] The case delayed the redevelopment of the Cabrini-Green site itself, but over the next couple of years, other aspects of Shuldiner's plan moved forward. In the late 1990s, the neighborhood saw an explosion of private development, which included the large Old Town Square Shopping Center with many national chains like Crate & Barrel, as well as roughly a dozen new apartment complexes.[66] The area would also benefit from important changes to federal public housing law in the late 1990s.

HARDBALL

When Republican presidential candidate Bob Dole told a national
real estate convention in 1996 that public housing was "one of
the last bastions of socialism in the world," he had to eat crow.[67]
Many people—especially his opponent—quickly pointed out all
the market-based transformations to public housing enacted by
the Clinton administration. Al Gore pledged that the administration would go even further and demolish one hundred thousand
dilapidated units by the end of 2000. Relying on a series of racialized and sensationalist tropes, Gore denounced the high-rises as
"warehouses for the poor" and stated that these "crime-infested
monuments to a failed policy are killing the neighborhoods around
them." He declared that "by tearing them down and replacing them
with apartments and town homes, we lay the foundations for vibrant neighborhoods that will bring our inner cities back to life."[68]

HUD, after avoiding demolition itself, became emboldened to
enact this vision and push for new legislation to make permanent
many of the reforms it had temporarily secured through appropri-
ations bills. HUD also sought to make public housing reform more
central to Clinton's priorities by tying it directly to the president's
anticrime and welfare agendas. The quest for the legislation's passage outlived the tenure of Cisneros, who resigned amid an investigation into payments he gave to a former mistress. His successor,
Andrew Cuomo, largely carried on his vision and legislative plan.
After a debate on Capitol Hill that stretched over several years,
Congress finally passed the Quality Housing and Work Responsibility Act in the fall of 1998. Cuomo celebrated how it would enable
HUD to "change the culture" of public housing.[69]

The new law effectively overhauled the 1937 Housing Act and
replaced it with the HOPE VI approach. It expanded a rule initially passed in 1996 requiring that any large public housing development undergo a viability test to determine whether the cost to
rehabilitate it was worth it. The law encouraged lower-density development by explicitly requiring that the number of apartments
put on an old site would be "significantly fewer than the number

of units demolished."[70] In a radical move, the legislation officially endorsed the move away from the idea that public housing was a right and should serve the poor. Instead, it gave preference to employed people who abided by middle-class norms. Local authorities had to target between 30 and 40 percent of its developments for extremely low-income households. For the remainder of low-income families, the Quality Housing and Work Responsibility Act sanctioned the use of Section 8 vouchers rather than hard units. HUD and White House officials believed these changes would "empower residents" and ensure they had "the opportunity to participate in decisions affecting their lives."[71] The law, however, included several other components that explicitly limited the freedom of people receiving public housing assistance.

Fulfilling the work and responsibility components of the legislation's title, the act contained mechanisms to "encourage and reward work," drawing direct connections to welfare-to-work initiatives.[72] Even before the passage of the 1996 welfare reform law, HUD explored ways to encourage responsibility among residents.[73] Officials discussed ways to establish policies that might elicit certain behaviors in tenants to make them more responsible and self-sufficient.[74] The 1998 Quality Housing and Work Responsibility Act built on these discussions and the behavioral components of the welfare reform initiative. The housing law included a requirement that residents have a job and those who did not would have to spend at least eight hours per month in either a community service or job readiness program. This work incentive became critical in making public housing less of an entitlement and more of a reward.[75] Other mechanisms in the law that restricted who was entitled to public housing upheld the president's anticrime agenda.

Throughout his presidency, Clinton had tied public housing to his anticrime initiatives. He singled out and visited places like Cabrini-Green and the Robert Taylor Homes as examples to justify his punitive crime policies. The Clinton administration also embraced public housing as a way to further penalize criminal offenders. It directly linked access to public housing units to the 1994 crime bill, especially the infamous three-strikes provision.

The rule mandated life imprisonment for anyone convicted of a third felony and served as a symbol of the severity of the sweeping legislation, which in total led to a tripling of the Black incarceration rate by 2000.[76] When it came to public housing, the Clinton administration was even harsher. "Criminal gang members and drug dealers are destroying the lives of decent tenants," Clinton fearmongered in the 1996 State of the Union. "From now on, the rule for residents who commit crimes and peddle drugs should be 'one strike and you're out.'"[77] He immediately followed up with an executive order known as "One Strike and You're Out." The order demanded the eviction of an entire family from their public housing unit if anyone in the household was convicted of a crime and directed housing authorities to deny residency to convicted felons. These rules had already existed as part of the 1988 Anti-Drug Abuse Act, but Clinton took it a step further by extending penalties to encompass not just residents but their guests as well. The order also threatened penalties for public housing authorities that did not enforce the policy and gave them access to the FBI's crime databases to better screen the criminal records of applicants. Federal housing officials heralded the policy as the "toughest admission and eviction policy that HUD has implemented" and one that would "improve the quality of life for residents."[78] Members of the Clinton administration believed the provisions sent a message that public housing was a "privilege not a right" and "the only people who deserve to live in public housing are those who live responsibly there, and those who honor the rule of law."[79] Clinton admitted that it might sound "like hard ball" and that was the very idea.[80]

Like the administration's other antipoverty and welfare programs, the one-strike policy sought to create a sharp distinction between who were deserving and undeserving of government support. However, in actuality, those groups became conflated: a number of elderly residents were evicted from their units after the arrest of a relative for drug or gun possession, even if the offense occurred off the premises.[81] The administration, nevertheless, pressed on with the policy, citing anecdotal reports that many public residents strongly favored it and credited it with lessening crime in their buildings. The Quality Housing and Work Responsibility Act expanded the scope of the rule by authorizing housing authorities to evict felons automatically and gave local officials even more latitude over what constituted criminal activity. The law directed housing authorities to refuse applicants they suspected of using illegal drugs or abusing alcohol. It extended these provisions to the Section 8 program as well.[82] It also allowed ways to deny voucher payments to landlords who refused to evict Section 8 families for drug-related or violent criminal activity.[83] These stringent policies—in their effort to show that government-subsidized housing would only be available to those responsible and deserving, people who "work hard" and "play by the rules"— clearly circumscribed residents' sense of freedom of choice in the housing market.[84]

BUILDING COMMUNITIES, TRANSFORMING LIVES?

The administration sought to make homeownership another reward for hardworking and responsible public housing residents. The Quality Housing and Work Responsibility Act created an option to allow Section 8 recipients deemed "ready to take on homeownership" to use their vouchers toward mortgages rather than rental assistance. Over the ensuing years, this program would help a very limited number of recipients scattered throughout the country. In fact, just one person in the city of Chicago had used it by 2002.[85] In 1998, the administration secured $25 million for another small initiative, tellingly called the Play by the Rules program, which would assist approximately ten thousand families who were "responsible" and "paid their rent on time" become homeowners.[86]

The programs aligned with the Clinton administration's larger efforts to increase homeownership, especially among marginalized groups. In 1995, at Clinton's behest, HUD launched a public-private initiative called the National Homeownership Strategy, which aimed to create eight million new homeowners in the US by

2000. The program was a classic example of the New Democrats' "doing well by doing good" approach. It sought to address residential discrimination and the history of redlining while bolstering the housing industry and real estate market. Announcing the idea in an address to the National Association of Realtors, Clinton described how he wanted to "target new markets, underserved populations, tear down the barriers of discrimination wherever they are found," reach "the millions and millions and millions of people that the economy of the 1980's left behind," and "explode the American economic growth rate well into the next century."[87]

The hundred-point action plan focused on cutting production costs and liberalizing the private mortgage market by loosening lending standards and reducing down payment amounts to make mortgages and other housing loans more readily available.[88] HUD expressly directed Fannie Mae, Freddie Mac, and private mortgage brokers to expand credit options to "non-conforming borrowers," especially people of color, women, immigrants, married couples below the age of thirty-five, and public housing residents. HUD undersecretary Bruce Katz dubbed the strategy as a form of "trickle-up economics" that would create new jobs in construction, home sales, and related areas and at the same time offer new credit and opportunity to marginalized groups.[89] Many of the administration's economic officials, including Robert Rubin, also recognized the ways the strategy's "democratization of credit" could help lower interest rates, which had benefits for the entire economy, especially the financial services sector.[90]

The Clinton administration saw the strategy as yet another opportunity to use market-based tools to influence the behavior of public housing residents and members of other marginalized groups.[91] At the program's launch, Clinton contended that expanding homeownership would foster stability, lower crime, improve neighborhoods, and "reinforce family values in America, encourage two-parent households, get people to stay home."[92] The administration saw these forms of market disciplining as especially important for public housing recipients. HUD deemed the program as a way for public housing residents to "move up the ladder of success," "achieve economic self-sufficiency," and realize "the American Dream of private homeownership."[93] HUD acknowledged that it would be suitable only for residents who had stable employment (and clean criminal records), but in HUD's literature, they treated all people in public housing as potential homeowners. HUD suggested that even the promise of homeownership could make residents ascribe to middle-class norms. The program, HUD contended, would incentivize those who were unemployed or on welfare to "search more actively for paid employment" and "begin saving for a downpayment on their American Dream home."[94]

The National Homeownership Strategy, coupled with the Federal Reserve's lowering of interest rates, contributed to the United States achieving the highest rate of homeownership in history, surpassing the goal set by Clinton. By the middle of 2000, the homeownership rate was 67.7 percent, and 40 percent of the net new homeowners were people of color. In fact, the African American and Latinx homeownership rates grew twice as fast as the white homeownership rate.[95]

These rates, of course, would not continue to surge indefinitely and spiked in the other direction in 2007. The strategy and its emphasis on loosening the availability of credit and targeting marginalized groups was one of the many catalysts of the foreclosure crisis.[96] For millions of Americans, homeownership would prove not a source of upward mobility but the very opposite. The situation was all the more precarious because the public housing stock had dwindled so substantially that it was no longer an option to fall back on.

In the short term, the strategy helped a few public housing residents like Maria Givens, a single mother of two in Hamilton, Ohio. Givens pooled the income from her part-time job, child support, and public assistance, along with a lender who used the new flexible guidelines, to purchase her own home. "I love my house. It's something I always wanted. It's mine," Givens proudly declared.[97] However, the numbers of public housing residents able to take advantage of the program remained quite small.[98] In general, homeownership programs targeting public housing residents were very limited. HOPE VI itself included a few provisions for selling units in new developments to former residents. However, by the late 1990s, HUD put a much stronger emphasis on trying to recruit middle-class families to purchase homes in HOPE VI developments at market-rate prices. HUD both recognized the sales of the units could help fund the projects and believed middle-class homeowners would increase the stability of the developments and their surrounding neighborhoods. In promotional literature, HUD celebrated middle-class homeowners as "the bedrock of stable neighborhoods."[99] In such statements, HUD clearly tipped its hand.

The focus on luring middle-class residents to disinvested areas also continued to perpetuate the strong bias toward large cities like Chicago in HOPE VI and HUD's approach. This focus glossed over the fact that many smaller cities confronted the same, if not worse, economic and social problems and a similar shortage of subsidized housing.[100] For instance, in 1996 alone, HUD funded eight HOPE VI-affiliated projects in Chicago as opposed to three in Little Rock.[101] It funded none in Pine Bluff even though, by the late 1990s, the city had one of the nation's highest unemployment rates, and its violent crime and murder rate surpassed Chicago and every other city in the United States. The FBI uniform crime report in 1998 disclosed that Pine Bluff had 33.8 murders per 100,000 population; in second place was New Orleans, which had 22.1. The rate in United States as a whole was 6.3.[102] HUD did expressly single out Pine Bluff as one of the most extreme cases of poverty and unemployment in the country. Yet, the money the agency directed toward the city primarily focused on eliminating drug abuse and trafficking and crime in developments rather than producing new publicly funded units.[103] In fact, Cuomo declared the money, which was part of a national grant program, was focused on sending drug dealers to "another type of subsidized housing—a prison cell."[104] The turn of phrase reflected a deeper truth about the Clinton administration's priorities. The 1994 crime bill had contributed substantially to subsidizing a construction boom of state and federal correctional facilities, with a new prison opening every fifteen days in the mid-1990s.[105] Like many rural communities in the 1990s, Pine Bluff faced a substantial shortage of housing and jobs and began clinging to the growth in incarceration as an employment and economic development lifeline.[106]

In December 1999, HUD released a glossy booklet entitled *Hope VI: Building Communities, Transforming Lives*, which celebrated the success of HOPE VI and how it was "leading the way" for the bold reforms created by the 1998 housing law. The booklet included several before and after photographs of HOPE VI projects. The images further solidified the links between public housing and mass incarceration by juxtaposing large brutalist high-rises built in what it described as "penal colony modern" with tasteful New Urbanist rowhouses. HUD suggested that HOPE VI was liberating public housing residents from buildings that "were institutional—punitive—in both form and function" and "walled off from the surrounding community." It also stressed that the designs of the new projects had physical elements to improve security and foster community and several had resident patrols and other crime-prevention programs. HUD suggested that HOPE VI did not just liberate deserving and innocent public housing residents who had been "trapped" in buildings that looked like prisons and in "neighborhoods where gangs and drugs have long been entrenched." It was also freeing them from the lack of choice that came with involuntary confinement by giving them vouchers to decide where they wanted to live.[107] The booklet did not, however, mention the fact that formerly incarcerated people and their families would be ineligible for either HOPE VI housing or vouchers. And despite what the images of racially diverse faces smiling in the booklet might have tried to convey, the majority of public housing residents did not find the program liberating. Instead, it created a sense of confusion and outrage. Chicago would once again serve as the pacesetter.

From 1993 to 1998, Chicago received $150 million in HOPE VI funding, which was more than any other city in the nation. Much of the funding went to the infamous State Street Corridor. In addition to the funds to transform Cabrini-Green, in 1996 alone, Chicago got $18.4 million for the Henry Horner Homes, $24.5 million

Before being demolished, one of the Cabrini-
Green towers stands in the background of the
mixed-income townhouses and apartments that
HOPE VI ushered in to replace it, 2003
Credit: Reuters/Frank Polich

for the ABLA, and $25 million for the Robert Taylor Homes.[108]
Far more difficult than constructing new mixed-income developments was relocating former residents. The Robert Taylor Homes
brought that challenge into sharp relief.

CHA envisioned turning the site where the twenty-eight buildings stood into a light industrial park with some mixed-income
housing as well. CHA planned to gradually tear down the high-
rises, focusing first on the most decaying and gang-ridden ones.

At the time, the adult population of the Robert Taylor Homes was 99 percent African American, 96 percent unemployed, and 50 percent living on less than $5,000 a year. Many had disabilities, and few ventured outside its confines to other parts of the city.[109] Residents like Juanita Williams had lived in their units for decades and feared losing their building's strong sense of community. Some did not see the announcements or willfully ignored the notices and meetings about relocating.[110] The process of relocating proved challenging even for those residents willing to participate. Many residents found themselves in a double bind as they were disqualified from returning to their rebuilt developments or from other public housing projects due to their criminal and drug histories or that of their families. Even those Robert Taylor residents who did not have records faced difficulties.

Most residents hoped to receive vouchers to use in the private market, but many had lived in public housing for most of their lives and had little to no experience navigating the rental market. Though CHA hired a private relocation agency to help tenants with the process, such coaching did little to persuade landlords not to discriminate and reject public housing residents.[111] The Coalition to Protect Public Housing estimated in the late 1990s that about 30 percent of the families issued vouchers could not find housing.[112] Even residents who did receive vouchers experienced other problems. For instance, former Robert Taylor resident Katie Sistrunk used her voucher to move to an apartment in Rogers Park in Chicago's Far North Side. While there were no gunshots on her new block, she missed her old neighborhood and worried relocation was causing estrangement among her large and close-knit family.[113] The upheaval was but a preview, as the city resumed control of the Housing Authority at the turn of the twenty-first century.

REINVENTION OF CHICAGO

HUD's oversight of the Chicago Housing Authority created the kind of straightening up and cleaning of house it hoped for. By the end of 1998, HUD took CHA off its "troubled list" and announced it was ready to give control back to the city, contingent on it developing a plan for the future.[114] Mayor Richard Daley saw the transfer as a chance to create an even bolder plan, which could get rid of the large high-rises once and for all and facilitate the further economic redevelopment and revitalization of the city. In late 1999, Chicago unveiled the Plan for Transformation, which proposed clearing all the city's remaining high-rise projects and put mixed-income housing in their place. It would reduce the city's public housing stock by thirteen thousand units.[115] The plan also pledged to further reduce the size of CHA and privatize the management of the developments.[116] HUD approved the plan and made a commitment to provide the Chicago Housing Authority $1.5 billion over ten years for the program. Chicago planned to pay for the rest through a combination of tax breaks and private sector investment. "The only way to get public benefits funded," Julie Stasch, the main architect of the plan, explained, "is by harnessing the market motives of private entities."[117] Her comment reflected both the political realities of the late 1990s and the fact that the Plan for Transformation had a host of profit-making opportunities for private industry.

CHA quickly discovered that these "market motives" did not offer much appeal to the nearly one hundred thousand public housing residents facing relocation due to the Plan for Transformation. The relocation process quickly confronted the same challenges that had occurred at the Robert Taylor Homes and other HOPE VI projects, only on a much vaster scale. CHA assumed that residents would see leaving their run-down buildings as the most rational decision. Equally rational, many people wanted to stay put in a familiar place where they had an existing social network. City officials also operated with an optimistic view of just how free and open the city's private housing market was.[118] Many observers voiced immediate concerns that Chicago's rental market would not be able to handle the new demand, especially because Chicago had an overall rental vacancy rate of less than 5 percent, and the percentage of available affordable units was even lower.[119]

Landlords also consistently discriminated against former public housing residents, further circumscribing where residents could relocate. As a consequence, between 1995 and 2002, 82 percent of the displaced families using vouchers moved to neighborhoods that were more than 90 percent African American and half moved to neighborhoods with poverty rates in excess of 30 percent.[120] An independent monitor brought in to evaluate the relocation process charged that the "vertical ghettoes from which the families are being moved are being replaced with horizontal ghettos, located in well defined, highly segregated neighborhoods on the west and south sides."[121] Despite this sharp warning, the problem persisted.

The new mixed-income developments of HOPE VI and the Plan for Transformation offered little solace to those forced to move out of their homes. It took years for the projects to break ground, and even when they did, they offered very few units for low-income residents. CHA subjected applicants wanting to return to the new developments to a rigorous screening process that built directly on the behavioral provisions of the 1998 federal housing law. CHA required work or enrollment in school or a job-training program and screened out applicants with a criminal background, a pattern of drug or alcohol abuse, delinquent bills, and debt or whose children had a high rate of school absences.[122] It is difficult to calculate the exact number of residents who returned to the new developments on the sites where they once lived, but many estimates place it at around 11 percent.[123] While Chicago officials celebrated the reduction of poverty in the areas surrounding the HOPE VI and Plan for Transformation projects, a closer look showed the programs were merely pushing problems into other parts of the city.

No place better represented the tensions created by the new laws than South Shore. Starting in 1996, the home of ShoreBank absorbed the largest share of former public housing residents of any neighborhood in the city.[124] South Shore proved popular with residents from the high-rises because of its relative proximity to the location of the former South Side projects and large stock of multifamily buildings and affordable apartments.[125] South Shore residents, especially the ma-and-pa rehabbers who had long been

the bread and butter of ShoreBank's model, voiced fears that the
new tenants would drag down the neighborhood and blamed them
for a whole host of problems, from noise violations to overcrowd-
ing in the local schools. Revealing clear class prejudices, one resident complained that her building used to be "beautiful" but now
"there's drugs, people hanging out on the corner. I can't let my
grandson go out there to play."[126] Milton Davis of ShoreBank observed "that stigma of the CHA breeds the fear" of this resident and
others.[127] These tensions would only worsen in the coming years
as it coincided with other economic pressures on the community.

CHAPTER 8

PUBLIC SCHOOLS ARE OUR MOST IMPORTANT BUSINESS

In early 1997, Vice President Al Gore solidified his reputation as the "geek veep" and the quintessential Atari Democrat when he began organizing monthly meetings with leading executives and entrepreneurs from Silicon Valley.[1] The so-called Gore-Tech sessions often took place over pizza and beer, and Gore hoped for them to be a chance for the administration to learn from innovators of the New Economy and come up with practical solutions to important public policy issues.[2] One of these meetings focused on the problems of public education and the growing achievement gap between affluent white suburbanites and students of color in the inner city, which had the Clinton administration, among others, worried. Gore asked the participants: "If you Silicon Valley types are so smart, why can't you do something to create new schools?"[3]

The challenge gave venture capitalist John Doerr, who had become Gore's closest tech advisor, an idea. Doerr, a partner at the legendary venture capital firm Kleiner Perkins, was one of the most powerful figures in Silicon Valley with a knack for funding technology start-ups. He counted Netscape, Amazon, and Google as some of his many successes.[4] He firmly believed that a tech- and information-based economy relied on an educated citizenry. "Forty percent of eight-year-olds can't read," he observed. "If you can't read, you can't run a Web browser. You just fall further and further behind."[5] The tools of venture capital, Doerr thought, might offer a way to build new and better schools based on Silicon Valley's principles of accountability, choice, and competition.[6] "I guess if you are a carpenter with a hammer everything looks like a nail," he later explained.[7]

Doerr decided to pool money from several other Silicon Valley icons to start the NewSchools Venture Fund. NewSchools sat at the forefront of the concepts of venture philanthropy. Often known by the neologism *philanthrocapitalism*, venture or strategic philanthropy focused on taking tools from the private sector, especially entrepreneurialism, venture capitalism, and management consulting—the key ingredients in the 1990s tech boom—and applying them to philanthropic work. These new philanthropists like the founders of NewSchools and Bill and Melinda Gates—who owed their wealth in part to the growth-oriented policies of the Clinton administration—represented another way the New Democrats facilitated the spread of the "doing well by doing good" ethos.

Doerr and the NewSchools Fund became especially focused on charter schools, which the Clinton administration and the DLC were similarly encouraging in the 1990s. The New Democrats and their allies in Silicon Valley saw charters as an entrepreneurial and innovative way to improve public education, especially among low-income students of color in struggling urban schools who were at risk of being left behind by the knowledge-based tech-oriented economy. These efforts would not just lead to the substantial growth of charters but would also deepen ties between the tech industry and the Democratic Party at the end of the twentieth century.

There is a wide assumption that Republican politicians and donors—who wanted to privatize education—were the driving force behind the charter movement.[8] In fact, Republicans were largely late to the game on charters and through much of the 1990s promoted school vouchers as their favored form of school choice. The roots of charters lie deeper in the New Democrats' quest to reinvent the public sector and promote technology-based education as a route toward economic growth. This encouragement of charters demonstrates the New Democrats' effort to remake another core liberal issue—public education—in market-based terms. It also marked the New Democrats' long-standing goal of reorienting the base and priorities of the Democratic Party away from so-called special interests like organized labor and toward the engineers and entrepreneurs of Silicon Valley.

The Clinton administration and their allies in the tech industry and the DLC always emphasized that one of the things they liked most about charters was that the schools were not about making a profit. Rather, charters drew on market-oriented techniques of competition and data-based accountability purportedly to make the larger public school system more effective and better serve the needs of vulnerable students who were being "left behind." Clinton's successor George W. Bush would take up similar ideas and phrasing in the landmark No Child Left Behind legislation passed in 2001. The rise of the charter movement in the Clinton era proved critical in injecting the ideas of the private sector and language of the marketplace into discussions of education and making learning ever more focused on incentives and results. Like microenterprise and HOPE VI, charters served as another way the New Democrats embraced the seemingly neutral language and techniques of the market to impose meritocratic middle-class norms on poor people of color living in distressed communities.

Charters clearly had benefits for the tech industry and the New Democrats. For Silicon Valley luminaries like John Doerr and Netflix founder Reed Hastings, charters offered both an investment in a better-educated workforce in the future and a way to have a direct influence on policy issues. For Clinton, Gore, and other New Democrats, the issue became a way to earn the loyalty and campaign donations of what was increasingly becoming the pivotal sector of the economy. It also provided a means to enlist tech entrepreneurs and their foundations to bankroll new public schools, which had been traditionally the responsibility of government. Clinton, Gore, and the New Democrats liked to portray the issue of charters as another example of a win-win. The issue was ultimately more zero-sum. New Democrats and Silicon Valley tycoons became the winners at the direct expense of both teachers' unions and the nation's most vulnerable and marginalized students. Tracing the rise of charter schools reveals how efforts to harness the tools of the market and the values of the tech industry to promote equality came to do the opposite and weakened a key component of the social safety net in the process.

BUILDING A BRIDGE

Clinton and his advisors opted to make "building a bridge to the 21st century" the organizing metaphor of his 1996 reelection bid. The optimistic slogan was in part a subtle dig at his septuagenarian opponent Bob Dole. But it also embodied Clinton's relentless focus on the future. In the post–Cold War era, the metaphor aimed to give the nation the unifying goal and mission of transcending the nation's racial, class, and geographic divisions. The bridge imagery also represented Clinton and Gore's efforts to tighten its connections to the tech industry. Silicon Valley entrepreneurs, in fact, welcomed it as a validation of their role in late twentieth-century economic and social life.

Forging connections with the tech industry had been a key priority for the New Democrats from the start. Al Gore had played a leading role in that effort. Dating back to his time in the Senate, Gore evangelized about how computers provided key opportunities for expanding education, democracy, and economic growth.[9] Even if he didn't "invent the internet," Gore had played an essential role in expanding the nation's telecommunications infrastructure or the "information superhighway" as he christened it.[10] Gore brought this commitment to the 1992 presidential campaign. The Clinton-Gore ticket's support for tech and internet proved a key way to cultivate support and donations from Silicon Valley execs, whose pockets were quite deep but who had traditionally skewed Republican.[11]

To keep the momentum going during their first month in office, Clinton and Gore traveled to Silicon Valley to release their technology initiative called Technology for America's Economic Growth. The plan included many of the ideas that Atari Democrats had been floating for more than a decade, including $17 billion in investment in technological research, a corporate research and development tax credit, and funds for expanding "the national information infrastructure."[12] These policies abetted the further development of Silicon Valley industry and the internet. Over Clinton's first term, the tech sector expanded exponentially and proved an important driver of the nation's larger economic growth. From 1992 to 1996, Silicon Valley gained 3,100 new businesses, and the first IPOs of tech businesses were making billions. John Doerr declared the boom "the largest legal creation of wealth in the history of the planet" and *Newsweek* named 1995 "The Year of the Internet."[13] The internet would continue its exponential growth, especially after the Clinton administration helped push through passage of the Telecommunications Act of 1996, which encouraged competition and removed barriers between telephones, cable, and internet markets.

As he faced reelection, Clinton sought to tap the new wealth and power of Silicon Valley. The DLC proved to be a willing partner in this effort. Al From and the DLC recognized how the tech industry's entrepreneurial-based economic growth, opposition to bureaucracy, and antipathy to unions aligned with the New Democrats' core principles. To further facilitate these connections, From hired an ambitious operative, Wade Randlett, to further flip the Valley to the Democrats and the DLC.[14] Randlett knew that the first person he had to reach out to was John Doerr.

Doerr was as much a true believer in the ideals and far-reaching potential of the internet and New Economy as Al Gore. "The New Economy isn't just about high-tech products," Doerr liked to say. "It's about the politics of education, constant innovation and unlimited growth" and a nonhierarchical meritocracy where "the best ideas win."[15] He believed that the internet had the power to fuel unprecedented economic growth, social change, and income redistribution.[16] Although a registered Republican, he had been mostly apolitical, save for a brief stint in the summer of 1986 when he went to Capitol Hill and worked with Atari Democrat Tim Wirth on defense-related technology.[17] But in 1996, he was undergoing a political awakening as he led a campaign against a California ballot measure that would lower the barrier to shareholder class-action lawsuits. He had raised $40 million and turned the sleek Sand Hill Road office of Kleiner Perkins into a virtual war room. Although Clinton was initially reluctant to weigh in, Doerr donated to the re-election campaign and secured endorsements and donations from seventy-five other major tech executives, including Steve Jobs.[18] The president spoke out against the ballot measure; it went down in flames, and Clinton, of course, won re-election by a landslide. The experience whetted Doerr's appetite to make Silicon Valley more politically powerful and have more of a say on policy. One clear way to do this was to become even closer with the White House.[19]

In January 1997, Doerr along with twelve other Valley leaders flew to Washington to attend Clinton's second inauguration. When Clinton affirmed how "the forces of the Information Age" would "unleash the limitless potential of all our people" and called on the country to "build our bridge" to the twenty-first century, he seemed to be talking directly to the tech group.[20] Doerr was also heartened by Clinton's renewed promises to reinvent government. He believed it aligned with his own view and, more broadly, that of Silicon Valley, which he explained as: "We want less government, but we want it to be more effective."[21] The day before he gave the speech, Clinton and Gore met with Doerr and the Silicon Valley delegation to thank them for their support during the election. Clinton's appearance in the ornate White House conference room was relatively brief. But Gore stayed on for another two hours and "wowed" the group with his nuanced understanding of the tech industry.[22] The feeling was apparently mutual. Just weeks after the meeting, Gore and Doerr began hosting their monthly Gore-Tech sessions with executives and entrepreneurs from Silicon Valley's

most cutting-edge companies (many of them disciples or beneficiaries of Doerr).[23] Gore continued to impress the executives and
entrepreneurs. "We don't have to talk down to him" noted Marc
Andreessen, the cofounder of Netscape who regularly attended
the meetings. "He has a very good conceptual understanding of
technology."[24]

The conversations, nevertheless, quickly veered from a solely
technology-based agenda. The topic of education especially interested many of the executives. Computer companies had long
understood that getting a foothold in the nation's schools was a
potential goldmine.[25] Many Valley CEOs also bemoaned the lack
of a better-educated domestic workforce. They worried that the
perceived low quality of public education in science, math, and engineering, especially in California, hurt their ability to recruit the
best workers.[26] The New Democrats, influenced by the research of
Robert Reich, long touted the related argument that having better-
educated students could fuel postindustrial economic growth.
Thus, education was a way for both the nation and Silicon Valley to
do well by doing good and simultaneously help young people and
the economy as a whole. As the participants at the Gore-Tech sessions took up education reform, the conversation quickly turned
to the topic of charter schools, which were a favorite reform tool
of the president.[27]

FROM SCHOOL CHOICE TO CHARTER SCHOOLS

The mythology surrounding charter schools' origins often con-
jures images of a bottom-up assault on the failing behemoth of
American public education. But the rise of charter schools came
less from the grassroots and more from Democratic policymakers
and politicians at the national and state levels, well-known figures
like economist Milton Friedman and Albert Shanker, longtime
head of the American Federation of Teachers (AFT), and organizations like the DLC.

The release of the National Commission on Excellence in
Education's report *A Nation at Risk* in 1983 brought a renewed

urgency to the perennial topic of K–12 public education reform. However, there was a disagreement about the best way to enact improvements. Many liberal policymakers and education experts called for even more federal spending, and some urged reforms like stricter graduation requirements, a return to the basics, and a greater emphasis on test scores, similar to what Clinton pursued in Arkansas.[28] Still others began to argue that the solution lay in providing more choices.

Despite (or because of) its seemingly neutral-sounding name, the concept of school choice had a racially fraught history. During the era of massive resistance to school integration, many southern school officials sought to avoid integration by creating "freedom of choice" policies. These policies technically allowed students to enroll in any public school in the district, but in reality, they became a way to maintain the segregated status quo. Several districts went even further, encouraging the creation of private schools for white students that became known as "schools of choice" or "segregation academies."[29] Friedman also puzzled over the issue of school choice. Like the leaders of the massive resistance movement, the University of Chicago economist opposed government intrusion in education. He believed that the government should fund education but should not have oversight over it. In 1955, he published the article "The Role of Government in Education," which proposed the federal government supply vouchers to all students so that they could attend the school of their choice. Friedman argued that such a system would create competition that would improve schools and offer students and their parents a wider range of choices.[30]

The voucher idea didn't really gain serious political traction until the 1970s when Ronald Reagan took up the idea in his quest for national office.[31] After becoming president, Reagan championed several voucher proposals, but they provoked strong opposition from the Democratic-controlled Congress and never passed. Despite the resistance to vouchers, the larger idea of choice intrigued many liberal school reformers. In the 1970s and 1980s, several urban school districts experimented with school choice programs as a way to create more racial integration in the wake of the failures of mandatory desegregation. In 1988, Minnesota became the first state to institute a choice policy at the statewide level with Arkansas following closely behind.[32] These programs would lay the groundwork for charter schools.

Shanker, head of the AFT, the nation's largest teachers' union, was the first person to make the idea of charters truly part of the national discussion.[33] While unionization overall steadily declined in the United States beginning in the late 1950s, the inverse was true of public sector workers, especially teachers. In cities and states throughout the country, teachers' unions were able to secure collective bargaining rights.[34] The AFT and its counterpart, the National Education Association, also became an increasingly powerful force in Democratic Party politics, credited with playing a major role in Jimmy Carter's victory and his decision to establish the Department of Education in 1979. Yet, both Reagan's win and the findings of *A Nation of Risk* had put the teachers' unions on their heels.

Shanker was troubled by the growing momentum around vouchers and also believed that schools needed more systemic reform led by teachers. He learned of a somewhat obscure idea from an education professor named Ray Budde: a program where districts would grant a "charter" to teachers who wanted to take risks and explore new approaches.[35] Shanker built on that model to create his own proposal for charter schools in 1988. He envisioned that small groups of teachers could create "schools within schools" where they could experiment and then could share what they learned, which would help improve public schools writ large.[36] He believed that teachers' unions would play a central role at all stages—from approving plans to ensuring the schools maintained protections like collective bargaining. Shanker took his idea on the road, stopping in Minnesota where it caught the attention of a group of policy reformers and legislators who decided to transform the charter concept into a piece of state legislation. Though it built on Shanker's idea, the bill confronted immediate opposition from Minnesota teachers' unions, who saw it as a threat to public education and rights of teachers. The unions mobilized an aggressive countercampaign, but the legislation passed by a razor-thin margin in 1991.[37]

The DLC celebrated the Minnesota law. The organization had become one of the earliest promoters of charter schools, recognizing how the idea fit in with their goals of upsetting old bureaucratic modes of governance and limiting the power of organized labor in the Democratic Party. As the Minnesota legislature was still debating the charter issue, the DLC commissioned Ted Kolderie, who was one of the bill's leading architects, to write a report entitled *Beyond Choice to New Public Schools*, released in 1990, which touted charter schools as a "simple yet radical" way to "introduce choice, competition and innovation into America's public school system."[38] Clinton had recently become DLC chair. As he went around the country building support for the organization, he made charters a key example to demonstrate how the New Democrats offered an alternative to the traditional Democratic and Republican way of doing business.[39] Clinton would make a similar case in his bid for the presidency in 1992.

By the early 1990s, the GOP had reframed the voucher issue. Instead of focusing on deregulation and privatization, many Republican politicians and their conservative think tank allies contended that vouchers were a means to "empower low-income families" and give them the chance to receive quality schooling.[40] The Republicans' case strengthened when African American parents and educators in Milwaukee began pushing for voucher programs to allow low-income students in Milwaukee to attend private schools. As part of his effort to placate the conservative wing of the party and also potentially make inroads within urban Black constituencies, George H. W. Bush promised to create vouchers for all children during the 1992 election.[41] The Clinton campaign latched onto charters as the best counterpoint. Clinton stressed that he also wanted to create more options but wanted a model that would strengthen rather than abandon public schools. The argument worked. Vouchers proved unpopular with a large part of the electorate. Yet, many white middle-class moderates—whom the New Democrats were desperate to woo—liked the idea of having more choice over their children's education.

Clinton's victory in 1992 would ensure that charters had a very high-profile champion. By that time, charters were still a relatively obscure idea. When Clinton took office, City Academy in St. Paul was the only charter school in operation in the United States. And California, which in 1992 became the second state to allow charters, set a cap on the number of schools that could be established at a hundred. In a state that had more than eight thousand public schools, it thereby constituted a drop in the bucket. That would soon change.

Throughout his presidency, Bill Clinton liked to cite the number of charter schools that opened during his time to suggest his critical role in this growth. While the administration did not deserve full credit for the growth of charters, it did play a significant role. David Osborne, the coauthor of *Reinventing Government*, became a major champion of charters and later observed that Clinton's stated commitment to charters became "hugely important politically" and "hugely important practically."[42] He was referring to the Clinton administration's Public Charter School Program, passed in 1994, which provided new seed capital for opening charter schools.[43]

After the Republican takeover of Congress, the Clinton administration redoubled its commitment to charter schools. Newt Gingrich and his allies intensified the campaign for vouchers, and Clinton staffers recognized that charter schools remained one way to counter the push. In internal memos sent at the end of 1995, officials at the Department of Education advocated for placing "charter schools at the center of education reform discussions." Staffers intimated that the issue upheld the president's DLC-style commitment to creating a "leaner, more responsive government that catalyzes and supports grass roots, community initiatives."[44]

The DLC itself buttressed these suggestions. Throughout the 1990s, the DLC assumed the self-described role as "proselytizers" of charters.[45] It promoted the idea at DLC events and to its state chapters, underscoring that they were a "good example of the Third Way," which provided "two-way accountability" downward to parents and upward to the state and district.[46] The organization published a flurry of policy memos, articles, and newsletters connecting charters to its larger priorities of inserting more opportunity, responsibility, and competition into the public sector.[47] In 1994, the DLC's think tank, the Progressive Policy Institute, produced a handbook on how to spread the charter movement called *Blueprint for Change*. The guide included a draft bill for states that had not yet passed charter laws and advice for how to get such legislation enacted. The DLC went around the country working with state-level New Democrats in places like Colorado and Massachusetts to help pass charter school legislation and promote the cause.

The 1994 midterm elections only heightened the DLC's commitment to charters as both a policy solution and a political strategy for Clinton and the Democrats. Weeks after the election, Al From publicly declared that charter schools were central to the New Democrat politics that Clinton needed to adopt to win reelection in 1996. From called on him to "grab the mantle" of charters and school choice for the Democrats.[48] Privately, From stressed to the president that charter schools, along with welfare reform, were the most important ways to show his willingness to challenge "the old liberal Democratic Party orthodoxy" and special interest groups like organized labor.[49] Charters could appeal to the white moderate suburbanites whom the DLC believed to be critical to Clinton's reelection bid and who purportedly cared deeply about improving education. Clinton heeded this advice and made charters a key part of his education agenda as he developed the main themes of his reelection effort. The 1996 State of the Union was most notable for Clinton's declaration that the "era of big government is over." Elaborating on that theme, he also dared "every state to give all parents the right to choose which public school their children will attend; and to let teachers form new schools with a charter they can keep only if they do a good job."[50]

In promoting charters, the Clinton administration routinely praised the flexibility of the model—how it largely left it up to states to develop their own laws and individual schools to develop their own structure and focus. In practice, this meant that states adopted a wide variety of requirements, and a wide array of different types of schools emerged. The charters that incorporated in the mid-1990s ranged from those for at-risk Black and Latinx high school dropouts in urban neighborhoods to ones for affluent students in white suburban neighborhoods, from those with an African American–centered curriculum to ones that placed technological literacy at the center of their mission.

The Clinton administration did not promote all charters equally but became particularly focused on ones intended to serve poor children of color in urban areas. Bill and Hillary Clinton became particularly enamored with the Vaughn Next Century Learning Center in Los Angeles, which they promoted as a standard-bearer for how charters could improve public education efficiently in low-income communities. The school sat in Pacoima, which was one of the poorest parts of the city with increasing gang activity, drug use, and crimes. It primarily served the children of recent immigrants from Mexico and Central America who had limited English language skills and almost every student received free or reduced lunch.[51] Vaughn had a dynamic principal named Yvonne Chan who saw herself as "equal parts entrepreneur, politician and educator."[52] She abided by the mantra that "you can't be a school that just educates. You have to be a school that cares."[53] Putting that philosophy into practice, she focused attention on high parental and community involvement to get Vaughn to achieve high attendance rates and scores on state standardized tests. In its first year of operation, the school managed to create a $1.2 million budget surplus, which it used enhance its technology curriculum and build a computer lab on an adjacent lot by bulldozing a purported crackhouse.[54] Over the next few years, Vaughn racked up several awards and national media attention, and Chan earned acclaim as one of the "talented educators in America" and became a national spokesperson for the charter movement.[55]

Further burnishing Vaughn's image, Hillary Clinton selected the school as a stop to promote her book *It Takes a Village* in February 1996. The book focused on how families needed support from the larger community to raise children. According to nine-year-old Kathy Mariscal, Clinton chose Vaughn because "our school is like her book. It takes a village."[56] A reporter noted it helped that the school had a "'we are the world'" ethnic makeup, which made it perfect for a photo-op.[57] During the visit, Clinton toured a kindergarten computer class and met with fourth-, fifth-, and sixth-graders for a question-and-answer session, during which she showered praise on the school.[58] In subsequent speeches, the First Lady celebrated the level of parental and teacher involvement and deemed Vaughn "a village of caring."[59] The following year, Chan shared the stage with Bill Clinton and Al Gore at an education summit, where she impressed and charmed them as well. Clinton remarked that Chan showed how the charter school movement offered students "the power to change their own lives."[60]

The Clintons' heralding of Vaughn in many ways paralleled their promotion of community development banking and micro-enterprise. The first couple routinely highlighted the stories of low-income people of color who aligned with middle-class merito-cratic values of hard work, discipline, and academic achievement. This focus often obscured the substantial hardships and lack of success of many other charter schools. Vaughn itself faced dif-ficulties, especially a decline in its test scores after its first cou-ple of years. Skeptics and sympathetic observers alike questioned how dependent the school was on its charismatic principal and a set of other exceptional circumstances that would be difficult to replicate.[61] These questions were emerging not just about Vaughn and revealed that Bill Clinton's glowing calls for the transforma-tive power of charters to create individual and systemic change represented another case of him exaggerating a small solution to address a much larger structural problem. As his administra-tion began to intensify such arguments, the doubts from skeptics would follow suit.

The teachers' unions were first in line. The National Education Association (NEA), which was the larger of the nation's two teachers' unions with over two million members, was from the start a sharp critic of the schools. Al Shanker still thought that charters were preferable to vouchers, but by the mid-1990s, he believed the movement had deviated from his original idea and could be creating "a public form of privatization."[62] He and his staff grew worried that the wide range of different laws, standards, and oversight could exacerbate inequalities.[63] Aware that the majority of states' laws did not provide collective bargaining rights to teachers at charters and only a handful required that teachers be certified, the AFT was especially concerned the charters would dilute labor rights and union strength.[64] In private communication, AFT leaders expressed unease about the DLC's leading role in the charter school movement and voiced concern that the DLC did "not really care deeply" about the ways in which the charter movement could potentially undermine union power.[65]

The African American community's response to the charter issues also reflected the growing divisions and complex questions the schools raised. Several groups of Black educational activists across the country embraced the charter legislation to create African American–centered schools like Betty Shabazz International Charter School in Chicago, Nataki Talibah Schoolhouse in Detroit, and the West Oakland Community School. These schools emerged from the Black independent schools movement of the 1960s and 1970s. The founders believed that the concept of charters could create a sense of community control and self-determination they had long worked for, gain access to state funds for students of color, and provide African American parents a sense of choice long denied to them.[66] Representatives from other civil rights groups, including the NAACP and MALDEF, were far more skeptical. Activists voiced fears that the schools would only intensify the problems of educational inequality and magnify racial segregation by skimming parents and funds from traditional public schools and leaving other students of color in urban school districts "to sink or swim."[67] These critics also stressed there was no proof that charters were doing much to significantly lessen the achievement gap or reduce the unequitable allocation of public education funds.[68]

Clinton's decision to make charters a part of his reelection campaign in 1996 placed representatives from progressive groups, especially teachers' unions, in a difficult position. Like the larger labor movement, the Republican takeover of Congress motivated teachers' unions to intensify their political mobilization and focus on Clinton's reelection. The NEA had the largest share of delegates of any single organization at the 1996 Democratic National Convention in Chicago while its political action committee raised over $5 million to support Clinton.[69] Despite this clout, the NEA did not significantly challenge the official party platform, which called for expanding public school choice by promoting charter schools, nor did the union delegates vocally boo or hiss at Clinton's mention of charters in his acceptance address.[70] The teachers' unions' concerns about charters clearly did little to deter the Clinton administration from promoting the schools. In fact, after winning reelection, Clinton set a goal of having three thousand charter schools across the country by 2001. The quest to achieve that benchmark was abetted by the administration's bond with the tech industry, which had grown ever tighter after the 1996 election. Clinton and Gore were increasingly demonstrating that it was Silicon Valley entrepreneurs—not teachers' unions—who offered both the Democratic Party and the economy a bridge to the twenty-first century.

LIFTING THE CAP

On Friday, September 19, 1997, the Clintons dropped off their daughter Chelsea for her freshman year at Stanford University. The next morning, the first couple arrived at the gymnasium at the San Carlos Charter Learning Center, which was just a short drive from Palo Alto, to host a roundtable discussion about charter schools.[71] The school had received the first California state charter five years earlier. Bill Clinton opened the event by heralding his own early commitment to charter schools as a mechanism that allowed for innovation in public education. Clinton celebrated how charters like San Carlos and its founder Don Shalvey were "bringing new life, new energy, and new creativity into public education" and suggested "every school in the country has got to become like this one."[72] The San Carlos event galvanized momentum for charter schools. But in typical Silicon Valley fashion, the most important developments came in the informal networking that took place after the Clintons rushed off to three back-to-back fundraisers—including a $10,000 per plate lunch at an upscale San Francisco restaurant and a $50,000 per plate dinner at the mansion of Halsey Minor, the CEO of the media company C/NET.[73]

As the Clintons' motorcade sped away from the San Carlos Charter Learning Center, a thirty-something man with a goatee and Birkenstocks approached Shalvey and asked him, "Do you ever think that there'll be more than a hundred charter schools in California?"[74] The man was entrepreneur Reed Hastings. After graduating from college, Hastings spent three years as a Peace Corps volunteer teaching in Swaziland. He went on to get a master's degree in engineering and then founded a company called Pure Software, which he sold in early 1997 for roughly $750 million. With some time on his hands, he began studying education.[75] Hastings announced that he planned to begin a "new career in school reform" and enrolled in a master's program in education at Stanford, becoming by far the wealthiest student.[76] His coursework proved critical to convincing him that expanding charter schools offered a long-term solution to the nation's education crisis.[77]

Attending the San Carlos roundtable further persuaded Hastings of the need to increase the number of charters, especially in California. He knew, nevertheless, that the state's cap limited the number to a hundred, which it had reached in 1996.[78] There had been several attempts in the state legislature to raise the cap, but none had passed.[79] Hastings became increasingly convinced that a ballot initiative was the only way to get the cap lifted. Yet, as an education neophyte, he recognized that he would need someone like Shalvey to give the plan credibility, which was why he had chosen to approach him at the event.[80] Shalvey told him that he did not think it was possible to lift the cap, but Hastings persisted and eventually persuaded Shalvey to help him lead the campaign.

Soon after the roundtable, Hastings and Shalvey founded the organization Californians for Public School Excellence and hatched plans for their ballot initiative. They drew on Hastings's funds and connections to hire the state's most politically influential and seasoned lawyers, consultants, and lobbyists.[81] Hastings was also trying to start his new company Netflix (which led him to drop out of the master's program), but he still found time to raise substantial funds through his personal and professional networks, reaching out to many of the executives who had been participating in the Gore-Tech meetings. By the time they formally launched the campaign for the Charter Public Schools Initiative a few months after they met at the roundtable, Hastings and Shalvey had secured $15 million in funding.[82]

Assuming that vouchers more aptly fit with the libertarian and promarket ethos of the tech industry, some observers voiced surprise that a Silicon Valley entrepreneur like Hastings would support charters. But he maintained that he had a firm commitment to public education. "Vouchers are fundamentally about escaping public education, and I just don't believe in that," Hasting explained. "Charter schools are about improving the public school system."[83] He believed charters could inject the bedrock Silicon Valley values of innovation, competition, and accountability into public education.[84] There were some tech figures who favored vouchers. Venture capitalist Tim Draper pursued a quixotic quest to get a voucher measure on the California ballot into the next century.[85] Yet, many other Silicon Valley tycoons shared Hastings's belief that expanding the number of charter schools was the best way to revolutionize the existing education bureaucracy. The charter campaign earned the strong support of TechNet. The recently formed political action committee was founded by John Doerr and led by Wade Randlett, which like the Gore-Tech sessions focused on building closer relationships between technology executives and political leaders. The ballot initiative constituted TechNet's first serious venture into campaigning, and the deep-pocketed committee put up $3 million. "We can spend as much as it takes," Randlett warned the teachers' unions, whose members were beginning to organize in opposition to the measure.[86]

Representatives of the California Teachers Association and California Federation of Teachers were strongly against lifting the cap. The unions argued that charters were still at the experimental stage, and there was no empirical data to show that they enhanced educational opportunity. Union representatives also charged any new charter law should include more significant rights for teachers and school employees and require all teachers at the schools to have credentials.[87] The unions were well aware of the power of a deep-pocketed ballot initiative campaign in California as well as the clout of the tech sector.[88] The campaign also raised anxiety among members of the state legislature who favored creating policies through the legislative process rather than by voter referendum.[89] State assembly member Ted Lampert proposed that Hastings and Shalvey and the teachers' unions representatives come to the bargaining table to reach a legislative compromise.[90] Eventually, the two sides reached agreement on a bill that would increase the number of charters in the state from 250 immediately and add an additional 100 each year after that. While it still left the decision of giving teachers collective bargaining rights up to individual charter schools, it contained stricter credentialing requirements for charters, which union representatives saw as a win.[91] The California legislature approved it by a wide margin.

Governor Pete Wilson signed the bill at a ceremony on the playground at the San Carlos Learning Center on May 13, 1998, surrounded by the leading lights of the tech industry. Wilson praised the Silicon Valley figures for "demanding the same principles that govern their world-class operations" would be applied to the state's education system.[92] Wilson's kowtowing to the Valley entrepreneurs demonstrated their influence. "It took us just 45 days. Forty-five days and three and a half million dollars—yeah, I think people will pay attention when we raise other [education] issues," boasted Randlett. Hastings was slightly less arrogant.

"The initiative tipped the balance," he declared, "and made Sacramento understand it would be quite disadvantageous to oppose [Silicon Valley] on this issue."[93] John Doerr similarly spoke glowingly about how a few million dollars—to him a small amount of money—had been able to bring about "big, scalable social change." He suggested that similar types of action should be taken throughout the country.[94]

The legislation, nevertheless, marked the growing divisions over charters and the tech industry's involvement in their growth. The Progressive Policy Institute's Will Marshall applauded the interest of John Doerr and the tech community in charter schools, especially powerful figures who could (and already had) serve as a "countervailing force" to teachers' unions and other opponents.[95] Other observers were less ebullient about the implications for teachers' unions and were skeptical about the schools in general, especially since there was still very little evidence to support the claim that charter schools were creating superior outcomes or accountability. One of the first comprehensive studies of charters, which focused on California, was released the same year as the passage of the cap lift and, in fact, found the opposite.[96] Such warnings went unheeded by Doerr and Hastings, who were developing other ways to use their wealth and expertise to expand charter schools.

"PUBLIC SCHOOLS: OUR MOST IMPORTANT BUSINESS"

The surging stock market coupled with the Clinton administration's active role in spurring New Economy sectors like finance, real estate, and tech led to a substantial amassing of private wealth over the 1990s. Along with the cuts in the capital gains tax and changes to the tax code, the administration's encouragement of policies to make charitable giving more attractive created a corresponding explosion in private philanthropy during Clinton's time in office.[97]

Private sector giving almost doubled from $101.4 billion in 1990 to $203.5 billion by 2000, with foundation giving increasing 72 percent between 1995 and 1999 alone.[98] The stock market and dot-com boom enabled a substantial growth in the assets of existing foundations. Equally notable were the number of new foundations that incorporated in just a few years, as the richest Americans (and their wealth managers) identified the institutions as a win-win way to both do good and circumvent certain tax obligations.[99] In addition to the launch of thousands of small family founda-tions, many of them started by the young millionaires who had struck rich in tech, the end of the decade witnessed the formation of behemoths like the Eli and Edythe Broad Foundation and the Bill and Melinda Gates Foundation.

The Clinton administration sought to harness and accelerate this growth in giving by New Economy entrepreneurs and not just into campaign donations to the Democratic Party and Al Gore's presidential bid. At a 1999 White House conference devoted to philanthropy, Clinton spoke of the need of fostering "a new gen-eration of philanthropists" among "Silicon Valley and the whole venture capital, high-tech community."[100] Offering his own version of wealth redistribution, he candidly declared this outreach was important for the "same reason Willie Sutton robbed banks. That's where the money is." He then heralded how Silicon Valley donors were using the tools of the private sector to make philanthropic giving more cost effective and efficient.[101] Although he did not mention him by name, the final comment marked a validation of the approach of John Doerr and the NewSchools Venture Fund.

Despite his close alliance with Al Gore and the Clinton admin-istration, with typical Silicon Valley hubris, John Doerr came to believe that "the quest for education reform will fail if it's left to the politicians."[102] He realized that to truly reform the education system, to help disadvantaged children gain the skills to succeed in the New Economy, and to bring the charter model "to scale" would need the ingenuity and money of the tech industry. With Gore's comments as the apocryphal spark, Doerr created the NewSchools Venture Fund in 1997. Gore and Clinton overlooked Doerr's dig at the ineptitude of politicians. The early planning for the fund was on the agenda of more than one Gore-Tech session, and the administration allowed Doerr to officially unveil his idea at a White House conference in June 1997, while both the president and vice president looked on approvingly.[103]

NewSchools embraced and advanced the ideas of venture philanthropy and social entrepreneurship. By the late 1990s, these concepts had begun to percolate at business schools like Stanford and Harvard, which started to increase their offerings in social enterprise and nonprofit management.[104] Venture philanthropy was also a hot discussion topic at dinner parties and meetings with private wealth managers throughout Silicon Valley. Proponents advocated taking the techniques of the private sector—particularly the tech sector and management consulting—and applying them to philanthropy to do social good. For many adherents, this meant making investments in entrepreneurs trying to create social change. Microfinance, which represented another effort to use the entrepreneurial and market-based ideas of the private sector to address a problem of inequality, became especially popular with many of the early advocates of venture philanthropy. Several people, including Pierre Omidyar, the cofounder of eBay, started making major investments in microfinance organizations—with a variety of management-consultant-influenced strings attached.[105]

The idea of venture philanthropy clearly had natural appeal to Doerr and other venture capitalists as a way to apply their expertise toward pressing societal issues. It also gained currency with entrepreneurs like Reed Hastings who had been the direct beneficiaries of venture capital investment. Doerr quickly raised $20 million from allies in Silicon Valley drawing on the free-flowing money of the late 1990s dot-com boom. In addition to investing, Hastings and Marc Andreessen became founding board members and actively involved in getting the fund off the ground.[106] Hastings declared that he and the other founders were "admittedly amateurs at philanthropy (but) we're banding together to get better faster [and] want to create a new paradigm for venture philanthropy." Hastings was dismissive of traditional philanthropic foundations. He saw them as practicing the same entrenched thinking as other bureaucracies and were especially unwilling to take the kind of risks he saw as critical to creating social change.[107] The so-called investments that private donors like Hastings placed in the fund would, nevertheless, receive the same tax write-offs as a traditional philanthropic gift, which mitigated much of the risk for them personally.

NewSchool's early tagline, "Public Schools: Our most important business," aptly reflected its goals as well as the tensions embedded in it. NewSchools aimed to bring "New Economy principles to the problems facing public schools" by using the founders' expertise to support innovation by educational entrepreneurs.[108] Using typical Silicon Valley jargon, NewSchools specifically focused on identifying a "vulnerability" in the education system and finding a "scalable" solution, where impact could be quantified.[109] Instead of a grant proposal—the bread and butter of philanthropic funding—potential beneficiaries had to submit a detailed business plan.[110] Similar to venture capital executives, NewSchools staff members conducted significant due diligence on potential investments and had direct involvement in organizations it selected, including installing tech-oriented board members and providing the services of management consulting heavyweights like Bain, McKinsey, and Boston Consulting Group to ensure efficiency.[111]

Like traditional venture capitalists, NewSchools expected a return on its investment, but the return would be measured through educational achievement metrics like test scores rather than dollars. This focus on measurable achievement along with the emphasis on using the market-based techniques of the private sector to make the public sector more effective directly aligned with what the New Democrats had been advocating for decades. These goals explain, in part, why Clinton and Gore actively supported the effort. NewSchools' focus on charter schools marked another point of overlap with the New Democrats.

The NewSchools board and staff especially concentrated on ways to accelerate the scale and impact of the charter school model. At the time, most charters operated as individual independently run operations. There were also education management organizations, most notably Edison Schools, which were for-profit entities that districts contracted to run schools. NewSchools saw benefits in Edison's emphasis on scale and efficiency, but it recognized parents and teachers had become increasingly suspicious of its profit motives.[112] NewSchools developed a model of creating a charter network called a charter management organization (CMO), which would be nonprofit but draw on market-based ideas and practices. NewSchools worked closely on this idea with Hastings and Don Shalvey.

While traveling around California on the charter cap campaign, Shalvey and Hastings realized that lifting the cap was only the first step and a limited one. The law "wouldn't get schools built or kids served," Hastings explained. "We decided our next project should be a really big network of charter schools."[113] The two imagined creating a chain that would be so effective and big that it would pose a competitive threat to traditional public school districts and force them to improve. "We pray at the altar of competition; it's our lifeblood, our oxygen," Hastings observed about Silicon Valley, but in public education, competition was "considered weird."[114] He and Shalvey hoped to change that attitude.

Shalvey did most of the legwork in developing University Public Schools (it would later change to Aspire), which he envisioned as a "scalable model" that would bring "the customer focus and sense of responsibility of a top-notch service organization or consulting firm to public education."[115] The name derived from its goal that all the low-income students who enrolled would go on to college or at least "aspire" to do so. Shalvey began by opening schools in struggling California communities like Stockton, Modesto, and Oakland. NewSchools provided the initial funding but tied the money to student performance and achievement. Shalvey appreciated this pressure and said that it motivated him to improve.[116] He worked with consultants from McKinsey to create a "Balanced Scorecard" to evaluate effectiveness.[117] Shalvey poached Gloria Lee from McKinsey to serve as chief operating officer. Despite having no background in education, Lee saw similarities to what Aspire was trying to do and her experiences at

McKinsey. "Traditional schools operate on an old-fashioned factory model," she observed. But in a revealing comment she suggested that education is "more like strategy consulting," where each child needs an individualized approach.[118]

Shalvey made the same point slightly differently. He often compared his model to Starbucks, which provided a consistent product with some opportunities to individualize.[119] Also similar to Starbucks, Aspire did not provide tenure or union representation to its teachers. Instead, Shalvey offered them excitement and the chance to innovate. He told teachers that working at one of his schools "was like coming to work in a flotilla of kayaks, rather than sailing in on an ocean liner."[120] This promise was not appealing to all teachers, but Aspire did prove popular with many parents, and its schools started to amass long waitlists.

Watching the Aspire model in action convinced the staff and investors at NewSchools that CMOs offered the best and most efficient way to expand charter schools. In 2002, the organization created the Charter Accelerator Fund, committed to increasing the number and scale of CMOs.[121] The fund sought to capitalize on growing interest in public education reform and charter schools by three of the nation's newest and largest foundations.[122]

The combined funding from the Eli and Edythe Broad Foundation, established by real estate tycoon Eli Broad, the Bill and Melinda Gates Foundation, and the Walton Family Foundation, begun by Walmart founders Sam and Helen Walton, brought an unprecedented amount of money and resources to charter schools at the dawn of the twenty-first century.[123] Although the major legacy foundations started by Andrew Carnegie, John D. Rockefeller, and Henry Ford had an interest in public education and also increasingly utilized the tools of the market and the private sector, they were nothing on the scale of these three. As living donors who sought to actively shape the work of the organizations that bore their names, Gates and Broad were especially committed to deploying the strategies they had cultivated to earn vast sums of wealth to reforming education and making it better serve Black and brown low-income students.[124]

Bill Gates meeting with a group of students at the SEED charter
school in Washington, DC, June 6, 2000
Credit: Reuters/Jeff Christensen

Bill Gates and Eli Broad both demonstrated a personal interest in charter schools. While the Arkansas-based Walton Foundation had been a champion of school choice since its formation
in 1987, the funding of charter schools from other foundations
had remained relatively sparse and unsystematic through much
of the 1990s.[125] That trend changed with this new interest from
Gates and Broad. Gates especially liked the research and development aspect of charters, while they appealed to Broad's entrepreneurial instincts and desire to "challenge the status quo."[126] The
staff at their respective foundations saw charter management
organizations and NewSchools as effective means of spreading
the charter model. The two foundations became major investors
in NewSchools' Charter Accelerator Fund.[127] In 2002, the Broad
Foundation placed $10.5 million in the fund to incubate six CMOs
over the next three years.[128] Broad's donation became quickly
overshadowed when the Gates Foundation invested $22 million in
the fund in 2003.[129] The sizable gifts helped validate both charter

schools and venture philanthropy of NewSchools as innovative forms of disrupting old systems.[130]

For most of the 1990s, charters represented a small portion of the total schools in most urban districts. The growth of CMOs and the new philanthropic investment changed that in the next decade as NewSchools helped to launch or expand twenty CMOs. The schools of chains like Aspire, Green Dot, KIPP, Noble Network, and Success Academy (all of which were seeded by the fund) began to crisscross the low-income racially segregated neighborhoods of large urban districts like Los Angeles, Chicago, New York, Newark, New Orleans, and Washington, DC. By 2010, more than 30 percent of public school students attended a charter school in New Orleans and DC, while Los Angeles had the largest number of schools and total number of students enrolled (more than 68,000).[131] Parents in many of these districts put their students in lotteries for a coveted spot at the schools, which often offered smaller classes, more academic rigor, and also resources like computers and field trips furnished by private donors.[132] For the first time, public schools in struggling urban neighborhoods found charter schools making a significant dent in their enrollments and funding.[133] With the perpetual scarcity of funding and resources allocated for public education, it would have particularly deleterious consequences for many urban schools.

The spread of charters also threatened the tenuous power of the labor movement. Charters contributed to a decrease in the number of teachers who were unionized as well as weakening basic rights like seniority and tenure, which had cascading effects.[134] The rise of CMOs stirred outrage among the AFT and other teachers' groups. The AFT saw the chains as a symbol of how the charter school mission had "morphed," and rather than embody Shanker's vision of "teacher-developed laboratories," they had taken a "cookie-cutter approach to education."[135] The impact on union power was one of the things that many tech-centered philanthropists appreciated about charters. It was something the DLC still liked about them too. The DLC itself continued to play a prominent role in the expansion of charter schools by advocating in explicitly partisan terms to make them a key part of the Democratic platform. The issue provided an important way for the DLC to continue to disseminate the New Democrat ideas of expanding choice and using market-based techniques to make the public sector more effective and efficient. Many of the politicians associated with the New Democrats became some of the fiercest advocates for charters on Capitol Hill and in state houses around the country.

To many others, charters revealed the very problems in applying the market-based techniques of the tech industry to the public sector. The chains in which major philanthropists sunk the most money, like Aspire, Green Dot, Kipp, and Success Academy, contended that their "no excuses" achievement-oriented models helped students of color in poor neighborhoods to succeed academically and put them on the path for college.[136] Critics continued to question just how successful the schools were and whether they were helping or harming the students whom they enrolled and public education in general.[137] Many critics also argued that charters were doing nothing to address the problems of racial disparities in education. Instead, they were compounding it. In Los Angeles, Chicago, and other major cities, charter schools primarily enrolled students of color, but the teachers, administrators, and CMO executives were predominantly white. These dynamics intensified as programs like Teach for America began to place large percentages of its corps members in CMO-operated charters.[138] As Elizabeth Todd-Breland has pointed out, it has only further contributed to giving the schools "a colonial veneer."[139]

The controversy over the effectiveness of charter schools remains complex and ongoing.[140] Whether successful or not, charters remain effective symbols of the control that wealthy private forces have come to wield over public policy and the ways that the ethos of the New Democrats had a direct impact on the public sector. The Gates Foundation and the tech entrepreneurs of the NewSchools Venture Fund did not just get a seat at the decision-making table but wielded the financial power to control educational policy at the local, state, and federal level. Few of these foundations and their benefactors ever acknowledged that they themselves were accountable to basically no one, despite their relentless calls for more accountability from schools, teachers, and parents.[141] The efforts to expand the charter school movement opened up a new and powerful place for wealthy New Economy entrepreneurs to shape and potentially benefit from public policy. At the same time, Silicon Valley leaders were becoming some of the biggest donors to and voices in the Democratic Party, calling into question what and whose good charters ultimately served. Increasingly, business executives would not only impose market-based principles on nonprofits and the public sector as a means of "doing good." They would also suggest that buying their products and stock was a way of doing good in and of itself. That is where we turn next.

CHAPTER 9

THE FOX AND THE HENHOUSE

In the spring of 1996, Kathie Lee Gifford burst into tears in the middle of her popular television show *Live with Regis and Kathie Lee.* It was out of character for the indefatigably perky morning host. Gifford had crafted an image as "America's Wonder-Mom," with her kids Cody and Cassidy and her strong commitment to children's charities a central part of her public persona.[1] Gifford lent her name to a popular line of clothing for Walmart and pledged 10 percent of the $9 million she earned annually from the deal to help HIV-positive and crack-addicted babies in New York City. It was her own way of doing well by doing good.[2] Yet, the source of her tears were allegations that pants for the line had been produced in a dingy factory in Honduras that employed girls as young as thirteen. The owners paid the girls thirty-one cents an hour for fourteen- to sixteen-hour shifts, subjected them to verbal, physical, and sexual harassment, and prevented them from attending school.[3] Gifford's troubles went from bad to worse when it came to light that much closer to home—in fact, just steps from the *Live with Regis and Kathie Lee* studio in New York—a factory forced its largely undocumented female workforce to endure abusive conditions and extensive wage theft as they rushed to finish an order for fifty thousand Kathie Lee blouses.[4]

The dual revelations about Kathie Lee's clothing line revealed the complex dynamics of the apparel industry's global supply chain. The scandal illustrated how companies like Walmart were enlisting factories across the globe to complete various items based on where they could get the cheapest bid in a continual race to the bottom. Gifford served as the ideal symbol of the disparities of globalization, which enabled large companies like Walmart and celebrities to make huge profits while exploiting young brown women in the United States and throughout the world.[5] The Kathie Lee scandal was quickly surpassed, however, by allegations against Nike's own race-to-the-bottom practices and rampant abuses against women in Indonesia and Vietnam. The accusations against Kathie Lee, Nike, and many other top companies challenged the optimistic vision of globalization that Bill Clinton refined over his presidency, which presented free trade not just as a means of increasing US prosperity but also as a way to promote democracy, encourage freedom, and combat poverty throughout the world.[6]

The controversies brought attention to Robert Reich and the Labor Department's ongoing efforts to address the problems of sweatshop labor domestically by encouraging companies to self-monitor their subcontractors. In 1996, Reich and his staff suggested the White House build on this model of self-regulation to respond to the growing public outrage about sweatshop abuses around the world. Clinton established the Apparel Industry Partnership, which brought together representatives from major companies, unions, and human rights organizations, to formulate a standard code of conduct for the apparel industry in its practices in the US and around the world. The Apparel Industry Partnership aligned with the administration's faith in forging partnerships with the private sector and harnessing the power of businesses and the market to do the work of government and create social good. In this case, it tasked the regulation of industry—a role that at least since the New Deal had been one of the key functions of federal, state, and local government—largely to industry itself. By encouraging self-monitoring and corporate social responsibility, the Clinton administration aimed to avoid using the law to reform or regulate capitalism by holding companies accountable for the ways that they violated basic labor laws. Instead, the initiative rested on a belief that corporate responsibility and market forces could replace government regulation and union representation to address the exploitation of low-income garment workers.

This approach to the problem of sweatshop abuse focused on the concept of *responsibility*, which was a preferred term of the New Democrats. In fact, responsibility had been one of the organizing ideas of both the DLC and Clinton's presidency and was at the very heart of their doing well by doing good ethos. Yet, the sweatshop cases revealed that responsibility had different meanings for the New Democrats depending on the context. In the case of poor women of color and welfare reform, responsibility operated punitively to impel them into the workforce and to abide by middle-class norms. In the case of Kathie Lee Gifford, Nike, and other major corporations, it became an opportunity to avoid government regulation that could meaningfully alter their business practices in ways that would have helped the low-wage producers of their products but might have hurt their bottom lines. While the New Democrats contended that one of the main selling points of charter schools was that they held low-income students and their teachers more accountable, their solution to the sweatshop issue evaded asking the same of corporations like Nike and Walmart. Like charter schools, this focus on responsibility and self-monitoring abetted the New Democrats' long-standing quest to limit the influence and power of organized labor.

The emphasis on responsibility rather than accountability further emboldened the anti-sweatshop movement, which had been growing, especially on college campuses. These activists joined the larger movement that coalesced in protest at the World Trade Organization meetings in Seattle in November 1999. The protests demonstrated the variety of constituencies discontented with the Clinton administration's pursuit of neoliberal free trade and procorporate policies. The demonstrations represented the most significant challenge from the left Clinton had received for his

New Democrat faith in markets to address inequality in the US and globally. However, rather than take the charges of the protest seriously, the Clinton administration responded by redoubling its commitment to global trade and market-based reform, while companies like Nike repeated their promises that they would be more socially responsible. The bolstering of global trade, industry self-regulation, and corporate social responsibility did not just contribute to defusing the coalition that came together in Seattle. These claims prevented finding solutions to the problem of sweatshops and the larger forces that produced precarious conditions in which many poor women of color, both in the US and around the world, were working and living.

NO SWEAT

The first case to spark national outrage about modern sweatshop abuses did not occur in the maquiladoras in Mexico or a Nike factory in Indonesia but in an apartment complex in the Los Angeles suburb of El Monte. On August 2, 1995, a team of federal agents ripped through a razor-wire fence and sawed thick iron bars off the windows of a building to discover a group of seventy-two Thai garment workers who had been suffering in a state of involuntary servitude for several years. The factory's owners lured the young women to the United States with promises of good work only to confiscate their passports and withhold their earnings in repayment of their "debt." The owners subjected the women to slavery-like conditions, forcing them to work up to twenty-two hours a day, seven days a week, for an average of sixty-nine cents an hour. The workers endured threats of rape and murder as they produced clothes for forty of the nation's leading retailers, including Sears, Macy's, Filene's, Neiman Marcus, and Target.[7] The case became front-page news, with images of the cramped and dangerous conditions of the factory running alongside those of young women looking forlorn. Politicians from Bill Clinton and Robert Reich on down quickly denounced the return of the sweatshop on American soil.

The seeming eradication of sweatshops had long served as a case study of the effectiveness of New Deal–style regulatory law and labor protection. The Fair Labor Standards Act of 1938, a hallmark piece of New Deal legislation, established standards for minimum wage and overtime pay, required employers to keep records of employees' hours worked, and limited child labor. It also created the Wage and Hour Division within the Department of Labor to conduct workplace inspections. These regulations, coupled with high rates of unionization in the industry, created better conditions for garment workers after World War II.[8] Steadily liberalized trade policies, adopted in part to stem the spread of communism, however propelled many apparel companies to shift their production to Asia and Latin America, beginning as early as the 1960s.[9] As a means to maximize profits and minimize liability, brand-name manufacturers like Nike and the Gap and department stores like JC Penney and Macy's began contracting the manufacturing of their products to subcontractors who offered the lowest bid. A company like Levi Strauss, therefore, might produce one line of pants in El Salvador and another in China. These global supply chains contributed to the increased availability of cheap clothes for American consumers and record profits for retailers like Walmart and Target. By 1995, the Department of Labor estimated that the US garment industry was grossing over $45 billion a year with over 80 percent of its production occurring overseas.[10]

The statistics revealed that US-based brands had not exported all their garment production.[11] Companies often found it advantageous to produce "fast fashion" items domestically so that they could go immediately on the shelves. But the rise of foreign manufacturing placed substantial pressure on the domestic apparel industry to reduce costs to stay competitive. Garment workers saw their wages decline beginning in the 1970s, which corresponded with a drop in unionization rates.[12] Factory owners increasingly tapped into the rising flows of immigrants, many of whom came from the very countries like China, El Salvador, and the Dominican Republic to which apparel production had shifted. El Monte was perhaps an extreme example, but the peripheries of New York and Los Angeles began filling with small factories run by subcontractors that overwhelmingly employed undocumented and non-unionized women and paid less than two dollars an hour to work long hours in unsanitary and unsafe conditions. Exacerbating the situation, the enforcement of workplace law reached a nadir during the Reagan and Bush years. Between 1978 and 1993, the Wage and Hour Division experienced a 60 percent reduction in staff, and by 1993, 804 inspectors were responsible for monitoring conditions at six million firms and 110 million workers across the entire country and not just the garment industry but across all sectors.[13] This was the situation that Robert Reich inherited when he took over as head of the Department of Labor.

Reich was an unconventional choice for the position of secretary of labor and an even more unlikely champion of combating sweatshops. Reich had served as one of Clinton's key economic advisors during the 1992 campaign, and after he won, Clinton cajoled his old friend to head the Labor Department. The Harvard Kennedy School professor had little experience in government and none in a management position and was the first labor secretary in at least a generation to have no existing ties to organized labor. In fact, his position on industrial policy had earned him sharp condemnation from union leaders in the early 1980s. By the time he joined the Clinton team, Reich had abandoned some of his earlier views, but he continued to treat globalization as something of an inevitability. Reich believed free trade could be used for progressive good and as a means of lessening inequality if enough resources went toward helping Americans enhance their education and skills. In his 1990 book *The Work of Nations*, he stressed that the US should not focus on trying to save repetitive jobs like those in the garment industry. Instead, boosting highly skilled work that engaged in complex problem solving was the solution.[14] During his early days as labor secretary, Reich translated these ideas into a major stimulus and investment package.

After Clinton opted to pursue deficit reduction as the path toward domestic economic growth, Reich did not give up. He continued to push the administration to create jobs and retraining programs to help workers adjust to the realities of globalization. He identified that one way to pay for these kinds of programs would be by reducing the generous entitlements and subsidies directed toward corporations. In late 1994, in a speech before the Democratic Leadership Council, Reich provocatively repurposed Clinton's famed 1992 campaign promise. "Since we are committed to moving the disadvantaged from welfare to work," he proposed, "why not target corporate welfare as well, and use the savings to help all Americans get better work?"[15] The statement found a surprisingly receptive audience among the DLCers. The staff at the DLC's think tank had, in fact, recently released a list of frivolous tax breaks and subsidies to companies, which together amounted to over $100 billion a year.[16] It also linked with what Rep. Bernie Sanders (I-VT) had been saying since he arrived on Capitol Hill in 1991.

Reich's speech was less warmly received by senior officials inside the Clinton administration. In response, Commerce Secretary Ron Brown publicly defended corporate subsidies while Robert Rubin privately raised concerns that Reich's language would be perceived as anticorporate and might shake the confidence of the financial markets.[17] As a concession, Reich stopped using the phrase *corporate welfare* publicly and started using the term *corporate responsibility* instead. Reich found the term an effective way to criticize the focus of many companies on maximizing shareholder value rather than investing in the skills of its workers or communities.[18] Responsibility had other important valances as well. It represented an animating theme of the DLC's project to reinvent both the Democratic Party and government and Clinton's 1992 campaign. It was also a fundamental part of the welfare reform agenda. Reich clearly recognized that he could inject some economic populism into Clinton's agenda by capitalizing on the administration's hypocrisy of asking welfare mothers to take responsibility while not asking corporations to do the same.

Reich's idea and language tapped into the corporate social responsibility movement that was gaining steam in the mid-1990s. In 1970, Milton Friedman penned an influential polemic in the

New York Times Magazine entitled "The Social Responsibility of Business Is to Increase Its Profits." The avowed champion of unconstrained markets argued that the primary responsibility of corporations was to maximize profits, and they should not engage in activities that did not provide direct financial benefit to their shareholders.[19] A group of business owners and entrepreneurs who gained the spotlight in the 1980s and early 1990s flatly rejected Friedman's view.

The founders of companies like Ben & Jerry's, the Body Shop, and Patagonia firmly believed that profitability and socially and environmentally responsible practices were not only compatible but inextricably linked. These figures and their companies sought to show that it was possible to do well and do good at the same time and gained notoriety for inserting that idea into the popular consciousness.[20] Taking Friedman head on, Jerry Greenfield of Ben & Jerry's declared, "We think making a better world increases profits."[21] The proof was perhaps in the company's success, which was as much for the taste of its ice cream as its values. The popularity of the guidebooks like *Shopping for a Better World* in the late 1980s offered another indication of the desire of many people with disposable income to combine their social values with their consumer choices.[22] In the early 1990s, Ben Cohen and his allies founded the trade group Business for Social Responsibility, which focused on making corporate social responsibility an integral part of the business operations and strategies of large companies. It was clear that a desire to reconcile moral values with financial and consumer practices was beginning to appeal to more than a small niche of progressive customers. Even companies like Monsanto, Exxon, and Procter & Gamble had engaged their services and joined their ranks. So, too, had many of the companies whose names were on the labels confiscated during the El Monte raid.[23]

Reich and the Labor Department tried to use this interest in corporate social responsibility to their advantage in addressing the problems in the apparel industry. In the months after the El Monte raid, the Labor Department created an initiative called No Sweat, which sought to harness apparel companies' concern about protecting their public image by impelling their sense of responsibility. First, it focused on enforcement. The Labor Department increased its targeted sweeps of garment factories and began producing a quarterly Garment Enforcement Summary outlining in detail the results of the raids.[24] Labor officials worked more closely with the Immigration and Naturalization Service to coordinate the sweeps, both to expose companies that hired undocumented workers and discourage migrants from entering the country in search of work.[25]

Labor Department officials were well aware, however, that they did not have the resources to investigate or identify anywhere near every infraction. The department thus realized that the best way to ensure compliance was by enlisting the retailers and manufacturers to do the enforcement for them. Even before the El Monte case, the department had been cultivating a strategy that relied on a rarely invoked law called the "hot goods" provision. It prohibited the interstate shipment of goods made in violation of federal labor rules. Officials began offering companies a choice: they could endure a court injunction on the goods produced in domestic sweatshops and pay millions of dollars in fines, or they could conduct their own investigations of their subcontractors.[26] Reich proudly declared the tactic allowed "market forces to do the enforcing for us," since companies invariably selected the second option.[27]

Following the El Monte case, Reich confidently announced to the press: "This type of enforcement works."[28] He spoke of enlisting retailers "as adjunct policemen" and slightly tongue-in-cheek noted that "at a time when business says to government, 'Get off our back. We can do it ourselves,' we're giving them the opportunity."[29] As Reich fully admitted, this approach essentially constituted the privatization of regulation. It called on companies to conduct what had long been the function of government. Rather than holding companies *accountable* through a comprehensive investigation and then issuing fines and other penalties, it instead urged companies to take *responsibility* by monitoring their contractors themselves.

The No Sweat initiative took other steps to focus less on sticks and more on carrots. Several apparel executives complained that Labor officials only concentrated on "bad actors" and did not praise companies that were "trying to do the right thing."[30] In response, the department developed a "Trendsetter List," which spotlighted thirty-one retailers and manufacturers, including Lands' End, Levi Strauss, Liz Claiborne, Nordstrom, Patagonia, Guess, and several subsidiaries of The Limited, such as Abercrombie & Fitch, Express, Lane Bryant, and Victoria's Secret, who had agreed to monitor their subcontractors.[31] Reich pointed to the list as evidence that the department could convince companies that "good citizenship is often a wise business strategy."[32]

The No Sweat initiative marked an innovative way for Labor officials to adapt to the budgetary constraints they confronted in trying to regulate the apparel industry. Yet, the strategy had serious limitations, and even the revelations of El Monte led to only a minimal increase in the number of Wage and Hour inspectors the department could hire.[33] Representatives from organized labor and immigrant rights groups voiced skepticism about these forms of "industry self-policing" and dismissed them as simply a case of "the fox guarding the henhouse."[34] That the No Sweat initiative focused on celebrating good corporate actors rather than trying to strengthen union rights in apparel workplaces was revealing about the Labor Department's priorities. The initiative similarly failed to build or acknowledge the campaigns among grassroots immigrant rights groups like the Oakland-based Asian Immigrant Women Advocates and Los Angeles's Korean Immigrant Workers Advocates, who were fighting for garment workers to gain both a living wage and political empowerment.[35] These campaigns aligned with the full employment goals of Jesse Jackson as they focused on bringing decent paying jobs to low-income marginalized communities while also drawing attention to larger issues of racial and economic inequality.[36] The focus on self-regulation by companies instead shunted a serious discussion about the underlying structural conditions that forced poor women of color to work in garment factories with sweatshop-like conditions. The No Sweat initiative also did not target labor abuses outside the country, which many saw as a far bigger problem.[37] Yet, as the Kathie Lee Gifford scandal shifted national attention toward the problems of sweatshops in the developing world, it created new opportunities to address the problem at an international level.

"DO THE RIGHT THING"

The media could not get enough of the Kathie Lee Gifford story. Throughout the spring of 1996, Gifford's image was splashed across the covers of tabloids and magazines in the supermarket checkout line, and it was almost impossible to turn the TV on and not hear about it. After realizing that the attention would not go away, Gifford decided to lean into it. At the urging of Robert Reich (and her public relations team), she decided to transform herself into the lead spokesperson of the anti-sweatshop crusade.[38] She called on other celebrities to join her in doing "the right thing."[39]

Gifford hardly invented modern anti-sweatshop activism. Labor rights activists had been trying to address the problem in the Global South for almost a decade.[40] In the first years of the 1990s, the movement launched campaigns against several major companies, including Levi Strauss and the Gap. Similarly, investigative journalists had released a spate of reports uncovering sweatshop abuses. In 1992, *Dateline NBC* ran a story documenting how Walmart, the distributor of Kathie Lee's line, sold products made by children in Bangladesh.[41] Yet, the campaigns and reports were periodic and made it seem like they documented a set of isolated and aberrant incidents.[42] The Gifford story turned the tide. Following her tearful outburst, exposé after exposé appeared, indicting major companies and illustrating the hypocrisies of the system. Such instances were not that hard to find. Disney, it turned out, contracted the production of T-shirts and children's nightgowns with Pocahontas and Mickey Mouse on them to a factory in Haiti that had filthy toilets and contaminated drinking water and was crawling with rats. It paid workers so little that some had to feed their babies with sugar water to stave off malnutrition.[43]

Nike quickly became the preferred subject of scorn. Since the 1970s, Nike had been marching across Asia, moving from Japan and Korea to China and Indonesia in search of the cheapest production costs. At the same time, Nike's advertising campaigns used a racially diverse array of athletes and models to sell its sneakers, presenting itself as a symbol of personal transformation and progressive values. Activists like Jeffrey Ballinger of Press for Change and Medea Benjamin of Global Exchange rang alarm bells about Nike's practices in Indonesia, which had a long record of human rights abuses and disregard for workers' rights. But Nike's popularity and progressive image left it largely immune to sustained public scrutiny.

Demonstrators protest outside of the grand opening of the Niketown megastore in downtown San Francisco, 1997

Credit: Reuters/David Ake

In the summer of 1996, Nike's good luck ran out. Articles began appearing about workers in Indonesia who received less than a dollar to make Air Jordans, which retailed in the US for $140. *New York Times* columnist Bob Herbert penned a series of scathing op-eds pointing out the company's hypocrisy. He took particular aim at Nike's advertisements touting female empowerment, while its subcontractors overworked, underpaid, and discriminated against the women who made the company's shoes.[44] Protesters began having a field day coming up with ways to subvert the company's slogans and iconic swoosh.[45] Jesse Jackson, who had previously orchestrated a boycott of Nike because of the lack of Black representation on its board, joined in the outcry about the company's exploitation of its workers. He flew to Indonesia that summer and demanded to tour a factory that produced the company's shoes. After Nike rejected the request, Jackson led a delegation of US civil rights activists and labor organizers in a prayer circle outside the factory's gates and called on the company "to recognize the basic right of workers for free association into unions for their own protection and advancement." Never missing an opportunity to best its competitor, an executive from Reebok quickly boarded a plane from Boston to Jakarta to give Jackson and his delegation a tour of the Indonesian factories to which it subcontracted production.[46]

Nike executives deflected the charges of Herbert, Jackson, and other protesters with their own version of the "doing well by doing good" argument. The company presented itself as a leader in improving the working conditions and raising the minimum wage in Indonesia and other countries where it subcontracted production.[47] In 1992 Nike had adopted a code of conduct for its subcontractors, which banned the use of forced or child labor and required compliance with local laws on wages, benefits, and environmental protection.[48] The company's spokespeople pointed to the code as evidence that the company was a leader of good practices and suggested that the real beneficiaries of global trade were the workers who made their products.[49] Founder and CEO

Philip H. Knight contended that without Nike's business, workers in Indonesia and its counterparts would be in worse shape and their countries would see a decline in their overall standard of living.[50] "Whether you like Nike or don't like Nike, good corporations are the ones that lead these countries out of poverty," he unapologetically declared.[51] This argument echoed many prominent economists like Jeffrey Sachs and Paul Krugman who stressed "the growth of this kind of employment is tremendous good news for the world's poor."[52] Yet, reports emerged of workers who made Nike shoes in Indonesia living in run-down shacks without enough money to feed themselves. Few workers even knew of the company's code of conduct much less worked in factories that abided by it.[53] And after Indonesia raised its minimum wage from $1.25 to $2.20 per day in the mid-1990s, Nike began shifting much of its production to Vietnam, where labor costs were even lower.[54]

Even harder for Nike and Knight to explain away were images that appeared in the June 1996 issue of *Life* magazine of a young child in Pakistan sewing soccer balls emblazoned with the swoosh on it. His picture appeared under the headline "Six Cents an Hour," which was the amount that the boy received for his work.[55] The revelations about Nike's use of child labor proved the straw that broke the camel's back for members of Congress. "Parents have a right to know that the toys and clothes they buy for their children are not made by exploited children," Rep. George Miller (D-CA) fumed.[56] Weeks after the *Life* story appeared on newsstands, Miller organized a congressional hearing on child labor, which included testimony from Gifford and Reich. Miller followed up by suggesting legislation that would require companies to attach a "No Sweat" label to clothing and shoes certifying that no child labor had been used in manufacturing the apparel. Sen. Ted Kennedy (D-MA) and Rep. Bill Clay (D-MO) went even further. Building on what union leaders and activists had long argued was one of the best ways to address the issue of sweatshops, they proposed holding apparel manufacturers and retailers jointly liable for labor violations that occurred at their subcontractors.[57]

The outrage over sweatshops—most of it coming from members of his own party—put Bill Clinton in a difficult position. Since his days as chair of the DLC, Clinton had extended the New Democrat faith that globalization was good for American workers, could lead to economic growth, and was a way to spread freedom and democracy around the world. His case for NAFTA had rested largely on those terms and only intensified after its passage.[58] The signing of NAFTA had offered momentum to conclude the Uruguay Round of the General Agreement on Tariffs and Trade, which paved the way for the creation of the World Trade Organization (WTO) in 1995. With the goal of increasing the flow of capital among countries, the new multinational authority sought to standardize and regulate international trade. The Clinton administration had also been rapidly signing trade agreements with countries with large emerging markets, such as China, India, Indonesia, Brazil, Mexico, and South Africa.[59] Before he tragically died in a plane crash in the Balkans, Commerce Secretary Ron Brown had been leading corporate executives on trade missions to these places to secure lucrative contracts.[60] The Clinton administration had consistently described such trips as "doing well by doing good" and stressed that they were win-wins that were increasing the twin New Democrat ideals of growth and opportunity in the US and the emerging markets of the Global South. The exposure of sweatshop abuses at garment and shoe factories around the world challenged the main tenets of these promises.

For Clinton's team, the sweatshop controversies were all the more complicated because they occurred during an election year. The president's senior economic advisors feared the joint liability legislation proposed by Kennedy and Clay might alienate corporations, contradict his arguments about the humanitarian power of open markets, and violate the WTO's international trade rules.[61] Members of the administration, moreover, believed commerce with "big emerging markets" like Indonesia and Mexico was crucial for America's own continued prosperity and did not want to threaten those ties.[62] But members of the administration knew they had to do something.

Reich offered the most viable solution. In mid-July, as part of its effort to work with apparel companies, he and the Labor Department had organized the Fashion Industry Forum. The event brought together three hundred representatives of the industry to discuss the sweatshop problem and consider future steps.[63] "Government cannot do it all," Reich bluntly told the crowd.[64] The industry representatives expressed a willingness to help out. Afterward, Reich proposed the administration build on this momentum and create a fashion industry–led commission that could create a unified monitoring system and set of standards. The National Economic Council embraced the idea and endorsed it as a form of "industry self-monitoring." The members of the council advised Clinton it would be a way to "demonstrate your leadership on a compelling issue" but avoid "top-down regulatory or legislative remedies" and charges of favoring "big government solutions." They urged that he move quickly.[65]

THE APPAREL INDUSTRY PARTNERSHIP

On August 2, 1996, the one-year anniversary of the El Monte raid and a few days after Clinton had announced he would sign the major welfare reform bill, Clinton took to the podium at a ceremony in the Rose Garden and announced the formation of a White House–sponsored task force called the Apparel Industry Partnership (AIP). The audience included executives from L.L.Bean, Patagonia, Nicole Miller, and Liz Claiborne who had agreed to be part of the AIP and had met with Clinton, Reich, and Al Gore in a private meeting in the West Wing's Roosevelt Room just before the ceremony. Clinton explained the task force would work to end the problem of sweatshops both in the US and abroad by first getting companies to commit to making their products in "decent and humane conditions" and second developing a way to inform consumers of that fact.[66] Clinton admitted that the mandate of the task force was somewhat vague but voiced confidence the group would issue a more detailed plan in the next six months.

Clinton then yielded the microphone to the other people who joined him at the podium, including Kathie Lee Gifford, who spoke in a measured tone about the controversy surrounding her clothing line and how empowering it was to be able to be part of the solution.[67] Nike CEO Phil Knight also spoke in what was one of his first public statements about the accusations about his company's use of sweatshop labor. "We have been good citizens within our industry," he defensively began. But then he admitted that "there is clearly more that we can do and we can indeed be better."[68] He pledged that Nike would actively participate in the task force. Although the White House had hoped he would bring Michael Jordan with him, Knight's presence and statement was an important endorsement of the endeavor.[69] Many activists worried, however, that Nike was merely joining to evade addressing the problems in its supply chain. In general, activists were concerned that despite the fanfare, the voluntary nature of the task force was simply another opportunity for the apparel industry to police itself rather than for government to hold it accountable.[70]

Clinton had consistently taken organized labor for granted and tried to distance himself from unions out of fear it would hurt his political fortunes with white middle-class moderate voters. Yet, the Clinton administration recognized that it would need their involvement to make the AIP legitimate. Reich made an overture to the garment workers union UNITE, asking it to join the endeavor.[71] The sweatshop scandal coincided with an important turning point for UNITE. Garment workers unions, especially the International Ladies' Garment Workers' Union (ILGWU) in the early twentieth century, had been among the most powerful trade unions and played an important role in the fighting for the passage of the Fair Labor Standards Act and the National Labor Relations Act. By the 1960s, however, the rise of cheap imports and the flight of American factories overseas had led to a slow decline in membership. Despite outreach to immigrant workers and other initiatives, it had not been able to rebound, and by 1995, its membership had decreased to 125,000, down from 457,000 in 1968.[72] In 1995, the ILGWU joined forces with Amalgamated Clothing and Textile Workers, which made men's clothes, textiles, auto parts, and other products, to create UNITE.[73] The revamped union made sweatshops an immediate area of focus. In Los Angeles, UNITE was working in coalition with a group of immigrants' rights organizations to launch a unionization drive among the garment workers at factories that produced jeans and other clothing for Guess, which was the city's largest apparel manufacturer.[74]

UNITE's leaders voiced skepticism at the idea of the Apparel Industry Partnership as well as the larger efforts of the Labor Department to encourage the industry to self-regulate. UNITE president Jay Mazur stressed that joint liability legislation like that proposed by Miller and Kennedy, along with providing workers the full rights to organize and the power to bargain collectively at home and abroad, was the best way to provide humane labor conditions.[75] Despite reservations, UNITE representatives ultimately decided to accept Reich's invitation to join the AIP. However, UNITE required that the task force also include members of religious and human rights groups so that it might create a power bloc.[76] The task force's membership eventually expanded to eighteen members. In addition to UNITE, it included representatives from L.L.Bean, Patagonia, Liz Claiborne, Reebok, Phillips-Van Heusen, and Nike; the advocacy groups the National Consumers League and Business for Social Responsibility; and the human rights organizations the International Labor Rights Fund, the Lawyers Committee for Human Rights, and the Interfaith Center for Corporate Responsibility.

On the surface, the AIP looked like a return to the corporatist model when the government brokered arrangements between industry and labor.[77] It showed the administration's recognition that it needed to give organized labor a seat at the table, which also harkened back to liberalism of old. But the AIP was explicitly industry and consumer focused rather than union or worker focused. The main priorities were making sure consumers didn't buy clothes made in a sweatshop and companies did not take a hit to their reputations, rather than ensuring that workers or unions were truly empowered. In fact, the White House did not even invite any garment workers to attend the ceremony in the Rose Garden.

This absence was a stark contrast to the Clinton administration's approach to antipoverty and economic empowerment initiatives like microenterprise. Events devoted to microenterprise often featured remarks from a microcredit borrower or at least references to the individual stories and anecdotes of women in the United States and Global South who through hard work and discipline achieved success and self-sufficiency. Administration officials seldom heralded the hard work, discipline, or agency of individual garment workers and rarely invoked their names or personal stories. While officials frequently spoke of how microentrepreneurs were agents of change who had the power to have control over their own lives and the growth of the global economy, garment workers largely remained anonymous victims. In these depictions, the workers making Kathie Lee pants and Nike shoes had little agency, even though they earned wages and contributed to the global economy and many had taken great risks to organize to demand fair treatment. Tellingly at the Rose Garden event, Clinton celebrated both Gifford and Knight for their heroic willingness "to live up to their responsibilities." Yet, he spoke in vague terms about "the people who work under deplorable conditions."[78] Coming on the heels of Clinton's welfare-to-work announcement, it was an indication of the kind of poor women of color that Clinton and the New Democrats valued and those they did not.

Even if the Clinton administration avoided the tactic, anti-sweatshop and immigrant rights activists recognized the power of using individual garment workers' experiences to build support for their cause. Borrowing a tactic from the sanctuary movement of the 1980s, organizations began bringing garment workers from Latin America and Asia to the United States on speaking tours. Activists from the National Labor Committee arranged for Wendy Diaz, a four-foot, nine-inch fifteen-year-old Honduran girl who had sewn the famed Kathie Lee Gifford pants to come to Washington, just as the scandal surrounding the morning host was reaching fever pitch. Diaz delivered a series of press conferences and offered congressional testimony. In these forums, she described the harsh conditions and low pay of the factory she had worked at since she was thirteen. Her stories of being pelted with clothes and frequently groped by her supervisors horrified listeners.[79] A few weeks after, Global Exchange arranged a tour for an Indonesian worker named Cicih Sukaesih who been fired from her job with a Nike subcontractor after trying to organize her coworkers to demand they receive minimum wage. The tour coincided with the Labor Department's Fashion Industry Forum, but officials denied Sukaesih's request to participate, potentially for fear of alienating Nike.[80]

Unlike the Rose Garden ceremony a few weeks later, the forum's lineup did include one garment worker. At the forum, Nancy Penaloza, a migrant from Mexico who worked at a factory in the New York area making women's suits for JC Penney and Ann Taylor, recounted her experiences with long hours, wage theft, and abuse from her boss.[81] "When I'm working I'm very afraid," she explained. "Big mice and rats crawl at my feet."[82] Despite the applause she received from the distinguished audience, Penaloza ultimately regretted her decision to participate in the forum. The day after the event, Immigration and Naturalization Service (INS) officials raided the factory where she worked and arrested many of the workers. Penaloza's coworkers blamed her for speaking out.[83]

Ignoring warnings from labor rights activists that raids did little to control unauthorized migration, INS and the Department of Labor increased their coordinated sweeps of garment factories, arresting and deporting scores of workers in the aftermath of El Monte.[84] The raids served as another indication of the administration's limited commitment to protecting workers themselves, especially those who were undocumented. In fact, just a month after the formation of the AIP, Clinton signed the Illegal Immigration Reform and Immigrant Responsibility Act. The law substantially broadened who the federal government could deport and detain along with far more capacity to do so.[85] Like welfare reform, it showed the punitive potential of requiring "responsibility." And when put side by side with the Apparel Industry Partnership, the law revealed how the Clinton administration applied different meanings of responsibility for marginalized groups than for corporate actors, where it was less a punishment and more of a reward.

Despite the inclusion of "White House" in the name, Clinton's staff actually played a limited role in the Apparel Industry Partnership. The AIP was officially an informal private initiative, and the administration did not grant it money, a staff, or legal authority. Gene Sperling, the chair of the president's National Economic Council, served as the facilitator. But he and other members of the administration did not have a voice on the actual task force. The administration left the members to sort out the details and initial issues among themselves, which proved telling of how seriously the White House took the endeavor. Further hamstringing the work, Reich resigned as secretary of labor in early 1997. He remained committed to the sweatshop issue and even tried to work with UNITE to establish a concerned citizens group comprised of high-profile figures to ensure the issue did not fade from public attention.[86] Yet, there was significantly less that he could do from outside the administration. Moreover, Alexis Herman, his replacement, showed less interest in the problem of sweatshops.

During the first of its monthly sessions, the AIP members narrowed their broad mandate to the more focused goal of creating a universal code of conduct. The group came to quick agreement on issues of child labor, antiharassment measures, and overtime. As they began discussing how to determine a living wage and who should monitor the factories, the members fell into a prolonged stalemate.[87] As the group's negotiations extended well beyond its six-month deadline, Sperling hosted a seven-hour closed-door session at the White House where he all but forced the members to agree on creating a formal and permanent association called the Fair Labor Association (FLA), which would carry out the adoption of the code and monitor the process.[88] Yet, as the task force sought to develop the code of conduct, the disagreements among members became even more vehement, and they fell into a prolonged stalemate.

With the task force's negotiations stretching on over years, the White House was increasingly worried that the whole thing would fall apart.[89] Clinton's own interest in the issue also wavered, especially as he became embroiled in the Monica Lewinsky scandal. But he and his staff acknowledged that even though the task force was formally independent, it could hurt his image if it failed. Sperling thereby sanctioned a group of self-described centrists on the task force to hold private meetings to finalize the creation of the FLA. The group, which included representatives from Nike, deliberately excluded UNITE from these meetings. The union representatives interpreted it as a slight and a symbol of both the companies' and the administration's dismissive attitudes about organized labor. Just before the task force finished its work, the union publicly quit. The exodus was not a good omen for the FLA.[90]

In November 1998, the remaining members of the task force unveiled the details of the Fair Labor Association. Companies that decided to join would have to abide by the association's code and undergo periodic monitoring of a portion of their factories, but in exchange, they could promote that their products were sweatshop-free. Clinton hailed the association as a "historic step" and urged companies to sign on.[91] UNITE forcefully disagreed and issued several blistering statements, calling the FLA worse than nothing since it "provid[ed] the illusion of public oversight" while allowing corporations "to exert control in ways that weaken the power of unions."[92] Other activists used slightly less sharp language to point out that the voluntary nature of the association meant that companies committed to increasing profits regardless of the social harms had no incentive to join.[93] The FLA's code of conduct, moreover, was not an enforceable set of government rules and did not have any mechanisms to hold companies accountable for labor violations at home or abroad. Instead, it served as another instance of the government asking corporations to take responsibility and self-regulate. The members of the growing anti-sweatshop movement, based on college campuses, were not impressed.

THE BATTLE IN SEATTLE

Many activists had initially worried that the formation of the Apparel Industry Partnership and Fair Labor Association would defuse the anti-sweatshop movement. However, the movement only strengthened in the late 1990s, as college students across the country got involved. The campus anti-sweatshop movement had its origins in organized labor. In 1996, the AFL-CIO orchestrated a program to place college students in summer internships at unions to build support among young people who often saw organized labor as out of date and corrupt and to cultivate a new generation of organizers.[94] The interns at UNITE began thinking about how they could bring the anti-sweatshop movement to their schools. Enrolled at institutions like Duke, Michigan, and the University of North Carolina, they recognized that as college students they represented an important market share. Even more substantial was the value of the multibillion licensing contracts that their universities had with companies like Nike and Reebok.[95] The students returned to their campuses and launched campaigns to pressure their institutions to change their agreements. By the summer of 1998, the groups coalesced into United Students Against Sweatshops with the full support of UNITE. The activists used tactics like taking over administration buildings and hunger strikes. It grew into the largest outpouring of student activism in a generation and encompassed students not just from Duke, the University of Michigan, and UNC, but also from Harvard, the University of California system, and smaller schools like Haverford and Pitzer Colleges.[96]

The administrations of Harvard, Yale, Princeton, Duke, Notre Dame, and others decided joining the FLA would be a means to defuse the protest.[97] This decision was in part a response to high-profile pressure. The enthusiasm of corporations for signing on to the FLA had not been as robust as the Clinton administration had hoped. White House officials determined that prodding large and prestigious universities to join the FLA would bolster its reputation and credibility. Phil Knight also personally lobbied several university presidents to join.[98] These actions angered college activists even more and led them to turn their attention to opposing the FLA. Campus activists denounced the FLA as overly corporate controlled and too limited in its monitoring system.[99] Several student activists created an alternative monitoring association called the Workers Rights Consortium (WRC), which focused more on the rights of workers.[100] The student founders urged their universities to withdraw from the FLA and join the WRC instead. Schools like Brown and the University of Oregon agreed to do so. Ultimately, the students played a key role in challenging the legitimacy of the FLA and drawing public attention to the problems of sweatshop abuse. Campus activists saw the meeting of the World Trade Organization in Seattle in November 1999 as a chance to further press the issue.

For many people around the globe, the WTO had become a concrete symbol of neoliberalism and the ways governments had come to serve the interests of multinational corporations rather than workers and citizens.[101] Critics believed that the WTO's trade rules favored wealthy countries and allowed worker and environmental exploitation throughout the world, and its lack of transparency violated the basic principles of democracy. The vast majority of these opponents were not opposed to globalization as a whole but of the version of it embodied by the WTO.[102] When Bill Clinton invited the WTO to host a meeting in Seattle in November 1999, the meeting provided the ideal opportunity to protest.

Activists across the globe spent months coordinating and planning demonstrations to coincide with the Seattle meeting. The process brought together a wide range of groups and issues and revealed the range of frustrations with the WTO and the system it embodied. Despite their differences, the thousands of activists involved in the planning shared a desire to harness and channel the power of democratic institutions held in thrall by multinational corporations.[103] The AFL-CIO played a critical role in the planning efforts. The union's leadership had been working to insert the issue of workers' rights into the trade agreements that the US signed since 1992 and were fed up with the largely toothless side deals that the Clinton administration and protrade Democrats in Congress delivered instead. By the late 1990s, the AFL-CIO was involved in organizing drives in the Global South and provided resources to campaigns against sweatshops in Central America and Latin America. President John Sweeney had visited Mexico in 1998 to encourage more cross-border union cooperation.[104] Sweeney and the AFL-CIO saw the WTO protests as a chance to push for international labor standards, with mechanisms for enforcement and accountability that would limit the incentives for companies to shift their production to countries like Indonesia, Honduras, and China, which had rampant labor and human rights abuses.[105]

The organizers were ready to go from the start, with forty thousand demonstrators to back them up. On the opening morning of the meeting, activists from environmental, consumer rights, human rights, religious, and college anti-sweatshop groups created a blockade of the thirteen intersections around the Seattle Convention Center. Later in the day, the AFL-CIO orchestrated a huge peaceful parade of a wide array of union members, spanning from teamsters to teachers.[106] As the demonstrations continued, a more destructive faction of protesters smashed the downtown storefronts of major banks and corporations like Nordstrom, McDonald's, the Gap, and Niketown. Other protestors spray-painted messages such as "No Sweatshops" and "No WTO" on Nike and other chain stores.[107] Officials dispatched police to protect stores like Nike, which continued to be the target of anger throughout the week.

For Clinton, the demonstrations rendered visible how his administration's priorities were in tension with traditional Democratic constituencies like labor and environmental groups. He made his first order of business upon arriving in Seattle midweek to meet with the heads of the AFL-CIO, Sierra Club, and World Wildlife Fund, but it did little to heal the rifts.[108] Clinton confronted difficulties inside the convention hall as well. Many of the delegates from Africa and Asia saw the negotiations as rigged against them and balked at signing on to a new round of trade talks until they received more concessions from the US and other OECD countries.[109] The Seattle round of trade negotiations ultimately reached a stalemate, and all sides left empty-handed. The events both inside and outside the convention center permanently circumscribed the WTO and marked a fundamental turning point in discussions around globalization.[110] For many involved and watching the events on television, a sense of optimism took hold. Labor, environmental, consumer, religious, feminist, and human rights groups had created a unified coalition to challenge the neoliberal forces of global capitalism. The future political potential of the global justice movement was bright.[111]

GLOBALIZATION THE THIRD WAY

In the aftermath of the Seattle meeting, Clinton attempted to disprove the view that globalization produced poverty and impeded democracy. During his last year in office, he made more of a concerted effort to reach out to the countries who had voiced anger at the Seattle meeting about the inequities of the free trade system.[112] At the same time, extending a theme that informed policy initiatives from welfare reform to charter schools and harkened back to the core values of the Democratic Leadership Council, Clinton promised to offer the benefits of economic growth to those countries that demonstrated a sense of responsibility. He tellingly called it a "Third Way approach to globalization."[113]

Clinton's use of the *third way* was a deliberate reference to the ways that both he and the DLC began branding their politics at the end of the 1990s, with an emphasis on growth, opportunity, and responsibility.[114] The phrase differed from the idea of triangulation, Dick Morris's political strategy for Clinton's 1996 reelection bid, which the DLC strongly supported. Triangulation sought to appropriate ideas of the right in an effort to appeal to moderate swing voters. The DLC's Third Way harkened back to the organization's founding mission and was more ideological in nature. It focused on transcending the traditional ideologies of liberalism and conservatism and providing an alternative.[115] The DLC made both responsibility and free trade a central part of that vision. Al From proudly celebrated how the New Democrats rejected both "the laissez faire belief that the global economy is self-regulating and the protectionist belief that America can withdraw from the global economy."[116] Further solidifying its antipathy to organized labor, the DLCers flatly dismissed the claims of the AFL-CIO and other unions that free trade hurt American jobs and their calls for more rigorous labor standards in trade agreements.[117] In policy papers, the DLC directly confronted the accusations from many of the protesters in Seattle and contended that expanding trade did not cause "poverty and exploitation" but instead "form[ed] part of the solution." In fact, DLCers argued that "globalization brings new opportunities to raise standards of living around the world."[118]

The DLC and Clinton sought to use the idea of the Third Way to transcend national boundaries and create common cause with like-minded political leaders across the Atlantic.[119] The DLC and Clinton found an especially willing partner in Great Britain's prime minister Tony Blair. In October 1997, Blair hosted a retreat at Checquers, the British prime minister's stately country manor, to discuss the Third Way. Hillary Clinton led a US delegation, which included the DLC's Al From, Treasury Undersecretary Lawrence Summers, and HUD Secretary Andrew Cuomo. The delegation discussed with their counterparts from Britain's New Labour movement ways to create a shared philosophy rooted in equal opportunity, lean government, and international engagement.[120] The event marked the beginning of a series of retreats and conversations on the Third Way, either sponsored or attended by members of the DLC. The guest list for the discussions quickly expanded to include not just Bill Clinton but also the prime ministers of Germany, Italy, and the Netherlands.[121] Clinton proudly observed the meetings proved how DLC ideas were sweeping the globe.[122]

The trade deals that Clinton enacted in his last year in office further demonstrated this effort to implement the New Democrat commitment to growth and opportunity on a global scale. In May

2000, Clinton signed into law a major trade agreement with Africa. It tellingly was called the African Growth and Opportunity Act and rested on the idea that trade and market reform was the best way to eliminate poverty and address human rights crises on the continent.[123] A few months later, Clinton signed a historic trade deal agreement with Vietnam based on a similar premise.[124] To further spread that message, in late November 2000, Clinton became the first president to go to Vietnam since Richard M. Nixon visited US troops near Saigon in 1969. Clinton routinely emphasized that the trip was more about the future than the past. He also made clear that his administration's approach to countries like Vietnam—with their dubious human rights records, routine silencing of political dissent, and crackdown on unionization efforts—would be similar to their treatment of corporations like Nike. He essentially encouraged them to self-regulate and embrace market capitalism.[125]

As part of the tour, Clinton visited a container terminal on the Saigon River outside Ho Chi Minh City. Standing in front of large cranes and stacks of shipping containers filled with Nike sneakers and other products, he declared that the port's dock workers "know better than anyone that trade lifts wages, raises living standards and opens opportunities."[126] The comment encapsulated Clinton's steadfast faith in the New Democrat mantra that markets could create both growth and opportunity across the globe. What Clinton failed to mention was that the advantages were exponentially greater for Nike than the dock workers in Ho Chi Minh City or their counterparts at the Port of Long Beach, California. By 2000, Nike had become the biggest private employer in Vietnam and stood to directly benefit from the trade agreement Clinton signed.[127]

RESPONSIBILITY NOT ACCOUNTABILITY

By the time of Clinton's visit to Vietnam, Nike began to acknowledge the realities of the conditions in its factories in Vietnam and elsewhere. After Nike's sales and stock prices took a sizable dip,

Phil Knight delivered a speech before the National Press Club in the spring of 1998 where he admitted the "Nike product has become synonymous with slave wages, forced overtime and arbitrary abuse" and "the American consumer does not want to buy products made in abusive conditions."[128] He announced that Nike would do more to improve the working conditions in its factories and its process of monitoring them. However, he made no commitment to raising the wages of the hundreds of thousands of workers who made its products.

Instead, Nike followed another path toward purportedly improving the living conditions in countries it operated. It allocated funding for the creation of a new office of corporate social responsibility and eventually launched a separate foundation largely concentrated on empowering women and adolescent girls in the Global South. Grameen Bank became one of the many organizations to receive funds from Nike's foundation.[129] Furthering its commitment to microenterprise as a tool of empowerment, Nike started a program in the late 1990s to provide microloans to women who worked in its factories in Vietnam, Indonesia, and Thailand. While the company frequently cited the program as an example of its commitment to the economic mobility of its workers, in six years of operation, it distributed $250,000 in loans.[130] Such tactics combated the negative image that the company exploited young, marginalized women in its factories, but they did little to meaningfully empower the vast majority of those workers or help them achieve a living wage.

The actions of Nike revealed the larger challenges the anti-sweatshop movement faced in fighting the neoliberal forces of free trade. Few companies agreed to the type of actions advocated by unions like UNITE and the anti-sweatshop movement. Instead, the vast majority adopted codes of conduct or worked with the FLA to avoid such rigorous monitoring.[131] The student-created Workers Rights Consortium did achieve several signal victories for unionization and worker empowerment, especially at factories producing collegiate apparel.[132] Yet, even the best organizing campaign proved unable to alter international trade policies. The

impact of NAFTA and other WTO agreements on the apparel industry did not become fully clear until the turn of the twenty-first
century. The new millennium would see a continued race to the
bottom as apparel production became increasingly concentrated
in Mexico as well as Bangladesh and China, which had some of the
world's lowest wages and weakest labor standards.[133] At the same
time, Congress and the George W. Bush administration showed
ever-lessening willingness to insert vigorous labor and environmental standards or living wage agreements into trade policies.
Apart from the passage of an important law in California, the effort to pass legislation to make companies jointly liable for the
infractions of their subcontractors largely fizzled out in the early
2000s. It also became more difficult to maintain the large number
of groups that had coalesced in Seattle into a permanent and stable coalition, especially after 9/11.

The Seattle activists did, nevertheless, inadvertently embolden
the popularity of corporate social responsibility. In the aftermath
of the Seattle protests, customers, especially those with disposable income, showed an increasing preference for companies that
acted ethically and were good global citizens. By the dawn of the
twenty-first century, not paying lip service to social issues increasingly hurt a company's ability to make profits. Companies
like Starbucks and Whole Foods rooted their brand image in the
idea that they were addressing the world's problems.[134] Several apparel companies followed Nike's lead and sought to demonstrate
their commitment to ending sweatshop abuses by establishing
corporate social responsibility departments or separate foundations. Corporate social responsibility paralleled the concepts of
venture philanthropy and social enterprise embraced by Silicon
Valley tycoons as another market-based form of doing good;
though if social enterprise sought to use the tools of the market
to make nonprofits more effective, corporate social responsibility
contended that buying products from companies like Nike was itself a way of doing good.

Like social enterprise, corporate social responsibility captured
the imagination of a new generation of young people interested in

reconciling their values with their work. In response, Harvard, Stanford, and other leading MBA programs made both social enterprise and corporate social responsibility more significant parts of their curriculum. Firms like Citigroup and Goldman Sachs also started touting their socially responsible credentials to lure MBA graduates to work for them.[135] While the anti-sweatshop movement and the WTO protests marked one way that many college students and twenty-somethings responded to economic changes wrought by globalization and the New Economy, the commitment to corporate social responsibility was another. Yet, if the anti-sweatshop movement was a clear rejection of the "doing well by doing good" logic that had defined the policies of the Clinton administration, the corporate social responsibility movement played an important role in expanding it and further embedding it into the popular consciousness.

Assuring consumers that their purchases and investments could have social benefits—and workers that their employers had the power to do good—contributed to channeling demands for accountability further from the public sector. The philanthropic endeavors of companies like Nike and their founders lacked any meaningful accountability, and their priorities could and did change based on whim or what best helped their corporate image. This has led to a paradoxical set of circumstances. On the one hand, since 2000, more apparel companies than ever have made pledges of corporate responsibility, created their own foundations, and established codes of conduct. At the same time, in both the US and around the world, garment workers have experienced a decline in wages and confronted increased difficulty in gaining the right to unionize.[136]

The flourishing of corporate social responsibility lent more power to the idea that it was the private sector—and not the public sector and labor unions—that does good for the world. The ideas of corporate social responsibility embodied the New Democrat conviction that the private companies could do the work of government and that labor unions were outdated and unnecessary. There are obvious and serious shortcomings, however, in relying on companies to self-monitor and consumer markets to act as a mechanism for regulation and worker protection. Responsibility does not equal accountability. As the Clinton administration simultaneously sought to direct investment to address poverty domestically at the end of the 1990s, it similarly did not heed that important lesson.

CHAPTER 10

UNTAPPED MARKETS

The rain from a lingering summer thunderstorm did not deter the hundreds of people who stood in the parking lot of an East St. Louis Walgreens in early July 1999, awaiting the arrival of the presidential motorcade.[1] The crowd cheered loudly when Clinton finally rolled in, joined by an entourage that included Olympic gold medalist Jackie Joyner-Kersee, several corporate executives, politicians, and government officials along with Rev. Jesse Jackson. East St. Louis sat just across the Mississippi River and the Illinois border from its namesake. In its earlier days, the city served as a major rail and river depot and industrial center. The acres of stockyards, shipping yards, and steel and chemical factories sent pollutants into the air and river and brought streams of white and Black laborers to settle in the city starting in the late nineteenth century. East St. Louis earned national notoriety in 1917 when bands of white workers attacked their Black coworkers and neighbors in what was one of the worst race massacres of the twentieth century.[2] Since that time, the city steadily lost its white population along with much of its industry and revenue. The local government fell into such dire financial straits that it had auctioned off the city hall building to repay debts. By the time Clinton came to visit, the poverty rate of the 38,000 mostly Black residents hovered around 40 percent, and the unemployment rate sat at 9.2 percent. The city also had stubbornly high crime and incarceration rates.[3]

Boarded-up storefronts and run-down houses lined its streets, and the *Casino Queen* riverboat, docked along the gritty banks of the Mississippi, served as one of the few forms of economic revenue.

Clinton did not dwell on East St. Louis's fraught racial history but instead celebrated its future economic potential. The administration had recently named the city an Empowerment Zone, and the Walgreens Clinton stopped at was the first national chain to open in East St. Louis in decades. "We see in this community both poverty and great promise," Clinton announced to the crowd in the parking lot before going inside the store.[4] He then meandered through the fluorescent-lit aisles, stopping to talk with employees and reminisce in front of a display of Hostess fruit pies, which he explained had been a staple of his diet during his freshman year at Georgetown.[5]

The visit to the East St. Louis Walgreens was one stop on the three New Markets tours that Clinton led during the last year and a half of his presidency. The itineraries spanned from Appalachia to South Dakota's Pine Ridge Reservation, Arkansas to Chicago, and East Palo Alto to rural North Carolina. The tours covered issues ranging from increasing the flow of corporate and venture capital funds into underserved areas, the protection of the Community Reinvestment Act, and closing the digital divide. The White House deliberately modeled the tours to resemble the trips Ron Brown led to seek out business opportunities and spread freedom and democracy in the emerging markets abroad.

The New Markets tours also paralleled and drew on a program that Jesse Jackson started to bring corporate investment to distressed parts of the country. Clinton's former nemesis served as an active participant on the New Markets tour. The president and his entourage largely stopped in places where the residents were more the natural constituents of Jackson than Clinton. At every event, Jackson received equal or bigger cheers than the president. Over the chants, Jackson dutifully told audiences, "Don't take this giant for granted" and maintained Clinton was committed to the New Markets program not for political gain but "because he thinks this is right."[6] Jackson's role as the president's sidekick was revealing both about the civil rights leader's pragmatism and the power of the "doing well by doing good" ethos to overpower more progressive and redistributive solutions to poverty and inequality by the end of Clinton's presidency.

The New Markets program rested on the idea that forces of investment, credit, and technology could integrate places like East St. Louis and the people who inhabited them economically and socially into the nation. The program did not just aim to give poor people more access to markets and capital, it also sought to increase the access of corporations to poor people as a source of profit. It was the apogee of the effort that spanned Clinton's presidency to promote private sector investment as a route to addressing poverty and inequality in distressed communities. New Markets, and the tours to promote it, aimed to unify the often disparate aspects of this agenda—including Empowerment Zones, community development banking, reforming the Community Reinvestment Act, corporate social responsibility, and closing the digital divide—under the same umbrella. The initiative also marked an effort to secure and connect Clinton's legacy in improving both the economy and the plight of distressed communities and people.

By the time Clinton embarked on the first tour, the nation's overall economic statistics stood in stark contrast to those of East St. Louis. Since 1993, the GDP had grown at an average of 3.5 percent annually, there were more than seventeen million new private sector jobs, the unemployment rate was 4.3 percent (the lowest in twenty-nine years), and the inflation rate was under 2 percent.[7] Clinton's gamble on balancing the budget had paid off and in 1998, there was a surplus for the first time since 1969. In making the case for the New Markets idea, Clinton repeatedly emphasized that a time of unparalleled prosperity was the best moment to attack the problem of poverty. Clinton's case echoed the one that Lyndon Johnson made in the 1960s for launching the Great Society and War on Poverty.

Rather than see the roaring economy and balanced budget as an opportunity for the federal government to commit more resources to the problem of persistent inequality, the Clinton administration took a deliberately different tack. It advocated a very limited program with a distinctly market-based approach that deputized private corporations to do government's bidding and promised them a profit at the same time. In many ways, the New Markets program offered redistribution upward rather than downward, since it provided tax breaks, tax credits, regulatory rollbacks, and enhanced market access to large companies like Walgreens, Citigroup, and America Online rather than payments to poor people themselves. In return, the program promised that private companies would deliver social functions and services that had once been the obligation and domain of government. Like the Clinton administration's response to sweatshop abuses, the program called on companies to help address the problems that they had partially played a hand in creating to enhance their corporate image and improve their bottom lines.

The New Markets program personified the New Democrats' logic that the financial services, banking, technology, and retail industries could not only fuel economic growth but could also solve poverty and racial inequality. This equation never fully added up but was especially faulty as these sectors themselves were transforming in the 1990s. The Clinton administration's simultaneous pursuit of financial services and telecommunications deregulation made these sectors especially precarious sources of economic salvation. Enmeshing antipoverty programs ever more tightly with the forces of the New Economy ultimately failed to bring distressed and segregated communities like East St. Louis, Pine Ridge, or Chicago's Englewood neighborhood into the economic mainstream. Instead, it made them more vulnerable to predation.

TEARING DOWN THE WALLS ON WALL STREET

The New Markets tours made for fascinating political theater. Perhaps even odder than the sight of Clinton and a group of corporate executives touring blighted downtowns and ramshackle trailer parks and barrios was seeing Rev. Jesse Jackson enthusiastically walking beside them. In the late 1990s, the nation's most prominent champion of economic populism launched his own effort to bring finance capital to poor communities.

As part of his larger push for economic justice, Jackson long argued that earning a foothold in the market offered the next stage of the civil rights battle. He consistently deemed the fight for access to capital, or "silver rights," the "fourth stage of the freedom struggle," after emancipation, desegregation, and voting rights.[8] In the late 1990s, he decided to take that fight directly to the nation's financial capital. In early 1997, Jackson and the Rainbow/PUSH Coalition set up an office at 40 Wall Street just a block from the floor of the New York Stock Exchange in space loaned by Donald Trump. Evoking his reputation for using boycotts as a protest tactic, Jackson declared that Wall Street had long "boycotted" African Americans by not providing them key job opportunities. "The walls on Wall Street," he announced, "have to come down."[9] Jackson's Wall Street Project sought to tear down those barriers by encouraging companies to hire Black employees, award more contracts to Black-owned companies, and give Black people seats on their boards. The project also encouraged African Americans to invest more of their money in the stock market as an alternative way to pressure companies.

"We're on Wall Street," Jackson liked to say, "because that's where the capital is."[10] The explanation showed some of the signs of the fiery economic populism that had defined much of his career. In an important difference from his earlier campaigns, however, Jackson decided his battle would take place in the boardroom rather than on the picket line and focus on negotiations rather than protests.[11] At the press conference launching the Wall Street Project, Jackson said, "We are not looking for boycott targets. We are looking for partners."[12] He quickly amassed an impressive roster of corporate sponsors and connections through his charisma and his power to command the national spotlight. As corporate social responsibility became ever more important to consumers and investors, companies recognized how having the endorsement of Jackson could help to burnish their image. In some respects, Jackson had more success making inroads with major corporations than he had with the Democratic Party.[13]

Jackson cultivated an especially close relationship with Sanford Weill, the CEO of Travelers Insurance, who was the leading icon of the corporate consolidations that were remaking the financial services industry. When Jackson arrived on Wall Street, Weill was in the midst of brokering a deal to merge his insurance and securities firm with Citicorp.[14] When the $70 billion deal went through in early 1998, it was the largest merger in history. It created Citigroup, which became the biggest financial company in the world with more than one hundred million customers and four thousand offices worldwide. It marked the arrival of the new type of financial institution enabled in the Clinton era.[15] Despite his reputation as being ruthless and brash, Weill had a commitment to charitable work and especially efforts that promoted doing well by doing good. He became one of the earliest and most enthusiastic endorsers of the Wall Street Project. His involvement provided the program with an important source of legitimacy and funding. In turn, when community activists protested the Citicorp and Travelers merger, charging that both institutions had poor records providing services in low-income neighborhoods, Jackson publicly defended the firms.[16] This stance confirmed to many of Jackson's allies that the civil rights leader had sold out. Journalist George Packer, in an article called "Trickle-Down Civil Rights," described Jackson as "moving from civil rights advocate and mass leader to power broker."[17]

Jackson vigorously maintained that he was still a defender of the downtrodden. Rather than "selling out," Jackson, riffing on de Tocqueville, dubbed his approach "enlightened self-interest."[18] He argued that Wall Street had closed itself off to an important pool of talent by not making more of an effort to hire African Americans and give them seats on their boards. He contended that diversifying employee and customer bases was "good business—not the cost of doing business."[19] Jackson increasingly applied this argument to places as well as people. He pointed out to corporate executives that they were willing to pour billions of dollars into "high-risk emerging markets all over the world" and should instead "take a new look at your own backyard."[20] He returned to the economic populist roots of his presidential campaigns to address the problems of poverty in rural as well urban communities and for whites as well. In July 1998, he and Weill organized "The Trillion Dollar Roundtable," a one-day event whose attendees included the CEOs of NationsBank, Fannie Mae, and General Motors. The roundtable focused on creating new "vehicles for transport of capital from Wall Street to Appalachia and Mississippi."[21] Despite buy-in from the nation's top CEOs, Jackson became increasingly aware that this effort to bring private investment into the poor pockets of the nation required government involvement, especially from the president.

Clinton and Jackson's relationship had come a long way since the Sister Souljah flap. In an effort to repair their antagonistic rivalry, Clinton, when he became president, named Jackson a special envoy to Haiti. He also reached out to Jackson for spiritual guidance at the height of the Monica Lewinsky scandal (an ironic choice since Jackson himself was involved in an extramarital affair at the time).[22] Clinton spoke at the Wall Street Project's first annual conference in 1998. As part of a further effort to solidify those ties, National Economic Council chair Gene Sperling agreed to offer substantial input on Jackson and Weill's proposal for channeling equity capital into distressed areas.[23] In reviewing the proposal, Sperling recognized that the ideas closely resembled the president's own commitment to increasing private sector investment in poor places.[24] When making the case for programs like Empowerment Zones and community development banks, Clinton often noted that the United States was doing more to stimulate economic growth in Asia and Latin America than it did in rural Arkansas or South LA.[25] Sperling realized that the administration could use the momentum created by Jackson's calls for action to amplify its existing economic empowerment agenda. It might especially help boost the Empowerment Zone initiative, which was based on a similar idea of encouraging investment in underserved areas.

The Empowerment Zone program, which Clinton had unveiled to much fanfare in 1993, had fallen short of expectations. The zones had problems ranging from significant delays and red tape to questionable use of the funds by local administrators. At almost every site, community groups and residents complained that while officials had involved them in the application and planning process, they excluded them from the implementation. The projects instead focused on the needs of large companies. Community groups worried that the plans to build large retail complexes in places like Harlem and Atlanta would exacerbate gentrification and drive out local residents and businesses.[26] Despite these problems, Al Gore remained deeply committed to the program and prodded White House officials to expand it.[27] The administration eventually unveiled a scaled-back Round II, which offered a smaller package of tax breaks and abandoned the social service grants.

Sperling and the National Economic Council staff hoped adopting a more cohesive market-based initiative would increase the effectiveness and impact of the Empowerment Zones. It could also enhance the CDFI Fund, which had been more successful but remained limited.[28] The NEC envisioned an initiative that could reach beyond the handful of Empowerment Zones and community development banks dispersed throughout the country and potentially reach all underserved areas. Sperling assembled members of several agencies in an Untapped Markets Working Group to determine how the government "could act as a catalyst for greater private sector economic activity in America's untapped markets."[29]

In addition to drawing on the ideas and advice of the Wall Street Project, the working group relied heavily on the work of Harvard Business School professor Michael Porter. A leading expert on economic strategy who also played a key role in advancing venture philanthropy and social enterprise, Porter turned his attention in the 1990s to low-income neighborhoods. In 1995, he published an article in the *Harvard Business Review* called "The Competitive Advantage of the Inner City." In it, he argued that "inner cities hold untapped potential for profitable businesses" due to their "competitive advantages" such as a central location, an underemployed labor pool, and an underserved market for retailing, finance, and other services.[30] Porter expanded this idea in his subsequent work, estimating that the nation's low-income urban neighborhoods had a collective retail spending power between $85 and $100 billion per year, which was larger than that of Mexico.[31] He questioned why companies were racing to expand south of the border when roughly the same size market existed on the streets of New York, Boston, and Chicago. Porter was weary of direct government involvement. But he essentially argued what the New Democrats had been saying for years—that the federal government could "help create the conditions necessary for private, mainstream financial institutions to lend and invest profitably in inner city businesses."[32] Sperling's working group believed Porter's theory applied to rural areas as well, making the amount of money in these unexplored markets even larger.

With these ideas in mind, the working group decided to name the program the New Markets Initiative.[33] The program aimed to stimulate significant capital investment in inner cities and rural areas in a variety of ways. First, it sought to expand the growth of CDFIs and microenterprise organizations. Second, it would establish new venture capital firms that would match the equity funds of the private investors with government loan debt guarantees. Finally, the working group suggested developing a new tax credit that would make $1 billion available to community development banks, venture funds, and corporations investing in underserved areas. Staffers estimated the tax credit could leverage an additional $6 billion in investments in distressed communities.

The White House put the finishing touches on the proposal just in time for the Wall Street Project's annual conference in January

1999. The event was held at the Windows on the World restaurant on the 106th floor of the iconic World Trade Center building. Sperling recognized that having Clinton announce the program there could gain buy-in from Jackson and potentially pique the interest of the many CEOs and investment bankers in attendance.[34] In contrast to the blustery winter weather outside, the tone of the president's remarks was warm and energetic. Clinton began by joking that the most immediate and concrete result of the "marriage of Jesse Jackson and Wall Street" was that Jackson had started wearing fancier suits.[35]

References to Jackson's new wardrobe aside, Clinton's speech sounded many themes that would come to define his selling of the New Markets program. He spoke of the urgency of initiating the program when the economy was strong. "If we can't do it now, when in the wide world will we ever get around to it? If there was ever a time when none of us have an excuse, this is that time," he implored.[36] Other speeches and literature on the initiative invariably cited as a mandate the low unemployment rate, rise in real wage growth, drop in inflation, and historically high rate of home-ownership.[37] Clinton suggested the only way to keep this prosperity going was to find new markets. "How are we going to keep growing the economy, keep the unemployment rate low, with inflation down?" he rhetorically asked the audience of financial heavyweights. "The answer is, we've got to find more places to invest and more customers." Clinton cited Michael Porter's research that residents in poor neighborhoods like Harlem, Brooklyn, and the Bronx had more purchasing power than the entire retail market of Mexico. If Jackson liked the imagery of tearing down the walls of Wall Street, Clinton went back to his own preferred construction-based metaphor of building bridges. He heralded how the government could use tax credits and other incentives to "build a bridge between Wall Street and our greatest untapped markets." He could see many of these untapped markets from the tall windows at the top of the World Trade Center and others of which were beyond the horizon.

NOW IS THE TIME

To build those metaphorical bridges, the Clinton administration decided to arrange a tour in the summer of 1999 to connect the nation's leading corporate executives with the untapped markets of Appalachia, the Mississippi Delta, and South LA. "The goal is not to ask people to make charitable contributions," Sperling stressed repeatedly, "but to make companies take a second look in our backyard where there could be profitable business opportunities while also helping rebuild communities that have been left behind."[38] The administration recognized that designing the tour as a "domestic trade mission" would be a way to attract the interest of corporate executives. This design could also draw media attention, which would be crucial as the administration sought to build support for the New Markets legislative package.

The tour offered the Clinton administration an opportunity to potentially refocus national attention on the problem of poverty, which had often been forgotten amid the concentration on the economic boom of the late 1990s. In planning the trip, staffers deliberately developed an itinerary that illustrated the geographic scope and racial diversity of poverty in the United States.[39] Before embarking on the tour, Clinton described its purpose as "shin[ing] a spotlight on the pockets of poverty that remain in America."[40] He and his aides frequently adopted this language to explain how the tour and legislative package focused on "pockets of poverty" or the "places left behind by the new economy."[41] Some critics quickly pointed out that poverty was not confined to a few pockets and such descriptions diminished the extent of the problem.[42]

The "left behind" language treated poverty as a discreet issue and poor places and people as distinct and aberrant from the rest of the nation. Calling poor places and people *left behind* indirectly reaffirmed that the New Economy had primarily performed a positive role in creating the nation's economic growth. It also provided a convenient way to evade addressing the fact that the very things that made the stock market soar—global trade, finance, technology, and retail—were causing poverty in many of these areas. In addition, categorizing places as distinct as Appalachia, Clarksdale, East St. Louis, Pine Ridge, Phoenix, and Watts with the same "left behind" descriptor failed to account for the particular economic histories of these different rural and urban areas and the unique social needs and political challenges confronting them.

The New Markets trip did demonstrate Clinton's dexterity moving between Wall Street and the byways of the Mississippi Delta and the people who occupied each of these places. The entourage included executives from companies like Aetna, Bank of America, and Citigroup. The corporate executives welcomed the opportunity to go to parts of the country they had never before visited, scout out potential investment opportunities, earn positive media attention for their companies, and get significant face time with the president.[43] The four-day trip took the group to a wide variety of places and events. The stops included a cabinet-making company in Clarksdale, Mississippi, that had received funding from a community development bank, a neighborhood on the Pine Ridge Reservation, a tortilla business in Phoenix run by a Latina entrepreneur, and a high school in the heart of Watts, before concluding at a conference for an organization started by Sanford Weill that offered vocational training for at-risk adolescents. Every event showcased how a government or corporate initiative aimed at encouraging the flow of capital to low-income communities could potentially create more government and private funding for more such programs.[44]

The schedule of the tour had the frenetic speed of a presidential campaign. The pace and time away from Washington only served to relax and recharge Clinton, who could be found on Air Force One chewing on an unlit cigar while holding court with reporters and executives.[45] He added in his own unscheduled diversions to savor local cuisine, particularly indulging in heaping plates of southern barbecue.[46] After once such meal, he got the National Civil Rights Museum in Memphis to open its doors after hours for the group. Located on the site of the Lorraine Motel, the visit had extra meaning for Jesse Jackson, who had witnessed Martin

Luther King Jr.'s assassination. It inspired him to lead the group in a spontaneous prayer.[47] Equally memorable for members of the entourage was when Clinton persuaded the Secret Service to steer the motorcade for a late-night visit to Mount Rushmore.[48]

The most emotional moments of the tour came during the visit to the Ogala Sioux's Pine Ridge Reservation in the rolling plains of the South Dakota badlands. The reservation held a fabled place in American history as the home of Crazy Horse, the infamous Wounded Knee Massacre, and the American Indian Movement's siege in 1973. Yet, Pine Ridge had never before received a visit from a sitting president. In fact, since Franklin Roosevelt stopped at a Cherokee reservation in North Carolina while on vacation in 1936, no president had stepped foot on tribal land.[49] The two-million-acre reservation, located a hundred miles from the nearest interstate highway, contained the poorest census tract in the country. The official unemployment rate on Pine Ridge was 73 percent (though tribal leaders estimated it was closer to 85 percent). It had a median annual income of $17,000 per year and an average life expectancy of forty-five.[50] Pine Ridge's dusty unpaved roads lined with broken-down cars, wooden shacks, and run-down trailers resembled the towns of Bangladesh, Honduras, and Uganda that Bill and Hillary Clinton had visited during their travels abroad. The conditions undoubtedly lent credence to the idea that Pine Ridge and other poor communities had more in common with the developing world than the booming parts of the US. "No matter how good you are with words, you could not describe this," HUD Secretary Andrew Cuomo commented to a reporter as they followed behind Clinton while he walked around parts of Pine Ridge.[51]

Residents in Pine Ridge and the other communities the tour passed through waited hours in the midday July heat or late in the night to see Clinton speak or even catch a glimpse of the motorcade. For many, the tour brought much-needed hope. Beatrice Spencer Burton, who braved brutal Mississippi humidity to hear Clinton, called his visit "a blessing from God" and "a turning point for Clarksdale."[52] Others were less convinced. In Watts, members of ACORN met the tour with signs asking: "President Clinton, It

All Sounds Good. But Where Are the Living Wage Jobs?"[53] Billy Arnold, an unemployed warehouse worker in East St. Louis, asked the same thing. "I don't mean no disrespect, but words don't do a thing for me."[54]

The photo-ops of Clinton walking down desolate Main Streets flanked by CEOs further fueled critiques that the tour served as a form of corporate welfare.[55] Former secretary of labor Robert Reich voiced doubts that tax breaks alone would achieve the economic redevelopment and jobs that Beatrice Spencer Burton and Billy Arnold prayed for. "There's just no magic bullet" to business investment, Reich maintained.[56] Many others saw the tour as too little too late.[57] Cuomo, running cover for his boss, deflected such charges and instead suggested that the timing was perfect since Clinton had developed the economic and political clout to make it possible. "He couldn't have done this six or seven years ago," Cuomo stressed. "He has the economy at his back, he has credibility in his Government and business is more mobile. . . . Now is the time to use Government to tap those markets."[58]

Clinton unsurprisingly did not seize the moment of prosperity and his high approval ratings as a chance to complete the unfinished liberal agenda of the War on Poverty. Instead, he saw it as a chance to double down on his New Democrat roots. In both interviews and speeches, he framed the New Markets program as fulfilling the goals he established at the outset of his presidency and discussed how it encapsulated his view of the best way to address poverty and inequality. "This is a classic example . . . of the New Democratic or Third Way philosophy that I articulated back in 1991 and 1992," he said of the New Markets program. Essentially summarizing the main principles of the New Democrat theory of governance, he explained: "What we're doing basically is using the government to facilitate a public-private partnership at the grassroots level. It's not government alone, it's not private sector alone, but it's a partnership."[59] In an effort to connect the program to the DLC's philosophy, the White House had invited Al From to join the tour. From embraced the chance to rejoin his former travel buddy and even put aside old differences with Jesse Jackson.[60] He offered his seal of approval for the New Markets program, praising it as a "a way to use government resources effectively to leverage capital investment in these markets that have been left behind."[61] He proudly reported back to the members of the DLC that the trip offered "evidence of yet another way that New Democrats have reshaped the political debate" and "the dramatic paradigm shift that New Democrats have brought about in their party."[62]

In his speeches and interviews with reporters on the tour, Clinton framed the New Markets program in the New Democrats' preferred parlance of win-wins. As Clinton explained to an audience in Watts during the last day of tour: "Every time we hire a young person off the street in Watts and give him or her a better future, we are helping people who live in the ritziest suburb in America to continue to enjoy a rising stock market."[63] Clinton was speaking as much to the Republican members of Congress as he was to the crowd. He and his staff anticipated a battle to get the New Markets package passed, especially since they were already in a fierce struggle with the Republicans over the Community Reinvestment Act, which was another key flank of their market-based antipoverty program.

GOOD FOR BUSINESS

The Clinton administration never missed an opportunity to present the Community Reinvestment Act as a win-win for poor communities, banks, and government and stressed how it used market forces to help address inequality. In addition to unveiling the New Markets program, Clinton had gone to the 1999 Wall Street Project Conference to sell bankers on the importance of the CRA, which required that banks lend in areas where they did business. Clinton assured the Wall Street crowd: "This is not bad for business; this is good for business. It is not a welfare program; it is not a charity program." He explained, "We are not asking anybody to do anything we do not think they will make money out of."[64] The Clinton administration's advocacy for the CRA revealed its very real belief in the power of the banking industry to help poor communities.

These efforts, however, exposed the clear limitations to using the banking and the financial services sector as a way to lessen inequality, especially as the industry's landscape was changing dramatically.

Clinton made increasing the effectiveness of the CRA a major priority of his initial economic empowerment agenda in 1993. Throughout his presidency, he continued to tout it as an important way to redirect private sector capital into distressed areas. He proudly boasted that 95 percent of the commitments that banks had made in the CRA's twenty-plus year history had occurred since he had become president.[65] It was true. From 1993 to 1999, banks and thrifts subject to the CRA gave out $800 billion in home mortgage, small business, and community development loans to low- and moderate-income borrowers.[66] The CRA also contributed to a rise in lending to communities of color during the same period with the number of mortgage loans received by African Americans increasing 58 percent, to Latinx people by 62 percent, and to Asian Americans by 29 percent.[67] Clinton presented these figures as a sign that the changes to the CRA enabled financial institutions to profit while helping low-income communities. Banks were "doing well by doing good," he insisted.[68]

In truth, the main source of the growth of CRA lending was not the law reforms the Clinton administration implemented. Rather, it emerged as a by-product of the administration's support of the deregulation of the banking industry, which unleashed a historic wave of consolidation. In order to avoid having their merger applications held up for non-CRA compliance, the nation's major banks made hefty commitments to low-income lending in the 1990s. For instance, in advance of the Citicorp and Travelers merger, Sanford Weill announced Citigroup would invest $115 billion in moderate- and lower-income communities and small business over a ten-year period.[69] Bank of America went even bigger. When it joined with NationsBank in 1998, the bank pledged to spend $350 billion over the next decade.[70] Many bankers were quick to claim that they were making such commitments not just out of obligation but because of the profit-making potential of investing in low-income areas.[71] However, not everyone had grown to love the CRA.

Senator Phil Gramm of Texas had been a staunch opponent of the act since arriving on Capitol Hill in the late 1970s, but his vitriol grew as he assumed a leadership position on the powerful Senate Banking Committee. The former economics professor turned legislator and former Democrat turned Republican denounced the CRA as "legalized extortion" and complained that it enabled community groups "to hold up" banks for money.[72] While Clinton stressed that the CRA was a market-based solution, Gramm alleged it was a form of socialism that sought to reallocate wealth.[73] Over the years, Gramm made several attempts to repeal the CRA but came up short. Finally, he found an opening in the push to deregulate the financial services industry.

Since the Carter administration, Congress and the White House had been discussing revising the regulations around the financial services sector. At the top of the list of priorities was erasing the wall erected by the New Deal's Glass-Steagall Act to separate consumer, commercial, and investment banking and prohibit banks, securities firms, and insurance companies from merging and engaging in one another's business. Clinton's economic advisors supported such a change, taking the position that Glass-Steagall was out of date in the financial environment of the New Economy. The team also acknowledged that Congress and the Federal Reserve had already allowed substantial exemptions and loopholes, which made the rule weak. Gene Sperling, Robert Rubin, and other key advisors suggested in memos to the president that formally eliminating the wall would make financial services companies more competitive at home and abroad and would encourage innovation, offer more options to consumers, and streamline bureaucracy. Clinton's advisors were well aware, however, of the challenges of eradicating a staple of the New Deal and had delayed making a strong push for it.[74] But the formation of Citigroup in 1998 created new pressure to get something passed. The merger was in direct violation of Glass-Steagall, and without repeal of the law, the conglomerate would have to be broken up. This move ran the risk of creating substantial financial turmoil, something that the White House wanted to avoid.[75]

Gramm was also a firm advocate of overturning Glass-Steagall and led the drafting of several bills to do so. He also realized such a law provided a chance to defang the CRA. He inserted provisions in the proposed legislation that would exempt smaller banks from the CRA's requirements, make it harder for community groups to challenge a bank merger, and create a way to move certain assets and activities into holding companies where they would be outside the CRA's oversight. The proposal caused outrage among community groups as well as Clinton's economic advisors who interpreted the provisions as an "assault upon the CRA."[76] Clinton announced in the spring of 1999 that he would veto any bill that curtailed the power of the CRA.[77] The administration's stance made Citigroup's Weill nervous, and he met several times with Clinton's top advisors urging them to reconsider. This lobbying not surprisingly revealed that Weill's desire to keep Citigroup intact outweighed his concern for the plight of poor communities, regardless of his work with the Wall Street Project. Yet, the master dealmaker failed to make Clinton or Gramm budge.[78]

The New Markets tour in July provided Clinton a chance to make the case for preserving the CRA. Staffers deliberately inserted into Clinton's remarks at every stop on the tour a reference to the effectiveness of the CRA.[79] Returning to Washington, the CRA remained the final sticking point, preventing the passage of financial modernization legislation with both sides standing their ground.[80] During the fall of 1999, Gramm, Sperling, Larry Summers (who had recently replaced Rubin as treasury secretary), and their staffs engaged in protracted negotiations to work out a compromise. After days of twelve- to fourteen-hour sessions fighting over technical aspects of the CRA, they finally broke the impasse in the early morning hours of October 22. At 1:30 a.m., Gramm finally capitulated and said he would leave the CRA mostly intact if the administration agreed to a stipulation to make community groups more accountable.[81] He and Clinton's advisors announced the deal at 2:45 a.m. Glass-Steagall was no more! The news brought cheers from Wall Street, and the Dow immediately bounced over 170 points to 10,470.25 the next day.[82] Although exhausted, Sperling and Summers quickly moved to persuade community and civil rights groups that the agreement was the right thing to do and worked with both Weill and Bank of America's Cathy Bessant to put a positive spin on what the new legislation would mean for low-income communities.[83]

Weill needed little prodding. He and his co-CEO John Reed immediately released a joint statement hailing how the legislation, known as the Gramm-Leach-Bliley bill, would "unleash the creativity of our industry and insure our global competitiveness."[84] Citigroup employees later commissioned a large wooden plaque with Weill's image and the inscription: "The Man Who Shattered Glass-Steagall."[85] Late October would witness the erosion of not just the line between investment and commercial banks but also between the public and private sectors. Days after the late-night deal, Robert Rubin, who had left the Treasury Department only a few months before, announced that he was coming out of a very brief retirement to join Weill and Reed as the third co-CEO of Citigroup. This news only further crystallized who would be the main beneficiaries of the financial reforms.

Despite their efforts to stand their ground to preserve the CRA, Clinton and his staff avoided heeding the insistence of activists and some legislators that the law be extended to nonbanking services of financial institutions. Activists stressed that the erasure of Glass-Stegall would shift a large portion of financial activities beyond the parameters of the CRA. "More and more of the activities that CRA is about are being done outside of what CRA covers," Matthew Lee, a Bronx-based community activist warned lawmakers. "By not expanding CRA to those industries, you're weakening it."[86] He and others feared that without such an expansion, the new law would achieve Gramm's goal, just more slowly. This fear would increasingly pan out.

FROM DIGITAL DIVIDE TO DIGITAL OPPORTUNITY

On November 3, 1999, the day after Congress formally passed the Gramm-Leach-Bliley bill, Clinton appeared in the crowded gymnasium of Englewood High School in Chicago. The event was part of a second and shorter New Markets tour to focus on partnerships between the private sector and community organizations. The two-day tour bounced from Newark, where Clinton met with owners and members of several professional sports teams, to a tomato farming co-operative in Hermitage, Arkansas, before ending in Englewood. The South Side neighborhood served as the home base for the Women's Self-Employment Project. ShoreBank had also begun to focus attention on Englewood as had Jesse Jackson. The Wall Street Project recently launched an initiative to persuade Chicago-based banks and corporations of the potential development and employment opportunities amid the abandoned buildings, vacant lots, crumbling houses, and unemployed residents of the neighborhood.[87] "Englewood is less risky than Indonesia," Jackson stressed to corporate executives.[88] He publicly urged Clinton to make Englewood the model for the New Markets program and to come visit.[89]

When Clinton did come, he was greeted by more than two hundred local residents standing outside the high school who held signs declaring "Save Our Community. Save the CRA" and shouted for the president to veto the Gramm-Leach-Bliley bill.[90] Clinton deflected protestors' concerns and instead assured the audience inside that the legislation would preserve the CRA and help low-income neighborhoods. "This is the kind of thing we can do together," Clinton declared of the compromise that his administration reached with Gramm.[91] The statement was a direct pitch to Speaker of the House Dennis Hastert, who was standing alongside him on the gymnasium's makeshift dais. The administration had been working vigorously behind the scenes to get Hastert to support the New Markets legislation. Sperling even sent Weill as an emissary to make the case for the program to the Speaker.[92]

Hastert's decision to appear at the Englewood event was a promising sign.

Clinton's advisors still worried, however, that interest in the New Markets program was waning both on Capitol Hill and among the wider public. Returning to his office in the West Wing after the second tour, Sperling drafted a memo suggesting that one way to maintain momentum for the program would be to focus on the issue of the digital divide.[93] The racial and economic disparity in access to computers and the internet, especially among young people, had been a theme of Clinton-Gore's 1996 reelection campaign. It received a positive response from voters. Sperling recognized the issue naturally aligned with the New Markets program since both focused on creating public-private partnerships, giving the people and places left behind access to the benefits of the New Economy and reducing racial, economic, and geographic divisions.[94]

The internet revolution had personally passed Clinton by. He made jokes about his technical challenges, and staffers often had to prep him for tech-focused events with term sheets defining words like *e-mail*, *browser*, and *chat room*.[95] Yet, he long understood the economic and social significance of computers and internet-based technology. Al Gore, who remained far more tech savvy, was beginning to launch his presidential bid when Sperling wrote his memo. Pivoting the attention of the New Markets program to the digital divide was a way to spotlight Gore's record.[96] At the same time, it could build on the close relationships the vice president had cultivated with Silicon Valley heavyweights during his monthly Gore-Tech meetings and other outreach.

It was not as if Sperling was creating an issue where none existed. In the summer of 1999, the Commerce Department issued a report revealing that while there were dramatic gains in the number of Americans who had access to computers and the internet since 1995, the disparity between who had access had widened along race, class, and geographic lines.[97] Almost 50 percent of all white and Asian families owned computers, but fewer than half as many African Americans did and the number was even lower among Latinx households. The report also found that people living in rural areas, especially African Americans, were much less likely to have access to a computer or the internet than their urban counterparts. The issue caught the attention of the media, too, with stories appearing that featured images of wired suburban classrooms and towheaded children doing their homework on their family's PC juxtaposed with African American youth who lacked computers in their classrooms or homes.[98] The issue also attracted the philanthropic sector. The major legacy foundations began supporting initiatives to address the digital divide, as did the corporate foundations of several leading tech companies.[99] Bill and Melinda Gates, in fact, made their entry into philanthropy with an initiative to donate computers to libraries in areas with high rates of poverty.[100] The program had rapidly expanded side by side the Gates's other charitable work. In total, it helped install 47,200 computers in almost eleven thousand libraries across the United States.[101]

Recognizing the growing interest in the issue, the administration decided to make the digital divide a major organizing focus not just of the New Markets initiative but also of Clinton's final year in office. In the 2000 State of the Union, Clinton pledged to make computer and internet access available to all Americans. He spoke of how tragic it would be "if this instrument, that has done more to break down barriers between people than anything in all of human history, built a new wall because not everybody had access to it."[102] Clinton's staffers developed a plan to close the digital divide by breaking down the barriers between the public and private sector through a series of corporate tax breaks and loans. The proposal suggested $2 billion in tax incentives to encourage the private sector to donate computers to libraries, building on the model established by the Gateses.[103] It also sought to spur tech companies to sponsor technology centers in low-income communities and offer technology literacy programs for teachers in distressed areas. Finally, it gave corporations grant and loan guarantees to further accelerate private sector deployment of broadband networks in underserved urban and rural places.[104]

Like other elements of the New Markets program, the digital divide proposal reaffirmed the New Democrat principle that partnerships with the private sector were a more effective way to create economic equity and racial justice than direct government support. Though Clinton repeatedly claimed that computers and the internet were prerequisites to achieve educational or financial success in the New Economy, the initiative did not aim to make the internet a universal, free public utility, as some had advocated at the time and have continued to call for since. Instead, the administration focused on channeling the subsidies upward to private companies. This approach not surprisingly earned rapid buy-in from leading technology companies like America Online, Hewlett-Packard, and the like. Tech executives clearly appreciated how the initiative offered generous tax breaks and the potential to substantially expand their customer bases. Executives likewise recognized it was a relatively easy way to demonstrate corporate social responsibility and concern about the problems of low-income people, especially children, which could also help their bottom lines.

The final New Markets tour in April 2000, which focused specifically on the digital divide, further amplified these themes and ties. The tour began in East Palo Alto, a place that overtly exemplified the digital and financial gulf the tech industry was creating. The city sat in the center of Silicon Valley. Unlike its wealthy neighbors, the community had a predominantly Latinx and African American population, a fourth of whom lived below the poverty line and few of whom had jobs in the tech industry or PCs at home.[105] Jesse Jackson also recognized the symbolism of East Palo Alto, and just a month earlier the Wall Street Project had opened a West Coast outpost there called the Silicon Valley Project.[106] Jackson actively supported the Clinton's administration's digital divide initiative and joined the president during a stop at Plugged In, an East Palo Alto tech-based community center underwritten by Hewlett-Packard, Intel, and Sun Microsystems. At the event, Hewlett-Packard CEO Carly Fiorina and basketball star Rebecca Lobo spoke to a live audience of tech executives and youth from

Bill Clinton and Jesse Jackson at the Plugged In community center in East Palo Alto as part of the New Markets tour focused on the digital divide, April 2000
Credit: Getty Images

East Palo Alto, as well as to students around the country who joined from a webcast provided by AOL. The stop netted over $100 million in pledges from various tech firms to address the problem of the digital divide.[107]

Clinton then headed to Shiprock, New Mexico, with an entourage of tech and telecommunications executives in tow. Shiprock was part of the Navajo reservation, and most residents did not have phones, much less internet or computers. The president announced another round of commitments from private companies to provide equipment and training for American Indian tribes.[108] Clinton finished the trip in downtown Chicago at a large computer trade show. In addition to testing out a pager that could serve as a minicomputer, he exhorted the crowd "to devote more time and technology, more ideas and energy, to closing the digital divide." Borrowing a phrase from Jackson (and de Tocqueville), Clinton added that it "is actually in our enlightened self-interest."[109] The following week, Clinton added a brief postscript and traveled to Whiteville, North Carolina, to focus specifically on the problem of the rural digital divide. Standing in front of an abandoned train depot, against the backdrop of a banner reading "Rural America: From Digital Divide to Digital Opportunity," Clinton extolled the internet as the most important technological breakthrough ever to come to rural places (surpassing even the railroad, highways, and air travel). "It collapses time and distance," he declared, slapping his hands together repeatedly for dramatic effect. Clinton promised his audience of two thousand assembled Whiteville residents that the internet had the potential "to move more people out of poverty and unemployment" than any economic innovation that had come before.[110]

The promises of the digital divide initiative itself did not match this forceful claim and exposed the problems with the New Democrats' governing philosophy of trying to collapse the distance between the public and private sectors. Regardless of what Carly Fiorina and Steve Case might have professed during photo-ops with the president and how many computers they donated to urban schools, their companies' dedication to the people and places being left behind was quite shallow. So, too, was what the Clinton administration expected of their corporate allies. The administration's unwillingness to hold tech companies accountable for problems embodied by the digital divide ensured racial and economic inequality would only fester and deepen. The administration's proposals to close the digital divide did nothing to confront the impact of the tech industry on the rising prices of housing and goods in the Bay Area and other hubs, which would spark substantial displacement. It did not demand that these companies pay a living wage or allow their workers to unionize. And it did not force them to meaningfully consider relocating parts of their operations from factories in Asia to places like rural North Carolina or East St. Louis. Absent more consequential reforms, these private companies only did good in distressed communities to the extent it helped their bottom lines.

Clinton and the members of his administration never acknowledged that the digital divide might reflect a flaw or limitation in their macroeconomic policy and the New Economy's dependency on growth of sectors like technology. Instead, the program reinforced the notion that technology—like finance, banking, and retail—could solve larger systemic problems of economic inequality and racial discrimination. The consequences of this optimistic faith in the power of the private sector proved devastating.

"I SEE A MARKET"

As the first New Markets tour experienced its one-year anniversary in July 2000, the people in the places Clinton visited were growing disillusioned at the lack of change. Clarksdale, Missouri, still had waist-high weeds in vacant lots and trash piled up along its Main Street, and East St. Louis saw none of the new development promised by the president. Clarence Ellis, who ran a small childcare center, had gone to see Clinton speak in the East St. Louis Walgreens parking lot. Standing in the same parking lot the following year, Ellis complained, "He was talking about all the things he was going to bring here. But I don't see it. All talk and no action."[111]

Despite the energy and commitment engendered by the New Market tours, the administration struggled to push the initiatives through Congress. Staffers eventually decided to push the digital divide program down the road, betting that Gore would win the 2000 election. The administration was more committed to making the New Markets part of Clinton's legacy. The White House eventually reached a deal with congressional Republicans in fall 2000. The compromise jettisoned the idea of new venture capital firms but did include the New Markets Tax Credit. It also provided full funding for forty new Empowerment Zones, as well as the creation of forty Renewal Communities, an idea created by the Republicans, which essentially resurrected Jack Kemp's Enterprise Zone model.[112] Clinton signed the legislation on December 21, 2000, just a month before he left office. He heralded it as "the most significant effort ever to help hard-pressed communities lift themselves up through private investment and entrepreneurship."[113] The comment was a fitting capstone to Clinton's relentless overselling of what small market-based antipoverty programs could do.

The passage of the New Markets program simultaneously solidified the administration's case that Walgreens franchises and AOL dial-up, rather than an increase in social services and government funding, would solve the myriad problems of residents of East St. Louis, Clarksdale, Pine Ridge, and Englewood. A recollection of Jesse Jackson from the first New Markets tour illuminated the dangers in this market-oriented logic. During Clinton's speech at the Pine Ridge Reservation, one of the corporate leaders sitting next to Jackson on the dais looked out on the crowd and said: "I've always just seen Indian reservations. . . . Now, I see two supermarkets. I see a car dealership. I see 7,000 people wearing clothes. I see a market."[114] Larry Summers was actually one the few people within the administration to point out the drawbacks of relying so heavily on the private sector to help distressed communities. Soon after rising to the post of treasury secretary, Summers sent Clinton a memo about the New Markets program. He approved of the idea, but he suggested "the real test of what we are doing with the New Markets Initiative will be whether we can sustain the flow of capital and the business connections that are now being made when the next downturn comes."[115] While Clinton did not respond (at least in writing) to this observation, Summers's comment suggested the clear problems both in fusing antipoverty initiatives with economic growth and validating the role of the private sector investment to deliver social goods and services.

The foreclosure and financial crisis less than a decade later would bring into sharp relief the dangers of trying to connect poverty alleviation to private investment and capital. While the crisis occurred years after Clinton left office, many of the policies his administration approved played an important role in setting it into action. In fact, on December 21, 2000, the same day that Clinton signed the New Markets program into law, he also put his signature to the second part of the financial modernization program. Known as the Commodity Futures Modernization Act, it essentially prohibited the regulation of financial derivatives. Along with removal of Glass-Steagall, the law enabled banks to make far riskier investments, eventually fueling the subprime mortgage bubble of the early 2000s.

The combination of deregulation and market-based antipoverty initiatives led the nation's leading financial institutions to no longer see poor people of color living in places like East St. Louis or Englewood as a risk to avoid but instead as a profitable market to tap.[116] These communities transformed from places "left behind" to canaries in the coal mine. As has been extensively documented, it was such areas that the foreclosure crisis hit first and hardest. In neighborhoods like Englewood, the combination of a long history of systemic discrimination in the real estate market, capital flight, and chronic unemployment and the shrinking of social services made subprime mortgages especially alluring. Before the bubble even burst, the foreclosures started in Englewood at a rate seven times the national average. Many residents found themselves chided for being irresponsible for falling behind on their payments.[117] A drive through the sprawling neighborhood revealed that no block was left untouched, with thousands of houses and apartments stripped of their pipes and radiators, their windows covered in plywood. The protracted crisis exacerbated the area's interlocking problems of unemployment, violence, and lack of social welfare.[118]

The New Markets program could do little to stem these forces. The program contained no serious requirement or obligation that a corporation stay in an area if it was not profitable, just as charter school and microenterprise policies did not require philanthropies to support schools or programs if they were not performing as expected or a foundation's funding priorities changed. Corporations faced no consequences if they chose to leave a community they had purported to be improving, just as many faced limited repercussions for their role in the mortgage crisis. Although it was one of the most ambitious antipoverty programs of Clinton's presidency, with an allocation of $1.6 billion, its budget was a fraction of what the Gates Foundation and large philanthropies were doling out. By the time Clinton left office, the Gates Foundation had committed about the same amount to just one program that provided college and postgraduate scholarships to low-income students of color in science, math, and engineering.[119] This fact alone revealed the federal government's increased reliance on the private sector and philanthropy to address problems of poverty over the course of the 1990s.

Clinton's own move into philanthropy in his postpresidential career further abetted these trends. Through the Clinton Foundation, Bill Clinton continued to promote a market-based approach to addressing problems of inequity both in the United States and especially internationally. The foundation's New York headquarters not coincidentally sat at the intersection of 125th Street and Malcolm X Boulevard in the heart of Harlem's Empowerment Zone. From the large windows of its penthouse office, with views of both the brick blocks of Harlem and towering Manhattan skyscrapers, the foundation expanded Clinton's efforts to apply the tools of business and the market to the task of solving social problems. The Clinton Foundation developed a new model of philanthropy focused on creating partnerships among private companies and donors, NGOs, community organizations, and underserved communities.[120] Yet, tellingly, many in Harlem grew increasingly frustrated with the foundation's presence in their neighborhood. Residents alternatively blamed the former president and his foundation for contributing to the rapid gentrification of the neighborhood and for focusing more on the problems of Africa than those in their own backyard.[121] In the decades after Clinton left office, it became ever clearer that neither Walgreens, Citigroup, AOL, nor the Clinton Foundation could offer a cure for the many ills of urban and rural America and were weak, unreliable, and even predatory replacements for the state. Like the building itself, the foundation and its namesake gazed down at these problems mostly from above.

EPILOGUE

I n late February 2011, Al From announced that the Democratic
Leadership Council was closing its doors. After Bill Clinton left
office, the organization had struggled to find its lane in Washington
and found itself caught in fruitless and petty battles.[1] Following
the 2016 election, Bill and Hillary Clinton no longer held the sway
and stature in the Democratic Party they once had. Bill Clinton's
role especially diminished, and his political vision began looking
increasingly out of date. Yet, the ideas and policies that the DLC
and the Clintons helped to engender lived on. The New Democrat
worldview continued to influence and shape the agenda of the
Democratic Party throughout the first decades of the twenty-first
century and had a tangible impact on the lives of poor people and
the places where they live.

From Opportunity Zones and baby bonds to the perennial
promises of turning coal miners (and JC Penney workers) into
computer coders, New Democrat approaches and ideas have persisted. The administration of Barack Obama played an especially
important role in imprinting these ideas into the priorities of the
Democratic Party in the twenty-first century. Obama's promotion
of entrepreneurship, especially in the high-tech sector, would have
made his Atari Democrat predecessors proud. He and Education
Secretary Arne Duncan's Race to the Top program reinforced a
standards-and-competition-based approach to education. Race to

the Top incentivized states to lift their caps on charter schools, which, coupled with the infusion of billions of dollars from philanthropic funds, led to the opening of thousands of new charters, especially in low-income communities of color in the 2000s. The Obama administration also showed a strong commitment to "reinventing government" through market-based tools, such as competitive grantmaking, leveraging private funds, and data-driven solutions. The administration's much-touted Social and Behavioral Sciences Team sought to use market-oriented ideas to alter the behavior of Americans and included several techniques to make low-income people more responsible and reward work.[2]

Microenterprise advocates had hoped that Obama's presidency would ignite more interest in funding credit programs for low-income entrepreneurs in the US, especially given the fact that Obama's mother had worked for a microcredit organization in Indonesia.[3] In 2008, just before Obama became president, Grameen Bank once again started an offshoot in the United States and the second time was more successful. By 2020, Grameen had dispersed $1.5 billion in microloans to over 130,000 borrowers who were primarily immigrants.[4] Yet, microcredit programs have still never reached the scale domestically that its proponents had anticipated.

With the rise of the gig economy, however, ideas of self-employment flourished in the US. Companies like Etsy, Uber, Lyft, and Instacart led millions to turn to self-employment. Champions of the gig economy updated many of the claims about the liberating dimensions of self-employment and celebrated participants as entrepreneurs who demonstrated resourcefulness, resilience, and creativity. These celebrations ignored the multitude of hardships confronting the average self-employed person who had a more flexible schedule but none of the protections or security of stable employment. The gig economy, therefore, helped to perpetuate the idea that entrepreneurship could solve the problems of systemic inequality.[5] The fallacy of this notion was evident in, for example, the growing number of poor people in places like Chicago and the Mississippi Delta who had either received money from TANF, which was time limited, or were ineligible for it and were disqualified from public housing and so turned to off-the-books entrepreneurialism, like selling popsicles or tamales. For them, entrepreneurship was not a means of upward mobility but, rather, survival.[6]

Despite the ambitious promises made by the DLC in the 1990s, economic inequality has only intensified since 2000. A 2018 study commissioned by the United Nations found that the United States had the highest rate of wealth and income inequality in the developed world. It also had the highest youth poverty and infant mortality rates among wealthy democracies, which the study concluded was the result of years of neglecting the issue of poverty. The author of the study spent two weeks traveling the country, visiting some of the same places that Bill Clinton stopped at on his New Market tours. He concluded that the US was "a land of stark contrasts" and suggested the situation did not bode well for society as a whole.[7] While the stock market soared and the United States became home to 25 percent of the world's billionaires—including many of those who have set up private foundations trying to address poverty—median household income has declined in the twenty-first century. Median household income and assets also remain substantially higher for whites than people of color.[8] In 2019, the official poverty rate was 10.5 percent, and it is estimated that at least eight million more people have fallen into poverty since the start of 2020.[9]

Although the UN investigator did not stop in Chicago on his brief visit, the city starkly embodies these patterns of inequality. The successive mayoral administrations of Richard M. Daley and Rahm Emanuel, a Clinton and Obama administration alumnus, pursued an agenda that combined aggressive economic redevelopment and social welfare austerity. The new skyscrapers downtown and upscale chain stores and luxury condominiums on the site where Cabrini-Green once stood illustrate the fruits of this strategy. At the same time, the city's South Side has suffered from increased problems of poverty, foreclosures, evictions, drug addiction, violence, and hypersegregated schools, a problem compounded by Emanuel's approval of a mass closing of city schools.[10]

South Shore, the home of the community development bank ShoreBank, was not immune from these trends. The settlement of large numbers of displaced public housing residents kickstarted a large exodus of African American middle-class families from the neighborhood in the late 1990s.[11] The foreclosure crisis led others to follow suit either by choice or lack thereof. These forces had a reverberating effect on ShoreBank itself. The bank responded aggressively to the subprime mortgage crisis and helped residents in South Shore and other parts of the South Side refinance risky mortgages so that they could stay in their homes.[12] But ShoreBank's rapid expansion in the 1990s to Cleveland, Detroit, and the Pacific Northwest had come at a major cost and stretched its capacity thin. In addition, the combination of Community Reinvestment Act reforms and New Market Tax Credits led other many big financial institutions like Citigroup and Bank of America to invest in low-income markets, which often crowded out ShoreBank.[13] Freddie Mac started funding multifamily mortgage loans in these areas on terms that ShoreBank simply could not meet. As the foreclosure and financial crises deepened, the bank faltered.[14] ShoreBank officials then turned to Washington for help. The bank applied for some of the funds from the Troubled Asset Relief Program (TARP), which was established at the height of the recession to help faltering financial firms and rescued many of the banks that were "too big to fail." However, Republican members of Congress and conservative commentators raised eyebrows at ShoreBank's connections to the Clintons as well as Obama, who had attenuated ties to the bank dating back to his Chicago politics days.[15] Glenn Beck turned these connections into a wide and creative web that drew in Obama's mother and Treasury Secretary Timothy Geithner's father, who had been a senior officer at the Ford Foundation. The political turmoil contributed to the Treasury and Federal Reserve ultimately declining to provide ShoreBank with $75 million of TARP funds, even though it had raised $146 million in private investment to match it. And the organization, which at the time was by far the biggest CDFI in the country, had no choice but to close in the summer of 2010.

The fate of ShoreBank provides one of countless examples of the tragedies created by the conviction of members of the Clinton administration that financial deregulation and the tools of the New Economy provided a path to doing good. The institution's demise also reveals the limits of relying on nonprofits for the solutions to larger problems of economic underdevelopment and to provide a social safety net. Even an organization as innovative and well connected as ShoreBank, with visionary and committed leaders like Ron Grzywinski and Mary Houghton, proved unable to eradicate the root causes of poverty or comprehensively combat problems of capital disinvestment and structural inequality.

The CDFI industry has continued to offer an important source of credit in low-income areas. ShoreBank's Arkansas offshoot Southern Bancorp has grown substantially in the last several years with more than $1 billion in assets by 2020. It has worked to counter the payday lenders that have spread throughout the Mississippi and Arkansas Delta and to help its clients pay off their debts and reestablish credit.[16] In recent years, CDFIs have become an attractive source of investment for large tech and finance firms trying to address problems of systemic racism and inequality. In 2020 alone, Google promised $125 million, Netflix $100 million, Bank of America $250 million, and Goldman Sachs committed $750 million.[17] Yet, it is clear that solutions to the problem of structural inequality could never come from a community development bank alone, and the private dollars are but another drop in the bucket.

Things certainly got worse in South Shore, however, since ShoreBank closed. Many of the conditions that brought Grzywinski and Houghton to the neighborhood in the early 1970s reappeared as the foreclosure, eviction, and crime rates continued to accelerate.[18] Many businesses closed, as well, including the neighborhood's only supermarket. Little to none of Daley and Emanuel's redevelopment dollars reached the neighborhood, and its main commercial area, where the ShoreBank headquarters sat, became increasingly hollowed out.

The COVID-19 pandemic compounded South Shore's problems. By August 2020, the zip code that encompasses much of the neighborhood had Chicago's highest COVID-19 death rate.[19] And South Shore's unemployment rate surpassed 17 percent, which made residents' efforts to hold on to their homes and apartments increasingly tenuous.[20] Many residents pinned their hopes on the construction of the Obama Presidential Center, which will sit in Jackson Park on South Shore's northern edge. In addition to the presidential museum, the plan for the $500 million complex includes an event center and athletic space, outdoor movie theater, and sledding hill.[21] It will also house the headquarters of Barack and Michelle Obama's foundation, which has adopted as its mission to "inspire, empower, and connect people to change their world." Some South Shore residents and business owners bank on the project to deliver economic empowerment and change. Others worry it will only bring gentrification and further instability, much

Barack Obama presenting the design of the proposed Obama Presidential Center during a community meeting at the South Shore Cultural Center, May 3, 2017

Credit: Getty Images/Scott Olson

Downtown Pine Bluff, 2016
Credit: William Widmer

like what happened in Harlem with the Clinton Foundation, and have tried for years to block the groundbreaking.[22]

Things have been even bleaker in Pine Bluff, Arkansas. Since 2000, the site of the long-closed microenterprise program the Clintons helped to start has fallen into harder times. The city has consistently sat at the top of lists of the poorest, most racially segregated, and most dangerous metropolitan areas in the country.[23] Most of the buildings in Pine Bluff's downtown look like they are about to fall down, while others already have. Even minimum wage jobs are hard to come by. The area's large concentration of correctional facilities has offered one of the few sources of employment, with nursing homes and fast-food restaurants providing a few more. COVID-19 only heightened Pine Bluff's problems. The area's high rate of poverty coupled with its large concentration of older Black residents made it especially vulnerable to the disease. So too did its sizable number of assisted-living and correctional facilities, including the Cummings State Prison, which experienced one of the nation's largest outbreaks in the spring of 2020.[24]

The pandemic laid bare the consequences of the Democratic Party's half-century prioritizing of economic growth, opportunity, and individual responsibility over redistribution and government assistance. The interlocking crises ignited by COVID-19 revealed the very real downsides of decades of leaning on private corporations and philanthropic institutions to provide services and the basic functions of the state. These decisions have had political reverberations as well. The 2016 and 2020 elections coupled with the large protests that emerged in the aftermath of the murder of George Floyd exposed that many poor and low-income people across the country and across the political spectrum have become ever more alienated by government. Opportunity and responsibility, the shibboleths of the New Democrat ethos, no longer hold the power they once did nor does the promise that economic growth alone can provide it. Vast numbers of low-income people do not see the Democrats as addressing their concerns and needs nor have they been sold on the idea that market-based solutions can offer them the relief they need or that work incentives and the gig economy can be a source of upward mobility.[25] And they definitely don't see globalization as a source of good.

The successive and overlapping economic, political, and social crises of the twenty-first century reveal the limitations of the Democratic Party's commitment to making the market do good. Community development banking, microenterprise, Empowerment Zones, charter schools, free trade, and New Markets tax credits do not hold the answers to the problems caused by large-scale economic restructuring, persistent unemployment, foreclosures, and the retrenchment of direct cash assistance. These programs do not have the capabilities to eradicate the root causes of poverty or comprehensively combat problems of capital disinvestment and structural inequality. Instead, they have all too often provided a means for politicians, philanthropists, and corporations to avoid taking accountability for such problems and find more comprehensive and redistributive solutions.

No single politician is responsible for these conditions. It gets us nowhere to simply scapegoat the Clintons and the Democratic

Leadership Council. Nor is it useful to pin hope on the Biden administration to solve all these problems. The circumstances go beyond one president—Democrat or Republican. Instead, we must start by challenging the faith that public policy, private philanthropy, and the culture at large has placed in the market to accomplish humanitarian goals. We cannot begin to seek suitable and sustainable alternatives until we understand how deep that belief runs and how detrimental its consequences are.

One lesson of *Left Behind* is that ideas and policies have power. Yet, ideas and policies can change. The multifaceted problems facing places like South Shore and Pine Bluff and their countless counterparts around the country ultimately serve as reminders that the best way to solve the vexing problems of poverty, racism, and disinvestment is not by providing market-based microsolutions. Macroproblems need macrosolutions. It is time to stop trying to make the market do good. It is time to stop trying to fuse the functions of the federal government with the private sector. Instead, it is time to reimagine the relationship between the government and low-income and poor people in ways that restore democratic accountability and decision-making. This means erecting new barriers that will limit the reach of the private sector. We also need to reconstruct America's social safety net through the government. It is the government that should be providing well-paying jobs, quality schools, universal childcare and health care, affordable housing, and protections against surveillance and brutality from law enforcement. The devastating consequences of the pandemic make this approach more important than ever. It also might make the moment ripe for true change.

ACKNOWLEDGMENTS

I began working on this book in 2014, and it is remarkable how much has happened in the world since then and how conversations about the Democratic Party, inequality, and neoliberalism have changed. It often felt like I was chasing a moving target, and more than once I pondered giving up. I was fortunate to have the support of a large number of people and institutions that encouraged me not to abandon this project and offered me the insights and encouragement I needed to keep going. I am truly delighted to be able to officially thank them at long last.

The financial assistance I received from the Carnegie Corporation of New York, the Charles Warren Center for Studies in American History at Harvard University, and the American Council of Learned Societies (ACLS) was paramount in providing me the time and resources I needed to develop and complete this project. I appreciate these institutions for their continued commitment to the humanities, which is needed now more than ever. I especially thank grant officers Mary Gentile and John Paul Christy for their guidance and assistance and the UCLA Luskin Institute for Democracy and Inequality for hosting me as a scholar in residence. The year I spent at the Warren Center in 2015–2016, which was devoted to studying the history of American capitalism, proved critical in the formation of many of the core ideas and research for this project. I am grateful to the workshop's organizers and other fellows and people I got to know during my time at Harvard for their ideas and intellectual community.

I am deeply appreciative of the Dean of the Faculty's Office at Claremont McKenna College (CMC) for allowing me to take so much time from my teaching responsibilities to complete this project, along with their ongoing commitment to my scholarly development. I also thank Bridgette Stokes Conner, Cindi Guimond, Beth Jager, Jennifer Perez, and Dorlisa Tillman for their many forms of assistance. The members of the CMC History Department have offered continual encouragement of my work and provided a wonderful sense of community. I am especially grateful to Heather Ferguson, Gary Hamburg, Dan Livesay, Albert Park, Diana Selig, and Tamara Venit-Shelton for their mentorship and friendship. I thank Seth Lobis, Evan Kindley, and Ellen Rentz, as well. I am thankful to all my students at the 5Cs who have consistently sharpened and shaped my thinking in both subtle and obvious ways.

The research for this project took me to archives and libraries across the country, and I remain indebted to the assistance of so many archivists and librarians. I owe particular gratitude to Lee Hiltzik and other archivists at the Rockefeller Archive Center and the staff at the Special Collections Department at the University of Illinois Chicago, as well as the staff at the William J. Clinton Presidential Library, who answered my questions and digitized a trove of materials on my behalf. I am very appreciative of the many people who agreed to share their memories and reflections with me, including Sheryll Cashin, Paul Dimond, Connie Evans, Al From, Ron Gryzwinski, David Osborne, Will Marshall, Jan Piercy, and Paul Weinstein. I especially thank Mary Houghton and George Surgeon for both their flawless memories and profound generosity in helping me to get things right. I remain indebted to my fantastic research assistant Avery Raimondo. Even though he will probably never look at another ProQuest article again, Avery's tireless research and sharp insights undergird this project in so many ways. I also thank Alvita Akiboh, Jacqueline Brandon, Claire Cororaton, and Rebecca Zimmerman who provided critical archival materials and research help as well.

I had the opportunity to present and publish aspects of the project at various stages of its gestation. I thank the organizers and participants of workshops staged at the Charles Warren Center at Harvard University; the American Political History Institute Workshop at Boston University; the Business, Government, and International Economy Unit at Harvard Business School; the Center on Democracy, Development and the Rule of Law and the "Approaches to Capitalism" research workshop at Stanford University; the Center for the Study of Work, Labor, and Democracy at the University of California, Santa Barbara; and the Los Angeles and Metropolitan History Workshop. I also thank the commenters, fellow panelists, and audiences at a host of conferences. I am very grateful to Ananya Roy and the Luskin Institute for Democracy and Inequality for organizing a workshop devoted to my work, and the participants in that forum for their incisive and wide-ranging critiques and suggestions. I thank the editors and staff at *Dissent*, *Jacobin*, and the *Journal of American History* for their support of my work and their suggestions on ideas and writing that wound their way into the book.

Many others offered insights, encouragement, and feedback. I owe particular thanks to Brian Balogh, Megan Black, Anne Blaschke, Eileen Boris, Kathryn Cramer Brownell, Jennifer Burns, Marisa Chappell, Lizabeth Cohen, Claire Dunning, Lauren Hirschberg, Kevin Kruse, Nelson Lichtenstein, Joanne Meyerowitz, Margaret O'Mara, Alice O'Connor, Charles Petersen, Beryl Satter, Bruce Schulman, Kit Smemo, Michael Vorenberg, Danielle Wiggins, and Leah Wright Rigueur. Rebecca Marchiel and David Stein have provided a sense of solidarity and important perspective on both the political economy and the trials and tribulations of toddlers. Brent Cebul and Mason Williams have been my consummate co-collaborators and kept me true to my wonky roots. Clay Howard has remained my go-to sounding board for almost two decades, and I have appreciated all the time and energy he has devoted to listening to me and offering advice. Proving themselves to be the most giving of academic friends, Clay and Katherine Marino generously read the full manuscript and discussed it at the height of the 2020 election. I will also be forever grateful to Lila Corwin Berman, Brent Cebul, Matt Lassiter, and Bryant Simon for agreeing to participate in a virtual manuscript workshop. They all offered close engagement with the project, and their individual and collective ideas and astute feedback helped me to rethink key aspects at a critical stage. Matt long ago fulfilled his official duties as my advisor but has remained a selfless fountain of sage advice and a true inspiration.

It is perhaps not surprising that the two people who have been most central to making this project a reality are fellow Massachusetts natives. My agent, Katherine Flynn of Kneerim & Williams, encouraged me to see the broader potential of my research and patiently and expertly helped me navigate the uncharted waters of trade publishing. I am also grateful to her for guiding me to PublicAffairs and to Ben Adams. I am indebted to Ben for his patience, humanity, and penchant for puns and, most importantly, for giving me the space to develop the project but stepping in when it mattered. I thank Kelly Lenkevich for so efficiently guiding me through the production process and Kate Mueller for her meticulous and thoughtful copyediting. I am also grateful to indexer Don Glassman and proofreader Susan VanHecke, and to Pete Garceau for the wonderful cover design.

The friendship of Rebecca Hatkoff, Adriene Hill, Jeremy Soshenko, Jonah Lehrer, Sarah Liebowitz, Mirra Levitt, and Sarah Petrie has grounded me through stressful times and helped to make the process of book writing far less isolating and dispiriting. I am deeply indebted to Rubi Prieto, Katherine Gonzalez, Adam and Mary O'Connor, and the entire "Rubi school" family for the care, community, and sense of normalcy they provided under truly abnormal circumstances. I also thank the many other caregivers, teachers, and playdate partners who helped me find time to work on this book.

Even if the world has often felt like it was shrinking, I have relished the ways my own family has expanded. I am thankful to the Dangel, Geismer, and Kaufman clans and their many offshoots for all their encouragement and diversions. I am especially grateful to my in-laws, Sharon and Phil Kaufman, for their steadfast support and generosity. I would be remiss if I did not mention Beauford Kaufman, who has been my most constant work companion. I feel so fortunate to have Sarah Geismer as my sister and to get to live so close to her. Her eye for narrative, empathy, laughter, and brutal honesty have all propelled my work on this project. I am also appreciative of Josh Halloway for his encouragement and suggestions and his uncanny ability to turn a phrase. My parents, Alan Geismer and Susan Dangel, have always been my main source of motivation and knowledge on all things large and small. They remain my biggest fans even when I can be, at times, undeserving of their cheerleading and unwavering love.

My children, Gabriel and June Geismer, were both born over the course of my work on this project, and their wide smiles, boundless energy, and expansive curiosity have kept me on my toes and offered the best kinds of distractions. I quite simply could not have completed this book without the support and sacrifice of Michael Kaufman, especially as we became official coparents and unofficial coworkers. He has sustained me with his love, humor, patience, and insights, both on this project and everything beyond it.

July 2021

NOTES

ABBREVIATIONS FOR CITED ARCHIVAL COLLECTIONS

AFTR   AFT Records, Walter P. Reuther Library, Archives of Labor and Urban Affairs, Wayne State University Libraries, Detroit, Michigan

AHP   Alan Howard Papers, Records of the International Ladies' Garment Workers' Union, Kheel Center for Labor-Management Documentation and Archives, Cornell University Library, Ithaca, New York

AI   Accion International Records, Tufts University Special Collections, Medford, Massachusetts

CDL   Clinton Digital Library, the digitized collection of the William J. Clinton Library and Presidential Museum, Little Rock, Arkansas

DRP   Doug Ross Papers, Bentley Historical Library, University of Michigan, Ann Arbor

FF   Ford Foundation Records, Rockefeller Archive Center, Sleepy Hollow, New York

GKHC   Gary K. Hart Collection, Special Collections, Davidson Library, University of California, Santa Barbara

HDC   House Democratic Caucus Records, Manuscript Division, Library of Congress, Washington, DC

HUDR   Records of Department of Housing and Urban Development (RG 207), National Archives, College Park, Maryland

LAUSD   Los Angeles Unified School District Board of Education records (Collection 1923), UCLA Library Special Collections, Charles E. Young Research Library, University of California, Los Angeles

MEP   Mike Espy Papers, Congressional and Political Research Center, Mitchell Memorial Library, Mississippi State University, Starkville

SBC   ShoreBank Corporation Records, Richard J. Daley Library Special Collections and University Archives, University of Illinois Chicago

WE   Women Employed Records, Richard J. Daley Library Special Collections and University Archives, University of Illinois Chicago

WRF   Winthrop Rockefeller Foundation Records, Rockefeller Archive Center, Sleepy Hollow, New York

WWB   Women's World Banking Records, Public Policy Papers, Department of Rare Books and Special Collections, Princeton University Library, Princeton, New Jersey

INTRODUCTION: DOING WELL BY DOING GOOD

1. For depictions of this interaction see: John M. Broder, "Pledge of Federal Help for the Economic Byways," *New York Times*, July 7, 1999, 10; Susan Page, "Clinton Touts Investment Incentives in Appalachia," *USA Today*, July 6, 1999, 4A; Charles Babbington, "Clinton Urges Corporate Investment to Fight Pockets of Poverty," *Washington Post*, July 6, 1999, A2; Franklin Foer and Jodie T. Allen, "Is Poverty Fixable?," *U.S. News & World Report*, July 19, 1999, 18–20; Andrew Marshall, "Clinton Goes on Tour to Help Poor," *Independent*, July 7, 1999, 16; and James E. Casto, "Special Report: President Clinton Visits Appalachia," *Appalachia: Journal of the Appalachian Regional Commission* 32 (May–August 1999): 2–7.

2. Hillary Rodham Clinton, "Talking It Over," July 7, 1999, Clinton White House Archives, https://clintonwhitehouse4.archives.gov/WH/EOP/First_Lady/html/columns/hrc070799.html.

3. William J. Clinton, "Remarks to the Community in East St. Louis, Illinois," July 6, 1999, The American Presidency Project, www.presidency.ucsb.edu/node/227466.

4. James Gerstenzang, "Clinton Visits Appalachia, Hope in Hand," *Los Angeles Times*, July 6, 1999, 1.

5. Rick Hampson, "Revisiting a Scene from LBJ's War on Poverty," *USA Today*, April 16, 2014.

6. White House, Office of the Press Secretary, "President William Jefferson Clinton State of the Union," January 19, 1999, Clinton White House Archives, https://clintonwhitehouse4.archives.gov/WH/New/html/19990119-2656.html.

7. William J. Clinton, "Remarks by the President to the People of Appalachia," Main Street, Hazard, Kentucky, July 5, 1999, Clinton White House Archives, https://clintonwhitehouse4.archives.gov/textonly/WH/New/html/19990706.html.

8. See, for example, William J. Clinton, "Remarks on Presenting the Presidential Awards for Excellence in Microenterprise Development," February 5, 1999, The American Presidency Project, www.presidency.ucsb.edu/node/226762.

9. Democratic Leadership Council, "New Orleans Declaration," reprinted in *Mainstream Democrat* 2, no. 2 (May 1990).

10. William J. Clinton, "Interview with Jesse Jackson of CNN's 'Both Sides' in Torrance," July 9, 1999, The American Presidency Project, www.presidency.ucsb.edu/node/227645.

11. See, for example, Nancy MacLean, *Democracy in Chains: The Deep History of the Radical Right's Stealth Plan for America* (New York: Viking, 2017); Rick Perlstein, *Reaganland: America's Right Turn 1976–1980* (New York: Simon and Schuster, 2020); and Kim Phillips-Fein, *Invisible Hands: The Making of the Conservative Movement from the New Deal to Reagan* (New York: W. W. Norton, 2009).

12. For more on the standard interpretations of neoliberalism, see Wendy Brown, *Undoing the Demos: Neoliberalism's Stealth Revolution* (New York: Zone Books, 2015); David Harvey, *A Brief History of Neoliberalism* (New York: Oxford University Press, 2005); and Jaime Peck, *Constructions of Neoliberal Reason* (New York: Oxford University Press, 2010). For a discussion of historians' uses of neoliberalism, see Daniel Rodgers, "The Uses and Abuses of Neoliberalism," *Dissent*, Winter 2018; responses by Julia Ott et al., "Debating the Uses and Abuses of 'Neoliberalism': Forum," *Dissent*, January 22, 2018, www.dissent magazine.org/online_articles/debating-uses-abuses-neoliberalism-forum; Gary Gerstle, "The Rise and Fall (?) of America's Neoliberal Order," *Transactions of the Royal Historical Society* 28 (December 2018): 241–264; and Kim Phillips-Fein, "The History of Neoliberalism," in *Shaped by the State: Toward a New Political History of the Twentieth Century*, ed. Brent Cebul, Lily Geismer, and Mason B. Williams (Chicago: University of Chicago Press, 2019), 347–362.

13. These ideas build on a growing group of scholars who have aimed to provide more nuance and show the many origins of neoliberalism: see Brent Cebul, "Supply-Side Liberalism: Fiscal Crisis, Post-Industrial Policy, and the Rise of the New Democrats," *Modern American History* 2 (2019): 139–164; Stephanie L. Mudge, *Leftism Reinvented: Western Parties from Socialism to Neoliberalism* (Cambridge, MA: Harvard University Press, 2018); Amy C. Offner, *Sorting Out the Mixed Economy: The Rise and Fall of Welfare and Developmental States in the Americas* (Princeton, NJ: Princeton University Press, 2019); and Phillips-Fein, "The History of Neoliberalism."

14. Anand Giridharadas, *Winners Take All: The Elite Charade of Changing the World* (New York: Knopf, 2018), represents one effort to take a critical account of the corporate use of this idea.

15. See William J. Clinton, "Remarks at a Democratic National Committee Fundraiser," June 28, 1995, The American Presidency Project, www.presidency.ucsb.edu/node/221541.

16. See, for example, Steve Fraser and Gary Gerstle, eds., *The Rise and Fall of the New Deal Order, 1930–1980* (Princeton, NJ: Princeton

University Press, 1989); Alan Brinkley, *The End of Reform: New Deal Liberalism in Recession and War* (New York: Vintage, 1996); Lizabeth Cohen, *A Consumers' Republic: The Politics of Mass Consumption in Postwar America* (New York: Vintage, 2003); and Robert M. Collins, *More: The Politics of Economic Growth in Postwar America* (New York: Oxford University Press, 2000).

17. This idea builds directly on the work of Keeanga-Yamahtta Taylor, *Race for Profit: How Banks and the Real Estate Industry Undermined Black Homeownership* (Chapel Hill: University of North Carolina Press, 2015), 5–9; and Julia Elyachar, *Markets of Dispossession: NGOs, Economic Development, and the State in Cairo* (Durham, NC: Duke University Press, 2005), 3. For more on racial liberalism, see Martha Biondi, *To Stand and Fight: The Struggle for Civil Rights in Postwar New York City* (Cambridge, MA: Harvard University Press, 2006); and Thomas Sugrue, *Sweet Land of Liberty: The Forgotten Struggle for Civil Rights in the North* (New York: Random House, 2008).

18. Alyosha Goldstein, *Poverty in Common: The Politics of Community Action During the American Century* (Durham, NC: Duke University Press, 2012); Daniel Immerwahr, *Thinking Small: The United States and the Lure of Community Development* (Cambridge, MA: Harvard University Press, 2015); Nancy Kwak, *A World of Homeowners: American Power and the Politics of Housing Aid* (Chicago: University of Chicago Press, 2015); Joanne Meyerowitz, *A War on Global Poverty: The Lost Promise of Redistribution and the Rise of Microcredit* (Princeton, NJ: Princeton University Press, 2021); and Offner, *Sorting Out the Mixed Economy*.

19. See Cebul, "Supply-Side Liberalism," 141–145. This point builds on conversations with Brent Cebul and Mason Williams.

20. Sanford F. Schram, *Welfare Discipline: Discourse, Governance, and Globalization* (Philadelphia: Temple University Press, 2009), 108–109.

21. Ruth Wilson Gilmore, *Golden Gulag: Prisons, Surplus, Crisis, and Opposition in Globalizing California* (Berkeley: University of California Press, 2007); Julilly Kohler-Hausmann, *Getting Tough: Welfare and Imprisonment in 1970s America* (Princeton, NJ: Princeton University Press, 2017); and Elizabeth Kai Hinton, *From the War on Poverty to the War on Crime: The Making of Mass Incarceration in America* (Cambridge, MA: Harvard University Press, 2016).

22. David A. Fahrenthold, Tom Hamburger, and Rosalind S. Helderman, "The Inside Story of How the Clintons Built a $2 Billion Global Empire," *Washington Post*, June 2, 2015.

23. Emmanuel Saez and Gabriel Zucman, "Wealth Inequality in the United States Since 1913: Evidence from Capitalized Income Tax Data," National Bureau of Economic Research, Working Paper 20625, October 2014, www.nber.org/papers/w20625.

CHAPTER 1: GROWTH AND OPPORTUNITY

1. Barry Bearak, "As Popularity Rises, He Tries to Shed 'Aloof' Image," *Los Angeles Times*, March 12, 1984, B1.

2. Tony Fuller et al., "A Voice for the Yuppie Generation," *Newsweek*, November–December 1984.

3. Martin Tolchin, "Working Profile: Christopher J. Matthews; He Who Speaks for the Speaker," *New York Times*, June 21, 1985, A14.

4. Randall Rothenberg, "The Neoliberal Club," *Esquire*, February 1982.

5. Charles Peters, "A Neo-Liberal's Manifesto," *Washington Post*, September 5, 1982.

6. Gary Hart, interview by Robert MacNeil, *The MacNeil/Lehrer NewsHour*, PBS, March 16, 1984.

7. Walter Goodman, "As Neoliberals Search for Closest Fit, Hart Is Often Mentioned," *New York Times*, May 15, 1984.

8. Martha M. Hamilton, "Fragile Frontier; Atari's Departure Illustrates Flaws in High-Tech Job Solution," *Washington Post*, February 27, 1983.

9. Patrick Andelic, *Donkey Work: Congressional Democrats in Conservative America, 1974–1994* (Lawrence: University of Kansas Press, 2019), 21.

10. Randall Rothenberg, *The Neoliberals: Creating the New American Politics* (New York: Simon and Schuster, 1984), 20; and Anthony Lewis, "Why Gary Hart?," *New York Times*, March 8, 1984.

11. Rachel Guberman, "The Real Silent Majority: Denver and the Realignment of American Politics after the Sixties" (PhD diss., University of Pennsylvania, 2015).

12. Ben Bradlee Jr., "Gary Hart: The Long Trek from Kansas to Candidacy of New Ideas," *Boston Globe*, March 9, 1984, 1.

13. Gary Hart, *Right from the Start: A Chronicle of the McGovern Campaign* (New York: Quadrangle Books, 1973), 330.

14. Albin Krebs, "In Colorado, an Honesty Ticket," *New York Times*, November 13, 1973, 41.

15. Daryl Lembke, "Colorado's Hart: McGovern Liberal Moves into '70s as a 'Progressive,'" *Los Angeles Times*, November 10, 1974.

16. David S. Broder, "Big New Federal Programs Coming? Probably Not," *Los Angeles Times*, November 4, 1974.

17. Merrill Brown, "Spotlight Glows on Wirth as Leader in the Bell Debate," *Washington Post*, January 31, 1982.

18. Joseph Kraft, "Colorado Puts Emphasis on Ideology, Not Party," *Boston Globe*, October 30, 1974, 27.

19. Thomas Byrne Edsall, *The New Politics of Inequality* (New York: W. W. Norton, 1985), 31–32.

20. David S. Broder, "Zigzagging in Search of Identity," *Washington Post*, July 15, 1984.

21. Lembke, "Colorado's Hart"; and David Shribman, "A Closer Look at the Hart Generation," *New York Times*, May 27, 1984, A34.

22. Norman C. Miller, "The Transformation of Gary Hart," *Wall Street Journal*, October 28, 1974.

23. Miller, "The Transformation of Gary Hart."

24. Gary Hart, "Free Lunch Is Over," *New York Times*, April 21, 1975, 29.

25. Kurt Andersen, *Evil Geniuses: The Unmaking of America: A Recent History* (New York: Random House, 2020), 95.

26. See Alan Brinkley, *The End of Reform: New Deal Liberalism in Recession and War* (New York: Vintage, 1996).

27. Edsall, *New Politics of Inequality*, 14.

28. Robert M. Collins, *More: The Politics of Economic Growth in Postwar America* (New York: Oxford University Press, 2000), 52–53.

29. Collins, *More*, 58–60.

30. See Elizabeth Kai Hinton, *From the War on Poverty to the War on Crime: The Making of Mass Incarceration in America* (Cambridge, MA: Harvard University Press, 2016), 49–50; Collins, *More*, 60; and Marisa Chappell, *The War on Welfare: Family, Poverty, and Politics in Modern America* (Philadelphia: University of Pennsylvania Press, 2011), 40.

31. For more on the scope and transformative effects of the War on Poverty, see Annelise Orleck and Lisa Gayle Hazirjian, eds., *The War on Poverty: A New Grassroots History* (Athens: University of Georgia Press, 2011).

32. Collins, *More*, 55.

33. Chappell, *War on Welfare*, 40–41.

34. Rothenberg, "The Neoliberal Club."

35. Steven V. Roberts, "A Congressional Generation Gap Emerges on Role of Government," *New York Times*, April 1, 1979, 1.

36. Joshua Freeman, *American Empire: The Rise of a Global Power, The Democratic Revolution at Home, 1945–2000* (New York: Viking Press, 2012), 119–124; and Mike Davis, *Prisoners of the American Dream: Politics and Economy in the History of the U.S. Working Class* (New York: Verso, 1986), 96–104.

37. Daniel Schlozman, *When Movements Anchor Parties: Electoral Alignments in American History* (Princeton, NJ: Princeton University Press, 2015), 162–166.

38. Lily Geismer, *Don't Blame Us: Suburban Liberals and the Transformation of the Democratic Party* (Princeton, NJ: Princeton University Press, 2015), 165–166; and Judith Stein, *Pivotal Decade: How the United States Traded Factories for Finance in the Seventies* (New Haven: Yale University Press), 15–16.

39. Freeman, *American Empire*, 296–297.

40. Emma Rothschild, "Unemployment Figures Are Out of the 30's," *New York Times*, July 27, 1975, E1.

41. John R. Emshwiller, "Greener Pastures?," *Wall Street Journal*, October 9, 1975, 1.

42. Peter T. Kilborn, "Unemployment, Growing Daily, Takes Spotlight in Longest Recession Since the Depression," *New York Times*, January 16, 1975, 1.

43. Philip Revzin, "Bogged Down: Rising Unemployment Strains the Resources of Welfare Agencies," *Wall Street Journal*, March 14, 1975, 1.

44. Walter S. Mossberg, "Seeking a Solution: Black Jobless Problem Still Haunts President Despite New Programs," *Wall Street Journal*, November 28, 1977, 1.

45. Nadine Brozan, "Feminists Marshal Forces to Combat Job Layoffs of Women," *New York Times*, March 6, 1975.

46. Freeman, *American Empire*, 296.

47. William K. Stevens, "Dennis Dolan: Unemployed Since June," *New York Times*, October 13, 1974, 201.

48. For an overview of the economic conditions and mood of the 1970s, see Jefferson Cowie, *Stayin' Alive: The 1970s and the Last Days of the Working Class* (New York: New Press, 2010); Kim Phillips-Fein, *Fear City: New York's Fiscal Crisis and the Rise of Austerity Politics* (New York: Metropolitan Books, 2017); Bruce J. Schulman, *The Seventies: The Great Shift in American Culture, Society, and Politics* (New York: Free Press, 2001); and Stein, *Pivotal Decade*.

49. Robert Lindsey, "Economy Mars Belief in the American Dream," *New York Times*, October 26, 1975.

50. Members of American Studies Program at SUNY at Buffalo, "Down and Out in America," *New York Times*, February 9, 1975, 215.

51. Daniel T. Rodgers, *Age of Fracture* (Cambridge, MA: Harvard University Press, 2011), 49–50.

52. On the libertarian response to the recession, see Rodgers, *Age of Fracture*, 41–76; and Kim Phillips-Fein, *Invisible Hands: The Making of the Conservative Movement from the New Deal to Reagan* (New York: W. W. Norton, 2009). For the left response, see David P. Stein, *Fearing Inflation, Inflating Fears: The Civil Rights Struggle for Full Employment and the Rise of the Carceral State, 1929–1986* (Chapel Hill: University of North Carolina Press, forthcoming); and Chappell, *War on Welfare*, 106–139.

53. Rothenberg, *Neoliberals*, 46.

54. Paul Tsongas, *The Road from Here: Liberalism and Realities in the 1980s* (New York: Alfred A. Knopf, 1981), 5–7.

55. Tsongas, *Road from Here*, 128–134; and Fox Butterfield, "In Technology, Lowell, Mass. Finds New Life," *New York Times*, August 10, 1982, A1.

56. Tsongas, *Road from Here*, 20.

57. Steven V. Roberts, "Democrats with an Aye for Business," *New York Times*, March 1, 1981, A4.

58. Lester C. Thurow, *The Zero-Sum Society: Distribution and the Possibilities for Change* (New York: Basic Books, 1980).

59. "Education: The Cynical Idealists of '68," *Time*, June 7, 1968; and Randall Rothenberg, "Mr. Industrial Policy," *Esquire*, May 1, 1983.

60. Reich outlined his arguments in Ira Magaziner and Robert B. Reich, *Minding America's Business: The Decline and Rise of the American Economy* (New York: Harcourt Brace, 1982); Robert B. Reich, "Making Industrial Policy," *Foreign Affairs* 60, no. 4 (Spring 1982): 852–881; and Robert B. Reich, *The Next American Frontier* (New York: Penguin Books, 1984).

61. Otis Graham, *Losing Time: The Industrial Policy Debate* (Cambridge, MA: Harvard University Press, 1992).

62. Rothenberg, "Mr. Industrial Policy."

63. Rothenberg, "Mr. Industrial Policy."

64. Reich, *Next American Frontier*, 13, 208–209.

65. Leslie Wayne, "Designing a New Economics for the 'Atari Democrats,'" *New York Times*, September 26, 1982.

66. Rothenberg, *Neoliberals*, 91.

67. Reich, *Next American Frontier*, 20.

68. Robert B. Reich, "The Liberal Promise of Prosperity," *New Republic*, February 21, 1981.

69. Rothenberg, *Neoliberals*, 74–75.

70. Rothenberg, "The Neoliberal Agenda."

71. Steven V. Roberts, "Democrats with an Aye for Business," *New York Times*, March 1, 1981, A4.

72. Rothenberg, *Neoliberals*, 27.

73. Al From, interview with author, Bethesda, Maryland, September 26, 2019.

74. Al From, interview, William J. Clinton Presidential History Project, Miller Center, University of Virginia, April 27, 2006.

75. From, interview, April 27, 2006; and Al From with Alice McKeon, *The New Democrats and the Return to Power* (New York: Palgrave Mac-Millan, 2013), 15–16.

76. See, for example, Felicia Kornbluh, *The Battle for Welfare Rights: Politics and Poverty in Modern America* (Philadelphia: University of Pennsylvania Press, 2007).

77. From, *The New Democrats*, 18–19.

78. Mudge, *Leftism Reinvented*, 279–281.

79. From, interview, September 26, 2019; From, *The New Democrats*, 12; and Kenneth S. Baer, *Reinventing Democrats: The Politics of Liberalism from Reagan to Clinton* (Lawrence: University of Kansas Press, 2000), 37–38.

80. From, *The New Democrats*, 39; and Robert W. Merry, "Last Hurrah? Under Upbeat Surface, Democratic Party Is Beset with Problems," *Wall Street Journal*, July 16, 1984, 1.

81. Gillis W. Long and Geraldine Ferraro, Caucus Report for the 97th Cong., c. 1983, Box 63, Folder 1, HDC.

82. From, interview, April 27, 2006.

83. Gillis W. Long, chairman, Caucus Committee on Party Effective-ness, *Rebuilding the Road to Opportunity: A Democratic Direction for the 1980s*, September 1982, Box 63, Folder 2, HDC.

84. Chappell, *The War on Welfare*, 143–155, 199–214.

85. Edsall, *The New Politics of Inequality*, 211.

86. Timothy J. Minchin, "Together We Shall Be Heard: Exploring the 1981 'Solidarity Day' Mass March," *Labor Studies in Working-Class History of the Americas* 12, no. 3 (September 2015): 75–96.

87. Caucus Committee on Party Effectiveness, *Rebuilding the Road to Opportunity*.

88. Al From to GWL [Gillis Long], Subject: Today's Caucus Meeting Committee, September 16, 1982, Box 63, Folder 1, HDC.

89. Rothenberg, *The Neoliberals*, 163.

90. Caucus Committee on Party Effectiveness, *Rebuilding the Road to Opportunity*, 10.

91. Edward Cowan, "Democrats Offer New Policy to Sustain National Growth," *New York Times*, September 19, 1982.

92. From, interview, April 27, 2006.

93. For more on the differences between civil rights and economic opportunity, see Marcia Chatelain, *Franchise: The Golden Arches in Black America* (New York: Liveright, 2020), 75.

94. "Skirting the Fairness Issue," *Washington Post*, September 27, 1982.

95. Caucus Committee on Party Effectiveness, *Rebuilding the Road to Opportunity*, 70.

96. From, interview, April 27, 2006.

97. Memorandum from Al From to Reps. Frost, Gephardt, and Wirth, Subject: Strategy for New York.

98. Arthur M. Schlesinger Jr., "The Democratic Party After Ted Kennedy," *Wall Street Journal*, December 7, 1982; Robert M. Kaus, "Reaganism with a Human Face," *New Republic*, November 25, 1981; and Rothenberg, "The Neoliberal Club."

99. Rothenberg, "The Neoliberal Club."

100. David Osborne, "The Other Senator from Massachusetts," *Mother Jones*, July 1982, 27.

101. Rothenberg, "The Neoliberal Club."

102. Gary Hart, "An Economic Strategy for the 1980s," in *The World of Work: Careers and the Future*, ed. Howard F. Didsbury Jr. (Bethesda, MD: World Future Society, 1983), 151–154; see also Gary Hart, *A New Democracy: A Democratic Vision for the 1980s and Beyond* (New York: Quill, 1983).

103. Hart, *A New Democracy*, 9.

104. Wicker, "Democrats in Search of Ideas."

105. Andelic, *Donkey Work*, 154.

106. Bradlee, "Gary Hart: The Long Trek from Kansas."

107. Fuller, "A Voice for the Yuppie Generation."

108. Steven V. Roberts, "Hart Taps a Generation of Young Professionals," *New York Times*, March 16, 1984, 26.

109. From, interview, April 27, 2006; Merry, "Last Hurrah?"

110. Ronald Smothers, "Hart, Not Known Well to Blacks, Receives Few of Their Votes," *New York Times*, May 19, 1984, 1.

111. Ronald Smothers, "The Impact of Jesse Jackson," *New York Times*, March 4, 1984.

112. Manning Marable, *Beyond Black and White: Rethinking Race in American Politics and Society* (New York: Verso, 1995), 20.

113. David Harris, "Understanding Mondale," *New York Times*, June 19, 1983, SM26.

114. A. H. Raskin, "Labor's Gamble on Mondale, *New York Times*, January 22, 1984, A30.

115. Steven V. Roberts, "The Democratic Debate: Mondale Strategy Aimed at Miring Hart in Details," *New York Times*, March 30, 1984; Lewis, "Why Gary Hart?"

116. Jesse Jackson, "1984 Democratic National Convention Address," San Francisco, July 18, 1984, www.americanrhetoric.com/speeches/jesse jackson1984dnc.htm.

117. Rich Jaroslovsky and Jeanne Saddler, "Mondale Accepts the Nomination, Vows to Raise Taxes, Shrink Deficit," *Wall Street Journal*, July 20, 1984, 1.

118. Merry, "Last Hurrah?"

119. Baer, *Reinventing Democrats*, 59.

120. Hale, *Making of the New Democrats*, 214.

121. Will Marshall, interview with author, Washington, DC, July 15, 2019.

122. From, *The New Democrats*, 52.

123. Tom Sherwood and James R. Dickinson, "Robb Trying to Form New Party Policy Group: Would Project More Moderate Image," *Washington Post*, February 16, 1985.

124. From, *The New Democrats*, 57; and Richard Cohen, "Democratic Leadership Council Sees Party Void and Is Ready to Fill It," *National Journal*, February 1, 1986, 270.

125. Marshall, interview.

126. From, *The New Democrats*, 53–54.

127. Marshall, interview.

128. *Crashing the Party*, directed by David Sigal (Warren, NJ: Passion River Films, 2016), DVD.

129. Phil Gailey, "Dissidents Defy Top Democrats; Council Formed," *New York Times*, March 1, 1985.

130. Paul Taylor, "Democrats' New Centrists Preen for '88," *Washington Post*, November 10, 1985, A1.

131. Dan Balz and David S. Broder, "Rival Democratic Councils Forming," *Washington Post*, February 27, 1985.

132. Attlesley, "Both National Parties Focusing on Texas"; and Robert Lindsey, "Democratic Group Stumps California for Recruits," *New York Times*, August 19, 1985.

133. Baer, *Reinventing Democrats*, 76.

134. Arthur Schlesinger Jr., "For Democrats, Me-Too Reaganism Will Spell Disaster," *New York Times*, July 6, 1986; and Taylor, "Democrats' New Centrists."

135. Donald P. Baker, "Wilder Welcomed to the National Spotlight," *Washington Post*, November 14, 1989; and R. H. Melton, "While Trying to Close Rift Wilder Repeats Criticisms," *Washington Post*, December 5, 1986.

136. Paul A. Gigot, "Democrat Heretic Wants Party's Soul at Center," *Wall Street Journal*, April 22, 1988, 1.

137. From, *The New Democrats*, 61; and Baer, *Reinventing Democrats*, 82.

138. Tom Sherwood, "Robb Leads Democrats on Texas Blitz," *Washington Post*, July 2, 1985.

139. Dan Balz and David S. Broder, "Rival Democratic Councils Forming," *Washington Post*, February 27, 1985.

140. David S. Broder, "Democrats Ending a Cycle; Long Battle Expected for Party Leadership, *Washington Post*, December 21, 1985; and Jack Germond and Jules Witcover, "Warning Shots: Biden, Jackson Feuding," *Philadelphia Inquirer*, July 25, 1986.

141. Robin Toner, "Jackson Urges Support for 'Special Interests,'" *New York Times*, June 23, 1987.

142. Baer, *Reinventing Democrats*, 84.

143. Morton M. Kondracke, "Recriminations '88: Nunn's Story," *New Republic*, December 5, 1988.

144. Remarks of Gov. Charles S. Robb, Lyndon B. Johnson Presidential Conference, Hofstra University, April 12, 1986, Box 24, Folder 1, Richard A. Gephardt Collection, Library and Research Center, Missouri Historical Society, St. Louis, Missouri.

145. Remarks of Robb, Lyndon B. Johnson Presidential Conference.

146. Democratic Leadership Council, "New Directions, Enduring Values," 1987, Box 24, Folder 1, Richard A. Gephardt Collection.

CHAPTER 2: THE POWER OF CREDIT

1. David Osborne, "Bootstrap Banking," *Inc.*, August 1, 1987, www.inc .com /magazine/19870801/8543.html.

2. Mary Houghton, interview with author, by Zoom, September 9, 2020.

3. Houghton, interview.

4. Ronald Grzywinski, interview with author, by Zoom, November 5, 2020.

5. Grzywinski, interview. For more on the civil rights movement's promotion of Black business ownership as an avenue toward freedom, see Marcia Chatelain, *Franchise: The Golden Arches in Black America* (New

York: Liveright, 2020); and Mehrsa Baradaran, *The Color of Money: Black Banks and the Racial Wealth Gap* (Cambridge, MA: Harvard University Press, 2017).

6. Houghton, interview.

7. Ronald Grzywinski, "Forward to the New Eagle Bar: Inventing ShoreBank Again," State of the Corporation Address, September 24, 1996, Box 14, Folder 112, SBC.

8. For more on these processes in Chicago, see Beryl Satter, *Family Properties: Race, Real Estate and the Exploitation of Black Urban America* (New York: Metropolitan Books, 2009); and Arnold Hirsch, *Making the Second Ghetto: Race and Housing in Chicago, 1940–1960* (Chicago: University of Chicago Press, 1983).

9. Scott Jacobs, "Inner City Bank with Community Commitment," *Chicago Sun-Times*, November 4, 1973; and Ronald Grzywinski, "The New Old-Fashioned Banking," *Harvard Business Review*, May–June 1991, 88.

10. William Grady, "Chicago Bank Proves Profitability of Loans in Changing Neighborhood," *Baltimore Sun*, June 28, 1981.

11. Houghton, interview.

12. David Moberg, "The Left Bank," *Chicago Reader*, May 26, 1994.

13. Neal R. Pierce and Carol F. Steinbach, *Corrective Capitalism: The Rise of America's Community Development Corporations* (New York: Ford Foundation, 1987).

14. Memorandum from Ronald Grzywinski to Milton Davis et al., Subject: CDCs New Hope for the Inner City, July 19, 1971, Box 4, Folder 24, SBC.

15. Grzywinski, "The New Old-Fashioned Banking," 88. There was a long and established tradition of Black-owned and -operated banks that dated back to the post–Civil War era, but these banks had experienced a series of challenges, and none had an explicit focus on community redevelopment.

16. Lynn Pikholz and Ron Grzywinski, "On ShoreBank and Bumblebees," 1999, Box 26, Folder 208, SBC.

17. For more on this trend especially among Black-owned banks, see Baradaran, *Color of Money*.

18. Grzywinski, interview.

19. Neighborhood Development Group, "A Business Proposal," August 1972, Box 4, Folder 26, SBC.

20. Neighborhood Development Group, c. 1971, Box 4, Folder 24, SBC; Richard P. Taub, *Community Capitalism: The South Shore Bank's Strategy for Neighborhood Revitalization* (Boston: Harvard Business School Press, 1988), 2.

21. Moberg, "Left Bank"; Grzywinski, "The New Old-Fashioned Banking," 97–98.

22. For more on the urban reinvestment movement, see Rebecca Marchiel, *After Redlining: The Urban Reinvestment Movement in the Era of Financial Deregulation* (Chicago: University of Chicago Press, 2020).

23. Houghton, interview.

24. South Shore Bank of Chicago, "1977 Annual Report and Neighborhood Development Audit-1977," Box 2, Folder 11, SBC; and Houghton, interview.

25. Grzywinski, interview.

26. Michelle Obama, *Becoming* (New York: Crown, 2018), 2–29.

27. Judith Barnard, "Money Matters," *Chicago*, February 1977, Box 84, Folder 622, SBC.

28. Houghton, interview.

29. Woodstock Institute, "Evaluation of the Illinois Neighborhood Development Corporation," June 1, 1982, Box 2, Folder 10, SBC.

30. Pat Hansen, "Chicago Bank Setting Neighborhood Renewal Example," *American Banker*, May 22, 1978.

31. "Proposed Move of South Shore Bank Is Fought," *Chicago Tribune*, August 27, 1972.

32. Illinois Neighborhood Development Corporation, Offering Circular, October 2, 1972, Box 4, Folder 27, SBC; and Taub, *Community Capitalism*, 3.

33. Ron Grzywinski to Charles Rial, Re: Community Confidence Building, September 24, 1995, Box 86, Folder 633, SBC.

34. Barnard, "Money Matters"; Jacobs, "Inner City Bank with Community Commitment."

35. Barnard, "Money Matters."

36. Brian Nixon, "Chicago's Shorebank: A National Model," *Independent Banker*, April 1987; Grzywinski, "The New Old-Fashioned Banking," 89; and Taub, *Community Capitalism*, 52.

37. Bernard, "Money Matters"; and South Shore National Bank of Chicago, "1976 Annual Report and Neighborhood Development Audit-1976," Box 2, Folder 11, SBC.

38. South Shore National Bank of Chicago, "Neighborhood Development Audit-1974," Box 2, Folder 11, SBC; Hansen, "Chicago Bank Setting Neighborhood Renewal Example"; and Grzywinski to Rial, Re: Community Confidence Building.

39. Barnard, "Money Matters."

40. Taub, *Community Capitalism*, 43–44.

41. Nicholas von Hoffman, "Banking at Its Best," *Washington Post*, April 15, 1974.

42. South Shore National Bank of Chicago, "Neighborhood Development Audit-1975," Box 2, Folder 11, SBC.

43. Woodstock Institute, "Evaluation of the Illinois Neighborhood Development Corporation."

44. Bernard, "Money Matters."

45. George Surgeon, interview with author, by Zoom, November 13, 2020; and Grzywinski, interview.

46. Surgeon, interview.

47. Les Gray, "Losing Cause: Do-Good Mutual Funds Find Profits Elusive," *Wall Street Journal*, April 9, 1972.

48. South Shore Bank, Development Deposits: Account Application, no date, Box 89, Folder 10, WWB.

49. Taub, *Community Capitalism*, 63.

50. Nathaniel Sheppard Jr., "Chicago Bank Makes Money on Loans That Aid Deteriorating Neighborhood," *New York Times*, July 30, 1979.

51. Barnard, "Money Matters."

52. South Shore Bank, "1978 Annual Report Neighborhood Development Audit Program Report of Affiliates," Box 2, Folder 10, SBC.

53. David Osborne, *Laboratories of Democracy: A New Breed of Governor Creates Models for National Growth* (Boston: Harvard Business School Press, 1988), 306; and Brian Nixon, "Chicago's Shorebank: A National Model."

54. Surgeon, interview.

55. Grzywinski, interview.

56. For more on these patterns especially in Chicago, see Satter, *Family Properties*.

57. South Shore Bank, "1979 Annual Report."

58. Pasternack, "Chicago's Shorebank Earns Interest as Model for Rebirth"; and South Shore Bank and Affiliates, "Annual Report 1984," Box 2, Folder 10, SBC.

59. Hansen, "Chicago Bank Setting Neighborhood Renewal Example."

60. South Shore Bank and Affiliates, "Annual Report 1984."

61. South Shore Bank and Affiliates, "Annual Report 1984."

62. Pikholz and Grzywinski, "On ShoreBank and Bumblebees."

63. South Shore Bank, "1978 Annual Report."

64. South Shore Bank and Affiliates, "Annual Report 1984."

65. ShoreBank Corporation, "Annual Report 1992," Box 1, Folder 9, SBC.

66. Moberg, "The Left Reader."

67. Moberg, "The Left Reader."

68. Stanley Ziemba, "Commitment Turns the Tide in South Shore," *Chicago Tribune*, February 15, 1979.

69. South Shore Bank and Affiliates, "Ten-Year Report South Shore Bank and Affiliates 1973–1983," Box 2, Folder 10, SBC.

70. Grady, "Chicago Bank Proves Profitability"; Hansen, "Chicago Bank Setting Neighborhood Renewal Example."

71. Moberg, "Left Bank,"

72. Surgeon, interview.

73. ShoreBank Corporation, "Annual Report 1990," Box 1, Folder 9, SBC.

74. See, for example, Doris Crenshaw to Ron Grazywinski [*sic*], March 15, 1979, Box 84, Folder 616, SBC.

75. Muhammad Yunus testimony, "Microenterprise Credit," joint hearing before Select Committee on Hunger, Subcommittee on International Development Institutions and Finance, Committee on Banking, Finance and Urban Affairs, House of Representatives, 99th Cong., 2nd Sess.,

Washington, DC, February 25, 1986 (Washington, DC: Government Printing Office, 1986), 3–9.

76. Yunus testimony, February 25, 1986; Joan M. Dunlap to John D. Rockefeller III, Subject: Issues and Opportunities, Bangladesh and Pakistan, February–March 1976, Box 34, Folder 1, WWB.

77. Muhammad Yunus, *Banker to the Poor: Micro-lending and the Battle Against World Poverty* (New York: PublicAffairs, 1999), 71.

78. Helen Scheuer Cohen, "How Far Can Credit Travel?: A Comparative Study of the Grameen Bank in Bangladesh and the Women's Self-Employment Project in Chicago" (master's thesis, Massachusetts Institute of Technology, 1989).

79. Yunus, *Banker to the Poor*, 106–107.

80. Yunus, *Banker to the Poor*, 69.

81. Yunus, *Banker to the Poor*, 62–66.

82. Seth Mydans, "A Bank Battles Poverty," *New York Times*, July 12, 1987, A3; and Anwar Iqbal, "With This Bank, Poor Can Help the Poor," *Chicago Tribune*, July 22, 1987.

83. Yunus testimony, February 25, 1986, 5.

84. Itme-dad-ud-Doula, "Luck Returns to Bhagyarani," presented at "Bank Credit for Landless Women: A Study Tour of Grameen Bank in Bangladesh," organized by UN ESCAP, November 6–12, 1984, Dhaka, Bangladesh, Box 54, Folder: Study Tours of Grameen Bank, 1984, WWB.

85. Muhammad Yunus, "Obstacles to Participation in Economic Activity," June 1987, Box 43, Folder 331, SBC.

86. "Bangladesh Credit II: Grameen Bank Project Identification Report, First Draft," December 1983, Box 7, Folder 95, SBC.

87. Yunus, *Banker to the Poor*, 109–111.

88. Salma Khan, "Development of Women in Bangladesh," presented at "Bank Credit for Landless Women: A Study Tour of the Grameen Bank in Bangladesh," organized by UN ESCAP, November 6–12, 1984, Dhaka, Bangladesh, Box 54, Folder: Study Tours of Grameen Bank, 1984, WWB.

89. Yunus, "Obstacles to Participation in Economic Activity."

90. Muhammad Yunus, "Experience in Organizing Grass-root Initiatives and Mobilizing People's Participation: The Case of the Grameen Bank Project," July 1982, Box 33, Folder 11, WWB; and Kristin Helmore, "Banking on a Better Life," *Christian Science Monitor*, March 15, 1989.

91. See, for example, Joanne Meyerowitz, *A War on Global Poverty: The Lost Promise of Redistribution and the Rise of Microcredit* (Princeton, NJ: Princeton University Press, 2021), especially chapter 3; and Arvonne S. Fraser and Irene Tinker, eds., *Developing Power: How Women Transformed International Development* (New York: Feminist Press at CUNY, 2004).

92. David Bornstein, *The Price of a Dream: The Story of the Grameen Bank and the Idea That Is Helping the Poor to Change Their Lives* (New York: Simon and Schuster, 1996), 23.

93. Alex Counts, *Give Us Credit: How Muhammad Yunus's Micro-Lending Revolution Is Empowering Women from Bangladesh to Chicago* (New York: Times Books, 1996), 310.

94. Bornstein, *Price of a Dream*, 25–26.

95. Muhammad Yunus, *Jorimon and Others: Faces of Poverty* (Dhaka, Bangladesh: Grameen Bank, 1984); and Lamia Karim, *Microfinance and Its Discontents: Women in Debt in Bangladesh* (Minneapolis: University of Minnesota Press), 170–171.

96. Karim, *Microfinance and Its Discontents*, 170–171, 192. Although focused on the experiences of women in Grameen and other microcredit programs in the 1990s and 2000s, Karim's ethnography reveals borrowers' more complex narratives and experiences.

97. For the full Sixteen Decisions, see Counts, *Give Us Credit*, 347–348.

98. William D. Carmichael to Franklin A. Thomas, Recommendation for Grant: Grameen Bank, May 11, 1989, Grants E-G, July 1, 1985–January 1,1993, FF.

99. "Bank Credit for Landless Women: A Study Tour of Grameen Bank in Bangladesh," November 6–12, 1984, Dhaka, Bangladesh, Box 54, Folder: Study Tours of Grameen Bank, 1984, WWB.

100. Yunus, "Experience in Organizing Grass-root Initiatives and Mobilizing People's Participation"; Bornstein, *Price of a Dream*, 115–116.

101. William D. Carmichael to Franklin A. Thomas, Recommendation for Grant.

102. Karen Ferguson, *Top Down: The Ford Foundation, Black Power, and the Reinvention of Racial Liberalism* (Philadelphia: University of Pennsylvania Press, 2013), 210–260.

103. Kathleen Teltsch, "Transitional Pains at the Ford Foundation," *New York Times*, February 8, 1981; and Ford Foundation, "A Note on the Foundation's Program Concerned with Women in Development," Report 010968, 1977, FF.

104. Michelle Goldberg, *The Means of Reproduction: Sex, Power and the Future of the World* (New York: Penguin Books, 2009), 83–84.

105. Grzywinski, interview.

106. Houghton, interview.

107. Houghton, interview.

108. Carol Kleiman, "Village Capitalism Betters Women's Lot," *Chicago Tribune*, October 31, 1983.

109. For more on the language of empowerment, see Meyerowitz, *A War on Global Poverty*, 213–214.

110. Yunus, "Obstacles to Participation in Economic Activity"; Bornstein, *Price of a Dream*, 231.

111. Yunus, "Obstacles to Participation in Economic Activity."

112. Houghton, interview.

113. Ford Foundation, "Program-Related Investments: Program Review," June 1984, FF.

114. Houghton, interview.

115. Houghton, interview.

116. Muhammad Yunus to Dr. Anthony Betteral, Subject: Request for Ford Foundation Support to Setting up Monitoring and Evaluation Department at Grameen Bank, July 7, 1985, Grants E-G, July 1, 1985–January 1, 1993, FF; William D. Carmichael to Franklin A. Thomas, Recommendation for Grant: Grameen Bank, July 25, 1985, Grants E-G, July 1, 1985–January 1, 1993, FF; and Ford Foundation, "Program-Related Investments," FF.

117. Houghton, interview.

118. South Shore Bank, "Targeted Investment," January 1986, Box 89, Folder 10, WWB.

119. Yunus, "Experience in Organizing Grass-root Initiatives and Mobilizing People's Participation"; Yunus, "Obstacles to Participation in Economic Activity."

120. Yunus, "Obstacles to Participation in Economic Activity."

121. Yunus, "Experience in Organizing Grass-root Initiatives and Mobilizing People's Participation."

122. See Hernando de Soto, *The Other Path: The Invisible Revolution in the Third World* (New York: Harper Collins, 1989); and Hernando de Soto, *The Mystery of Capital: Why Capitalism Triumphs in the West and Fails Everywhere Else* (New York: Basic Books, 2000).

123. Julia Elyachar, *Markets of Dispossession: NGOs, Economic Development, and the State in Cairo* (Durham, NC: Duke University Press, 2005), 193–194. See also Meyerowitz, *A War on Global Poverty*, 183–184.

124. Nancy C. Jurik, *Bootstrap Dreams: US Microenterprise Development in an Era of Welfare Reform* (Ithaca, NY: Cornell University Press, 2005), 21.

125. Elyachar, *Markets of Dispossession*.

126. Select Committee on Hunger, *Banking for the Poor: Alleviating Poverty Through Credit Assistance to the Poorest Micro-Entrepreneurs in Developing Countries: Report of the Select Committee on Hunger, US House of Representatives*, vol. 4 (Washington, DC: Government Printing Office, May 1986).

127. Judith Tendler, *What Ever Happened to Poverty Alleviation? A Report Prepared for Mid-Decade Review of the Ford Foundation's Programs on Livelihood, Employment, and Income Generation*, May 1987, FF.

128. Rehman Sobhan, "Structural Maladjustment: Bangladesh's Experience with Market Reforms," *Economic and Political Weekly* 28, no. 19 (1993): 925–931.

129. Naomi Klein, *The Shock Doctrine: The Rise of Disaster Capitalism* (New York: Picador, 2007), 205–206; and Meyerowitz, *A War on Global Poverty*, 184–193.

130. Elyachar, *Markets of Dispossession*, 27; Tendler, *What Ever Happened to Poverty Alleviation?*

131. Galen Spencer Hull, *Experiments in Small- and Microenterprise Development*, A.I.D. Science and Technology Development Series

(Washington, DC: USAID, 1990), www.canr.msu.edu/afre/uploads/files/Mead/Experiments_in_Small_and_Microenterprise_Development_.pdf; and David Ekbladh, *The Great American Mission: Modernization and the Construction of an American World Order* (Princeton, NJ: Princeton University Press, 2010), 179.

132. Meyerowitz, *A War on Global Poverty*, 15–42; and Jamey Essex, *Development, Security, and Aid: Geopolitics and Geoeconomics at the U.S. Agency for International Development* (Athens: University of Georgia Press, 2013), 53–54.

133. Winifred Poster and Zakia Salime, "The Limits of Microcredit, Transnational Feminism in the United States and Morocco," in *Women's Activism and Globalization: Linking Local Struggles and Transnational Politics*, ed. Nancy A. Naples and Manisha Desai (New York: Routledge, 2002), 194.

134. Meyerowitz, *A War on Global Poverty*, 160–169.

135. Elisabeth Rhyne, *The Small Enterprise Approaches to Employment Project: How a Decade of A.I.D. Effort Contributed to the State of Knowledge on Small Enterprise Assistance*, USAID, October 1988, https://pdf.usaid.gov/pdf_docs/PNABH521.pdf.

136. Hull, *Experiments in Small- and Microenterprise Development*.

137. Yunus testimony, "Microenterprise Credit," 3–9.

138. Colman McCarthy, "Third World Bank That Lends a Hand," *Washington Post*, November 2, 1986; and Seth Mydans, "A Bank Battles Poverty," *New York Times*, July 12, 1987.

CHAPTER 3: BE YOUR OWN BOSS

1. Alex Chadwick, "Good Faith Fund Makes Small Loans," *All Things Considered*, Weekend Edition, NPR, Washington, DC, March 2, 1991.

2. Brian Kelley testimony, "Microloan Programs for New and Growing Small Businesses," hearing before the Committee on Small Business, US Senate, 102nd Cong., 1st Sess., Washington, DC, May 6, 1991 (Washington, DC: Government Printing Office, 1991).

3. Julie Stewart, "Little Bit of Help Goes a Long Way in Assisting the Poor," *Seattle Times*, May 13, 1990.

4. Karen M. Thomas, "Fund Gives Community a Bootstrap," *Chicago Tribune*, December 22, 1991.

5. Chadwick, "Good Faith Fund Makes Small Loans."

6. Wayne King, "Rapidly Growing Arkansas Turns to Liberal Politicians," *New York Times*, May 14, 1978, 26.

7. David Osborne, *Laboratories of Democracy: A New Breed of Governor Creates Models for National Growth* (Boston: Harvard Business School Press, 1988), 89–91; and Bill Rose, "Political Mandate in Arkansas: Don't Stray Too Far," *Miami Herald*, October 15, 1982, 1A.

8. James Morgan, "An Arkansas State of Mind," *Washington Post*, July 12, 1992.

9. Southern Development, Bancorporation, Arkansas Development Bank Holding Model Company Model, Supplemental Report, September 1, 1986, Box 62, Folder 489, SBC.

10. Osborne, *Laboratories of Democracy*, 83.

11. John A. Conway, "Growing Your Own," *Forbes*, October 15, 1979.

12. David Maraniss, *First in His Class: A Biography of Bill Clinton* (New York: Touchstone, 1995), 406; and Osborne, *Laboratories of Democracy*, 84–90.

13. Robert M. Press, "Arkansas' Clinton on Democrats in the South," *Christian Science Monitor*, July 15, 1985, 8; and Brent Cebul, *Illusions of Progress: Business, Poverty, and Liberalism in the American Century* (Philadelphia: University of Pennsylvania Press, forthcoming).

14. National Commission on Excellence in Education, *A Nation at Risk: The Imperative for Educational Reform: A Report to the Nation and the Secretary of Education, United States Department of Education*, Washington, DC, April 1983, www2.ed.gov/pubs/NatAtRisk/risk.html.

15. Joel Brinkley, "Clinton Remakes Home State in his Own Image," *New York Times*, March 31, 1992, A1.

16. "Arkansas Overhauling Its Education System," *New York Times*, November 20, 1983, A62.

17. David Maraniss, "How Clinton Moved to Handle the State's Economy," *Washington Post*, October 18, 1992; and "Arkansas Governor and His Spouse Both Put Education First," *Christian Science Monitor*, August 25, 1986.

18. "Arkansas Governor and His Spouse."

19. "Educators' Union Condemns Arkansas Plan to Test," *Miami Herald*, December 11, 1983, 12D.

20. David Lauter, "Clinton Arkansas Record: He Won a Few, Lost a Few," *Los Angeles Times*, May 23, 1992, A1.

21. Amy Kaslow, "Education Record Shines for Clinton," *Christian Science Monitor*, April 13, 1992, 11.

22. Ellie McGrath, "No More Dragging Up the Rear," *Time*, December 26, 1983.

23. Osborne, *Laboratories of Democracy*, 102–108; Cebul, *Illusions of Progress*; and Ernest Dumas, "The Democrat: Bootstrapper or Just Busy?" *Planning* 58, no. 10 (October 1992).

24. Dumas, "The Democrat: Bootstrapper or Just Busy?"

25. Dumas, "The Democrat: Bootstrapper or Just Busy?"

26. Ron Grzywinski, interview with author, by Zoom, November 5, 2020.

27. Jan Piercy, interview with author, by Zoom, December 15, 2020.

28. Piercy, interview.

29. Todd Cohen, "Leaders Expected to Lean on Non-Profits," *Raleigh News & Observer*, November 15, 1992, F1.

30. Jim McKenzie, "Twelve Obstacles to Economic Development in the Land of Opportunity," Staff Report by the Winthrop Rockefeller Foundation, October 1982, Reel 115, "Economic Development in Arkansas,

1982–1987," WRF; and Winthrop Rockefeller Foundation, "Capital Formation in Arkansas: Program Related Investment," Reel 145, Chronological Files, 1983, WRF.

31. Winthrop Rockefeller Foundation, "Context for Economic Development and Banking Activities," c. 1986, Box 61, Folder 482, SBC; and George Surgeon, interview with author, by Zoom, November 13, 2020.

32. Winthrop Rockefeller Foundation, "Context for Economic Development and Banking Activities."

33. Grzywinski, interview.

34. Winthrop Rockefeller Foundation, "Context for Economic Development and Banking Activities."

35. Surgeon, interview, November 13, 2020; and Mary Houghton to Arkansas Work Group, Re: Notes of Meeting on June 20, 1985, at W[inthrop] R[ockefeller] F[oundation] with McRae, McKindra, Grzywinski, and Houghton, June 22, 1985, Reel 125, Chronological Files, 1985, WRF.

36. Surgeon, interview, November 13, 2020.

37. Grzywinski, interview.

38. Houghton, interview; Grzywinski, interview.

39. Houghton, interview.

40. Houghton, interview.

41. Ron Grzywinski to Bill Clinton, August 15, 1985, Reel 125, Chronological Files, 1985, WRF.

42. Grzywinski, interview.

43. Grzywinski, interview.

44. Robert M. Garsson, "Clinton's Rx Relies on Small Banks," *American Banker*, July 13, 1992.

45. Piercy, interview.

46. W. Wilson Jones to Tom McRae, June 11, 1986, Reel 126, Chronological Files, January–March 1986, WRF.

47. Southern Bancorporation, Board of Directors Minutes, January 22, 1987, Reel 126, Chronological Files, January–March 1986, WRF.

48. Grzywinski, interview.

49. Proposed Principles of INDC Relationship to Arkrock, November 19, 1985, Reel 125, Chronological Files, 1985, WRF.

50. Houghton, interview.

51. Illinois Neighborhood Development Corporation, "An Arkansas Development Bank Holding Company Model Supplemental Report," May 20, 1986, Box 61, Folder 485, SBC.

52. David Wessel and Alex Kotlowitz, "Banker Who Battled Urban Blight in Chicago Takes on New Economic Challenge in Arkansas," *Wall Street Journal*, June 28, 1988.

53. George Surgeon, interview with author, by Zoom, November 20, 2020.

54. Surgeon, interview, November 20, 2020.

55. George Surgeon to Delmer D. Weisz, vice president, Federal Reserve Bank of St. Louis, February 8, 1988, Reel 128, Chronological Files,

January–March 1988, WRF; and Southern Bancorporation, Arkansas Development Bank, c. 1986, Reel 125, Chronological Files, 1983, WRF.

56. Piercy, interview.

57. Thomas F. Miller to George Surgeon, November 4, 1987, Box 62, Folder 489, SBC.

58. From Thomas F. Miller and Norman Collins to Susan V. Berresford, Re: Delegated Authority Grant, Neighborhood Institute, February 10, 1986, Grant 86-269, FF.

59. Southern Development Bancorporation Investors, January 12, 1988, Reel 128, Chronological Files, January–March 1988, WRF.

60. Arkansas Development Bank Holding Company Model, Supplemental Report, September 1, 1986, Box 62, Folder 489, SBC; and Osborne, *Laboratories of Democracy*, 105.

61. Garsson, "Clinton's Rx Relies on Small Banks."

62. Piercy, interview.

63. Surgeon, interview, November 20, 2020.

64. Surgeon, interview, November 20, 2020.

65. Surgeon, interview, November 13, 2020.

66. Grzywinski, interview; Surgeon, interview, November 13, 2020.

67. Surgeon, interview, November 13, 2020.

68. Southern Development Bancorporation, Inc., Application to the Board of Governors of the Federal Reserve Bank.

69. Richard P. Taub, *Doing Development in Arkansas: Using Credit to Create Opportunity for Entrepreneurs Outside the Mainstream* (Fayetteville: University of Arkansas Press, 2004), 14.

70. Taub, *Doing Development in Arkansas*, 15.

71. Surgeon, interview, November 13, 2020.

72. Surgeon, interview, November 13, 2020.

73. Surgeon, interview, November 13, 2020; and Taub, *Doing Development in Arkansas*, 46.

74. Surgeon, interview, November 20, 2020.

75. Houghton, interview.

76. Karen Maru File, "The Invisible Entrepreneurs," Edges, c. 1989, Box 170, Folder 1951, WE.

77. Cheryl Rene Rodriguez, *Women, Microenterprise, and the Politics of Self-Help* (New York: Garland, 1995), 44; and Counts, *Give Us Credit*, xvii.

78. Surgeon, interview, November 20, 2020.

79. Piercy, interview.

80. Piercy, interview.

81. Counts, *Give Us Credit*, 94–96; and Muhammad Yunus, *Banker to the Poor: Micro-lending and the Battle Against World Poverty* (New York: PublicAffairs, 1999), 204–205.

82. Yunus, *Banker to the Poor*, 205.

83. Mary Houghton to Tom McRae, Re: Winrock Conference Report, February 19, 1986, Box 61, Folder 480, SBC.

84. Jeffrey Ashe, "A Development Bank to Assist Small Businesses in Arkansas," Accion International, 1986, Box 61, Folder 481, SBC.

85. William Greider, "Credit Where Credit's Due," *Rolling Stone*, September 1993.

86. Bill Clinton, *My Life* (New York: Alfred A. Knopf, 2004), 271.

87. Clinton, *My Life*, 329.

88. William Greider et al., "The Rolling Stone Interview," *Rolling Stone*, September 17, 1992.

89. Counts, *Give Us Credit*, 96.

90. Yunus, *Banker to the Poor*, 201–202.

91. Tom Leander, "Julia Vindasius," *American Banker*, January 23, 1992.

92. Leander, "Julia Vindasius."

93. Yunus, *Banker to the Poor*, 80–81.

94. Kim Harper, "Banking on the Delta," *Arkansas Business*, February 10, 1992.

95. A. C. Moncrief, "Peer Approved Revolving Loans," *Economic Development Review*, Spring 1992.

96. Osborne, *Laboratories of Democracy*, 104.

97. Taub, *Doing Development in Arkansas*, 26; and Maraniss, "How Clinton Moved to Handle the State's Economy."

98. Alexandra Brown, Jackie Khor, and David Stern, "The Good Faith Fund: Managing a Grass Roots Organization in Rural Arkansas," Yale School of Management, Spring 1991, Box 64, Folder 506, SBC; and Ruth Anne Tune, "The Good Faith Fund, First Annual Report," Summer 1990, presented to the Aspen Institute, Box 64, Folder 506, SBC.

99. Ford Foundation, "Development Banking: Giving Credit Where Credit is Overdue," Ford Foundation letter, November 1989, Box 64, Folder 504, SBC.

100. Good Faith Fund Flyer, 1990, Box 63, Folder 501, SBC.

101. Mary Houghton and Ron Grzywinski to board of directors, Winthrop Rockefeller Foundation, Re: Progress Report, Southern Development Bancorporation, August 31, 1989, Box 62, Folder 493, SBC.

102. Tune, "The Good Faith Fund, First Annual Report"; and Taub, *Doing Development in Arkansas*, 89.

103. Tom Leander, "They're Banking on the Poor," *American Banker*, Monday December 2, 1991.

104. Katti Gray, "Loan Program Shows Faith in the Poor," *Newsday*, September 2, 1990.

105. For more on these depictions of the poor, see Michael B. Katz, *The Undeserving Poor: America's Enduring Confrontation with Poverty* (New York: Oxford University Press, 2013), 9–29, 168–187, 205–220.

106. Leander, "They're Banking on the Poor."

107. Richard P. Taub, "South Arkansas Rural Development Study: First Annual Report," 1990, Box 62, Folder 493, SBC.

108. David Wessel, "Doing Business in the Inner City," *Wall Street Journal*, June 23, 1992, A1.

109. Taub, *Doing Development in Arkansas*, 91.

110. Judith Tendler, *What Ever Happened to Poverty Alleviation? A Report Prepared for Mid-Decade Review of the Ford Foundation's Programs on Livelihood, Employment and Income Generation*, May 1987, FF.

111. Surgeon, interview, November 20, 2020.

112. Wessel, "Doing Business in the Inner City."

113. Kamal Ahmad to Catherine Gwin, Subject: Grameen Trust, November 1, 1990, Box 43, Folder 331, SBC. For more on early criticisms of Grameen and other microcredit programs, see Joanne Meyerowitz, *A War on Global Poverty: The Lost Promise of Redistribution and the Rise of Microcredit* (Princeton, NJ: Princeton University Press, 2021), 213–215.

114. Southern Development Bancorporation, "Lessons Learned About Economic Development in Rural Arkansas," c. 1992, Box 62, Folder 492, SBC.

115. Surgeon, interview, November 20, 2020.

116. Britt Talent, "A New Way to Get Off Welfare," *Pine Bluff Commercial*, September 18, 1994.

117. Houghton, interview; and Connie Evans, interview with author, by Zoom, September 21, 2020.

118. Jennifer Roback, "Torn Between Family and Career? Give Birth to a Business," *Wall Street Journal*, November 14, 1983.

119. Carol Kleiman, "Self-Employment: Yet Another Way to Get Off Welfare," *Chicago Tribune*, May 23, 1988; and Evans, interview.

120. Nancy Bearden Henderson, "Joint Venture: The Mentor-Mentee Relationship Delivers Rewards for Both Parties," *Chicago Tribune*, August 22, 2001.

121. Evans, interview.

122. Evans, interview.

123. Maudylne Ihejirika, "Women's Self-Employment Project Celebrates 10 Years," *Chicago Sun-Times*, March 15, 1996.

124. Connie Evans to Julie Abrams, January 23, 1987, Box 60, Folder 2, WWB.

125. Robert McClory, "Our Bosses, Ourselves: Turning Wage Slaves and Welfare Women into Entrepreneurs," *Chicago Reader*, July 6, 1989.

126. Mary Schimich, "It's Not Just a Job, It's the Principle," *Chicago Tribune*, April 7, 1993.

127. Evans, interview.

128. McClory, "Our Bosses, Ourselves."

129. McClory, "Our Bosses, Ourselves."

130. Robert Friedman, *The Safety Net as Ladder: Transfer Payments and Economic Development* (Washington, DC: Council of State Planning Agencies, 1988), 116.

131. Rodriguez, *Women, Microenterprise, and the Politics of Self-Help*, 44.

132. Counts, *Give Us Credit*, 247.

133. Evans, interview.

134. Women's Self-Employment Project, press release, October 16, 1987, Box 170, Folder 1951, WE.

135. Counts, *Give Us Credit*, 103.

136. Wessel, "Doing Business in the Inner City."

137. Yunus, *Banker to the Poor*, 197.

138. Robert Koehler, "A $30 Loan, A Global Assault on Poverty," *News-Star* (Chicago), September 26, 1990, Box 170, Folder 1951, WE.

139. Kim Harper, "Supporting Small Business: Pine Bluff's Good Faith Fund Selected as Recipient of SBA Loan," *Arkansas Business*, July 6, 1992.

140. Small Business Association, "Microloan Demonstration Project Fact Sheet," c. 1993, Office of Speechwriting and Jonathan Prince, "5/93 Microloans [1]," CDL.

141. Dale Bumpers testimony, "Microloan Programs for New and Growing Small Businesses," hearing before the Committee on Small Business, US Senate, 102nd Cong., 1st Sess., Washington, DC, May 6, 1991 (Washington, DC: Government Printing Office, 1991).

142. Opening statement of Tony P. Hall, "New Strategies for Alleviating Poverty: Building Hope by Building Assets," hearing before the Select Committee on Hunger, House of Representatives, 102nd Cong., 1st Sess., Washington, DC, October 9, 1991 (Washington, DC: Government Printing Office, 1992).

143. Statement of Mike Espy, "New Perspectives on Urban Poverty and Microeconomic Development," hearing before the Select Committee on Hunger, House of Representatives, 102nd Cong., 1st Sess., Washington, DC, October 9, 1991 (Washington, DC: Government Printing Office, 1992), pp. 3–5.

144. ShoreBank Corporation, "Annual Report 1991," Box 2, Folder 9, SBC.

145. Surgeon, interview, November 20, 2020.

146. Mary Ann Zehr, "Imported from Bangladesh," *Foundation News* 33, no. 6 (November–December 1992): 28.

147. Scott Bailey, "Winners' Circles: Chicago's Experiment in Low-Income Enterprise," *Policy Review* (Winter 1993): 64.

148. Richard P. Taub, "The Southern Development Bancorporation: The First Five Years," 1993, Box 63, Folder 498, SBC.

CHAPTER 4: REINVENTING LIBERALISM

1. Bill Clinton, "Keynote Address of Gov. Bill Clinton to the DLC's Cleveland Convention," May 6, 1991, New Democrats Online, https://web.archive.org/web/20020821195710/http://www.ndol.org/print.cfm?content id=3166.

2. Clinton, "Keynote Address of Gov. Bill Clinton."

3. Democratic Leadership Council, "New Orleans Declaration," reprinted in *Mainstream Democrat* 2, no. 2 (May 1990).

4. Al From with Alice McKeon, *The New Democrats and the Return to Power* (New York: Palgrave MacMillan, 2013), 94.

5. Phil Gailey, "From Biden to Babbitt to Nunn," *New York Times*, May 18, 1986.

6. Marjorie Hunter, "Some New Political Figures Have Emerged," *New York Times*, November 4, 1976.

7. Randall Rothenberg, *The Neoliberals: Creating the New American Politics* (New York: Simon and Schuster, 1984), 136.

8. Phil Gailey, "Gore Announces Plan to Declare for the Presidency Later in the Spring," *New York Times*, April 11, 1987.

9. Keith Love, "Gore a Favorite with Moderates' Group," *Los Angeles Times*, November 13, 1987, 20.

10. Paul A. Gigot, "Democrat Heretic Wants Party's Soul at Center," *Wall Street Journal*, April 22, 1988, 1.

11. David S. Broder, "Building Party Consensus," *Washington Post*, July 17, 1988; and "Jesse Jackson Close Up," Associated Press, March 30, 1988.

12. Jesse Jackson, "The Fundamentals of Economic Growth and Economic Justice," position paper, c. 1988, 63–72; and Jesse Jackson, "Paying for Our Dreams: A Budget Plan for Jobs, Peace and Justice," c. 1988, 73–92, reprinted in Jesse Jackson, Frank Clemente, and Frank E. Watkins, *Keep Hope Alive: Jesse Jackson's 1988 Presidential Campaign: A Collection of Major Speeches, Issue Papers, Photographs, and Campaign Analysis* (Washington, DC: Keep Hope Alive PAC, 1989).

13. Jesse Jackson, "Investing in America," issue brief in Jackson et al., *Keep Hope Alive*, 92–93

14. See Lily Geismer, *Don't Blame Us: Suburban Liberals and the Transformation of the Democratic Party* (Princeton, NJ: Princeton University Press, 2015), 251–281.

15. Gigot, "Democrat Heretic."

16. Dennis Farney, "The Democrats Recast the Party to Win Back Suburban Voters They Lost to Reagan," *Wall Street Journal*, July 19, 1988.

17. Al From, interview with author, Bethesda, Maryland, September 26, 2019.

18. From, *The New Democrats*, 100–101; and Kenneth S. Baer, *Reinventing Democrats: The Politics of Liberalism from Reagan to Clinton* (Lawrence: University of Kansas Press, 2000), 118.

19. William Galston, interview, William J. Clinton Presidential History Project, Miller Center, University of Virginia, April 22–23, 2004.

20. Morton M. Kondracke, "Recriminations '88: Nunn's Story," *New Republic*, December 5, 1988, 5; and Farney, "The Democrats Recast the Party."

21. William Galston and Elaine Cuilla Kamarck, *The Politics of Evasion: Democrats and the Presidency*, Progressive Policy Institute, September 1989, www.progressivepolicy.org/wp-content/uploads/2013/03/Politics_of_Evasion.pdf.

22. Broder, "Building Party Consensus."

23. Albert R. Hunt, "Jackson Says Woes of Democrats Stem from Trying to Placate Conservatives," *Wall Street Journal*, November 1, 1988.

24. Galston, interview.

25. Paul Taylor and Maralee Schwartz, "Jackson's Unity Address Baffles, Irks Some Moderate Democrats," *Washington Post*, March 25, 1990.

26. For more on these think tanks and their role in the rise of the New Right and Reagan, see Kim Phillips-Fein, *Invisible Hands: The Making of the Conservative Movement from the New Deal to Reagan* (New York: W. W. Norton, 2009).

27. Baer, *Reinventing Democrats*, 161.

28. Robert Dreyfuss, "How the DLC Does It," *American Prospect*, December 19, 2001.

29. From, *The New Democrats*, 113.

30. "Progressive Challenge to Political Orthodoxy," *Mainstream Democrat* 1, no. 1 (September–October 1989).

31. Baer, *Reinventing Democrats*, 136.

32. "Progressive Challenge to Political Orthodoxy," *Mainstream Democrat*.

33. Bruce Reed, interview, William J. Clinton Presidential History Project, Miller Center, University of Virginia, February 19–20, 2004.

34. Bruce N. Reed, interview, Diane D. Blair Papers, Special Collections, University of Arkansas Libraries, November 18, 1992; and Baer, *Reinventing Democrats*, 139.

35. Peter T. Kilborn, "Rise in Minimum Wage Offers Minimum Joy," *New York Times*, March 29, 1990.

36. Robert J. Shapiro, *Work and Poverty: A Progressive View of the Minimum Wage and the Earned Income Tax Credit*, Policy Report No. 1, Progressive Policy Institute, June 1989; Robert J. Shapiro, "The Minimum Wage Deal," *Washington Post*, July 3, 1989; and Robert J. Shapiro, "An American Working Wage," *Mainstream Democrat* 2, no. 1 (March 1990).

37. From, interview.

38. E. J. Dionne Jr., "The New Think Tank on the Block," *New York Times*, June 28, 1989, A20.

39. Dan Balz, "Moderate Democratic Think Tank Criticizes Party Support of Base Wage," *Los Angeles Times*, July 23, 1989.

40. Ford Foundation, "Asset Building for Social Change: Pathways to Large-Scale Impact," c. 2002, https://fordfoundcontent.blob.core.windows.net/media/1730/2004-assets_pathways.pdf.

41. For a full elaboration of Sherraden's argument, see Michael Sherraden, *Assets and the Poor: A New American Welfare Policy* (Armonk, NY: M. E. Sharpe, 1991).

42. Michael Sherraden, "From Research to Policy: Lessons from Individual Development Accounts," *Journal of Consumer Affairs* 34, no. 2 (2000): 159–181.

43. David Osborne, interview with author, Gloucester, Massachusetts, July 18, 2019.

44. Dan Goodgame, "David Osborne: A Prophet of Innovation," *Time*, December 14, 1992.

45. David Osborne, "A Poverty Program That Works," *New Republic*, May 8, 1989.

46. ShoreBank Corporation, "Annual Report 1993," April 1994, Box 1, Folder 9, SBC.

47. David Osborne, "Bootstrap Banking," *Inc.*, August 1, 1987.

48. David Osborne and Ted Gaebler, *Reinventing Government: How the Entrepreneurial Spirit is Transforming the Public Sector* (Reading, MA: Addison-Wesley, 1992), xviii.

49. Osborne and Gaebler, *Reinventing Government*, 30–32.

50. Osborne and Gaebler, *Reinventing Government*, 282–283.

51. Baer, *Reinventing Democrats*, 179-180.

52. From, *The New Democrats*, 118; and Will Marshall, interview with author, Washington, DC, July 15, 2019.

53. From, *The New Democrats*, 118.

54. Democratic Leadership Council, "New Orleans Declaration," reprinted in *Mainstream Democrat* 2, no. 2 (May 1990).

55. Bruce Reed, "The New Orleans Declaration: A Reader's Guide," *Mainstream Democrat* 2, no. 2 (May 1990).

56. Reed, "The New Orleans Declaration: A Reader's Guide."

57. Democratic Leadership Council, "New Orleans Declaration."

58. Marshall, interview.

59. Marshall, interview.

60. Paul Taylor and Maralee Schwartz, "Jackson's Unity Address Baffles, Irks Some Moderate Democrats," *Washington Post*, March 25, 1990, A10.

61. Robin Toner, "Eyes to Left, Democrats Edge Toward the Center," *New York Times*, March 25, 1990, A26.

62. From, *The New Democrats*, 113; and Marshall, interview.

63. *Crashing the Party*, directed by David Sigal (Warren, NJ: Passion River Films, 2016), DVD.

64. Bill Clinton, "Road Ahead," *Mainstream Democrat* 2, no. 2 (May 1990).

65. George Volsky, "Southern Leaders Cast Eyes Abroad," *New York Times*, September 8, 1985, A33; and John Herbers, "Arkansas Tries to Regain Its Footing," *New York Times*, April 27, 1986, A5.

66. Taylor and Schwartz, "Jackson's Unity Address."

67. From, interview.

68. Ronald Brownstein, "Democrats Search for an Identity," *Los Angeles Times*, July 2, 1991.

69. Donald Lambro, "Reaching for the Donkey's Reins," *Washington Times*, January 21, 1991.

70. From, *The New Democrats*, 154.

71. Marshall, interview; Reed, interview, February 19–20, 2004.

72. Lewis D. Solomon, *Microenterprise: Human Reconstruction in America's Inner Cities*, Policy Report No. 10, Progressive Policy Institute, June 1991.

73. Paul Weinstein, interview with author, by telephone, July 29, 2020.

74. Marisa Chappell, *The War on Welfare: Family, Poverty, and Politics in Modern America* (Philadelphia: University of Pennsylvania Press, 2011), 90–94.

75. Jason DeParle, *American Dream: Three Women, Ten Kids, and a Nation's Drive to End Welfare* (New York: Viking, 2004), 92, 85–100.

76. Robert Scheer, "Trouble Still in Forrest City," *Nation*, March 22, 1993, 370–374.

77. Jason DeParle, "Arkansas Pushes Plan to Break Welfare Cycle," *New York Times*, March 14, 1992, 10.

78. Reed, interview, November 18, 1992.

79. Reed, interview, November 18, 1992.

80. Reed, interview, February 19–20, 2004.

81. Robert A. Jordon, "DLC Gets Jesse Jackson's Dander Up," *Boston Globe*, May 5, 1991.

82. Steve Daley, "Democrats Likely to Do Battle at Meeting," *Chicago Tribune*, May 6, 1991, 2.

83. Jesse Jackson, "For the Democrats, a Strategy of Inclusion," *Washington Post*, May 22, 1991, A21.

84. David S. Broder, "'Mainstream' Democratic Group Stakes Claim on Party's Future," *Washington Post*, May 3, 1991.

85. David S. Broder, "Hill Liberals Launch Democratic Coalition," *Washington Post*, May 14, 1990; and Robert Shogan, "Rival Factions Vie to Mold Democratic Agenda," *Los Angeles Times*, May 5, 1991.

86. Al From, interview, William J. Clinton Presidential History Project, Miller Center, University of Virginia, April 27, 2006.

87. David S. Broder, "The DLC at Six: It's Gone About as Far as It Can Go," *Washington Post*, May 12, 1991, C7.

88. Bill Clinton, Keynote Address, DLC's Cleveland Convention.

89. Gwen Ifill, "Democratic Group Argues Over Goals," *New York Times*, May 7, 1991.

90. "The New American Choice Resolutions," adopted at the DLC Convention, Cleveland, Ohio, May 1, 1991, Box 10, Folder 7, Congressional Series, MEP.

91. "The New American Choice Resolutions."

92. "The New American Choice Resolutions."

93. "The New American Choice Resolutions."

94. Baer, *Reinventing Democrats*, 180.

95. Gwen Ifill, "Centrist Council Exults in Success of a Member," *New York Times*, May 3, 1992, 29.

96. From, *The New Democrats*, 162–164.

97. Dan Balz and E. J. Dionne Jr., "Clinton: Groundwork and a Lot of Breaks," *Washington Post*, January 12, 1992, A01.

98. Bill Clinton, "The New Covenant: Responsibility and Rebuilding the American Community," Georgetown University, October 23, 1991.

99. Reed, interview, William J. Clinton Presidential History Project.

100. DeParle, *American Dream*, 102–103.

101. David Ellwood, *Poor Support: Poverty in the American Family* (New York: Basic Books, 1988).

102. Governor Bill Clinton, "Responsibility and Rebuilding the American Community," October 23, 1991, Office of Communications and Don Baer, "Georgetown Speeches," CDL.

103. William Greider et al., "The Rolling Stone Interview," *Rolling Stone*, September 17, 1992.

104. William J. Clinton: "Address Accepting the Presidential Nomination at the Democratic National Convention in New York," July 16, 1992, The American Presidency Project, www.presidency.ucsb.edu/node/220260.

105. Alan Murray, "Clintonomics: Presidential Candidate Backs Industrial Policy with a Populist Twist," *Wall Street Journal*, April 23, 1992.

106. E. J. Dionne Jr., "Inventing Clintonomics," *Washington Post*, October 15, 1992, A7.

107. Murray, "Clintonomics"; and Ronald Brownstein, "Clinton Revives Debate Over Industrial Policy: Economy," *Los Angeles Times*, May 20, 1992, A10.

108. Robert B. Reich, *Locked in the Cabinet* (New York: Alfred A. Knopf, 1997), 12.

109. Bill Clinton and Al Gore, *Putting People First: How We Can All Change America* (New York: Times Books, 1992), 143–145.

110. Sidney Weintraub, *The Case for Free Trade with Mexico: Why Progressives Should Support a North American Free Trade Area*, Policy Report No. 9, Progressive Policy Institute, April 1991; and Ron Scheman, "Good Neighbors," *New Democrat*, May 1991.

111. Peter Behr, "Clinton's Conversion on NAFTA," *Washington Post*, September 19, 1993.

112. Gwen Ifill, "With Reservations, Clinton Endorses Free-Trade Pact," *New York Times*, October 5, 1992.

113. Thomas B. Edsall, "Show of Party Unity Masks Scars of Ideological Battle," *Washington Post*, July 13, 1992, A1.

114. Mike Causey, "Yep, He Really Said It," *Washington Post*, June 19, 1992; and Sam Fullwood II, "Clinton Tells Union He'd Cut Back on Jobs," *Los Angeles Times*, June 18, 1992.

115. Edsall, "Show of Party Unity Masks Scars of Ideological Battle."

116. Jesse L. Jackson, "Ominous Portents from Chicago," *Philadelphia Daily News*, April 20, 1992, 39.

117. Bill Clinton, "Remarks of Governor Bill Clinton to the Rainbow Coalition National Convention," Washington, DC, June 13, 1992, Box 4, Folder 44, Congressional Series, MEP.

118. Clinton, "Remarks of Governor Bill Clinton to the Rainbow Coalition National Convention."

119. David S. Broder and Thomas B. Edsall, "Clinton Finds Biracial Support for Criticism of Rap Singer," *Washington Post*, June 16, 1992, A7.

120. Thomas B. Edsall, "Clinton Stuns Rainbow Coalition," *Washington Post*, June 14, 1992, A1; and Gwen Ifill, "Clinton Stands by Remark on Rapper," *New York Times*, June 15, 1992, A16.

121. Thomas B. Edsall, "Black Leaders View Clinton Strategy with Mix of Pragmatism, Optimism," *Washington Post*, October 28, 1992, A16.

122. Edsall, "Black Leaders View Clinton Strategy."

123. Manning Marable, *Beyond Black and White: Rethinking Race in American Politics and Society* (New York: Verso, 1995), 69–70.

124. Clinton and Gore, *Putting People First*, 5.

125. Robert Pears, "In a Final Draft, Democrats Reject a Part of Their Past," *New York Times*, June 26, 1992, A13.

126. Democratic Party Platforms, "1992 Democratic Party Platform," The American Presidency Project, www.presidency.ucsb.edu/node/273264.

127. For more on the racial and class connotations of this type of language, which has a long history, see Matthew D. Lassiter, *The Silent Majority: Suburban Politics in the Sunbelt South* (Princeton, NJ: Princeton University Press, 2005).

128. David Lauter, "Clinton Picks Gore as Running Mate in Break from Tradition," *Los Angeles Times*, July 10, 1992.

129. Lloyd Grove, "Al From, the Life of the Party," *Washington Post*, July 24, 1992.

130. Grove, "Al From, the Life of the Party."

131. Grove, "Al From, the Life of the Party."

132. John B. Judis and Ruy Teixeira, *The Emerging Democratic Majority* (New York: Scribner, 2002), 28–30; Roper Center for Public Opinion Research, "How Groups Voted in 1992," https://ropercenter.cornell.edu/how-groups-voted-1992; and Paul Taylor, "The Growing Electoral Clout of Blacks Is Driven by Turnout, Not Demographics," Pew Research Center, www.pewresearch.org/wp-content/uploads/sites/3/2013/01/2012_Black_Voter_Project_revised_1-9.pdf.

133. Marshall, interview.

134. Al From and Will Marshall, "Preface," in *Mandate for Change*, ed. Will Marshall and Martin Schram (New York: Berkeley Books, 1992), xvi–vxiii.

135. From and Marshall, "Preface."

136. E. J. Dionne Jr., "After Exile, Democrats Reenter the Ideas Business," *Washington Post*, November 18, 1992, A21.

137. "The Clinton Revolution: A Domestic Policy Agenda for the First 100 Days [binder] [1]," Office of Speechwriting and Josh Gottheimer, CDL.

138. "The Clinton Revolution."

CHAPTER 5: BETTER THAN WELFARE

1. Mike Davis, *City of Quartz: Excavating the Future in Los Angeles* (New York: Vintage Books, 1992), 302–309.

2. Lou Cannon and Paul Taylor, "Uneasy Calm Prevails as LA Starts Cleanup," *Washington Post*, May 3, 1992; and Max Felker-Kantor, *Policing Los Angeles: Race, Resistance and the Rise of the LAPD* (Chapel Hill: University of North Carolina Press, 2018), 229.

3. Cannon and Taylor, "Uneasy Calm Prevails as LA Starts Cleanup."

4. William Greider et al., "The Rolling Stone Interview," *Rolling Stone*, September 17, 1992.

5. Greider et al., "The Rolling Stone Interview."

6. Carol Jouzaitis, "Clinton: Start Accounts for Poor," *Chicago Tribune*, September 17, 1992.

7. William J. Clinton, "Remarks on Empowerment Zones and Enterprise Communities," January 17, 1994, The American Presidency Project, www.presidency.ucsb.edu/node/219793.

8. William J. Clinton, "Remarks at Session I of the Southern Regional Economic Conference in Atlanta," March 29, 1995, The American Presidency Project, www.presidency.ucsb.edu/node/221629.

9. Robert Pear, "Clinton Tours City's Damaged Areas and Chides Bush," *New York Times*, May 5, 1992, A26.

10. While it is more accurate to call the events in Los Angeles in 1992 an uprising, I use the term *riots* here because that is how they were referred to at the time. For more on problems of the riot terminology, see Elizabeth Hinton, *America on Fire: The Untold History of Police Violence and Black Rebellion Since the 1960s* (New York: Liveright, 2021).

11. Ann Devroy, "White House Blames Liberal Programs for Unrest," *Washington Post*, May 5, 1992.

12. Maralee Schwartz, "Clinton Calls for National Day of Reflection," *Washington Post*, May 2, 1992, A12.

13. Schwartz, "Clinton Calls for National Day of Reflection."

14. See, for example, Bill Clinton, "A Plan for America's Future," c. 1992, Box 4, Folder 43, Congressional Series, MEP; "Clinton Outlines Ideas for Inner City to Persian Gulf," *Los Angeles Times*, August 14, 1992; and Bill Clinton, *My Life* (New York: Alfred A. Knopf, 2004), 209.

15. Jason DeParle, "How to Lift the Poor," *New York Times*, November 10, 1992.

16. Paul Weinstein, interview with author, by telephone, July 28, 2020.

17. Weinstein, interview.

18. Weinstein, interview.

19. Nelson Lichtenstein, "A Fabulous Failure: Clinton's 1990s and the Origins of Our Times," *American Prospect*, January 29, 2018.

20. Judith Stein, *Pivotal Decade: How the United States Traded Factories for Finance in the Seventies* (New Haven: Yale University Press), 281–282.

21. Lichtenstein, "A Fabulous Failure."

22. Mickey Kantor, "At Long Last, a Trade Pact to Be Proud of," *Wall Street Journal*, August 17, 1993, A14; and Lichtenstein, "A Fabulous Failure."

23. Michael K. Frisby, "Clinton Assembles a Panel to Develop His Domestic Plans," *Wall Street Journal*, February 24, 1993, A4.

24. Robin Toner, "A Clinton Whiz Kid Who's Still There and Still a Believer," *New York Times*, October 25, 1999.

25. Robert B. Reich, *Locked in the Cabinet* (New York: Alfred A. Knopf, 1997), 25; and Toner, "A Clinton Whiz Kid."

26. David S. Hilzenrath and Steven Mufson, "Keeper of the Flame," *Washington Post*, May 9, 1993.

27. Kevin Sack, "Andrew Cuomo: Born to Politics, Married to Politics," *New York Times*, March 27, 1994, 213.

28. Sack, "Andrew Cuomo."

29. Memorandum from Paul Dimond to Bruce Reed and Gene Sperling, Re: A Place Called Hope, February 21, 1993, Domestic Policy Council, Bruce Reed, and Subject Files, "Community Empowerment," CDL.

30. Nicholas Lemann, "The Myth of Community Development," *New York Times*, January 9, 1994.

31. Memorandum for the President from the Community Empowerment Working Group, Subject: Overview of the Enterprise Proposal, Draft 7, March 29, 1993, Domestic Policy Council, Bruce Reed, and Subject Files, "Enterprise Zones [2]," CDL.

32. Memorandum for the President from Bruce Reed and Gene Sperling, Subject: Economic Empowerment Agenda, April 19, 1993, History of the Office of the Vice President and Clinton Administration History Project, "[OVP—Community Empowerment Program—Presidential Decision Memos]," CDL.

33. Michael B. Katz, *The Price of Citizenship: Redefining the American Welfare State* (New York: Metropolitan Press, 2001), 126.

34. Karen Mossberger, *The Politics of Ideas and the Spread of Enterprise Zones* (Washington, DC: Georgetown University Press, 2000), 55–56.

35. Heritage Foundation, "New Life for Federal Enterprise Zone Legislation: Seven Lessons from the States," Heritage Foundation Backgrounder, No. 833, June 4, 1991, Congressional Series, Box 12, Folder 10, MEP.

36. Clifford D. May, "Theorist with a Heart: Jack French Hart," *New York Times*, December 20, 1988.

37. Department of Housing and Urban Development, "Secretary Jack Kemp Talks About a New War on Poverty," remarks at the Heritage

Foundation, Washington DC, June 6, 1990, Congressional Series, Box 16, Folder 17, MEP; and Jason DeParle, "How Jack Kemp Lost the War on Poverty," *New York Times*, February 28, 1993, A26.

38. Guy Gugliotta, "Clinton Mixes Strategies for Anti-Poverty Policy; Initiative Could Cost Up to $7.5 Billion a Year," *Washington Post*, December 3, 1992, A9.

39. Paul Dimond and Sheryll Cashin to Gene Sperling, Bruce Reed, and Paul Weinstein, Subject: Decision Memo for EP Proposal, March 17, 1993, Domestic Policy Council, Bruce Reed, and Subject Files, "Enterprise Zones [2]," CDL.

40. Sheryll Cashin, interview with author by Zoom, September 4, 2020.

41. Cashin, interview.

42. Lemann, "Myth of Community Development."

43. Dimond and Cashin to Sperling et al., Subject: Decision Memo for EP Proposal.

44. Dimond and Cashin to Sperling et al., Subject: Decision Memo for EP Proposal; and Gene [Sperling] to Bruce Reed, March 29, 1993, Domestic Policy Council, Bruce Reed, and Subject Files, "Enterprise Zones [2]," CDL.

45. Memorandum for the President from Reed and Sperling, Subject: Economic Empowerment Agenda.

46. US Department of Housing and Urban Development, Office of Community Planning and Development, US Department of Agriculture, Office of Rural Community and Economic Development, Building Communities Together: Application for Designation as a Federal Empowerment Zone & Enterprise Community, c. 1993, Domestic Policy Council, Carol Rasco, and Subject Series, "[Empowerment Zones] [1]," CDL.

47. Memorandum for the President from Reed and Sperling, Subject: Economic Empowerment Agenda.

48. Gene Sperling, *The Pro-Growth Progressive: An Economic Strategy for Shared Prosperity* (New York: Simon and Schuster, 2005), 72.

49. Cashin, interview.

50. Dimond and Cashin to Sperling et al., Subject: Decision Memo for EP Proposal.

51. Dimond and Cashin to Sperling et al., Subject: Decision Memo for EP Proposal.

52. Lemann, "Myth of Community Development."

53. Jeffrey L. Katz, "Enterprise Zones Struggle to Make Their Mark," *Congressional Quarterly*, July 17, 1993.

54. Cashin, interview.

55. Cashin, interview.

56. David Wessel and David Rogers, "Clinton Places Priority on Deficit Cuts," *Wall Street Journal*, June 23, 1993.

57. Stein, *Pivotal Decade*, 282.

58. Kevin M. Kruse and Julian E. Zelizer, *Fault Lines: A History of the United States Since 1974* (New York: Basic Books, 2019), 209–210.

59. Monte Piliawsky, "Racism or Realpolitik?: The Clinton Administration and African-Americans," *Black Scholar* 24, no. 2 (Spring 1994).

60. Piliawsky, "Racism or Realpolitik?"

61. Robin Toner, "King's Speech Commemorated by Thousands," *New York Times*, August 28, 1993, A18.

62. Toner, "King's Speech Commemorated by Thousands."

63. Sack, "Andrew Cuomo."

64. See, for example, Mrs. Connie Graves letter, May 17, 1994, Domestic Policy Council, Carol Rasco, and Subject Series, "Empowerment Zones [4]," CDL.

65. Neal R. Peirce, "Empowerment Zones: How Successful Are They?," *Baltimore Sun*, March 3, 1997.

66. "President Clinton Announces Designation of More Than 100 Empowerment Zones and Enterprise Communities," December 21, 1994, Domestic Policy Council, Carol Rasco, and Issues Series, "EZ/EC [Empowerment Zones/Enterprise Communities]," CDL; and Peter Necheles to Secretary Mike Espy, Subject: Empowerment Zone and Enterprise Community Update, October 5, 1994, USDA, Box 6, Folder 19, MEP.

67. "President Clinton Announces Designation of More Than 100 Empowerment Zones and Enterprise Communities."

68. Gebe Martinez, "South-Central L.A. Likely Focus for New Aid Program Cities," *Los Angeles Times*, January 24, 1993, 4.

69. Hugo Martin, "L.A. OKs Map of 'Empowerment Zone' Redevelopment," *Los Angeles Times*, April 14,1994, 4.

70. Robert J. Lopez, "City to Vie for Federal Zoning Plan Designation Urban Agenda," *Los Angeles Times*, June 23, 1994, 4.

71. Rich Connell, "Delays, Lack of Focus Dogged L.A.'s Grant Bid Aid," *Los Angeles Times*, December 25, 1994, 1.

72. Eric Lichtblau, "L.A. Intensifies Effort as Hope Fades for $100 Million in Aid," *Los Angeles Times*, December 19, 1994, 1.

73. Cashin, interview.

74. Cleveland also earned that designation.

75. Nathan Gorenstein, "A Big Aid Plan Comes Up Small: Philadelphia's Empowerment Zone Has Made Only Modest Gains," *Philadelphia Inquirer*, July 24, 1997; and Jeffrey Ball, "GAO Probe Calls into Question Atlanta's Empowerment Zone," *Wall Street Journal*, October 22, 1997. For more on the delays and the wide variety of outcomes in various cities, see Michael J. Rich and Robert P. Stoker, *Collaborative Governance for Urban Revitalization: Lessons from Empowerment Zones* (Ithaca, NY: Cornell University Press, 2014).

76. Mark Caro, "A Political Message for Holiday Inmates," *Chicago Tribune*, December 26, 1994, 1.

77. Mike Davis, *Ecology of Fear: Los Angeles and the Imagination of Disaster* (New York: Henry Holt, 1998), chap. 7.

78. Piliawsky, "Racism or Realpolitik?"

79. Cashin, interview.

80. Sharon Stangenes, "South Shore Bank Thrust into Spotlight," *Chicago Tribune*, November 15, 1992.

81. Michael Quint, "A Bank Shows It Can Profit and Follow a Social Agenda," *New York Times*, May 24, 1992.

82. Paul Wiseman, "Investing in Inner City," *USA Today*, January 8, 1993, B1.

83. Stangenes, "South Shore Bank Thrust into Spotlight."

84. Ronald Grzywinski, interview with author, by Zoom, November 5, 2020.

85. Quint, "A Bank Shows It Can Profit and Follow a Social Agenda."

86. Guy Gugliotta, "Banking on Community Development," *Washington Post*, December 20, 1992, A1.

87. NEC-DPC Interagency Working Group on Community Development and Empowerment, Subject: Community Lending Proposal, Draft 8, April 10, 1993, Domestic Policy Council, Bruce Reed, and Subject Files, "Community Development Banks [1]," CDL.

88. NEC-DPC Interagency Working Group on Community Development and Empowerment to the President [Bill Clinton], Subject: Enterprise Zones, April 20, 1993, History of the Office of the Vice President and Clinton Administration History Project, "[OVP—Community Empowerment Program—Presidential Decision Memos]," CDL.

89. "Highlights of the CDFI Proposal," c. 1993, Domestic Policy Council, Bruce Reed, and Subject Files, "Community Development Banks [1]," CDL.

90. "Highlights of the CDFI Proposal."

91. Robert B. Cox, "Fringe Lenders Unite to Seek Central Role in Clinton Plan," *American Banker*, January 29, 1993. For more on these tensions, see Clifford N. Rosenthal, *Democratizing Finance: Origins of the Community Development Financial Institutions Movement* (Victoria, BC: Friesen Press, 2018), Kindle edition.

92. George Surgeon, interview with author, by Zoom, November 13, 2020; and Paul Weinstein to Bruce Reed and Gene Sperling, Subject: Legislative Strategy on Community Development Financial Institutions Proposal, May 10, 1993, Domestic Policy Council, Bruce Reed, and Subject Files, "Community Development Banks [2]," CDL.

93. "The Clinton Revolution: A Domestic Policy Agenda for the First Hundred Days," prepared for the President-Elect and the Vice-President-Elect by the Presidential Transition Domestic Policy Staff, December 1992, History of the Domestic Policy Council and Clinton Administration History Project, "Domestic Policy Council—Documentary Annex II [6]," CDL; and Weinstein, interview.

94. Osborne, "A Poverty Program That Works."

95. Clinton administration, "Principles of the Administration's Community Development Financial Institutions Proposal," c. 1993, Domestic Policy Council, Carol Rasco, and Subject Series, "Community Development Banks [2]," CDL.

96. Gene Sperling and Bruce Reed to the President, Subject Tomorrow's CD Bank/CRA Reform Event, July 14, 1993, History of the Office of the Vice President and Clinton Administration History Project, "[OVP—CEP—CDFI/CRA—Memos]," CDL.

97. "Creating a Nationwide Network of Community Development Banks and Financial Institutions," c. 1994, National Security Council, Speechwriting Office, and Robert Boorstin, "Economic Conference of the President & Vice President—Briefing Papers on Select Administration Policies [4]," CDL.

98. "Creating a Nationwide Network of Community Development Banks and Financial Institutions."

99. Weinstein, interview; Surgeon, interview.

100. Paul Weinstein to the Interagency Task Force on Enterprise Zones/Community Development Financial Institutions, Subject: Community development financial institutions proposals (discussion draft), February 24, 1993, Domestic Policy Council, Bruce Reed, and Subject Files, "Community Empowerment," CDL.

101. Yi-Hsin Chang, "Fund to Help Poor Areas Clears Congress," *Wall Street Journal*, August 11, 1994.

102. "Clinton Signs Bill to Spur Spending in Poor Areas," *San Francisco Chronicle*, September 24, 1994.

103. William J. Clinton, "Remarks on Signing the Riegle Community Development and Regulatory Improvement Act of 1994," September 23, 1994, The American Presidency Project, www.presidency.ucsb.edu/node /217688.

104. Clinton, "Remarks on Signing the Riegle Community Development and Regulatory Improvement Act of 1994."

105. Rosenthal, *Democratizing Finance*.

106. Robert E. Rubin with Jacob Weisberg, *In an Uncertain World: Tough Choices from Wall Street to Washington* (New York: Random House, 2003), 94–95; and James Risen, "On Economic Matters, Man to See is Clinton Aide Rubin," *Los Angeles Times*, February 10, 1993.

107. Ann Reilly Dowd, "Clinton's Point Man on the Economy Robert Rubin Directs the National Economic Council," *Fortune*, May 3, 1993, https://money.cnn.com/magazines/fortune/fortune_archive/1993/05/03 /77801/index.htm.

108. Rubin, *In an Uncertain World*, 95.

109. Reich, *Locked in the Cabinet*, 211.

110. Rosenthal, *Democratizing Finance*; and Weinstein, interview.

111. Bob Rubin to the Honorable Bob Livingston, March 28, 1996, "History of the Department of the Treasury," CDL.

112. Rosenthal, *Democratizing Finance*; and Department of the Treasury, *Community Development Financial Institutions Fund*, Fiscal Year 1997, Annual Report, www.treasury.gov/press-center/press-releases /pages/cdfi97.aspx.

113. Department of the Treasury, "Overview of the Community Development Financial Institutions Fund," September 2, 1999, First Lady's

Office, Ruby Shamir, and Subject Files, "New Markets/Interagency Meetings [1]," CDL.

114. Department of the Treasury, "Overview of the Community Development Financial Institutions Fund," July 7, 1999, Office of Policy Development and Lisa Green, "CDFIs [Community Development Financial Institutions] [4]," CDL.

115. Bob Rubin to the Hon. Bob Livingston, March 28, 1996.

116. Mehrsa Baradaran, *How the Other Half Banks: Exclusion, Exploitation, and the Threat to Democracy* (Cambridge, MA: Harvard University Press, 2015), 169.

117. For more on the urban reinvestment movement and its role in the passage of the CRA, see Rebecca Marchiel, *After Redlining: The Urban Reinvestment Movement in the Era of Financial Deregulation* (Chicago: University of Chicago Press, 2020).

118. Office of the Comptroller of the Currency, "Community Reinvestment Act," March 2014, www.occ.gov/publications-and-resources /publications/community-affairs/community-developments-fact-sheets /pub-fact-sheet-cra-reinvestment-act-mar-2014.pdf.

119. Grzywinski, interview.

120. "Community Reinvestment Act Short Term Legislative and Administrative Agenda," c. 1993, Domestic Policy Council, Bruce Reed, and Subject Files, "Community Empowerment," CDL.

121. Weinstein, interview.

122. William J. Clinton, "Press Briefing by Secretary of the Treasury, Lloyd Bentsen, Robert Rubin, Assistant to the President for Economic Policy and Eugene Ludwig, Comptroller of the Currency," December 8, 1993, The American Presidency Project. www.presidency.ucsb.edu/node /269135.

123. President Bill Clinton Memorandum for Eugene Allan Ludwig et al., July 15, 1993, Domestic Policy Council, Bruce Reed, and Subject Files, "Community Reinvestment Act," CDL.

124. Office of the Comptroller of the Currency, "Remarks of Eugene A. Ludwig Comptroller of the Currency Before the National Urban League," news release, August 5, 1997, www.occ.gov/news-issuances/news-releases /1997/nr-occ-1997-78.html.

125. William J. Clinton, "Statement on Reform of Regulations Implementing the Community Reinvestment Act," April 19, 1995, The American Presidency Project, www.presidency.ucsb.edu/node/220805.

126. See, for example, Beryl Satter, *Family Properties: Race, Real Estate, and the Exploitation of Black Urban America* (New York: Metropolitan Books, 2009); and Keeanga-Yamahtta Taylor, *Race for Profit: How Banks and the Real Estate Industry Undermined Black Homeownership* (Chapel Hill: University of North Carolina Press, 2019).

127. William J. Clinton, "Remarks on Signing the Riegle-Neal Interstate Banking and Branching Efficiency Act of 1994," September 29, 1994, The American Presidency Project www.presidency.ucsb.edu/node /217946.

128. Nicholas Lemann, *Transaction Man: The Rise of the Deal and the Decline of the American Dream* (New York: Farrar, Straus and Giroux, 2019), 163–164.

129. William J. Clinton, "Remarks on Empowerment Zones and Enterprise Communities," January 17, 1994, The American Presidency Project, www.presidency.ucsb.edu/node/219793.

130. Judy Pasternack, "Chicago's Shorebank Earns Interest as Model for Rebirth Renewal," *Los Angeles Times*, February 22, 1993, 1.

131. Michael Quint, "Lender for Low-Income Areas Gets Boost," *New York Times*, March 19, 1993.

132. ShoreBank Corporation, "Annual Report 1993," Box 1, Folder 9, SBC.

133. David Moberg, "The Left Bank," *Chicago Reader*, May 26, 1994.

134. Stangenes, "South Shore Bank Thrust into the Spotlight."

135. Moberg, "The Left Bank."

136. Moberg, "The Left Bank."

137. Surgeon, interview.

138. Barbara F. Bronstein, "Shorebank, a Community Lending Model, Takes Heat Over Bid for Black-Owned Bank," *American Banker*, August 10, 1995.

139. Surgeon, interview.

140. Grzywinski, interview.

141. ShoreBank, Executive Summary, August 1994, Box 44, Folder 338, SBC.

142. Moberg, "The Left Bank."

143. Julie Johnsson, "Banking on Baku," *Crain's Chicago Business*, March 27, 2000.

144. ShoreBank Corporation, "Annual Report 1998," Box 1, Folder 8, SBC.

CHAPTER 6: CHANGE THEIR HEADS

1. Microcredit Summit, *1997 Microcredit Summit Report* (last accessed January 5, 2020).

2. *Accion International Bulletin* 33, no. 1 (Spring 1997), Box 1, Folder 22, AI.

3. White House, Office of the Press Secretary, "Remarks by the First Lady at the Microcredit Summit," Sheraton Hotel, Washington, DC, February 3, 1997, First Lady's Office, Press Office, and Lissa Muscatine, "[Speeches and Remarks] [binder]-[Remarks to the Microcredit Summit, 2/3/97] [Folder 1]," CDL.

4. Grameen Bank, Bangladesh, Voice of America, c. 1996, http://www.gdrc.org/icm/grameen-voa.html.

5. Meg McSherry Breslin and Annie Sweeney, "First Lady's Wish Is to Help Women, Children Overcome," *Chicago Tribune*, February 19, 1997.

6. Julia Elyachar, *Markets of Dispossession: NGOs, Economic Development, and the State in Cairo* (Durham, NC: Duke University Press, 2005), 81.

7. Michael B. Katz, *The Undeserving Poor: America's Enduring Confrontation with Poverty* (New York: Oxford University Press, 2013), 251–255.

8. Sanford F. Schram, *Welfare Discipline: Discourse, Governance, and Globalization* (Philadelphia: Temple University Press, 2009), 108–109.

9. Schram, *Welfare Discipline*, 255.

10. Jason DeParle, "From Pledge to Plan: The Campaign to End Welfare," *New York Times*, July 15, 1994.

11. For more on the Clinton health-care plan and controversy, see Colin Gordon, *Dead on Arrival: The Politics of Health Care in Twentieth-Century America*, rev. ed. (Princeton, NJ: Princeton University Press, 2004), 42–44; and Theda Skocpol, *Boomerang: Health Care Reform and the Turn Against Government*, 2nd rev. ed. (New York: W. W. Norton, 1997).

12. Sheryl Gay Stolberg and Astead W. Herndon, "'Lock the S.O.B.s Up': Joe Biden and the Era of Mass Incarceration," *New York Times*, June 25, 2019.

13. Keeanga-Yamahtta Taylor, *From #BlackLivesMatter to Black Liberation* (Chicago: Haymarket Books, 2019), 120.

14. William J. Clinton, "Remarks to the Convocation of the Church of God in Christ at Memphis, Tennessee," November 13, 1993, The American Presidency Project, www.presidency.ucsb.edu/node/217857.

15. See James Forman Jr., *Locking Up Our Own: Crime and Punishment in Black America* (New York: Farrar, Straus and Giroux, 2017); and Ronald Brownstein, "Clinton's 'New Democrat' Agenda Reopens Racial Divisions," *Los Angeles Times*, February 9, 1994, 5.

16. Dinah Wisenberg Brin, "Jesse Jackson Voices His Views on the Clinton Admin," *Philadelphia Tribune*, July 1, 1994, 4B.

17. "Adding a Federal Antipoverty Development Package to Welfare Reform, A Preliminary Proposal," no date, Domestic Policy Council, Bruce Reed, and Subject Files, "IDAs [Individual Development Accounts]," CDL; and Mike Alexander to Mary Jo Bane and David Ellwood, Subject: Comments on Welfare Reform Recommendations, November 23, 1993, Domestic Policy Council, Bruce Reed, and Welfare Reform Series, "Welfare Group Comments," CDL.

18. Bruce Reed to Bill Clinton, Subject: The Politics of Welfare Reform, May 30, 1994, Domestic Policy Council, Bruce Reed, and Welfare Reform Series, "Memos to the President (5/30/94)," CDL.

19. Jeremy Ben-Ami to Bruce Reed, Kathie Way, Paul Weinstein, and Sheryll Cashin, May 25, 1994, Domestic Policy Council, Bruce Reed, and Welfare Reform Series, "Assets," CDL.

20. Ruth Marcus and Dan Balz, "Clinton Outlines Plan to Break Welfare Cycle," *Washington Post*, June 15, 1994; and Jason DeParle, "Skirmish on

Welfare Highlights the Chasm Between Left and Right," *New York Times*, July 31, 1994, A22.

21. David Corn, "What's Left in the Party?," *Nation*, September 23, 1996, 20.

22. For more on Gingrich, see Julian Zelizer, *Burning Down the House: Newt Gingrich, the Fall of a Speaker, and the Rise of the New Republican Party* (New York: Penguin Press, 2020); and Kevin M. Kruse and Julian E. Zelizer, *Fault Lines: A History of the United States Since 1974* (New York: Basic Books, 2019), 216–217.

23. Al From and Will Marshall, "A Fresh Start," *New Democrat*, January–February 1995, 5.

24. Al From to the President, Subject: Improving Your Politics, May 4, 1993, Box 4, Folder: DLC Memos to Bill Clinton, 1992–1993, DRP.

25. Will Marshall to Al From, Re: BC's "PC Problem," May 3, 1993, Box 4, Folder: DLC Memos to Bill Clinton, 1992–1993, DRP.

26. Al From, interview with author, Bethesda, Maryland, September 26, 2019; and Will Marshall, interview with author, Washington, DC, July 15, 2019.

27. Will Marshall, "Replacing Welfare with Work," Policy Briefing, Progressive Policy Institute, July 1994.

28. Bill Galston to the President, Subject: DLC/Progressive Policy Institute Recommendations, December 23, 1994, Domestic Policy Council, Carol Rasco, Subject Series, "Progressive Policy Institute Recommendations," CDL.

29. Sean Wilentz, *The Age of Reagan: A History, 1974–2008* (New York: HarperCollins, 2008), 350–315.

30. Jason DeParle, *American Dream: Three Women, Ten Kids, and a Nation's Drive to End Welfare* (New York: Viking, 2004), 123.

31. DeParle, *American Dream*, 124–125.

32. Robin Toner, "New Senate Push on Welfare Revives Tensions in Both Parties," *New York Times*, September 9, 1995, 9.

33. Barbara Vobejda, "Welfare Bill Opponents Turn Up Pressure," *Washington Post*, July 27, 1996, A4.

34. Vobejda, "Welfare Bill Opponents Turn Up Pressure."

35. Gregg Zoroya, "Taking a Stand for Women and Children," *Los Angeles Times*, August 9, 1996.

36. DeParle, *American Dream*, 154.

37. William J. Clinton, "Remarks on Welfare Reform Legislation and an Exchange with Reporters," July 31, 1996, The American Presidency Project, www.presidency.ucsb.edu/node/223295.

38. Lyn Hogan to Carolyn O'Brien, Re: Microenterprise and Individual Development Accounts, November 12, 1996, Domestic Policy Council and Elena Kagan, "Ideas—Welfare," CDL.

39. "What We're Fighting For," *New Democrat* 8, no. 3 (September–October 1996).

40. Robert Pear, "Millions Affected," *New York Times*, August 1, 1996.

41. "Grapes of Wrath," *Nation*, August 26–September 2, 1996, 3.

42. Francis X. Clines, "Clinton Signs Bill Cutting Welfare," *New York Times*, August 23, 1996.

43. David Broder, "Divided Democrats, After November Façade of Unity Likely to Crack Wide Open," *Orlando Sentinel*, August 27, 1996, A9.

44. Brin, "Jesse Jackson Voices His Views"; and James Warren, "Jesse Jackson's Protest of Welfare Bill is Rich in Sad Twists," *Chicago Tribune*, August 4, 1996, 4.

45. Robert G. Beckel, "Where Have all the Liberal Voices Gone?" *Los Angeles Times*, September 15, 1996, 2.

46. Paul Richter and Sarah Fritz, "Clinton Would Soften Welfare Law, Gore Says," *Los Angeles Times*, August 26, 1996.

47. James Wright, "Jesse Jackson Differs with Clinton on Welfare, Backs Him for President," *Afro-American Red Star*, August 31,1996, A1.

48. Corn, "What's Left in the Party?," 20.

49. Corn, "What's Left in the Party?," 21–22.

50. Anand Giridharadas, *Winners Take All: The Elite Charade of Changing the World* (New York: Knopf, 2018), 237–238. See also Hillary Rodham Clinton, *Living History* (New York: Houghton Mifflin, 2003), 368–370; and Sidney Blumenthal, *The Clinton Wars* (New York Farrar, Straus and Giroux, 2003).

51. Lyn Hogan to Bruce Reed, Re: Welfare Reform Signing Ceremony Suggestion, August 14, 1996, Domestic Policy Council, Bruce Reed, and Welfare Reform Series, "Signing [3]," CDL.

52. "Biographies of Welfare Recipients," c. 1986, Domestic Policy Council, Carol Rasco, and Meetings, Trips, Events Series, "Welfare Reform Bill Signing Ceremony Thursday, August 22, 1996," CDL.

53. Memorandum from Julia Moffett to Don Baer, Subject: Updated Anecdotes, July 4, 1996, Office of Communications and Don Baer, "Updated Anecdotes," CDL.

54. "Lillie Harden Speaks About Her Life," clip of Welfare Reform Bill signing, C-SPAN video, 2:48, August 22, 1996, posted November 23, 2015, www.c-span.org/video/?c4562242/user-clip-lillie-harden-speaks-life.

55. DeParle, *American Dream*, 151–152.

56. DeParle, *American Dream*, 112. DeParle suggests that Clinton's commitment to this view came from his own experiences as the son of a single mother in a family that struggled economically.

57. Alfred E. Eckes and Thomas W. Zeiler, *Globalization and the American Century* (New York: Cambridge University Press, 2003), 220.

58. Ann Van Dusen testimony, "The Value of Microenterprise Development," hearing before the Committee on International Relations, House of Representatives, 104th Cong., 1st Sess., Washington, DC, June 27, 1995 (Washington DC: Government Printing Office, 1995); and USAID, *Reaching Down and Scaling Up in the Next Century: U.S. Agency for International Development Microenterprise Results Reporting for 1998*, September 1999, https://mrr.usaid.gov/docs/MRR_Annual_Report_FY1998.pdf.

59. US Agency for International Development, "The USAID Microenterprise Initiative Statement of Renewal," June 30, 1997, http://pdf.usaid.gov/pdf_docs/Pdacg146.pdf.

60. Kathryn Moeller, *The Gender Effect: Capitalism, Feminism, and the Corporate Politics of Development* (Berkeley: University of California Press, 2018), 70–73.

61. US Agency for International Development, "The USAID Microenterprise Initiative Statement of Renewal."

62. White House Press Office, "Remarks of the First Lady, Secretary of the Treasury Bob Rubin and AID Administrator Brian Atwood in Press Briefing," January 30, 1997, First Lady's Office, Press Office, and Lissa Muscatine, "FLOTUS Statements and Speeches 1/22/97—7/14/97 [Binder]- [Briefing with Secretary Rubin and USAID's Atwood 1/30/1997]," CDL.

63. Jan Piercy, interview with author, by Zoom, December 15, 2020.

64. Piercy, interview.

65. White House Press Office, "Remarks of the First Lady, Secretary of the Treasury Bob Rubin and AID Administrator Brian Atwood"; and Alan Friedman, "50 Years On, 2 U.S. Official Signal Shift: Women and Bretton Woods," *New York Times*, September 30, 1994.

66. Hillary Rodham Clinton to Mary Houghton, December 4, 1992, Box 63, Folder 495, SBC.

67. For more on the culture wars of the 1990s, see Robert O. Self, *All in the Family: The Realignment of American Democracy Since the 1960s* (New York: Hill and Wang, 2012), 399–419.

68. Clinton, *Living History*, 268–286.

69. Clinton, *Living History*, 269.

70. David Bornstein, *The Price of a Dream: The Story of the Grameen Bank and the Idea That Is Helping the Poor to Change Their Lives* (New York: Simon and Schuster, 1996), 20–21.

71. Clinton, *Living History*, 283–286.

72. Todd Purdum, "Bengali Women Are Candid with Hillary Clinton," *New York Times*, April 4,1995.

73. Hillary Rodham Clinton, "Remarks of the First Lady, Meeting on Southeast Asia," Washington, DC, April 26, 1995, First Lady's Office, Press Office, and Lissa Muscatine, "FLOTUS Statements and Speeches 10/1/94—6/1/95 [Binder] [4/26/95 Southeast Asia Meeting]," CDL.

74. White House Office of the Press Secretary, "First Lady Hillary Rodham Clinton Remarks to the United Nations Development Fund for Women 'Women's Economic Empowerment' Panel Beijing China," September 6, 1995, First Lady's Office and First Lady's Press Office, "Speeches—Beijing & Ulaambaatar [Mongolia]," CDL.

75. "Chronology of the First Lady's Involvement in Promoting Microenterprise Development," January 2000, First Lady's Office, Ruby Shamir, and Subject Files, "Some HRC Record Documents," CDL.

76. William J. Clinton, "Remarks on Presenting the Presidential Awards for Excellence in Microenterprise Development" January 30, 1997, The American Presidency Project, www.presidency.ucsb.edu/node/224221.

77. Clinton, "Remarks by the First Lady at the Microcredit Summit."

78. Clinton, "Remarks by the First Lady at the Microcredit Summit."

79. Winifred Poster and Zakia Salime, "The Limits of Microcredit: Transnational Feminism in the United States and Morocco," in *Women's Activism and Globalization: Linking Local Struggles and Transnational Politics*, ed. Nancy A. Naples and Manisha Desai (New York: Routledge, 2002), 200.

80. USAID, Department of the Treasury, "U.S. Government Statement on Microenterprise Development and Microfinance for the Microcredit Summit, February 2–4, 1997," 1996, Box 7, Folder 23, AI.

81. Accion International, Annual Report 1994, Box 1, Folder 26, AI; and "Accion International," c. 1995, Box 1, Folder 22, AI.

82. *Accion International Bulletin* 33, no. 1 (Spring 1997), Box 1, Folder 22, AI; and Marguerite S. Robinson, *The Microfinance Revolution: Sustainable Finance for the Poor* (Washington, DC: World Bank and Open Society Institute, 2001), 97.

83. Martha M. Hamilton, "Small Enterprises Gain Global Lenders' Favor," *Washington Post*, November 23, 1995.

84. Accion International, Annual Report 1999 and Annual Report 1998, Box 1, Folder 27, AI.

85. White House Press Office, "Remarks of the First Lady, Secretary of the Treasury Bob Rubin and AID Administrator Brian Atwood."

86. Treasury News, "Microlending Awards Program Announced," May 2, 1996, Domestic Policy Council, Bruce Reed, and Welfare Reform Series, "Event (Micro Event/WH, 1/29/97)," CDL.

87. Associated Press, "Arkansas Starts New Welfare Plan—'Any Job Is a Good Job,' Program Director Says," *Commercial Appeal*, July 2, 1997.

88. Rich Huddleston and Angela Duran, *Breaking the Cycle: A Special Report by Arkansas Kids Count*, Arkansas Kids Count, 1999, https://files.eric.ed.gov/fulltext/ED433963.pdf.

89. Southern Development Bancorporation, 2000 Annual Report, https://banksouthern.com/wp-content/uploads/2016/04/annual_report_2000.pdf; and George Surgeon, interview with author by Zoom, November 13, 2020.

90. Mark Elliott and Elisabeth King, "Labor Market Leverage: Sectoral Employment Field Report," Charles Mott Foundation 1999, https://eric.ed.gov/?id=ED428270.

91. Brian Kelley, Penny Pennrose, and Deborah Slayton to board of directors, AEG, board of directors, SDB, Re: May 14, 1997, Board Report, May 5, 1997, Box 62, Folder 492, SBC; and Southern Development Bancorporation, 1999 Annual Report, Box 62, Folder 492, SBC.

92. Elliott and King, "Labor Market Leverage."

93. George Surgeon, interview with author by Zoom, November 20, 2020.

94. Surgeon, interview, November 20, 2020.

95. Mary Houghton and Ron Grzywinski to Winthrop Rockefeller Foundation, Re: Talking Points, June 1997, phone interview, May 29, 1997, Box 62, Folder 493, SBC; and Good Faith Fund, MS Foundation Grant Proposal, Good Faith Fund, c. June 1996, Box 64, Folder 506, SBC.

96. Good Faith Fund, MS Foundation Grant Proposal.

97. Southern Development Bancorporation, Grant Proposal 1999 (Grant #9951687), September 1, 1999–January 31, 2004, Reel R9214, FF.

98. Taub, *Doing Development in Arkansas*, 94.

99. Houghton and Grzywinski to Winthrop Rockefeller Foundation, Re: Talking Points; and Nancy C. Jurik, *Bootstrap Dreams: US Microenterprise Development in an Era of Welfare Reform* (Ithaca, NY: Cornell University Press, 2005), 175–176.

100. Connie Evans, interview with author, by Zoom, September 21, 2020.

101. Evans, interview.

102. Evans, interview.

103. Jason DeParle, "Welfare to Work: A Sequel," *New York Times*, December 28, 1997.

104. Evans, interview.

105. Michael Sherraden, *Assets and the Poor: A New American Welfare Policy* (Armonk, NY: M. E. Sharpe, 1991).

106. Sherraden, *Assets and the Poor*, 6.

107. Evans, interview.

108. Connie Evans, Women's Self-Employment Project Proposal to the Ford Foundation, April 1989, Ford Foundation Grants, U to Z Women's Self-Employment Project, July 1, 1989–June 30, 1991, FF.

109. Connie Evans testimony, Congressional Hunger Caucus Roundtable on Asset Based Welfare Strategies, May 25, 1994, Domestic Policy Council, Bruce Reed, and Welfare Reform Series, "Assets," CDL.

110. Harris Bank, "New Individual Development Accounts Allow Low Income Businesswomen to Accumulate Assets," PR Newswire, July 8, 1996.

111. Michael Sherraden, "From Research to Policy: Lessons from Individual Development Accounts," *Journal of Consumer Affairs* 34, no. 2 (Winter 2000): 165–167.

112. Sherraden, "From Research to Policy," 164.

113. Schram, *Welfare Discipline*, 121–122.

114. Susan Saegert, J. Phillip Thompson, and Mark R. Warren, eds., *Social Capital and Poor Communities* (New York: Russell Sage Foundation, 2005), xi.

115. Mark Schreiner and Michael Sherraden, *Can the Poor Save? Saving and Asset Building in Individual Development Accounts* (New York: Routledge, 2005), 55.

116. Merrill Goozner, "Matching Savings of the Poor Gives Extra Tug to Bootstrap," *Chicago Tribune*, January 30, 2000.

117. Corporation for Enterprise Development, "IDAs Part of the New Welfare Reform Law," *Assets: A Quarterly Update for Innovators* 2, no. 2 (August 1996); and Hogan to O'Brien, Re: Microenterprise and Individual Development Accounts.

118. Barbara Vobejda, "Interest Grows in Assisted Savings Plans," *Washington Post*, April 25, 1997, 8.

119. Corporation for Enterprise Development, American Dream Demonstration, Semi-Annual Progress Report, February 1999, Corporation for Enterprise Development, May 1, 1997–June 30, 2002, Grants C-D, FF.

120. Goozner, "Matching Savings of the Poor Gives Extra Tug to Bootstrap."

121. Corporation for Enterprise Development, Downpayments on the American Dream Demonstration Semi-Annual Progress Report, April 2002, Corporation for Enterprise Development, May 1, 1997–June 30, 2002, Grants C-D, FF.

122. Margaret Sherrard Sherraden and Amanda Moore McBride, *Striving to Save: Creating Policies for Financial Security of Low-Income Families* (Ann Arbor: University of Michigan Press, 2010), 199.

123. Schreiner and Sherraden, *Can the Poor Save?*, 7, 123.

124. Sherraden and McBride, *Striving to Save*, 214.

125. Jared Bernstein, "Savings Incentives for the Poor," *American Prospect*, April 16, 2003.

126. Guy Feldman, "Saving from Poverty: A Critical Review of Individual Development Accounts" *Critical Social Policy* 38, no. 2 (May 2018): 181–200.

127. Corporation for Enterprise Development, The Assets and Enterprise Welfare Reform Initiative, Proposal to Ford Foundation c. 1995, Grants C-D, Corporation for Enterprise Development, October 1, 1995–March 31, 1996, Ford Foundation Records.

128. Corporation for Enterprise Development, The Assets and Enterprise Welfare Reform Initiative.

129. Bernstein, "Savings Incentives for the Poor."

130. Jurik, *Bootstrap Dreams*, 70.

131. Jurik, *Bootstrap Dreams*, 65.

132. Angela Bonavoglia with Anna Wadia, *Building Businesses, Rebuilding Lives: Microenterprise and Welfare Reform*, Ms. Foundation for Women, Collaborative Fund for Women's Economic Development, 2001, www.findevgateway.org/sites/default/files/publications/files/mfg-en-paper-building-businesses-rebuilding-lives-microenterprise-and-welfare-reform-2001.pdf.

133. Evans, interview.

134. Donna M. Goldstein, "Microenterprise Training Programs, Neoliberal Common Sense, and the Discourses of Self-Esteem," in *The New Poverty Studies: The Ethnography of Power, Politics and Impoverished*

People in the United States (New York: New York University Press, 2001), 250–251.

135. William J. Clinton, "Remarks on Presenting the Presidential Awards for Excellence in Microenterprise Development," February 5, 1999, The American Presidency Project, www.presidency.ucsb.edu/node/226762.

136. Clinton, "Remarks on Presenting the Presidential Awards for Excellence in Microenterprise Development."

137. Wendell Primus, "The Safety Net Delivers: The Effects of Government Benefit Programs in Reducing Poverty," Center on Budget and Policy Priorities, November 15, 1996, www.cbpp.org/sites/default/files/archive/SAFETY.htm.

138. "President Clinton and Vice President Gore's Accomplishments: Arkansas," January 1, 2001, Office of Speechwriting and Heather Hurlburt, "Points for Arkansas Arrival 1/17/00 [Talking Points]," CDL.

139. Huddleston and Duran, "Breaking the Cycle."

140. De Parle, *American Dream*, 325.

141. Jamey Dunn-Thomason, "Does Welfare to Work, Work? Assistance to Needy Families Program was Slow to Respond to Recession," NPR Illinois, October 1, 2012.

142. Douglas Holt, "Welfare-to-Work Mom Still in Big Trouble," *Chicago Tribune*, August 3, 1999.

143. Muhammad Yunus, *Creating a World Without Poverty: Social Business and the Future of Capitalism* (New York: PublicAffairs, 2009).

144. Lydia Polgreen and Vikas Bajaj, "India Microcredit Faces Collapse from Defaults," *New York Times*, November 17, 2010.

145. Connie Bruck, "Millions for Millions," *New Yorker*, October 30, 2006; and Muhammad Yunus, "Sacrificing Microcredit for Megaprofits," *New York Times*, January 14, 2011.

146. Neil MacFarquhar, "Banks Making Big Profits from Tiny Loans," *New York Times*, April 23, 2010.

147. See, for example, Kevin Sieff, "The Migrant Debt Cycle," *Washington Post*, November 4, 2019.

CHAPTER 7: FROM A RIGHT TO A REWARD

1. Ed Vulliamy, "Ghetto Blasting," *Observer Life*, September 27, 1998, 14.

2. Pam Belluck, "End of a Ghetto: A Special Report," *New York Times*, September 6, 1998.

3. Patrick Reardon and Bonita Brodt, "Public Housing Draws the Dividing Line," *Chicago Tribune*, November 30, 1986.

4. Ben Austen, *High-Risers: Cabrini-Green and the Fate of American Public Housing* (New York: Harper, 2018), 41.

5. Lawrence J. Vale, *Purging the Poorest: Public Housing and the Design Politics of Twice-Cleared Communities* (Chicago: University of Chicago Press, 2013), 17–18; and D. Bradford Hunt, *Blueprint for Disaster:*

The Unraveling of Chicago Public Housing (Chicago: University of Chicago Press, 2009), 150.

6. Vale, *Purging the Poorest*, 17–18.

7. Keeanga-Yamahtta Taylor, *Race for Profit: How Banks and the Real Estate Industry Undermined Black Homeownership* (Chapel Hill: University of North Carolina Press, 2019), 246–248; and Andrea M. K. Gill, "Moving to Integration? The Origins of Chicago's Gautreaux Program and the Limits of Voucher-Based Housing Mobility," *Journal of Urban History* 38, no. 4 (February 2012): 662–686.

8. Gill, "Moving to Integration?," 667, 671.

9. Edward G. Goetz, *New Deal Ruins: Race, Economic Justice, and Public Housing Policy* (Ithaca, NY: Cornell University Press, 2013), 49.

10. Jorge Casuso, "High Hopes: Many Think Public Housing Is a Lost Cause," *Chicago Tribune*, July 22 1990, 12.

11. Patrick Reardon, "CHA Links Projects' Managers to Gangs," *Chicago Tribune*, July 2, 1988.

12. Reardon, "CHA Links Projects' Managers to Gangs."

13. Alex Kotlowitz, *There Are No Children Here: The Story of Two Boys Growing Up in the Other America* (New York: Doubleday, 1992), 12–13.

14. Joe Davidson, "Kemp Bubbles with Enthusiasm as He Preaches 'Progressive Conservatism' for Fighting Poverty," *Wall Street Journal*, February 16, 1989, 1.

15. Housing and Urban Development, "Homeownership and Affordable Housing: The Opportunities," no date, Congressional Series, Box 16, Folder 16, MEP.

16. "Homeownership for the Poor: Facts About HOPE," c. 1992, Congressional Series, Box 16, Folder 12, MEP; and Lawrence J. Vale, "Jack Kemp's Pet Delusion," *Washington Post*, August 3, 1992.

17. Goetz, *New Deal Ruins*, 64.

18. Henry G. Cisneros, "A New Moment for Cities and People," chap. 1 in *From Despair to Hope: HOPE VI and the New Promise of Public Housing in America's Cities*, ed. Henry G. Cisneros and Lora Engdahl (Washington, DC: Brookings Institution Press), 5.

19. Henry G. Cisneros, "Rights and Responsibilities: The Health of the Urban Polity," presentation, Notre Dame Club Hesburgh Forum, Chicago, Illinois, April 15, 1994, Office of Speechwriting and Carolyn Curiel, "Shender, Stephen R.," CDL.

20. Memorandum from Christine A. Varney to the Chiefs of Staff, Subject: February 6 Meeting, February 5, 1993, Box 20, Folder 27, USDA Series, MEP.

21. Al Gore to Distribution, July 8, 1993, Office of Communications and Mark Gearan, "RIGO [Reinventing Government] [1]," CDL.

22. Gore to Distribution, July 8, 1993.

23. Stephen Barr, "From Gore, Clues About New Directions: 'Reinventing Government' Review Looks Toward a Transformation," *Washington Post*, August 3, 1993; and Stephen Barr, "Gore, Cisneros Have Hard Sell at

HUD; 'It Is Time for the Quality Revolution,' Vice President Tells Workers," *Washington Post*, March 27, 1993.

24. Barr, "Gore, Cisneros Have Hard Sell at HUD."

25. Gwen Ifill, "Federal Cutbacks Proposed by Gore in 5-Year Program," *New York Times*, September 8, 1993.

26. Reuel Schiller, "Regulation and the Collapse of the New Deal Order, or How I Learned to Stop Worrying and Love the Market," chap. 9 in *Beyond the New Deal Order: U.S. Politics from the Great Depression to the Great Recession*, ed. Gary Gerstle, Nelson Lichtenstein, and Alice O'Connor (Philadelphia: University of Pennsylvania Press, 2019), 168–185; and David Osborne, interview with author, Gloucester, Massachusetts, July 18, 2019.

27. Otto J. Hetzel, "Cutting HUD's Red Tape: The Gore Report's National Performance Review," *Journal of Housing*, July–August 1994.

28. Transcript of Clinton and Gore remarks in presenting National Performance Review, September 7, 1993, US Newswire.

29. Guy Gugliotta, "Henry Cisneros Goes for Broke," *Washington Post*, October 8, 1995.

30. US Department of Housing and Urban Development, "HUD Reinvention: From Blueprint to Action," March 1995, Office of the Assistant Secretary for Public and Indian Housing, General Files 1993–1995, Container 8, Reinventing Folder, HUDR.

31. HUD, "HUD Reinvention."

32. Mindy Turbov to Joseph Shuldiner et al., Subject: Leveraged Public Housing and the Blueprint for Reinvention, January 18, 1995, Office of the Assistant Secretary for Public and Indian Housing, General Files 1993, Container 8, Reinvention Blueprint Folder, HUDR.

33. Gugliotta, "Henry Cisneros Goes for Broke."

34. Guy Gugliotta, "Plan to Save Agency Is Gaining Momentum," *Washington Post*, May 25, 1995.

35. Clifford A. Pearson, "HUD Pushes 'New Urbanist' Principles for Inner-Cities," *Architectural Record*, October 1996.

36. Goetz, *New Deal Ruins*, 64.

37. Lawrence J. Vale, *After the Projects: Public Housing Redevelopment and the Governance of the Poorest Americans* (New York: Oxford University Press, 2018), 23.

38. Turbov to Shuldiner et al., Subject: Leveraged Public Housing and the Blueprint for Reinvention.

39. Yan Zhang and Gretchen Weismann, "Public Housing's Cinderella: Policy Dynamics of HOPE VI in the Mid-1990s," chap. 2 in *Where Are Poor People to Live? Transforming Public Housing Communities*, ed. Larry Bennett, Janet L. Smith, and Patricia A. Wright (New York: Routledge, 2015), 56–57.

40. Memorandum from Kevin Marchman to All URD Awardees, no date, Office of the Assistant Secretary for Public and Indian Housing, General Files 1993–1995, Container 5, HOPE VI Folder, HUDR.

41. Goetz, *New Deal Ruins*, 12.

42. Congress for New Urbanism and US Department of Housing and Urban Development, *Principles for Inner City Neighborhood Design: HOPE VI and the New Urbanism*, 2000, www.huduser.gov/Publications /pdf/principles.pdf.

43. Susan Cohen, "We Know We Want It. But Does Anyone Know What 'Community' Really Means?," *Washington Post*, July 31, 1994; and Roger K. Lewis, "'New Urbanism Congress Crusades for Change," *Washington Post*, October 16, 1993. For a critique of New Urbanism, especially its definition and application of community, see David Harvey, "The New Urbanism and the Communitarian Trap," *Harvard Design Magazine*, Winter–Spring 1997, 68–69. Catherine Fennell's *Last Project Standing: Civics and Sympathy in Post-Welfare Chicago* (Minneapolis: University of Minnesota Press, 2013) offers a nuanced perspective on the benefits and drawbacks of this approach.

44. Bruce Katz, "The Origins of HOPE VI," chap. 2 in *From Despair to Hope*, 26.

45. Roger K. Lewis, "'New Urbanist' Charter Returns to Old-Fashioned Architectural Ideals," *Washington Post*, June 15, 1996, F1; and Jerry Adler and Maggie Malone, "Toppling Towers," *Newsweek*, November 4, 1996.

46. For a discussion of the surveillance components of New Urbanism and HOPE VI, see Fennell, *Last Project Standing*, 145–149.

47. Pearson, "HUD Pushes 'New Urbanist' Principles for Inner-Cities."

48. Mathew Zeiler Reed, "Moving Out: Section 8 and Public Housing Relocation in Chicago" (PhD diss., Northwestern University, 2007).

49. US Department of Housing and Urban Development, "Older, Deteriorating Public Housing Demolished as HUD Seeks to Transform Inner-City Communities," press release, May 1, 1995, History of the Department of Housing and Urban Development and Clinton Administration History Project, "Housing and Urban Development] [3]," CDL.

50. Vale, *Purging the Poorest*, 24.

51. Goetz, *New Deal Ruins*, 166–167.

52. Hans Dekker testimony, Affordable Housing Programs, Congressional Housing Financial Services Committee, Washington, DC, April 23, 2002; and Michael Van Sickler, "Lakeland Housing Program Denied $20.4 Million," *Ledger* (Lakeland, FL), September 4, 1998.

53. Cisneros, "A New Moment for People and Cities," 4.

54. Casuso, "High Hopes."

55. Vale, *Purging the Poorest*, 252, 254; and Frank James, "CHA Plans a Facelift for Cabrini," *Chicago Tribune*, December 25, 1992.

56. Hunt, *Blueprint for Disaster*, 277.

57. Patrick T. Reardon and John Kass, "Facing Takeover, CHA Board Quits Lane, Others Clear Out Before HUD Comes In," *Chicago Tribune*, May 27, 1995, 1.

58. Flynn McRoberts and John Kass, "Demolishing Some High Rises Job 1 New Team Arrives Cisneros Vows Red Tape Will Crumble Too," *Chicago Tribune*, June 1, 1995.

59. James Warren and Patrick T. Reardon, "HUD Tired of CHA Failures, Cisneros Explains Shakeup," *Chicago Tribune*, May 28, 1995.

60. Joel Kaplan and Flynn McRoberts, "Officially, HUD Takes Over CHA: Cleveland Housing Boss May Get Top Job," *Chicago Tribune*, May 31, 1995, 1; and Vulliamy, "Ghetto Blasting."

61. Patricia A. Wright, with Richard M. Wheelock and Carol Steele, "The Case of Cabrini-Green," chap. 6 in *Where Are Poor People to Live?*, 168.

62. Larry Bennett and Adolph Reed, "The New Face of Urban Renewal," in Adolph Reed, *Without Justice for All: The New Liberalism and Our Retreat From Racial Equality* (New York: Routledge, 1999), 177–178; and Patrick T. Reardon, "Cabrini Is Prime Real Estate, but Not for Sale," *Chicago Tribune*, October 16, 1992, 1.

63. Vale, *Purging the Poorest*, 262.

64. Vale, *Purging the Poorest*, 264.

65. Wright et al., "The Case of Cabrini-Green," 168; Larry Bennett, Janet L. Smith, and Patricia A. Wright, "Introduction," in *Where Should Poor People Live?*, 11–12; and Vale, *Purging the Poores*, 264.

66. Vale, *Purging the Poorest*, 268.

67. Nicholas Lemann, "The Public Housing That Succeeds," *New York Times*, May 5, 1996.

68. Guy Gugliotta, "Redoubled Effort Targets Derelict Public Housing," *Washington Post*, May 31, 1996.

69. Ray Suarez, "Public Housing," *Talk of the Nation*, NPR, October 21, 1998.

70. Andrew Cuomo and Harold Lucas, *A Promise Being Fulfilled: The Transformation of America's Public Housing*, report to the president, US Department of Housing and Urban Development, July 2000.

71. Andrew Cuomo to conferees, 1998 Public Housing Reform Bills, Draft 6/19/98, Automated Records Management System and OPD, "[06/18/1998—07/06/1998]," CDL.

72. Cuomo to conferees, 1998 Public Housing Reform Bills.

73. Office of Policy Development and Research, US Department of Housing and Urban Development, "Reinventing Housing Assistance: Options for Enhancing Tenant Responsibility," October 18, 1994, Office of the Assistant Secretary for Public and Indian Housing, General Files, 1993–1995, Container 8, Police through Rescission Folder, HUDR.

74. Office of Policy Development and Research, "Reinventing Housing Assistance."

75. Joe Soss, Richard C. Fording, and Sanford F. Schram, *Disciplining the Poor: Neoliberal Paternalism and the Persistent Power of Race* (Chicago: University of Chicago Press, 2011). See also, Rhiannon Patterson et al., *Evaluation of the Welfare to Work Voucher Program: Report to*

Congress, prepared for US Department of Housing and Urban Development, Office of Policy Development and Research, March 2004, www .huduser.gov/portal//Publications/pdf/welfrwrkVchrPrg.pdf.

76. Michelle Alexander, *The New Jim Crow: Mass Incarceration in the Age of Colorblindness* (New York: New Press, 2010), 56; and Justice Policy Institute, *Too Little Too Late: President Clinton's Prison Legacy* (Washington, DC, and San Francisco: Justice Policy Institute, February 2001), www.prisonpolicy.org/scans/clinton.pdf.

77. William J. Clinton, "Address Before a Joint Session of the Congress on the State of the Union," January 23, 1996, The American Presidency Project, www.presidency.ucsb.edu/node/223046.

78. US Department of Housing and Urban Development, Office of Crime Prevention and Safety, *Meeting the Challenge: Public Housing Authorities Respond to the "One Strike and You're Out" Initiative* (Washington, DC: US Dept. of Housing and Urban Development, 1997).

79. US Department of Housing and Urban Development, "One Strike and You're Out" Policy in Public Housing, c. 1996, Domestic Policy Council, Bruce Reed, and Crime Series, "Public Housing," CDL; and White House, Office of the Press Secretary, "Remarks by the President at One Strike Crime Symposium," March 28, 1996, CDL.

80. White House, Office of the Press Secretary, "Remarks by the President at One Strike Crime Symposium."

81. See, for example, Peter Katel, "Elderly Caught in Drug Evictions," *USA Today*, April 9, 1998; and Gina Holland, "Public Housing Policy Faces Legal Assault," Associated Press, May 1, 2001.

82. See Alexander, *New Jim Crow*, 44–48 for the impact and consequences of these policies.

83. Cuomo and Luca, *A Promise Being Fulfilled*.

84. White House, Office of the Press Secretary, "Remarks by the President at One Strike Crime Symposium."

85. S. Lynn Martinez, "Section 8 Homeownership," *Journal of Housing and Community Development* 59, no. 2 (March–April 2002): 22–25; and William Grady, "Section 8 Ownership Plan Gets into Gear," *Chicago Tribune*, July 19, 2002.

86. Andrew Cuomo, *The State of the Cities 1998*, US Department of Housing and Urban Development, June 1998, www.huduser.gov /Publications/PDF/soc_98.pdf.

87. William J. Clinton, "Remarks to the National Association of Realtors in Anaheim, California," November 5, 1994, The American Presidency Project, www.presidency.ucsb.edu/node/218256.

88. US Department of Housing and Urban Development, *The National Homeownership Strategy: Partners in the American Dream* (Washington, DC: US Dept. of Housing and Urban Development, 1995).

89. Bruce Katz to Kitty Higgins, Re: National Homeownership Strategy Rollout, April 17, 1995, Office of Speechwriting; and Carolyn Curiel, "Home Ownership Files," CDL.

90. Melinda Cooper, *Family Values: Between Neoliberalism and the New Social Conservatism* (Princeton, NJ: Princeton University Press, 2017), 142; and Alyssa Katz, *Our Lot: How Real Estate Came to Own Us* (New York: Bloomsbury, 2009), 31–33.

91. Cooper, *Family Values*, 140–152; and Katz, *Our Lot*, 33.

92. William J. Clinton, "Remarks on the National Homeownership Strategy," June 5, 1995, The American Presidency Project, www.presidency.ucsb.edu/node/220941.

93. US Department of Housing and Urban Development, *Moving Up to the American Dream: From Public Housing to Private Homeownership* (Washington, DC: US Dept. of Housing and Urban Development, 1996).

94. HUD, *Moving Up to the American Dream*.

95. Frederick J. Egger, "Homeownership: A Housing Success Story," *Cityscape: A Journal of Policy Development and Research* 5, no. 2 (2001), www.huduser.gov/Periodicals/CITYSCPE/VOL5NUM2/eggers.pdf.

96. There has been disagreement about the National Homeownership Strategy's role in the foreclosure crisis. See, for example, Peter Coy, "Bill Clinton's Drive to Increase Homeownership Went Way Too Far," *Bloomberg*, February 26, 2008; David Streifeld and Gretchen Morgenson, "Building Flawed American Dreams," *New York Times*, October 18, 2008; and Vincent J. Cannato, "A Home of One's Own," *National Affairs*, Spring 2010.

97. Henry G. Cisneros, "Achieving the American Dream," *Christian Science Monitor*, November 28, 1995.

98. Cuomo, *State of the Cities 1998*.

99. Andrew Cuomo, *HOPE VI: Building Communities, Transforming Lives*, US Department of Housing and Urban Development, December 1999, www.huduser.gov/publications/pdf/hope.pdf.

100. Ray Suarez, "Andrew Cuomo," *Talk of the Nation*, NPR, March 3, 1997.

101. Department of Housing and Urban Development, *Public Housing That Works: The Transformation of America's Public Housing* (May 1996).

102. R. W. Apple Jr., "Flashin' Those Dreamy Eyes Way Down Yonder," *New York Times*, November 24, 2000.

103. Department of Housing and Urban Development, *Now Is the Time: Places Left Behind in the New Economy*, October 1999, https://archives.hud.gov/news/1999/leftbehind/toc.html.

104. "Cuomo Awards $3,339,228 in Grants to Fight Drugs, Crime in Public and Assisted Housing in Arkansas," US Newswire, October 23, 1998.

105. Suzanne M. Kirchoff, "Economic Impacts of Prison Growth," Congressional Research Service, April 13, 2010, https://fas.org/sgp/crs/misc/R41177.pdf.

106. Ryan S. King, Marc Mauer, and Tracy Huling, "Big Prisons, Small Towns: Prison Economics in Urban America," The Sentencing Project, February 2003.

107. Cuomo, *HOPE VI*.

108. Goetz, *New Deal Ruins*, 80.

109. Belluck, "End of a Ghetto: A Special Report."

110. Austen, *High-Risers*, 263.

111. Belluck, "End of a Ghetto: A Special Report."

112. Jonathan Eig, "House Hunting," *New Republic*, December 1, 1997.

113. Natalie Y. Moore, "The Good Ol' Days," *Chicago Reader*, September 26, 2007.

114. Austen, *High-Risers*, 253–254.

115. William Claiborne, "Chicago Unveils $1.5 Billion Housing Plan," *Washington Post*, October 2, 1999.

116. Vale, *Purging the Poorest*, 284; and Chicago Housing Authority, *Chicago Housing Authority: Plan for Transformation: Improving Public Housing in Chicago and the Quality of Life*, January 6, 2000, www .hud.gov/sites/documents/CHAFY2000-ANNUAL-PLAN.PDF.

117. Austen, *High-Risers*, 255.

118. Reed, "Moving Out: Section 8 and Public Housing Relocation in Chicago."

119. Goetz, *New Deal Ruins*, 84.

120. Goetz, *New Deal Ruins*, 84.

121. Austen, *High-Risers*, 265.

122. Vale, *Purging the Poorest*, 294.

123. Vale, *Purging the Poorest*, 305.

124. Flynn McRoberts and Abdon M. Pallasch, "Neighbors Wary of New Arrivals," *Chicago Tribune*, December 28, 1998.

125. Reed, "Moving Out: Section 8 and Public Housing Relocation in Chicago."

126. McRoberts and Pallasch, "Neighbors Wary of New Arrivals."

127. McRoberts and Pallasch, "Neighbors Wary of New Arrivals."

CHAPTER 8: PUBLIC SCHOOLS ARE OUR MOST IMPORTANT BUSINESS

1. "Meeting w/High Tech CEOS," April 2, 1997, History of the Office of the Vice President and Clinton Administration History Project, "OVP— Gore Tech/Tech Outreach [1]," CDL.

2. "Talking Points on High-Tech Industry," c. 1997, History of the Office of the Vice President and Clinton Administration History Project, "OVP— Gore Tech/Tech Outreach [1]," CDL; and Elizabeth Shogren, "Gore Finds Brain Trust in Silicon Valley Group," *Los Angeles Times*, August 25, 1997.

3. Jeffrey L. Badrach and Nicole Tempest, "New Schools Venture Fund Case," Harvard Business School, October 13, 2000.

4. John Markoff, "A Political Fight Marks a Coming of Age for a Silicon Valley Titan," *New York Times*, October 21, 1996; and Michael Lewis, "The Little Creepy Crawlers Who Will Eat You in the Night," *New York Times Magazine*, March 1, 1998, 40.

5. Susan Wolf, "VC Luminary John Doerr: Education Reform Critical to Success of New Economy," Harbus, June 2000, www.alumni.hbs.edu /stories/Pages/story-bulletin.aspx?num=5074.

6. Sara Miles, *How to Hack a Party Line: The Democrats and Silicon Valley* (New York: Farrar, Straus and Giroux 2001), 55–56.

7. Badrach and Tempest, "New Schools Venture Fund Case."

8. See, for example, Diane Ravitch, *The Death and Life of the Great American School System: How Testing and Choice Are Undermining Education* (New York: Basic Books, 2010); Diane Ravitch, *Reign of Error: The Hoax of the Privatization Movement and the Danger to America's Public Schools* (New York: Knopf, 2013); and Jay P. Greene and Frederick Hess, "Education Reform's Deep Blue Hue," Education Next, www.educationnext.org/education-reform-deep-blue-hue-are-school-reformers-right-wingers-centrists-neither/.

9. Margaret O'Mara, *The Code: Silicon Valley and the Remaking of America* (New York: Penguin, 2019), 291–292.

10. Walter Isaacson, *The Innovators: How a Group of Hackers, Geniuses, and Geeks Created the Digital Revolution* (New York: Simon and Schuster, 2014), 402–403.

11. O'Mara, *Code*, 294–296.

12. O'Mara, *Code*, 297–298.

13. Miles, *How to Hack a Party Line*, 8–9.

14. See Miles, *How to Hack a Party Line*, 11, 18–21.

15. "How Tech Leaders Talk Politics," *San Francisco Chronicle*, November 13, 1997, A19.

16. Wolf, "VC Luminary John Doerr."

17. Miles, *How to Hack a Party Line*, 26.

18. Markoff, "A Political Fight."

19. Miles, *How to Hack a Party Line*, 37.

20. William J. Clinton, "Inaugural Address," January 20, 1997, The American Presidency Project, www.presidency.ucsb.edu/node/224843.

21. Miles, *How to Hack a Party Line*, 48.

22. Miles, *How to Hack a Party Line*, 46–47; and Tim Newell to Al Gore, "Meeting with Technology Leaders," January 16, 1997, History of the Office of the Vice President and Clinton Administration History Project, "OVP—Gore Tech/Tech Outreach [1]," CDL.

23. "Meeting w/High Tech CEOS," April 2, 1997, History of the Office of the Vice President and Clinton Administration History Project, "OVP—Gore Tech/Tech Outreach [1]," CDL.

24. Rajiv Chandrasekaran, "This Vice President's Best Friend is His Computer," *Washington Post*, November 29, 1997, A3.

25. O'Mara, *Code*, 216–221.

26. Michael Bazely, "Execs Get into School Issues," *San Jose Mercury News*, March 13, 1997.

27. Al Gore, "Talking Points for High Tech CEO Meeting," c. April 1997, History of the Office of the Vice President and Clinton Administration History Project, "OVP—Gore Tech/Tech Outreach [1]," CDL.

28. Ravitch, *Death and Life*, 25–34; and Amy Stuart Wells, "The Sociology of School Choice: Why Some Win and Others Lose in the Educa-

tional Marketplace," in *School Choice: Examining the Evidence*, ed. E. Rassell and Richard Rothstein (New York: Teachers College Press, 1993), 29.

29. On "freedom of choice" policies, see Matthew D. Lassiter, *The Silent Majority: Suburban Politics in the Sunbelt South* (Princeton, NJ: Princeton University Press, 2005); on freedom of choice schools, see Joseph Crespino, *In Search of Another Country: Mississippi and the Conservative Counterrevolution* (Princeton, NJ: Princeton University Press, 2007).

30. Milton Friedman, "The Role of Government in Education," in *Economics and the Public Interest*, ed. Robert A. Solo (New Brunswick, NJ: Rutgers University Press, 1955), 123–144. Friedman further developed these ideas in *Capitalism and Freedom* (Chicago: University of Chicago Press, 1962).

31. Ravitch, *Death and Life*, 121–122.

32. David Osborne and Ted Gaebler, *Reinventing Government: How the Entrepreneurial Spirit Is Transforming the Public Sector* (Reading, MA: Addison-Wesley, 1992), 99.

33. Ted Kolderie, "How the Idea of 'Chartering' Schools Came About," *Minnesota Journal*, June 2008, www.educationevolving.org/pdf/Origins -of-Chartering-Citizens-League-Role.pdf.

34. Richard Kalenberg, *Tough Liberal: Albert Shanker and the Battles Over Schools, Unions, Race, and Democracy* (New York: Columbia University Press, 2007), Kindle edition.

35. Ray Budde to Albert Shanker, June 14, 1986, Box 8, Folder 2, Bella Rosenberg Files, AFTR.

36. Albert Shanker, National Press Club Speech, Washington, DC, March 31, 1988, https://reuther.wayne.edu/files/64.43.pdf); and "Let's Get Together and Charter a School," no date, Box 97, Folder 135, AFT Educational Issues Department Records, AFTR.

37. Ember Reichgott Junge, *Zero Chance of Passage: The Pioneering Charter School Story* (Edina, MN: Beaver's Pond Press, 2012), 149.

38. Ted Kolderie, *Beyond Choice to New Public Schools: Withdrawing the Exclusive Franchise in Public Education*, Policy Report No. 8, Progressive Policy Institute, November 1990.

39. Will Marshall, interview with author, Washington, DC, July 15, 2019.

40. Patrick J. McGuinn, *No Child Left Behind and the Transformation of Federal Education Policy, 1965–2005* (Lawrence: University Press of Kansas, 2006), 51–54.

41. Karen De Witt, "Fanfare and Catcalls for Voucher Plan," *New York Times*, June 24, 1992, A17; and McGuinn, *No Child Left Behind*, 68.

42. David Osborne, interview with author, Gloucester, Massachusetts, July 18, 2019.

43. Republican Senator David Durenberger and Democrat Joe Lieberman in 1991 proposed the "Public School Redefinition Act," which would have established federal support for charter schools. It did not pass.

44. Office of Deputy Secretary of Education, Briefing Memo on Charter Schools, c. 1996, Domestic Policy Council, Bruce Reed, and Education Series, "Charter Schools [2]," CDL.

45. Marshall, interview.

46. Marshall, interview.

47. Keith A. Halpern and Eliza R. Culbertson, DLC, "Blueprint for Change: Charter Schools Handbook for Action," Domestic Policy Council, Bruce Reed, and Education Series, "Charter Schools [2]," CDL.

48. News Conference with Democratic Leadership Council, Subject: Release of Voter Study, Participants: Al From, Democratic Leadership Council, Will Marshall, Progressive Policy Institute, Stanley Greenberg, White House Pollster, Federal News Service, November 17, 1994.

49. Memorandum for the President from Al From, Subject: Improving Your Politics, May 4, 1993, Box 4, Political Involvement 1990s, DLC, Memos to Bill Clinton, 1992–1993, DRP.

50. William J. Clinton, "Address Before a Joint Session of the Congress on the State of the Union," January 23, 1996, The American Presidency Project, www.presidency.ucsb.edu/node/223046.

51. Vaughn Next Century Learning Center, a Charter School Petition submitted to the Los Angeles Unified School District (SB 1448), February 4, 1993, Box 1035, Folder 1, LAUSD; and Yvonne Chan testimony, "Education at a Crossroads: What Works and What's Wasted?," hearings before the Subcommittee on Oversight and Investigations, Committee on Education and the Workforce, House of Representatives, 105th Cong., 1st Sess., Napa, California, January 29, San Fernando, California, January 30, and Phoenix, Arizona, January 31, 1997.

52. Beth Shuster, "A Special Educator: Yvonne Chan Isn't Shy About Butting Heads," Los Angeles Times, April 16, 1995.

53. Henry Chu, "Charting Her Own Path in Education Profile: Principal Yvonne Chan Is Dynamic and Savvy," Los Angeles Times, August 29, 1993, 1.

54. Maki Becker, "Vaughn Charter School Sets Sail for Expansion," Los Angeles Times, October 11, 1994.

55. Shuster, "A Special Educator."

56. Margaret Ramirez, "Vaughn Elementary Prepares for Visit by Hillary Clinton," Los Angeles Time, February 8, 1996.

57. Amy Pyle, "Textbook Example: First Lady Visits a School Where Her Message Is Taken to Heart," Los Angeles Times, February 9, 1996, 1.

58. Pyle, "Textbook Example."

59. Rick Orlov, "1st Lady Woos California in Speech to Democrats," Los Angeles Daily News, April 14, 1996.

60. Bill Clinton speaks, clip of "Involving Parents in Education Conference," panel discussion, Vanderbilt University, Nashville, Tennessee, C-SPAN video, June 25, 1997, 1:29:06, www.c-span.org/video/?87228-1/involving-families-education.

61. Duke Helfand, "With Its Permit Up for Renewal, Vaughn Elementary Prepares Its Case," *Los Angeles Times*, June 1, 1998.

62. Albert Shanker to Ray Budde, June 15, 1993, Box 8, Folder 2, Bella Rosenberg Files, AFTR.

63. Albert Shanker, "Charter Schools: More Mediocrity?," *American Teacher*, October 1994, 5; and American Federation of Teachers, "Charter School Resolution Draft," December 15, 1999, Box 28, Folder 8, Bella Rosenberg Files, AFTR.

64. American Federation of Teachers, "Charter School Laws: Do They Measure Up?," 1996, Box 8, Folder 1, Bella Rosenberg Files, AFTR.

65. Joan A. Buckley to Al Shanker and Eugenia Kemble, April 9, 1996, Re: Charter school information, Box 8, Folder 1, Bella Rosenberg Files, AFTR.

66. Elizabeth Todd-Breland, *A Political Education: Black Politics and Education Reform in Chicago Since the 1960s* (Chapel Hill: University of North Carolina Press, 2018), 206–208; Patty Yancey, "Independent Schools and the Charter Movement," in *Parents Founding Charter Schools: Dilemmas of Empowerment and Decentralization* (New York: Peter Lang, 2000), 125–158; and Lisa M. Stulberg, *Race, Schools and Hope: African Americans and School Choice After Brown* (New York: Teachers College Press, 2008).

67. Teresa Blossom, "The New School: Charters Offer Parents More Choice," *Essence*, August 1999.

68. Genethia H. Hayes et al. to Gary Hart, April 11, 1994, Box 221, Folder SB1264, GKHC.

69. Sam Fullwood III, "Teachers Feel a Lot More Welcome in Democrats' Camp," *Los Angeles Times*, August 28, 1996; and "The Battle Over Schools," *Wall Street Journal*, August 26, 1996, A10.

70. Democratic Party Platforms, 1996 Democratic Party Platform, The American Presidency Project, www.presidency.ucsb.edu/node/273267.

71. Elizabeth Shogren, "Clinton Threatens Veto of School Bills," *Los Angeles Times*, September 21, 1997.

72. William J. Clinton, "Remarks in a Roundtable Discussion on Charter Schools at the San Carlos Charter Learning Center in San Carlos, California," September 20, 1997, The American Presidency Project, www.presidency.ucsb.edu/node/224862.

73. Brad Hayward, "Educational Efforts Touted by President," *Sacramento Bee*, September 21, 1997; and Julian Guthrie, "Clintons Tout Charter Schools in San Carlos," *San Francisco Examiner*, September 21, 1997.

74. Sarah Tantillo, *Hit the Drum: An Insider's Account of How the Charter School Idea Became a National Movement* (Pennsauken Township, NJ: BookBaby, 2019), Kindle edition.

75. Ed Mendel, "Entrepreneur Aids Charter School Growth," *San Diego Union-Tribune*, February 1, 1998.

76. Badrach and Tempest, "New Schools Venture Fund Case."

77. Nick Anderson, "A New Lesson Plan," *Los Angeles Times*, February 25, 1998, 2; and Joanne Jacobs, "Disrupting the Education Monopoly: A Conversation with Netflix CEO Reed Hastings," *Education Next*, Winter 2015, www.educationnext.org/disrupting-the-education-monopoly-reed -hastings-interview/.

78. Sidney A. Thompson, Board of Education Report No. 1, "Establishment of Deadline for Submission of Charter School Petitions and Board of Education Decision on Pending Petitions and Those Received by Such Deadline," October 11, 1993, Box 1034, Folder 4, LAUSD.

79. Interoffice Memorandum, Los Angeles Unified School District from Ron Prescott to Members of the Board of Education, Sidney A. Thompson, Subject: Status of Charter School Legislation, May 16, 1994, Box 1034, Folder 2, LAUSD.

80. Dan Morain, "Making of a Ballot Initiative," *Los Angeles Times*, April 16, 1998.

81. Tantillo, *Hit the Drum*; and Morain, "Making of a Ballot Initiative."

82. "Technology Network Endorses, Kicks Off Statewide Signature Gathering Campaign for Charter Public Schools Initiative," *Business Wire*, February 27, 1998, 1.

83. Mendel, "Entrepreneur Aids Charter School Growth," *San Diego Union-Tribune*, February 1, 1998.

84. Peter Schrag, "Governor Touches Down at San Carlos Charter School," *Sacramento Bee*, May 13, 1998.

85. "The Education Reformers of Silicon Valley," NewSchools Venture Fund, August 17, 1999, www.newschools.org/blog/education-reformers -of-silicon-valley/.

86. Miles, *How to Hack a Party Line*, 71.

87. Ernest F. Ciarrocchi to Delaine Eastin, June 13, 1994, Box 221, Folder SB1264, GKHC; Sue Burr Letter, June 21, 1994, Box 221, Folder SB1264, GKHC; and Allen Davenport to Gary Hart, April 11, 1994, Re: SB 1264—Oppose, Box 238, Folder SB1264, GKHC.

88. Miles, *How to Hack a Party Line*, 100–101.

89. "How Initiative Threat Prodded the Legislature," *San Francisco Chronicle*, May 5, 1998.

90. Dan Morain, "Legislators May Offer Charter School Deal," *Los Angeles Times*, April 24, 1998, 3.

91. Dan Morain, "Wilson Expected to OK Bill on Charter Schools," *Los Angeles Times*, April 29, 1998, 3.

92. "The Technology Network Hails Charter Public School Legislation," Business Wire, May 7, 1998.

93. Sara Miles, "Tech Lobby's Schools Victory," *Wired*, May 7, 1998.

94. Wolf, "VC Luminary John Doerr."

95. Marshall, interview.

96. Amy Stuart Wells et al., *Beyond the Rhetoric of Charter School Reform: A Study of Ten California Districts*, UCLA Charter School Study, 1998.

97. Nicholas Lemann, "Citizen 510(c)(3)," *Atlantic*, February 1997, 18–20.

98. Council of Economic Advisers, *Philanthropy in the American Economy: A Report by the Council of Economic Advisers*, 1999, Clinton White House Archives, https://clintonwhitehouse4.archives.gov/media /pdf/philanthropy.pdf.

99. Stephanie Strom, "The Newly Rich Are Fueling a New Era in Philanthropy," *New York Times*, April 27, 2002.

100. White House, Office of the Press Secretary, "White House Conference on Philanthropy," October 22, 1999, First Lady's Office, Press Office, and Lissa Muscatine, "FLOTUS Statement and Speeches 10/16/99—4/28/00 [Binder]/[White House Conference on Philanthropy—White House 10/22/ 1999][1]," CDL.

101. Charles Babbington, "Clinton Urges New Web of Giving," *Washington Post*, October 23, 1999.

102. Miles, *How to Hack a Party Line*, 55.

103. "Involving Families in Education Conference," panel discussion, Vanderbilt University, Nashville, Tennessee, June 25, 1997, C-SPAN video, June 25, 1997.

104. For one of the earliest arguments for venture philanthropy, see Christine W. Letts, William P. Ryan, and Allen S. Grossman, "Virtuous Capital: What Foundations Can Learn from Venture Capitalists," *Harvard Business Review*, March–April 1997; and Karen Brandon, "Venture Capitalists Alter Face of Charity," *Chicago Tribune*, August 22, 1999.

105. Bruck, "Millions for Millions."

106. "Investors Go Back to School: Venture Capital Votes Yes on Charter Schools," *Upside*, September 11, 2000, https://web.archive.org/web /20050212005720/http://www.newschools.org/viewpoints/sept_11_00 .html; Monika Guttman, "Cyber Saints Dot-com Millionaires Are Willing to Risk Their Money in New Charities," *USA Weekend*, September 17, 2000.

107. "New Schools Fund Hopes to Distribute $20 Million for Education," *San Jose Mercury News*, July 25, 1999, https://web.archive.org /web/20050209235340/http://www.newschools.org/viewpoints/july_25_00 .html/.

108. NewSchools Venture Fund, *Investing in a Revolution: Newschools Venture Fund and America's Education Entrepreneurs*, 2009, www .newschools.org/wp-content/uploads/2016/01/10YearReport4.pdf; and NewSchools FAQs, https://web.archive.org/web/20001007230958/http:// www.newschools.org/aboutus/faqs.html.

109. Badrach and Tempest, "New Schools Venture Fund Case."

110. NewSchools Venture Fund, Our Investment Process, https://web .archive.org/web/20030621133816/http://www.newschools.org/strategy /investment_process.htm.

111. NewSchools FAQs.

112. Rand Quinn, Megan Tompkins-Stange, and Debra Meyerson, "Beyond Grantmaking: Philanthropic Foundations as Agents of Change and Institutional Entrepreneurs," *Nonprofit and Voluntary Sector Quarterly* 43, no. 6 (December 2014): 954, 956.

113. June Kronholz, "Defying Convention, Superintendent Takes a Chance on Charters," *Wall Street Journal*, April 11, 2000.

114. Kronholz, "Defying Convention."

115. Sara Terry, "Schools That Think," *Fast Company*, March 31, 2000.

116. "New Schools Venture," *All Things Considered*, NPR, February 5, 2001.

117. Aspire Public Schools, "Balanced Scorecard," 2001, https://web.archive.org/web/20010812225341/http://aspirepublicschools.org/results.html.

118. Terry, "Schools That Think."

119. Charles Taylor Kerchner et al., *Learning from L.A.: Institutional Change in American Public Education* (Cambridge, MA: Harvard Education Press, 2008), 189–190.

120. Terry, "Schools That Think."

121. NewSchools Venture Fund, *Investing in a Revolution*.

122. NewSchools Venture Fund, *Investing in a Revolution*.

123. Ravitch, *Death and Life*, 209.

124. Ravitch, *Death and Life*, 209–210.

125. Ravitch, *Death and Life*, 212–215.

126. David Callahan, *The Givers: Wealth, Power and Philanthropy in a New Gilded Age* (New York: Penguin Random House, 2017), 169; and "Broad Foundation Invests in Charter Schools," U.S. Newswire, December 10, 2002.

127. Ravitch, *Death and Life*, 225–226.

128. "Broad Foundation Invests in Charter Schools."

129. Erik W. Robelen, "Venture Fund Fueling Push for NewSchools," *Education Week* 26, no. 19 (January 1, 2007): 26–29. By 2007, the Gates Foundation had invested $57 million in the fund.

130. Peter Loftus, "Gates Foundation Gift Reaffirms 'Venture Philanthropy' Concept," *Wall Street Journal*, September 3, 2003, 1.

131. National Alliance for Public Charter Schools, *A Growing Movement: America's Largest Charter School Communities*, 5th annual ed., November 2010, www.publiccharters.org/sites/default/files/migrated/wp-content/uploads/2014/01/AllianceMarket_Share_Report_FINAL_Nov2010.pdf_20110330T165253.pdf.

132. Ravitch, *Death and Life*, 144.

133. Ravitch, *Death and Life*, 155.

134. See, for example, the documentary *Waiting for Superman*, written and directed by Davis Guggenheim (Los Angeles: Walden Media, Participant, 2010).

135. "AFT Conference Explores Union Role in Charter School Movement," *American Teacher*, March–April 2006, 20.

136. Richard D. Kahlenberg and Halley Potter, "Restoring Shanker's Vision for Charter Schools," *American Educator*, Winter 2014–2015, www .aft.org/ae/winter2014-2015/kahlenberg_potter.

137. Ravitch, *Death and Life*, 155.

138. By 2018, TFA placed almost 40 percent of its 6,736 corps members in charters. In Los Angeles, over 70 percent of corps members taught at charters. Annie Waldman, "How Teach for America Evolved into an Arm of the Charter Movement," ProPublica, June 18, 2019, www.propublica .org/article/how-teach-for-america-evolved-into-an-arm-of-the-charter -school-movement.

139. Todd-Breland, *A Political Education*, 209.

140. Eve L. Ewing, "Can We Stop Fighting About Charter Schools?," *New York Times*, February 22, 2021.

141. Ravitch, *Death and Life*, 211; see also Rob Reich, *Just Giving: Why Philanthropy Is Failing Democracy and How It Can Do Better* (Princeton, NJ: Princeton University Press, 2018).

CHAPTER 9: THE FOX AND THE HENHOUSE

1. Tom Shales, "WonderMom Can't Take Heat in the Kitchen," *Los Angeles Times*, May 31, 1996, 24.

2. Eyal Press, "No Sweat: The Fashion Imagery Patches Its Image," *The Progressive*, September 1996.

3. D'Jamila Salem, "Human Rights Group Targets Disney, Kathie Lee Apparel Lines," *Los Angeles Times*, April 30, 1996; and Charles Bowden, "Charlie Kernaghan, Keeper of the Fire," *Mother Jones*, July–August 2003.

4. Rob Howe, "Labor Pains," *People*, June 10, 1996.

5. Naomi Klein, *No Logo*, 10th anniversary ed. (New York: Picador, 2009), 329.

6. "Clinton's Foreign Policy," *Foreign Policy*, no. 121 (November–December 2000): 18–29.

7. Patrick J. McDonnell and Paul Feldman, "Monitoring of Sweatshops Said to Be Inadequate," *Los Angeles Times*, August 16, 1995, 1; and William Branigin, "Sweatshop Instead of Paradise: Thais Lived in Fear as Slaves at L.A. Garment Factories," *Washington Post*, September 10, 1995, A1.

8. US General Accounting Office, *"Sweatshops" in the U.S.: Opinions on Their Extent and Possible Enforcement Options*, briefing to the Hon. Charles E. Schumer, House of Representatives, Washington, DC, August 1988, www.gao.gov/assets/80/77185.pdf. For more on the midcentury decline in sweatshops, see Robert J. S. Ross, *Slaves to Fashion: Poverty and Abuse in the New Sweatshops* (Ann Arbor: University of Michigan Press, 2004), 72–96.

9. Ellen Israel Rosen, *Making Sweatshops: The Globalization of the U.S. Apparel Industry* (Berkeley: University of California Press, 2002), 106.

10. "Garment Initiative Options," July 18, 1996, National Economic Council and Mark Silverman, "Sweatshop Initiative," CDL.

11. Government Accountability Office, *Garment Industry: Efforts to Address the Prevalence and Conditions of Sweatshops*, November 2, 1994, www.gpo.gov/fdsys/pkg/GAOREPORTS-HEHS-95-29/html/GAOREPORTS-HEHS-95-29.htm.

12. Ross, *Slaves to Fashion*, 99.

13. "Wage and Hour's Mission," Office of Speechwriting and Michael Waldman, "DOL [Department of Labor] Regulatory Reform [Binder]," CDL.

14. Robert B. Reich, *The Work of Nations: Preparing Ourselves for 21st Century Capitalism* (New York, Vintage, 1991), 213.

15. US Labor Secretary Robert B. Reich, "The Revolt of the Anxious Class," Democratic Leadership Council Washington, DC, November 22, 1994, Office of Speechwriting and Michael Waldman, "[Robert] Reich's 'Corporate Welfare' Speech," CDL.

16. Robert B. Reich, *Locked in the Cabinet* (New York: Alfred A. Knopf, 1997), 208.

17. Reich, *Locked in the Cabinet*, 206–212.

18. Reich, *Locked in the Cabinet*, 292–297; RBR [Robert B. Reich] to the President, Re: Corporate Responsibility, January 4, 1996, Domestic Policy Council, Bruce Reed, and Subject Files, "Corporate Responsibility," CDL; and Robert E. Rubin to the President, Subject: Your State of the Union Address, January 16, 1996, Domestic Policy Council, Bruce Reed, and Subject Files, "Corporate Responsibility," CDL.

19. Milton Friedman, "The Social Responsibility of Business Is to Increase Its Profits," *New York Times Magazine*, September 13, 1970.

20. Joel Makower, *Beyond the Bottom Line: Putting Social Responsibility to Work for Your Business and the World* (New York: Simon and Schuster, 1994).

21. Claudia Dreifus, "Passing the Scoop," *New York Times Magazine*, December 18, 1994.

22. "Helping Shoppers Buy on Principle," *New York Times*, December 7, 1988.

23. Karen Springen and Annetta Miller, "Doing the Right Thing," *Newsweek*, January 7, 1991, 42; and Craig Cox, "Executives of the World Unite!," *Business Ethics*, September–October 1992, 17–22.

24. "No Sweat, Garment Enforcement Summary," October 1995–March 1996, Department of Labor website, https://web.archive.org/web/20001218002500/http://www.dol.gov/dol/esa/public/nosweat/table.htm.

25. Office of the Deputy Attorney General, Interagency Group for Sweatshop Strategy Coordination, October 10, 1995, Domestic Policy Council and Stephen Warnath, "Sweatshops [Folder 1] [1]," CDL.

26. Edna Bonacich and Richard P. Appelbaum, *Behind the Label: Inequality in the Los Angeles Apparel Industry* (Berkeley: University of California Press, 2000), 229–230.

27. Department of Labor, "Press Release: Labor Secretary Announces Sweeping Garment Enforcement Success in L.A. Garment Industry," June 1995, https://web.archive.org/web/19970112144422/http://www.dol.gov:80/dol/opa/public/media/press/opa/opa95229.htm.

28. Patrick J. McDonnell and Paul Feldman, "New Approaches to Sweatshop Problem Urged," *Los Angeles Times*, August 16, 1995.

29. Susan Chandler, "Look Who's Sweating Now," *BusinessWeek*, November 11, 1995.

30. Statement of Suzanne B. Seiden, acting deputy administrator, Wage and Hour Division, Employment Standards Administration, US Department of Labor, hearing before the Subcommittee on Oversight and Investigations, Committee on Education and the Workforce, House of Representatives, 105th Cong., 2nd Sess., Washington, DC, June 19, 1998.

31. US Department of Labor, "Labor Secretary Robert B. Reich Releases Trendsetter List of Retailers, Manufacturers Committed to Eradicating Sweatshops," news release, December 5, 1995, Box 2 Folder: Correspondence, 1996, Andrew Ross Papers, Tamiment Library and Robert F. Wagner Labor Archive, New York University.

32. Robert B. Reich, "Slips, Profits, and Paychecks: Corporate Citizenship in an Era of Smaller Government," George Washington University School of Business and Public Management, February 6, 1996, Office of Communications and Don Baer, "Reich," CDL.

33. Kitty Higgens to Stephanie Street/Anno Hawley, Scheduling Request, June 14, 1996, Office of Communications and Don Baer, "POTUS Requests (Sched.)," CDL.

34. McDonnell and Feldman, "New Approaches to Sweatshop Problem Urged."

35. Randy Shaw, *Reclaiming America: Nike, Clean Air, and the New National Activism* (Berkeley: University of California Press, 1999), 99–113.

36. Shaw, *Reclaiming America*, 98.

37. Stuart Silverstein and George White, "'Good Guy' Labor List Gets a Bad Rap," *Los Angeles Times*, December 6, 1995.

38. Robert B. Reich testimony, "International Child Labor," hearing, Subcommittee on International Operations, House Committee on International Relations, House of Representatives, Washington, DC, C-SPAN video, July 15, 1996, 2:07:18, www.c-span.org/video/?73611-1/international-child-labor.

39. Steven Greenhouse, "Live with Kathie Lee and Apparel Workers," *New York Times*, May 31, 1996.

40. Ethel Carolyn Brooks, *Unraveling the Garment Industry: Transnational Organizing and Women's Work* (Minneapolis: University of Minnesota Press, 2007), 33.

41. Stephanie Strom, "A Sweetheart Becomes Suspect: Looking Behind Those Kathie Lee Labels," *New York Times*, June 27, 1996.

42. Ross, *Slaves to Fashion*, 209.

43. Barry Bearak, "Group Switches Focus from Kathie to Mickey," *Los Angeles Times*, June 6, 1996; "Santa's Sweatshop," *U.S. News & World Report*, December 16, 1996; and Klein, *No Logo*, 328.

44. Bob Herbert, "From Sweatshops to Aerobics," *New York Times*, June 24, 1996.

45. Klein, *No Logo*, 366–367.

46. Associated Press, "Nike Rejects Jackson Request to Visit Factory," *Chicago Tribune*, July 21, 1996, 4.

47. Ira Berkow, "Jordan's Bunker View on Sneaker Factories," *New York Times*, July 12, 1996; and Philip H. Knight, Letter to the Editor, *New York Times*, June 21, 1996.

48. Shaw, *Reclaiming America*, 20–21.

49. Shaw, *Reclaiming America*, 34–35.

50. Knight, Letter to the Editor.

51. Keith B. Richburg and Anne Swardson, "Sweatshop or Job Source? Indonesians Praise Work at Nike Factory," *Washington Post*, July 28, 1996.

52. Allen R. Myerson, "In Principle, a Case for More 'Sweatshops,'" *New York Times*, June 22, 1997; Paul Krugman, "In Praise of Cheap Labor," *Slate*, March 21, 1997; and Klein, *No Logo*, 227–228.

53. Bob Herbert, "Trampled Dreams," *New York Times*, July 12, 1996.

54. Bob Herbert, "Nike's Pyramid Scheme," *New York Times*, June 10, 1996.

55. Sydney H. Schanberg, "Six Cents an Hour," *Life*, June 1996.

56. Gary Borg, "Child Sweatshop Worker Tells of Beatings," *Chicago Tribune*, May 30, 1996.

57. Thomas A. Hemphill, "The White House Apparel Industry Partnership Agreement: Will Self-Regulation Be Successful?," *Business and Society Review* 104, no. 2 (1999): 121–137.

58. William J. Clinton, "Remarks at a Democratic National Committee Fundraiser," June 28, 1995, The American Presidency Project, www.presidency.ucsb.edu/node/221541.

59. Peter Behr, "The Commerce Comet," *Washington Post*, December 25, 1994; David E. Sanger, "How Washington Inc. Makes a Sale," *New York Times*, February 19, 1995; and Jeffrey E. Garten, *The Big Ten: The Big Emerging Markets and How They Will Change Our Lives* (New York: Basic Books, 1997).

60. "Hiller Group Chief Heads for South Africa," *St. Petersburg Times*, November 29, 1993; and "News Conference by Secretary of Commerce Ron Brown, Subject: Trade and Investment Mission to South Africa and Trade Mission to Mexico," Federal News Service, December 3, 1993.

61. Laura Tyson to the President, Proposed Garment Labeling Initiative, July 22, 1996, Office of Chief of Staff to the President and Harold Ickes, "Sweatshop-General," CDL.

62. Allen R. Myerson, "In Principle, a Case for More 'Sweatshops,'" *New York Times*, June 22, 1997.

63. US Department of Labor, Office of Public Affairs, "'No Sweat' Will Be in Fashion at Labor Department's Fashion Industry Forum on July 16; Every Aspect of Apparel Industry to Be Represented or Participate," press release, July 12, 1996, https://web.archive.org/web/19981202232549 /http://dol.gov:80/dol/opa/public/media/press/opa/opa96287.htm.

64. Robert B. Reich, "Opening Remarks Fashion Industry Forum," July 16, 1996, https://web.archive.org/web/19990219164343/http://www.dol .gov:80/dol/opa/public/forum/reich_1.txt.

65. Tyson to the President, July 22, 1996; "Garment Initiative Options," July 18, 1996, National Economic Council and Mark Silverman, "Sweatshop Initiative," CDL.

66. William J. Clinton, "Remarks Announcing Measures to Improve Working Conditions in the Apparel Industry and an Exchange with Reporters," August 2, 1996, The American Presidency Project, www.presidency .ucsb.edu/node/223324.

67. William J. Clinton, "Fair Labor Practices," C-SPAN video, August 2, 1996, 23:18, www.c-span.org/video/?74080-1/fair-labor-practices&start=581.

68. Clinton, "Fair Labor Practices."

69. Emil Parker to Gene Sperling, July 30, 1996, National Economic Council and Gene Sperling, "Sweatshop Initiative [Binder] [1]," CDL.

70. Kevin Danaher and Jason Mark, *Insurrection Citizen: Citizen Challenges to Corporate Power* (New York: Routledge, 2003), 77.

71. Alan Howard to Jay Mazur, Re: Labeling issues/Reich Meeting, July 29, 1996, Box 4, Folder 3, AHP.

72. Steven Greenhouse, "Its Heart Is Still 7th Avenue," *New York Times*, December 3, 1995.

73. Greenhouse, "Its Heart Is Still 7th Avenue."

74. Shaw, *Reclaiming America*, 113–116; and Scott L. Cummings, "Hemmed In: Legal Mobilization in the Los Angeles Anti-Sweatshop Movement," *Berkeley Journal of Employment & Labor Law* 30, no. 1 (2009): 28–36.

75. Statement of Jay Mazur, Box 2, Fashion Industry Forum Folder, Andrew Ross Papers.

76. Alan Howard to Jay Mazur, Re: Labeling issues/Reich Meeting, July 29, 1996, Box 4, Folder 3, AHP; and Notes for Meeting with Secretary Reich 7/30, 1997, Box 4, Folder 3, AHP.

77. Nelson Lichtenstein, *State of the Union: A Century of American Labor* (Princeton, NJ: Princeton University Press, 2013), 101–105.

78. Clinton, "Remarks Announcing Measures to Improve Working Conditions in the Apparel Industry."

79. Greenhouse, "Live with Kathie Lee and the Apparel Workers"; and Barry Bearak, "Kathie Lee and the Sweatshop Crusade," *Los Angeles Times*, June 14, 1996.

80. Shaw, *Reclaiming America*, 38–43.

81. William Branigin, "Reaping Abuse for What They Sew," *Washington Post*, February 16, 1997.

82. Peter McKay, "Cooperation Urged to Fight Sweatshops," *Washington Post*, July 17, 1996.

83. Jay Mazur to Secretary Reich, Ref: INS Factory Raids, July 29, 1996, Domestic Policy Council and Stephen Warnath, "Sweatshops [Folder 2] [3]," CDL.

84. US Department of Justice, Immigration and Naturalization Service, "INS and DOL Bust Alleged Sweatshop, 52 Illegal Workers Arrested," news release, July 26, 1996, Domestic Policy Council and Stephen Warnath, "Sweatshops [Folder 2] [3]," CDL; US Department of Justice, Immigration and Naturalization Service, INS Arrests 33 Illegal Aliens at Houston Worksites, July 31, 1996, Domestic Policy Council; and Stephen Warnath, "Sweatshops [Folder 2] [3]," CDL.

85. For more on the law, see Adam Goodman, *The Deportation Machine: America's Long History of Expelling Immigrants* (Princeton, NJ: Princeton University Press, 2020), 176–179.

86. Bob Reich to John Sweeney and Jay Mazur, February 8, 1997, Re: "Committee on the Condition of Work in America," Box 24, Folder 21, Susan Cowell Papers, Records of the International Ladies' Garment Workers' Union, Kheel Center for Labor-Management Documentation and Archives, Cornell University Library, Ithaca, New York.

87. Steven Greenhouse, "Voluntary Rules on Apparel Labor Prove Hard to Set," *New York Times*, February 1, 1997.

88. Jill Louise Esbenshade, *Monitoring Sweatshops: Workers, Consumers, and the Global Apparel Industry* (Philadelphia: Temple University Press, 2004), 177, 244; Steven Greenhouse, "Apparel Industry Group Moves to End Sweatshops," *New York Times*, April 9, 1997; and Details on the Apparel Industry Partnership Agreement OPD and Automated Records Management System, "[04/11/1997—04/14/1997]," CDL.

89. Gene Sperling to President, Re: NEC Weekly Report, April 24, 1998, History of the National Economic Council and Clinton Administration History Project, "NEC—Budget Surplus to Strengthen Social Security & Medicare II [4]," CDL.

90. Peter DeSimone, "AIP Surprises Critics with Accord," November 13, 1998, Box 3, Folder 9, AHP.

91. Steven Greenhouse, "Groups Reach Agreement for Curtailing Sweatshops," *New York Times*, November 5, 1998.

92. Alan Howard, "Why Unions Can't Support the Apparel Industry Sweatshop Code," *Working USA* 3, no. 2, (July–August 1999).

93. Danaher and Mark, *Insurrection Citizen*, 103.

94. Steven Greenhouse, "Lessons in Labor: A Course for Summer," *New York Times*, August 9, 1996, B1; and Steven Greenhouse, "Students Looking to Unions for Careers in Social Change," *New York Times*, March 11, 1996.

95. Steven Greenhouse, "Duke to Adopt a Code to Prevent Apparel from Being Made in Sweatshops," *New York Times*, March 8, 1998, 16.

96. Mark Asher, "Campus Activists Target Offshore Sweatshops," *Washington Post*, March 28, 1999, D07; and Kelly Greene, "Duke Students Give Lessons on Fighting Sweatshops," *Wall Street Journal*, March 17, 1999, S1.

97. Steven Greenhouse, "Student Critics Push Attacks on an Association Meant to Prevent Sweatshops," *New York Times*, April 25, 1999, 18; and Steven Greenhouse, "17 Colleges Join Against Sweatshops," *New York Times*, March 16, 1999, 22.

98. Phil Knight to University President, c. March 1999, Box 3, Folder 9, AHP.

99. Esbenshade, *Monitoring Sweatshops*, 183; and Ross, *Slaves to Fashion*, 170.

100. Alison Maxwell, "Students Protest FLA Inaction on Sweatshops," *WWD*, July 12, 1999, 24; and Esbenshade, *Monitoring Sweatshops*, 12.

101. Madeleine Bunting and Larry Elliott, "The Battle Over Trade," *Guardian* (Manchester, UK), November 25, 1999, 1.

102. Elaine Bernard, "The Battle in Seattle: What Was That All About?," *Washington Post*, December 5, 1999; and Quinn Slobodian, "20 Years After Seattle, the Clash of Globalizations Rages On," *Nation*, November 20, 2019.

103. Robert L. Borosage, "A WTO Celebration Faces People Power," *Los Angeles Times*, November 28, 1999, M1.

104. Shaw, *Reclaiming America*, 117–188.

105. Steve Early, "New Tyrant to Labor: WTO Protests Embody Worldwide Anger," *Boston Globe*, November 28, 1999, D1.

106. John Burgess and Steven Pearlstein, "Protests Delay WTO Opening," *Washington Post*, December 1, 1999, A1.

107. Helene Cooper, "Waves of Protest Disrupt WTO Meeting," *Wall Street Journal*, December 1, 1999.

108. Cooper, "Waves of Protest Disrupt WTO Meeting."

109. Cooper, "Waves of Protest Disrupt WTO Meeting."

110. Elizabeth Olson, "Patching Up Morale at the World Trade Organization," *New York Times*, October 31, 2000.

111. Early, "New Tyrant to Labor."

112. David E. Sanger, "Economic Engine for Foreign Policy," *New York Times*, December 28, 2000.

113. Bill Clinton, *My Life* (New York: Alfred A. Knopf, 2004), 894. See also, White House, "The Clinton Presidency: A Foreign Policy for the Global Age," c. 2000, Clinton White House Archives, https://clintonwhitehouse5.archives.gov/WH/Accomplishments/eightyears-10.html.

114. Kenneth S. Baer, *Reinventing Democrats: The Politics of Liberalism from Reagan to Clinton* (Lawrence: University of Kansas Press, 2000), 243; and Al From to the President, January 18, 1999, Subject: The State of the Union, Office of Speechwriting and Michael Waldman, "SOTU [State of the Union] 1999 Speech Drafts 1/18/99 [Binder] [5]," CDL.

115. Al From, "The New Democrat Decade," *New Democrat*, January–February 1999, 27, 29.

116. Al From, "The Vital Center Starts Here," 1999 DLC Annual Conference, Washington, DC, October 14, 1999, Office of Speechwriting and James (Terry) Edmonds, "SOTU [State of the Union] 2K [5]," CDL.

117. Jenny Bates, "Lifting Labor," *Blueprint*, June 1, 2000.

118. Jenny Bates and Greg Principato, *A Third Way on Trade and Globalization*, Policy Report, Progressive Policy Institute, July 18, 2000.

119. For more on the rise of Third Way politics in Western Europe, see Stephanie L. Mudge, "Making Western European Leftism 'Progressive,'" chap. 8 in *Leftism Reinvented: Western Parties from Socialism to Neoliberalism* (Cambridge, MA: Harvard University Press), 304–364.

120. Al From with Alice McKeon, *The New Democrats and the Return to Power* (New York: Palgrave MacMillan, 2013), 240–241.

121. Al From to the President, Subject: Possible New Democrat-New Labor Third Way Event, February 8, 1999; and Democratic Leadership Council Roundtable Discussion, Re: Progressive Governance, April 25, 1999, First Lady's Office, Speechwriting, and Laura Schiller, "Third Way—4/99 [1]," CDL.

122. From, "The New Democrat Decade."

123. US Department of Commerce, International Trade Administration, "African Growth and Opportunity Act," https://legacy.trade.gov/agoa/.

124. Rajiv Chandrasekaran, "Plugging into Capitalism," *Washington Post*, July 15, 2000, A1.

125. Samuel Berger and Stephanie Streett to the President, Subject: Themes for Your Trip Vietnam/Discussion of Key Issues, c. 2000, "FOIA 2008-0703-F—Thomas Rosshirt, Speechwriter," CDL.

126. Clay Chandler, "Clinton Urges Vietnam to Open Its Markets," *Washington Post*, November 20, 2000, A18.

127. Helene Cooper, "Vietnam Signs Trade Accord," *Wall Street Journal*, July 14, 2000, A4; and Clay Chandler, "Clinton Urges Vietnam to Open Its Markets," *Washington Post*, November 20, 2000, A18.

128. John H. Cushman Jr., "Nike Pledges to End Child Labor and Apply U.S. Rules Abroad," *New York Times*, May 13, 1998.

129. For an excellent exploration of the Nike Foundation's efforts, see Kathryn Moeller, *The Gender Effect: Capitalism, Feminism, and the Corporate Politics of Development* (Berkeley: University of California Press, 2018).

130. David Vogel, *The Market for Virtue: The Potential and Limits of Corporate Social Responsibility* (Washington, DC: Brookings Institution Press, 2005), 81; and Feminist Majority Foundation, "Nike Announces Plan to Improve Conditions for Asian Workers," May 13, 1998, https://feminist.org/news/nike-announces-plan-to-improve-conditions-for-asian-workers/.

131. Richard P. Appelbaum and Nelson Lichtenstein, "Introduction," in *Achieving Workers' Rights in the Global Economy*, ed. Richard P.

Appelbaum and Nelson Lichtenstein (Ithaca, NY: Cornell University Press, 2016), 1–14.

132. Ross, *Slaves to Fashion*, 249–283.

133. Cummings, "Hemmed In," 71.

134. Bryant Simon, *Everything but the Coffee: Learning About America From Starbucks* (Berkeley: University of California Press, 2009), 201–238.

135. See Vogel, *Market for Virtue*, 27–29; Kerry A. Dolan, "Kinder, Gentler M.B.A.'s," *Forbes*, June 2, 1997; and Jennifer Kingston Bloom, "Career Tracks: In Scouting Talent, Citi Is in Another League," *American Banker*, July 30, 199.

136. Appelbaum and Lichtenstein, "Introduction," 1–14.

CHAPTER 10: UNTAPPED MARKETS

1. "Clinton's Promise of New Cash Goes Over Well in East St. Louis," Associated Press, July 7, 1999.

2. Walter Johnson, *The Broken Heart of America: St. Louis and the Violent History of the United States* (New York: Basic Books, 2020), 217–249.

3. White House, "Fact Sheet: President's Clinton's New Markets Trip," July 6, 1999, Clinton White House Archives, https://clintonwhitehouse2. archives.gov/WH/New/New_Markets/cities/east_st_louis_facts.html; and Carl M. Cannon, "Looking for an Open Door in the Gateway's Shadow," *Baltimore Sun*, July 29, 1996.

4. William J. Clinton, "Remarks by the President to the East St. Louis Community," Office of the Press Secretary, White House, July 6, 1999, Clinton White House Archives, Office of Speechwriting and Jeff Shesol, "New Markets 7/99 Drafts—East St. Louis," CDL.

5. Jo Mannies and Mark Schlinkman, "Clinton Urges End to Racial Hatred," *St. Louis Post-Dispatch*, July 7, 1999, A1.

6. Mannies and Schlinkman, "Clinton Urges End to Racial Hatred."

7. "The Clinton/Gore Economic Record: Continued Strong Growth Across the Board," July 5, 1999, Clinton White House Archives, https://clintonwhitehouse2.archives.gov/WH/New/New_Markets/economic.html.

8. Marcia Chatelain, *Franchise: The Golden Arches in Black America* (New York: Liveright, 2020), 216–217; see also, for example, Julianne Malveaux, "From Jump Street to Wall Street," *Essence*, October 1999, 90.

9. "Jackson Opens Wall Street Office to Monitor Racism in Corporate America," Associated Press, March 12, 1997.

10. George Packer, "Trickle-Down Civil Rights," *New York Times*, December 12, 1999, SM75.

11. Joseph Kahn, "Jackson Challenges 'Capital of Capital,'" *New York Times*, January 16, 1999, 3.

12. "Jackson Opens Wall Street Office."

13. Packer, "Trickle-Down Civil Rights."

14. Leslie Eaton and Laura M. Holson, "Travelers Chief at 65, Lands 'The Deal of a Life of Deals,'" *New York Times*, April 11, 1998.

15. Nicholas Lemann, *Transaction Man: The Rise of the Deal and the Decline of the American Dream* (New York: Farrar, Straus and Giroux, 2019), 168–169.

16. Jacqueline Gold, "Uncommon Partnership: Citi's Weill and Jesse Jackson," *American Banker*, May 24, 2000.

17. Gold, "Uncommon Partnership"; and Packer, "Trickle-Down Civil Rights."

18. Tim Jones, "Jesse Jackson's Tough Sell," *Chicago Tribune*, July 19, 1998.

19. David Whitford, "Jesse Shakes the Money Tree," *Fortune*, June 21, 1999, https://money.cnn.com/magazines/fortune/fortune_archive/1999/06/21/261713/.

20. Eric L. Smith, "The Wall Street Project: What Does It Mean for You?" *Black Enterprise*, October 1998, 110.

21. Whitford, "Jesse Shakes the Money Tree."

22. Charles Babington, "For President and Jackson, A Friendship of Mutual Aid," *Washington Post*, January 13, 2000.

23. Gene Sperling and Maria Echaveste, "Press Briefing by National Economic Advisor Gene Sperling and Deputy Chief of Staff Maria Echaveste," Office of the Press Secretary, White House, July 2, 1999, Clinton White House Archives, https://clintonwhitehouse2.archives.gov/WH/New/New_Markets/briefing.html.

24. Gene Sperling to the President, Subject: Background for Meeting with Reverend Jackson—Your Untapped Markets Agenda, December 29, 1998, History of the National Economic Council and Clinton Administration History Project, "NEC—New Markets [1]," CDL.

25. See, for example, William J. Clinton, "Remarks on Empowerment Zones and Enterprise Communities," January 17, 1994, The American Presidency Project, www.presidency.ucsb.edu/node/219793.

26. Brian Goldstein, *The Roots of Urban Renaissance: Gentrification and the Struggle Over Harlem* (Cambridge; Harvard University Press, 2017), 238–277; and Derek S. Hyra, *The New Urban Renewal: The Economic Transformation of Harlem and Bronzeville* (Chicago: University of Chicago Press, 2008), 30.

27. Paul J. Weinstein to Bruce N. Reed and Gene B. Sperling, Subject: Empowerment Zones Round II, October 10, 1997, Domestic Policy Council and Elena Kagan, "Urban Policy—Empowerment Zones," CDL.

28. Gene Sperling, "White House Roundtable and Rose Garden Announcement with CEOs," May 10, 1999, History of the National Economic Council and Clinton Administration History Project, "NEC—New Markets [1]," CDL.

29. Sperling to the President, Subject: Background for Meeting with Reverend Jackson.

30. Michael E. Porter, "The Competitive Advantage of the Inner City," *Harvard Business Review*, May–June 1995, 55–71.

31. Chris Reidy, "Inner Cities' Retail Punch," *Boston Globe*, June 12, 1998.

32. Porter, "The Competitive Advantage of the Inner City."

33. Gene Sperling to the President, Subject: Edley Memo, January 13, 1999, History of the National Economic Council and Clinton Administration History Project, "NEC—New Markets [1]," CDL.

34. Sperling to the President, Subject: Background for Meeting with Reverend Jackson.

35. William J. Clinton, "Remarks to the Wall Street Project Conference in New York City," January 15, 1999, The American Presidency Project, www.presidency.ucsb.edu/node/229465.

36. Clinton, "Remarks to the Wall Street Project Conference in New York City."

37. White House, "An Overview of Clinton's New Markets Trip," c. 1999, Clinton White House Archives (last accessed July 8, 2021); and Department of Housing and Urban Development, *New Markets: The Untapped Retail Buying Power in America's Inner Cities* (Washington, DC: HUD, July 1999).

38. John M. Broder, "Clinton, in Poverty Tour, Focuses on Profits," *New York Times*, July 7, 1999.

39. Sperling and Echaveste, "Press Briefing."

40. William J. Clinton, "Remarks to the Presidential Scholars," June 25, 1999, The American Presidency Project, www.presidency.ucsb.edu/node/226915.

41. "President Clinton's Challenge to Invest in America's New Markets, c. 1999," Domestic Policy Council, Bruce Reed, and Subject Files, "New Markets," CDL; William J. Clinton, "Remarks on the New Markets Initiative," May 11, 1999, The American Presidency Project; and Department of Housing and Urban Development, "New Markets."

42. Jason DeParle, "Making a Belated Pilgrimage," *New York Times*, July 9, 1999, 10.

43. Jeanne Cummings, "Clinton Will Tow Executives to Poorest U.S. Areas to Spur Investment Under New Markets Initiative," *Wall Street Journal*, July 2, 1999.

44. Memorandum for the President from Gene Sperling, Re: Presidential Trip to America's New Markets, April 12, 1999, History of the National Economic Council and Clinton Administration History Project, "NEC—New Markets [1]," CDL.

45. Ronald Brownstein, "Clinton Urges Paying Off US Debt with Surplus," *Los Angeles Times*, July 8, 1999, A1.

46. Marsha Mercer, "Travels with Clinton: 8 Meals a Day the Norm," *Richmond Times-Dispatch*, July 11, 1999.

47. Kevin Galvin, "Clinton Offers $64 Million Aid Package for Poor Areas, *Atlanta Journal-Constitution*, July 6, 1999.

48. Al From, interview with author, Bethesda, Maryland, September 26, 2019.

49. Peter T. Kilborn, "Clinton, Amid the Despair on a Reservation, Again Pledges Help," *New York Times*, July 8, 1999.

50. "President Clinton's New Markets Trip: Highlighting the Need for Investment in Native American Communities on the Pine Ridge Indian Reservation," July 7, 1999, Clinton White House Archives, https://clinton whitehouse2.archives.gov/WH/New/New_Markets/cities/pine_ridge _reservation_facts.html; and James Gerstenzang, "Clinton Visit Illuminates Depth of Poverty on Sioux Reservation," *Los Angeles Times*, July 8, 1999.

51. Alex Tizon, "President Clinton's Poverty Tour," *Seattle Times*, July 8, 1999.

52. Charles Babington, "Desperation Despite a VIP Visit," *Washington Post*, July 7, 1999.

53. Matea Gold and James Gerstenzang, "In Watts Visit Clinton Vows Job, Education Aid," *Los Angeles Times*, July 9, 1999.

54. "Clinton's Promise of New Cash."

55. Jonathan Alter, "Trade Mission to Misery, USA," *Newsweek*, July 12, 1999, 34.

56. Cummings, "Clinton Will Tow Executives."

57. John M. Broder, "A Pledge of Federal Help for the Economic Byways: Clinton Seeks an Investment in Appalachia," *New York Times*, July 6, 1999.

58. John M. Broder, "Clinton, in Poverty Tour, Focuses on Profits," *New York Times*, July 7, 1999.

59. Charles Babington, "Clinton's 'Third Way' to Beat Poverty," *Washington Post*, July 9, 1999, www.washingtonpost.com/archive/politics/1999 /07/09/clintons-third-way-to-beat-poverty/416d61c9-3578-4afc-8c9a -1a5ac11e6ece/.

60. From, interview.

61. Babington, "Clinton's 'Third Way' to Beat Poverty."

62. Al From, "Ending Poverty the Third Way," *New Democrat*, September 1, 1999.

63. William J. Clinton, "Remarks in a Discussion on Youth Opportunities in Los Angeles, California," July 8, 1999, The American Presidency Project, www.presidency.ucsb.edu/node/227566.

64. Clinton, "Remarks to the Wall Street Project Conference in New York City."

65. Clinton, "Remarks to the Wall Street Project Conference in New York City."

66. Department of the Treasury, "History of the Department of the Treasury During the Clinton Administration 1993–2001," prepared for Clinton Administration History Project, Washington DC, 2001, [History of the Department of the Treasury], CDL.

67. "CRA Fact Sheet," c. 1999, Office of Policy Development and Lisa Green, "Paper—CRA [Community Reinvestment Act]," CDL.

68. William J. Clinton, "Remarks on Presenting the Presidential Awards for Excellence in Microenterprise Development," February 5, 1999, The American Presidency Project, www.presidency.ucsb.edu/node/226762.

69. Timothy L. O'Brien, "For Banks, a Big Nudge to Do More," *New York Times*, July 5, 1998, 1.

70. Jacob M. Schlesinger and Michael Schroeder, "Law Requiring Banks to Aid Poor Communities Faces Uncertain Future as Gramm Mounts Attack," *Wall Street Journal*, July 27, 1999.

71. Richard A. Oppel Jr., "Many Banks Make Money on Lending in Poor Areas," *New York Times*, October 22, 1999.

72. Kathleen Day, "Gramm Threatens Bank Bill," *Washington Post*, October 7, 1998.

73. Schlesinger and Schroeder, "Law Requiring Banks to Aid Poor Communities Faces Uncertain Future."

74. Ellen Seidman and Paul Dimond to Gene Sperling, Subject: Financial Services Modernization and Community Concerns, February 24, 1997, History of the National Economic Council and Clinton Administration History Project, "NEC—Financial Modernization [1]," CDL; and Gene Sperling to NEC Principals, Subject: Treasury's Proposed Financial Services Modernization Legislation, March 17, 1997, History of the National Economic Council and Clinton Administration History Project, "NEC—Financial Modernization [1]," CDL.

75. Lemann, *Transaction Man*, 169–170.

76. Executive Office of the President, Office of Budget and Management, Statement of Administration Policy, S.900-Financial Services Modernization Act of 1999, May 3, 1999, History of the National Economic Council and Clinton Administration History Project, "NEC—Financial Modernization [5]," CDL.

77. Bill Clinton to Phil Gramm, March 2, 1999, Office of Policy Development and Lisa Green, "CRA [Community Reinvestment Act] [Folder 1] [1]," CDL.

78. Jay Dunn to Gene Sperling, Re: Meeting with Travelers CEO and Citicorp CEO John Reed, September 22, 1998, "FOIA 2010-0385-F-Citicorp and Travelers Group Merger," CDL.

79. Sarah Rosen Wartell to Jonathan A. Kaplan et al., Subject: CRA and New Markets, May 17, 1999, Office of Policy Development and Lisa Green, "President's Speeches on CRA [Community Reinvestment Act]," CDL.

80. Stephen Labaton, "Political Stalemate Continues over Banking Bill," *New York Times*, October 20, 1999.

81. Michael Schroeder, "Glass-Steagall Compromise Is Reached," *Wall Street Journal*, October 25, 1999, A2; and Stephen Laboton, "Deal on Bank Bill Was Helped Along by Midnight Talks," *New York Times*, October 24, 1999, A1.

82. Kathleen Day, "Banking Accord Likely to Be Law: Clinton Hails Hard-Reached Agreement," *Washington Post*, October 23, 1999.

83. Memorandum for the President from Gene Sperling, Subject: NEC Weekly Reports, October 22, 1999, History of the National Economic Council and Clinton Administration History Project, "NEC—Financial Modernization [6]," CDL.

84. Joseph Kahn, "Financial Services Industry Faces a New World," *New York Times*, October 23, 1999, 1.

85. Timothy L. O'Brien and Julie Creswell, "Laughing All the Way to the Bank," *New York Times*, September 11, 2005.

86. Schlesinger and Schroeder, "Law Requiring Banks to Aid Poor Communities."

87. Megan O'Matz, "Jesse Jackson Leads Rally to Rebuild Area's Image," *Chicago Tribune*, July 31, 1999.

88. Packer, "Trickle-Down Civil Rights."

89. O'Matz, "Jesse Jackson Leads Rally."

90. Melissa Wahl, "Clinton Sees Bank Bill Aiding Englewood," *Chicago Tribune*, November 6, 1999.

91. Wahl, "Clinton Sees Bank Bill Aiding Englewood."

92. Gene Sperling to the President, Subject: New Markets Initiative Legislation, July 12, 1999; and Gene Sperling to Sandy [Weill], July 10, 1999, History of the National Economic Council and Clinton Administration History Project, "NEC—New Markets [2]," CDL.

93. Gene Sperling to John Podesta, Maria Echaveste, and Stephanie Street, Subject: Upcoming New Markets Tour, November 22, 1999, History of the National Economic Council and Clinton Administration History Project, "NEC—Digital Divide," CDL.

94. Lorriane Woellerg, "One Wired Nation, Indivisible? Or One Big Boondoggle?" *BusinessWeek*, February 14, 2000.

95. Loretta Ucelli et al. to the President, Subject: Monday Online Town Hall Meeting, November 5, 1999, Office of Speechwriting and Josh Gottheimer, "DLC [Democratic Leadership Council] On-Line Meeting 11/8/99 [1]," CDL.

96. See, for example, Katharine Q. Seelye, "Gore's Plan for Success in 2000: Wide Array of Specific Positions," *New York Times*, July 29, 1999, 1.

97. National Telecommunications and Information Administration, *Falling Through the Net: Defining the Digital Divide*, Department of Commerce, 1999, www.ntia.doc.gov/legacy/ntiahome/fttn99/FTTN.pdf.

98. See, for example, John Schwartz, "Kids and Computers," *Washington Post*, September 8, 1998, Z07; Jennifer 8. Lee, "Some Schools Can't Afford Hardware and Training," *New York Times*, September 2, 1999, 7; and Pam Belluck, "What Price Will Be Paid by Those Not on the Net?," *New York Times*, September 22, 1999, 12.

99. Nicole Wallace, "'Digital Divide' Draws Grant Makers' Attention," *Chronicle of Philanthropy*, January 27, 2000.

100. Steve Lohr, "Gates to Help Libraries Acquire Gear to Go On Line," *New York Times*, June 24, 1997, 1.

101. Siobhan Stevenson, "Digital Divide: A Discursive Move Away from the Real Inequities," *Information Society* 25, no. 1 (2009): 13.

102. William J. Clinton, "Remarks at Frank W. Ballou Senior High School," February 2, 2000, The American Presidency Project, www .presidency.ucsb.edu/node/227611.

103. Stevenson, "Digital Divide," 13.

104. "From Digital Divide to Digital Opportunity, Draft," December 12, 1999, History of the National Economic Council and Clinton Administration History Project, "NEC—Digital Divide," CDL.

105. *Wired* Staff, "Clinton Starts 'New Market' Tour," *Wired*, April 17, 2000; Zachary Coile, "Across the Digital Divide," *San Francisco Examiner*, April 16, 2000; and White House, Office of the Press Secretary, "Background on the Digital Divide and East Palo Alto, California," April 17, 2000, Clinton White House Archives, https://clintonwhitehouse4.archives .gov/WH/New/New_Markets-0004/20000417-5.html.

106. Reverend Jesse L. Jackson, "A Five Point Education and Job Plan to Move from Digital Divide to Digital Opportunity," December 13, 1999, Office of Speechwriting and Lowell Weiss, "[Digital Divide Navajo 4/17/00— Rainbow PUSH (People United to Save Humanity) Coalition]," CDL.

107. Tracy Seipel, "Clinton Lauds Connection of Business, Community Firms to Give $100 Million for Internet Access," *San Jose Mercury News*, April 18, 2000.

108. White House, Office of the Press Secretary, "The President's New Markets Trip: From Digital Divide to Digital Opportunity: Highlighting Technology's Economic Opportunity in Shiprock," April 17, 2000, Clinton White House Archives, https://clintonwhitehouse3.archives.gov/WH/New /New_Markets-0004/20000417-3.html.

109. William J. Clinton, "Remarks to the COMDEX 2000 Spring Conference in Chicago, Illinois," April 18, 2000, The American Presidency Project, www.presidency.ucsb.edu/node/226889.

110. William J. Clinton, "Remarks to the Community in Whiteville, North Carolina," April 26, 2000, The American Presidency Project, www .presidency.ucsb.edu/node/227020; and Ryan Koresko, "President Bill Clinton Visits Whiteville, April 26, 2000," posted April 23, 2014, YouTube video, 18:30, www.youtube.com/watch?v=hQGFDzoHTos.

111. David Usborne, "Across the Mississippi: A City Left Behind by Clinton Boom," *Independent*, October 19, 2000, 17.

112. White House, Office of the Press Secretary, "President Clinton and Speaker Hastert Announce Bipartisan Agreement on New Markets and Renewal Communities," May 23, 2000, Clinton White House Archives, https:// clintonwhitehouse4.archives.gov/WH/New/html/20000531_17.html.

113. White House, Office of the Press Secretary, Radio Address by the President to the Nation, Oval Office, December 16, 2000, Office of Speechwriting and James (Terry) Edmonds, "New Markets," CDL.

114. William J. Clinton, "Interview with Jesse Jackson of CNN's 'Both Sides' in Torrance," July 9, 1999, The American Presidency Project, www .presidency.ucsb.edu/node/227645.

115. Memorandum for the President from Lawrence H. Summers, Subject: New Markets: Report on Visit to Harlem, USA and New York BusinessLINC, July 15, 1999, History of the Department of the Treasury and Clinton Administration History Project, "[History of the Department of the Treasury—Supplementary Documents] [22]," CDL.

116. Lemann, *Transaction Man*, 170–183.

117. Becky Yerak and Sharon Stangenes, "Subprime Lending Worries Hit Home," *Chicago Tribune*, March 18, 2007.

118. Meribah Knight and Bridget O'Shea, "Foreclosures Leave Pockets of Neglect and Decay," *New York Times*, October 27, 2011; and Jenny Lee, "Why West Englewood Has High Unemployment," Social Justice News Nexus, June 27, 2016, https://sjnnchicago.medill.northwestern.edu/blog /2016/06/27/west-englewood-high-unemployment-jenny-lee/.

119. Packer, "Trickle-Down Civil Rights"; and Sam Howe Verhovek, "Gates Pledges $1 Billion Gift for Students," *New York Times*, September 16, 1999, 1.

120. Jonathan Rauch, "This Is Not Charity," *Atlantic*, October 2007; David A. Fahrenthold, Tom Hamburger, and Rosalind S. Helderman, "The Inside Story of How the Clintons Built a $2 Billion Global Empire," *Washington Post*, June 2, 2015; and Anand Giridharadas, *Winners Take All: The Elite Charade of Changing the World* (New York: Knopf, 2018), 204–244.

121. John Freeman Gill, "Cold Shoulders," *New York Times*, July 27, 2008; and Alan Feuer, "Mr. Clinton, Your Harlem Neighbors Need to See You More Often," *New York Times*, November 17, 2003.

EPILOGUE

1. Mark Schmitt, "When the Democratic Leadership Council Mattered," *American Prospect*, February 10, 2011.

2. Cass R. Sunstein, "Making Government More Logical," *New York Times*, September 19, 2015.

3. Connie Evans, interview with author, by Zoom, September 21, 2020.

4. Grameen America, "Grameen America Receives $25 Million Grant from MacKenzie Scott," PR Newswire, July 28, 2020, www.prnewswire .com/news-releases/grameen-america-receives-25-million-grant-from -mackenzie-scott-301101706.html.

5. For critiques of the gig economy, see Evgeny Morozov, "Don't Believe the Hype, the 'Sharing Economy' Masks a Failing Economy," *Guardian* (Manchester, UK), September 27, 2014, www.theguardian .com/commentisfree/2014/sep/28/sharing-economy-internet-hype -benefits-overstated-evgeny-morozov; and Cara Waters, "Uber Claims Drivers Are 'Entrepreneurs' Not Employees," *Smart Company*, Septem-

ber 15, 2015, www.smartcompany.com.au/technology/uber-claims-drivers
-are-entrepreneurs-not-employees/.

6. Kathryn Edin and H. Luke Shaefer, *$2.00 a Day: Living on Almost
Nothing in America* (New York: Houghton Mifflin, 2015).

7. UN General Assembly, *Report of the Special Rapporteur on Extreme Poverty and Human Rights on His Mission to the United States of
America*, Human Rights Council, 38th session, June 18–July 6, 2018,
agenda item 3, May 4, 2018, https://undocs.org/A/HRC/38/33/ADD.1.

8. Nicholas Kristof and Sheryl WuDunn, *Tightrope: Americans Reaching for Hope* (New York: Knopf Doubleday, 2020), 33; and Jessica Semega
et al., *Income and Poverty in the United States: 2019*, Report Number
P60-270, US Census Bureau, September 15, 2020, www.census.gov/library
/publications/2020/demo/p60-270.html.

9. Semega et al., "Income and Poverty in the United States"; and Jason
DeParle, "8 Million Have Slipped into Poverty Since May," *New York
Times*, October 15, 2020.

10. See, for example, Natalie Y. Moore, *The South Side: A Portrait of
Chicago and American Segregation* (New York: Picador, 2016); and
Eve L. Ewing, *Ghosts in the Schoolyard: Racism and School Closings on
Chicago's South Side* (Chicago: University of Chicago Press, 2018).

11. Kathy Bergen et al., "South Shore, Once Thriving, Struggles amid
Economic Erosion and Crime," *Chicago Tribune*, May 2, 2017.

12. ShoreBank Corporation, "Annual Report 2007," Box 1, Folder 8,
SBC.

13. George Surgeon, interview with author, by Zoom, November 20,
2020.

14. James E. Post and Fiona S. Wilson, "Too Good to Fail," *Stanford
Social Innovation Review*, Fall 2011; and Robert Kuttner, "Zillions for
Wall Street, Zippo for Barack's Old Neighborhood," *Huffington Post*, Au-
gust 22, 2010.

15. "Shore Bank Exposure," Glenn Beck, Fox News, May 21, 2010.

16. Jeff Green and Peter Robison, "One of Finance's Few Black CEOs
Thrives Where Big Banks Fled," *Bloomberg Businessweek*, September 21,
2020.

17. Amara Omeokwe, "Renewed Focus on Race Triggers Surge of Interest in Community-Based Lenders," *Wall Street Journal*, August 18, 2020;
and "Netflix to Shift $100 Million in Black-Run Banks, Credit Unions,"
American Banker, June 30, 2020.

18. Maya Dukmasova, "South Shore Is Chicago's Eviction Capital," *Chicago Reader*, April 17, 2017, www.chicagoreader.com/Bleader/archives
/2017/04/17/south-shore-is-chicagos-eviction-capital.

19. Esther Yoon-Ji Kang, Natalie Moore, and María Inés Zamudio, "50
Lives in 4 Zip Codes," WBEZ, August 17, 2020, www.wbez.org/stories
/a-perfect-storm-50-lives-and-4-zip-codes-tell-chicagos-story-of-covid-19
-inequality/50b822ae-523e-47fa-a823-3c6a1c3ee12f.

20. Kang et al., "50 Lives in 4 Zip Codes."

21. Jennifer Schuessler, "The Obama Presidential Library That Isn't," *New York Times*, February 20, 2019.

22. Lolly Bowean, "Amid Heated Debate City Approves Plan for Obama Presidential Center," *Chicago Tribune*, May 17, 2018.

23. David Usborne, "Pine Bluff: On Patrol in the Most Dangerous Little Town in America," *Independent*, February 17, 2013; "Study Says Pine Bluff Most Segregated City in US," *Pine Bluff Commercial*, August 6, 2019; and Chico Harlan, "The 25-Cent Raise: What Life Is Like After a Minimum Wage Increase," *Washington Post*, February 17, 2015.

24. Rachel Aviv, "Punishment by Pandemic," *New Yorker*, June 22, 2020.

25. Anand Giridharadas, *Winners Take All: The Elite Charade of Changing the World* (New York: Knopf, 2018), 210–211.

INDEX

Lily Geismer is an associate professor of history at Claremont McKenna College. She researches and teaches about recent political and urban history in the United States with a focus on liberalism and the Democratic Party. She is the author of *Don't Blame Us: Suburban Liberals and the Transformation of the Democratic Party,* and her work has appeared in the *New York Times, Washington Post, New Republic, Jacobin,* and *Dissent* and on NPR and other podcasts. A native of Massachusetts, Geismer currently resides in Los Angeles.

PublicAffairs is a publishing house founded in 1997. It is a tribute to the standards, values, and flair of three persons who have served as mentors to countless reporters, writers, editors, and book people of all kinds, including me.

I. F. STONE, proprietor of *I. F. Stone's Weekly*, combined a commitment to the First Amendment with entrepreneurial zeal and reporting skill and became one of the great independent journalists in American history. At the age of eighty, Izzy published *The Trial of Socrates*, which was a national bestseller. He wrote the book after he taught himself ancient Greek.

BENJAMIN C. BRADLEE was for nearly thirty years the charismatic editorial leader of *The Washington Post*. It was Ben who gave the *Post* the range and courage to pursue such historic issues as Watergate. He supported his reporters with a tenacity that made them fearless and it is no accident that so many became authors of influential, best-selling books.

ROBERT L. BERNSTEIN, the chief executive of Random House for more than a quarter century, guided one of the nation's premier publishing houses. Bob was personally responsible for many books of political dissent and argument that challenged tyranny around the globe. He is also the founder and longtime chair of Human Rights Watch, one of the most respected human rights organizations in the world.

·   ·   ·

For fifty years, the banner of Public Affairs Press was carried by its owner Morris B. Schnapper, who published Gandhi, Nasser, Toynbee, Truman, and about 1,500 other authors. In 1983, Schnapper was described by *The Washington Post* as "a redoubtable gadfly." His legacy will endure in the books to come.

Peter Osnos, *Founder*